John Beames

Comparative grammer of the modern Aryan languages of India

Volume 3

John Beames

Comparative grammer of the modern Aryan languages of India
Volume 3

ISBN/EAN: 9783337413934

Printed in Europe, USA, Canada, Australia, Japan

Cover: Foto ©Paul-Georg Meister /pixelio.de

More available books at **www.hansebooks.com**

A

COMPARATIVE GRAMMAR

OF THE

MODERN ARYAN LANGUAGES

OF INDIA:

TO WIT,

HINDI, PANJABI, SINDHI, GUJARATI, MARATHI, ORIYA AND BANGALI.

BY

JOHN BEAMES,

BENGAL CIVIL SERVICE,

FELLOW OF THE UNIVERSITY OF CALCUTTA,

MEMBER OF THE ROYAL ASIATIC SOCIETY, THE GERMAN ORIENTAL SOCIETY,

ETC., ETC.

VOL. III.

THE VERB.

LONDON:

TRÜBNER & CO., 57 AND 59, LUDGATE HILL.

1879.

TABLE OF CONTENTS.

BOOK III.—THE VERB.

Chapter I.—Structure of Verbal Stems.

PAGE

§ 1. Structure of the Sanskrit Verb 1
§ 2. Beginnings of the Analytical System in Sanskrit . 6
§ 3. Conjugations of the Pali Verb 9
§ 4. Tenses of the Pali Verb 11
§§ 5, 6. The Verb in Jaina Prakrit 16
§ 7. Sauraseni Prakrit Verb 22
§ 8. Apabhramsa Verbal Forms 24
§ 9. The Modern Verbal Stem 28
§ 10. Phases of the Verb 29
§ 11. Single and Double Stems 32
§ 12. Single Neuter Stems from Sanskrit BHŪ Roots . . 33
§ 13. The same from other Classes of Sanskrit Roots . 36
§ 14. Modern Neuter Stems from Sanskrit Past Participles . 37
§ 15. Single Active Stems 40
§ 16. Treatment of Sanskrit Roots ending in a Vowel . 42
§ 17. The Stem DEKH 45
§ 18. Double Verbs 46
§ 19. Siddha Double Stems Differing in the Final Consonant 48
§ 20. Double Stems Differing in Vowel and Final Consonant . 52
§ 21. Double Stems Differing only in the Vowel . . 54
§ 22. Examples and Illustrations . . . 58
§ 23. Laws of the Formation of Modern Stems . . 66
§ 24. The Passive Intransitive 69
§ 25. The Passive 71
§ 26. The Causal 75
§ 27. The Passive Causal . . . 82

PAGE
§ 28. The Causal in a Neuter Sense 84
§ 29. Secondary Stems 87
§ 30. Reduplicated and Imitative Stems 89
§ 31. Gipsy Verbal Stems 95

CHAPTER II.—THE SIMPLE TENSES.

§ 32. Classification of Tenses 99
§ 33. The Simple Present or Aorist 101
§ 34. The Imperative 106
§ 35. The Future in Old-Hindi and Gujarati . . . 112
§ 36. Type of the Active Verb in Sindhi and Marathi . . 115
§ 37. Synopsis of the Simple Tenses in all Seven Languages 118
§ 38. Simple Tenses in the Gipsy Verb 119

CHAPTER III.—THE PARTICIPIAL TENSES.

§ 39. Definition of the Participial Tenses 121
§ 40. The Present Participle Active 123
§ 41. Tenses formed thereby—the Sindhi Future . . 126
§ 42. Marathi Indicative and Conditional Present . . 127
§ 43. Bangali and Oriya Conditional 129
§ 44. Hindi, Panjabi, and Gujarati Present . . . 131
§ 45. The Past Participle Passive 132
§ 46. Early Tadbhava Participles in Sindhi and Panjabi . 136
§ 47. The same in Gujarati and Marathi 141
§ 48. The same in Old and New Hindi 144
§ 49. Tenses formed from the Past Participle . . . 147
§ 50. The *Prayoga* 151
§ 51. The Future Participle Passive 152
§ 52. Tenses formed from it in Sindhi, Gujarati, and Marathi . 155
§ 53. The Future in Oriya, Bengali, and Eastern Hindi . 158
§ 54. The Hindi and Panjabi Future 160
§ 55. Marathi Future compared with that in certain Hindi Dialects 161
§ 56. Synopsis of the Participial Tenses in all Seven Languages 164
§ 57. Participial Tenses in the Gipsy Verb . . . 168

CHAPTER IV.—THE COMPOUND TENSES.

	PAGE
§ 58. Definition of the Compound Tenses and Auxiliary Verbs	170
§ 59. The Root AS—Present Tense	171
§ 60. Imperfect in Panjabi and Gipsy	175
§ 61. AS, with a Negative	178
§ 62. Compound Tenses formed with AS	179
§ 63. The Root ACHH—Discussion as to its Origin	180
§ 64. Tenses derived therefrom	184
§ 65. Compound Tenses formed therewith	187
§ 66. BHÛ—the Simple Tenses	194
§ 67. *Id.*—the Participial Tenses	201
§ 68. Compound Tenses formed therewith	203
§ 69. STHÂ	206
§ 70. YÂ	213
§ 71. Ancillary Verbs Defined	215
§ 72. Examples of Ancillaries	216

CHAPTER V.—OTHER VERBAL FORMS.

§ 73. The Conjunctive Participle	229
§ 74. The Infinitive	234
§ 75. The Agent	238
§ 76. Sindhi Verbs with Pronominal Suffixes	241
§ 77. Conjugation of Stems ending in Vowels in Hindi, Panjabi, and Sindhi	246
§ 78. The same in Marathi	251
§ 79. The same in Bangali and Oriya	254

CHAPTER VI.—THE PARTICLE.

§ 80. Adverbs, Nominal and Pronominal	256
§ 81. Pronominal Adverbs of Time, Place, and Manner	257
§ 82. Adverbs Derived from Nouns and Verbs	264
§ 83. Conjunctions	270
§ 84. Interjections	272
§ 85. Postpositions	275
§ 86. Conclusion	275
GENERAL INDEX TO THE THREE VOLUMES	279

ERRATA.

PAGE LINE

3, 19, for *this much* read *such*.

10, 9, for मझुति read मझुति.

14, 23, for *different* read *difficult*.

19, 21, for पुरवति read पुर वति.

21, 26, for चिवोतितवे read चिवी-
हितवे.

34, 3 from below, for *Pali* read *Prakrit*

36, 6, for *khila* read *khula*.

39, 26, for वनिहत् read वनिहत्.

44, 2, for *detu* read *dehi*.

47, 26, *dele* that.

50, 16, for अचय read अचय.

50, 18, after *word* a full stop instead
of a comma.

52, 13, for *discharged* read *discharge*.

56, 5, for 00 read 38 (ed. Stenzler).

56, 7, for °विघम° read °विघम°.

57, 28, for ड्य read डड.

58, 5, after *Pali* a full stop instead
of a comma.

61, 25, for *khalid* read *khalu*.

63, 4, for *maj* read *majj*.

66, 9, for चछ read चछ.

70, 12, for *phrase* read *phase*.

73, 16, for वारी read मारी.

83, 24, for माहात्म्य read माहात्म्य.

105, 6, for वर्षे read वर्षे.

112, last but one, for अरसो read अरसी

114, 21, for चस read चस.

PAGE LINE

124, 1, *dele* comma after *bearing*.

131, 6, for छोडियो read छोडियी.

135, 29, after *dalala* insert *f.*; for
dalal', etc., read *dalal*', etc.

140, 31, for सिवचा read सिठचा.

141, 19, for मति read मीत.

149, 24, for *asmuh* read *asmuh*.

154, 29, for वावचा read वावचा.

162, 7, for माइंवौ read माइंवो.

163, 2, the words '*aorist* मुठी' should
be put between brackets.

173, 29, for *Ludhiana* read *Ludiana*.

176, 3 from below, for *Pr.* read *P.*

178, 18, for *Nuauti* read *Nukauti*.

179, 24, for दूचा read देचा.

195, 10, for 'Daughter' read 'laughter.'

196, 17, for चरिच read दरिच.

202, 2 from below, for 59 read 60.

214, 4, for *Imperfect* read *Imperative*.

225, 29, for वहती read रहती.

250, 17, for *Imperfect* read *Imperative*.

254, 3, for *Origa* read *Aryan*.

257, 3, for नावा read रावा.

262, 22, for वच्च read वचा.

262, 23, for प्रसाणे read प्रसारु.

262, 23, for चोधे read चोधे.

262, 23, for *its* read *as*.

263, 6, for *H.-D.* read *K.-D.*

267, 9, for संहित read सहित.

COMPARATIVE GRAMMAR

OF THE

MODERN ARYAN LANGUAGES OF INDIA.

CHAPTER I.

STRUCTURE OF VERBAL STEMS.

CONTENTS.—§ 1. Structure of the Sanskrit Verb.—§ 2. Beginnings of the Analytical System in Sanskrit.—§ 3. Conjugations of the Pali Verb.—§ 4. Tenses of the Pali Verb.—§§ 5, 6. The Verb in Jaina Prakrit.—§ 7. Scenic Prakrit Verb.—§ 8. Apabhramça Verbal Forms.—§ 9. The Modern Verbal Stem.—§ 10. Phases of the Verb.—§ 11. Single and Double Stems.—§ 12. Single Neuter Stems from Sanskrit *Bhū* Roots.—§ 13. The same from other Classes of Sanskrit Roots.—§ 14. Modern Neuter Stems from Sanskrit Passive Past Participles.—§ 15. Single Active Stems.—§ 16. Treatment of Sanskrit Roots ending in a Vowel.—§ 17. The Stem *dekh*.—§ 18. Double Verbs.—§ 19. Similar Double Stems Differing in the Final Consonant.—§ 20. Double Stems Differing in Vowel and Final Consonant.—§ 21. Double Stems Differing only in the Vowel.—§ 22. Examples and Illustrations.—§ 23. Laws of the Formation of Modern Stems.—§ 24. The Passive Intransitive.—§ 25. The Passive.—§ 26. The Causal.—§ 27. The Passive Causal.—§ 28. The Causal in a Neuter Sense.—§ 29. Secondary Stems.—§ 30. Reduplicated and Imitative Stems.—§ 31. Other Verbal Stems.

§ 1. The Sanskrit verb, with its long array of tenses, intricate phonetic changes, and elaborate rules of formation, seems to have been subjected at a very early period to processes of simplification. Indeed, we may be permitted to hold that some, at least, of the forms laid down in the works of Sanskrit grammarians, were never actually in use in the spoken language, and with all due deference to the opinions of scholars, it may be urged that much of this elaborate development arose in an age when the speech of the people had wandered very far away from the classical type. Even if it were not so, even if there ever were a time when the Aryan peasant used polysyllabic desideratives, and was familiar with multiform aorists, it is clear that he began to satisfy himself with a simpler system at a very distant epoch, for the range of forms in Pali and the other Prakrits is far narrower than in classical Sanskrit.

Simplification is in fact the rule in all branches of the Indo-European family of languages, and in those we are now discussing, the verb follows this general law. To make this clear, it may be well to give here, as a preliminary matter, a slight sketch of the structure of the verb as it stands in the Sanskrit and Prakrit stages of development.

In that stage of the Sanskrit language which is usually accepted as the classical one, the verb is synthetical throughout, except in one or two tenses where, as will be hereafter shown, the analytical method has already begun to show itself. By separating the inflectional additions, and unravelling the euphonic changes necessitated by them, we may arrive at a residuum or grammarian's abstraction called the root. These roots, which have no real existence in spoken language, serve as useful and indispensable pegs on which to hang the long chain of forms which would otherwise defy all attempts at reducing them to order. Some writers have lately thought fit to sneer at the philologist and his roots, and have made themselves merry over imaginary pictures of a time when the human race talked to each other in roots only. These gentleman set up a bugbear of their own creation for the purpose of pulling it to pieces again. No one, as far as I am aware, has ever asserted that at a given period of the world's history a certain race of men used such words as *bhú*, *gam*, or *kar*, till some one hit on the ingenious device of adding to *bhú* the word *ami*, and, modifying *bhú* into *bhava*, burst upon his astonished countrymen with the newly-discovered word *bhavámi*, "I am." What has been asserted, and truly too, is that in Sanskrit we find a large number of words expressing the idea of "being," in which the consonantal sound *bh* is followed by various vowels and semivowels, which, according to phonetic laws, spring from the vowel *ú*, and that as, for scientific purposes, some common generic term is required to enable us to include under one head all parts of the verb, we are justified in putting together these two constant unvarying elements, and so obtaining a neat technical expression *bhú*, to which, as to a common factor, can be referred all the words expressive of "being" in its relations of time, person, and condition. Analysis and arrangement of this sort is an essential part of every science, and the native grammarians had done this much work for us before European skill was brought to bear on the subject.

Verbal roots, then, are grammarians' tickets, by which actual spoken words are classified and arranged in groups for convenience of investigation. The roots in Sanskrit are mostly monosyllabic, consisting of a consonant followed by a vowel, as *bhú*, *yá*, *ni*, or of a vowel followed by a consonant, as *ad*, *ish*, *ubh*, or of a vowel between two consonants, as *kar*, *gam*, *pad*. Roots may also consist of a single vowel, as *i*, and in the place of a single consonant there may be a nexus, as *grah*, *pinj*, *mlai*. Those roots which have more than one syllable are usually of a secondary nature, being in some cases produced by reduplication, as *jágar*, in others made from nouns, as *kumár*.

Each verbal root presents six phases or grades of action: active, neuter, passive, causal, desiderative, intensive. All these are distinguished by certain modifications of the letters of the root, and by certain prefixed and affixed syllables. Thus भू *bhû*, "to be," undergoes the following modifications:

Active / *Neuter*	bhava.
Passive	bhûya.
Causal	bhâvaya.
Desiderative	bubhûsha.
Intensive	bobhûya.

The causal also is in some cases treated as primary stem, and gives rise to subsidiary forms; thus from *pâtaya* "cause to fall," is made a passive *pâtya*, whence comes a desiderative causal *pipâtayisha*.

Each of these six phases may be conjugated throughout thirteen tenses, in each of which are nine forms representing the three persons of the singular, dual, and plural. It rarely happens in practice that any one verbal root exhibits the whole of these forms, but if we regard the general type, we may fairly say that a Sanskrit verb, as an individual entity, is an aggregate of seven hundred and two words, all agreeing in expressing modifications of the idea contained in the root-syllable, which is the common inheritance of them all.[1] Of the thirteen tenses, nine are conjugated according to certain rules which, with some exceptions, hold good for all verbs in the language, but the remaining four tenses are subject to rules by which they are divided into ten classes or conjugations. These four are the present, imperfect, imperative, and optative; and before we can determine what form a verbal

[1] Namely, 6 phases × 13 tenses × 9 persons = 702. But this is an extreme calculation, for the Subjunctive (Leṭ) is only found in Vedic Sanskrit; and the two forms of the Perfect (Liṭ) may be regarded as variations of the same tense. Thus the number of tenses may be reduced to ten, viz. Present (Laṭ), Imperfect (Laṅ), Optative (Liṅ), Imperative (Loṭ), Perfect (Liṭ), Aorist (Luṅ), Future (Lṛṭ), Conditional (Lṛṅ), Second Future (Luṭ), Benedictive (âśir Liṅ). By this reckoning the number of forms would be 6 × 10 × 9 = 540.

root can take in any of these tenses, we must know what conjugation it belongs to.

Inasmuch also as the Sanskrit grammarians class the active and neuter phases together, we must find out which of these two phases any given verb employs, for the terminations of the tenses and persons are different. Some verbs employ both, but the majority are conjugated only in one of the two, and as there is no rule as to which of the two is to be used, the dictionary is our only guide. The active, or Parasmaipada, as it is called, stands to the neuter, or Âtmanepada, in the same relation as the active in Greek does to the middle voice, and the resemblance is the greater, in that the Âtmanepada, like the middle voice in Greek, uses the terminations of the passive.

Although each of the seven hundred and two words which make up the complete typical Sanskrit verb contains the common root-syllable, yet this syllable does not appear in the same form in each word, but is subject to certain euphonic and other influences which affect both the vowels and consonants composing it, and often materially alter its shape. Thus the verbal root *KAR*, "do," appears in classical Sanskrit in the following forms:

1. कृ *Kṛi*, in 1 du. pf. Par. *chakṛiva*, 1 pl. id. *chakṛima*, 2 s. pf. Âtm. *chakṛishe*, 1 du., 1 and 2 pl. id. *chakṛivahe*, *chakṛimahe*, *chakṛidhve*; in the whole of the 1 aor. Âtm., as *akṛishi*, *akṛithâh*, *akṛita*, etc.; in the pass. part. *kṛitah*, and gerund *kṛitvâ*, and in the benedictive Âtm., as *kṛishîshṭa*, etc.

2. क्रि *kri*, in bened. Par., as *kriyâsam*, *kriyâh*, *kriyât*, etc., and in the passive present, as *kriye*, *kriyase*, *kriyate*, etc.

3. कर् *kar*, in pres. Par., as *karomi*, *karoshi*, *karoti*, and before all weak terminations.

4. कुर् *kur*, in pres. Âtm., as *kurve*, *kurvahe*, *kurvate*, and before strong terminations.

5. कार् *kâr*, in pf. Par., as *chakâra*, and 1 aor. Par., as *akârsham*, also in the causal, as *kârayati*.

6. कृ *kr*, in 2 and 3 pl. pf. Par., *chakru*, *chakruh*, and 1 and 3 s. pf. Âtm. *chakre*.

In the same way the root *ÇRU* "hear," appears in some parts of the verb as *çri*, in others as *çru*, *çrû*, *çrin*, and *çrûr*. In the whole range of verbal roots there is perhaps not one which does not undergo more or less modification in the course of being conjugated.

Not only does the root-syllable present itself in various forms in the several tenses, but the terminations of the nine persons differ in each tense, and sometimes one tense will have two sets of terminations. Moreover, the endings of any given tense in one phase, differ from the corresponding ones of the same tense in another phase. Thus the terminations of the present tense are in the active phase

Singular	1. mi.	2. si.	3. ti.
Dual	1. avah.	2. thah.	3. tah.
Plural	1. amah.	2. tha.	3. nti.

But in the middle phase the same tense ends in

Singular	1. i.	2. se.	3. te.
Dual	1. avahe.	2. ithe.	3. ite.
Plural	1. amahe.	2. dhve.	3. nte.

This slight outline will suffice to show how vast and intricate are the ramifications of the Sanskrit verb. The reader who has followed the steps by which the noun has been simplified, as shown in the second volume of this work, will not be surprised to find in the present volume how widely the modern verb differs from that of Sanskrit. It was impossible to reduce the verb to anything like the simplicity required by modern speakers without sacrificing by far the greater portion of the immense and unwieldy apparatus of ancient times.

§ 2. Owing to the want of a continuous succession of literary documents, such as exists in the case of the modern Romance languages of Europe, it is scarcely possible to trace step by step the changes which have occurred in the verb. It is necessary, however, to make the attempt, and to piece together such evidence as we have, because the modern verb is an undoubted descendant of the ancient one, though only a slight trait here and there recalls the features of its parent, and its structure in many points can only be rendered intelligible by tracing it back to the ancient stock whence it sprung.

The first steps in the direction of simplification occur in Sanskrit itself. Many of the elaborate forms cited by grammarians are of very rare occurrence in actual literature, and some of them seem almost to have been invented for the sake of uniformity. Three instances of this tendency in classical Sanskrit may here be noticed.

The perfect tense in Sanskrit, as in Greek, is usually formed by reduplication, so we have from √ तप् "burn," pf. तताप, √ दृश् "see," pf. ददर्श, just as λείπω makes λέλοιπα and τρέπω, τέτροφα. But there are certain roots which cannot take reduplication, and these form their perfect by an analytical process. The root is formed into a sort of abstract substantive in the accusative case, and the perfect of an auxiliary verb is added to it. The verbs भू "be," अस् "be," and कृ "do," are the auxiliaries principally employed for this purpose. Thus—

√ उन्द् "wet," makes pf. उन्दां चकार, उन्दां बभूव or उन्दां आस.

√ चकास् "shine," „ „ चकासां चकार, etc.

√ बोधय "explain," „ „ बोधयां चकार, etc.[1]

Another instance of the analytical formation is seen in the future tense made out of the agent of the verb with the present tense of the auxiliary अस् "be." Thus from √ बुध् "know," comes the agent बोधिता, which with the present of अस् makes

S. 1. बोधितास्मि	P. 1. बोधितास्मः
2. बोधितासि	2. बोधितास्थ.

[1] Max Müller's Sanskrit Grammar, p. 172.

A third instance is a form of phrase in which the passive past participle is combined with this same auxiliary अस् to form a perfect definite, as आगतोऽस्मि "I have come," or, as more faithfully represented by other European languages, "*je suis venu*," and as we sometimes say ourselves, "I am come." Here an analytical construction supplies the place of the perfect. Closely allied to this is the frequent habit in writers of the classical style of expressing the same tense by the neuter of the p.p.p. with the subject in the instrumental, as तेन गतं "by him gone," *i.e.* "he went," instead of अगमत्.

These are the first faint indications of a method which, in the course of ages, has developed to such an extent as to constitute the leading principle in the organization of the modern verb. By this system a greater facility for expressing nice shades of meaning is obtained. अगमत् may mean "he went," or, "he has gone," but by the other system each of these two meanings has a phrase peculiar to itself, गतोऽस्ति meaning "he has gone," and तेन गतं "he went." Precisely in the same way the Latin had only *ego amavi* for "I loved" and "I have loved," but the Romance languages found this insufficient, and they have—

	"I loved."	"I have loved."
French	j'aimai	j'ai aimé.
Italian	io amai	io ho amato.
Spanish	yo amé	yo he amado.

§ 3. The next step in the reduction of the numerous Sanskrit tenses to a more manageable compass is seen in Pali, originally an Indian Prakrit, but which became the sacred language of the Buddhists of Ceylon, having been carried thither in the middle of the third century[1] before Christ, by Mahendra, son of King Açoka, and spread thence to Burmah and Siam.

[1] Kuhn, Beiträge zur Pali Grammatik, p. 1. But Turnour, Mahawanso xxix., gives B.C. 307. So also Childers, preface, p. ix.

Although the Pali grammarians, in their anxiety to exalt their sacred speech, tell us that the verb has ten conjugations, yet examples of all these are but rarely found.[1] Four of the ten Sanskrit conjugations, the first, fourth, sixth, and tenth, resemble each other very closely even in that language, and are easily brought down to one in Pali. The seventh of Sanskrit also loses somewhat of its peculiar type, which consists in inserting न् between the vowel of the root and the final consonant, or न before weak terminations. Thus in Skr. √ रुध् *rudh*, "to obstruct," makes its present रुणद्धि *ruṇaddhi*, but in Pali, while the न is retained, the present is *rundhati*, after the type of the first class.

Five out of the ten Sanskrit conjugations are thus reduced almost, if not entirely, to one. Of the remaining five, the second of Sanskrit in roots which end in a vowel exhibits some traces of Sanskrit forms, while in those which end in a consonant the types of the first, or, *Bhû*, class prevail. Thus Skr. √या "to go," pr. याति, Pali also *yâti*, but

Skr. √ मृज् "to rub," pr. मार्ष्टि. Pali *majjati*, as if from a Skr. मर्जति.
√ दुह् "to milk," „ दोग्धि. „ *dohati*.
√ लिह् "to lick," „ लेढि. „ *lehati*.

The third conjugation occasionally takes the reduplication as in Sanskrit, but in many instances prefers the Bhû type. Thus

Skr. √ भी "to fear," बिभेति. Pali भायति.
√ धा "to hold," दधाति. „ दधाति and दहति.

The verb *dâ*, "to give," which belongs to this conjugation, has special developments of its own, and is discussed in § 16.

The fifth, eighth, and ninth classes are very similar even in Sanskrit, for while the fifth adds नु to its root, the eighth adds उ; but as all its roots except one already end in न्, it

[1] Seven classes are given by Kaccâyana. See Senart, Journal Asiatique, vi. série, vol. xvii. p. 439.

comes practically to pretty much the same thing as the fifth. The ninth adds न्, ना, and नी to the root before various terminations. Here Pali draws very slight distinctions, making verbs of the fifth class take नु and ना indifferently, and both fifth and ninth appear occasionally in the guise of the first. Thus—

Skr. √श्रु "hear," v.	शृणोति.	Pali	सुणोति and सुणाति.
√बन्ध् "bind," ix.	बध्नाति.	,,	बंधति.
√कृ "do," viii.	करोति.	,,	करोति.
√मन् "think," viii.	मनुते.	,,	मञ्ञति.

The reason why the forms of the Bhû conjugation exercise so great an influence, and, like the -a-stem in nouns, so largely displace all the other types, is probably that the first conjugation is by far the largest, containing upwards of nine hundred out of the two thousand roots said to exist in Sanskrit. The second conjugation has only seventy-three, the third but twenty-five, the fourth and sixth about one hundred and forty each. The tenth, it is true, contains four hundred, but it is identical in form with the causal. The fifth has only thirty-three, the ninth sixty-one, while under the seventh class are twenty-five, and under the eighth only nine. These figures, it must be added, are taken from the Dhâtupâṭha, a grammarian's list of roots,[1] which contains many roots seldom, if ever, found in use, so that for all practical purposes the first conjugation covers more than half the verbs in the language. When it is also remembered that the fourth, sixth, and tenth differ but slightly from the first, it is not surprising that the terminations common to these four conjugations should have fixed themselves in the popular mind, and been added by the vulgar to all roots indiscriminately. Nearly all those verbs which retain the type of any conjugation, except the first, are words of extremely common use, which would naturally keep their

[1] Westergaard, Radices Sanskr. p. 342.

well-known forms in the mouths of the people in spite of all rules and tendencies to the contrary.

§ 4. The dual number has entirely disappeared from Pali, and the Atmanepada, or middle phase, has practically merged into the active, for although Kaccâyana (J. As., vol. xvii. p. 429, sûtra 18) gives terminations for it, yet it is admitted that those of the active may be used instead, and practically it would appear that they are so used. The other phases, as causal, passive, desiderative, and intensive, have their own forms as in Sanskrit.

Among the tenses the chief is the present, and it is in Pali that we first find a tendency to retain throughout the whole verb that form of the root which is in use in the present. This tendency grows stronger in the later Prakrits, and becomes an almost invariable rule in the modern languages. Thus—

Skr. √ पच् "cook,"	present	पचति.	Pa.	पचति.
	future	पक्ष्यति.	"	पचिस्सति.
	aorist	अपाक्षीत्.	"	अपचि.
	gerund	पक्त्वा.	"	पचित्वा.

Phonetic influences in Sanskrit change this root as regards its final consonant in the different tenses, but Pali, having got hold of the form *pach* in the present tense, retains it throughout the verb. It is still, however, only a tendency, and not a law, for we find instances in which Pali forms are derived directly from the corresponding tense in Sanskrit. One who should attempt to learn Pali without reference to Sanskrit would find it difficult to understand how the words *karoti*, *kubbati*, *kayirâ*, *kâhâmi*, *akâsi*, *kattum*, could all spring from the same verbal root. It is only when the corresponding Sanskrit forms *karoti*, *kurvate*, *kuryât*,[1] *karishyâmi*, *akârshît*, *kartum*, are put by their

[1] Or more strictly from an older *kuryât* not in use in classical Sanskrit. Kuhn, Beiträge, 106.

side, that the thread which connects them all becomes evident. Just so in the Romance languages, Italian *so, sa, sapete, sanno, seppi*, seem to have very little beyond the initial *s* in common, till it is perceived that they come from the Latin *sapio, sapit, sapitis, sapiunt, sapui*; thus, also, *ho* and *ebbi* can only be seen to be parts of the same verb when their origin from Latin *habeo* and *habui* is recognized. In Spanish there is the same difficulty, as will be seen by comparing *hacer, hago, hice, haré*, and *hecho*, with their Latin originals *facere, facio, feci, facere habeo*, and *factum*. In Portuguese, which seems to be the lowest and most corrupt Apabhramça of the Romance Prakrits, the changes are such as almost to defy analysis. For instance, *ter, tenho, tinha, tive, terei*, correspond to Latin *tenere, teneo, tenebam, tenui, tenere habeo*: also *hei, houve, haja*, to *habeo, habui, habeam*, and *sou, he, fui, seja*, to *sum, est, fui, sit*.[1]

The tenses of the Pali verb are eight in number.[2] These correspond to the tenses of the Sanskrit verb, omitting the periphrastic or second future (luṭ), the benedictive (âçir liṅ), and the subjunctive (leṭ). The present active is almost exactly the same as the Sanskrit as regards its terminations in the Bhû form, and the middle only differs, and even then very slightly, in the 1 and 2 plural. Thus—

Skr. 1 pl. पचामहे. 2. पचध्वे.
Pa. 1. पचाम्हे. 2. पचव्हे.

In this tense, as in many others, Pali is not very instructive, it clings too closely to the Sanskrit. It is, however, necessary to give a sketch of its forms, because they exhibit the first traces of that gradual change which has led to the modern conjugation. Even when the Pali conjugates a verb according to

[1] Diez, Gramm. d. Romanischen Sprachen, vol. ii. p. 126.
[2] The materials for this section are taken chiefly from Kuhn, Beiträge, p. 92 seqq., with some additions from Childers's Dictionary, and a few remarks of my own.

any class other than the Bhû, it still keeps the personal endings of Sanskrit for that conjugation; thus from √ या "go," we have—

Pa. S. 1. यामि, 2. यासि, 3. याति; P. 1. याम, 2. याथ, 3. यन्ति.

which differs from Sanskrit only in omitting the visarga in P. 1.

The imperative follows the type of the present, and may be thus compared with Sanskrit Parasmaipada,

Skr. S. 1. पचानि, 2. पच, 3. पचतु; P. 1. पचाम, 2. पचत, 3. पचन्तु.
Pa. S. 1. पचामि, 2. पचाहि, 3. पचतु; P. 1. पचाम, 2. पचथ, 3. पचन्तु.

and with the Âtmanepada, thus—

Skr. S. 1. पचै, 2. पचस्व, 3. पचताम्; P. 1. पचामहै, 2. पचध्वं, 3. पचन्ताम्.
Pa. S. 1. पचे, 2. पचस्सु, 3. पचतं; P. 1. पचामसे, 2. पचव्हो, 3. पचन्तं.

Here the S. 1 Parasmai seems to have arisen from some confusion with the present, as also P. 2. Noteworthy is S. 2, with its ending हि, which, though only found in classical Sanskrit in the second, third, seventh, and ninth conjugations, has crept into all in Pali, and has continued on into the mediæval period, thus Chand

तिन सु सद्द अक्खी कहहि।
"*Say thou* a good word of them."—Pr. R. i. 9.

where कहहि = Skr. कथय (हि). In Vedic Skr. हि appears in all the conjugations. Of the Âtmane forms P. 1 seems to be derived from an older form, *masi*. P. 2 should perhaps be read *hvo*, not *vho*, in which case it is a regular resultant from Sanskrit *dhve*.

The potential is the Sanskrit optative (liṅ), thus—

PARASMAI.

Skr. S. 1. पचेयं, 2. पचेः, 3. पचेत्; P. 1. पचेम, 2. पचेत, 3. पचेयुः.
Pa. S. 1. पचेय्यामि, 2. °य्यासि, 3. °य्य; P. 1. °य्याम, 2. °य्याथ, 3. °य्युं.

ÂTMANE.

Sk. S. 1. पचेय. 2. पचेथाः. 3. पचेत; P. 1. पचेमहि. 2. पचेध्वं. 3. पचेरन्.

Pa. S. 1. पचेय्यं. 2. पचेथो. 3. पचेथ; P. 1. पचेय्याम्हे. 2. °य्यव्हो. 3. पचेरं.

In this tense the point specially to be noticed is the tendency to simplify not only the root-syllable, but the range of terminations also. Having got the syllable *eyya* as the type of the tense, Pali seeks to avoid all further distinctions, and to use as much as possible the personal endings of the present tense. It sometimes conjugates the potential according to the types of other classes, and in this respect follows the lead of the present less faithfully in this tense than in the imperative. Thus, though in the present and imperative of *kar*, it follows the Sanskrit, and has *karoti*, *karotu*, yet in the potential it treats *kar* as if it belonged to the Bhû class, and has *kareyyâmi* as though from a Sanskrit *kareyam* instead of the actual *kuryâm*. There are other peculiarities about this tense which are not here noticed, as having no bearing upon the subject of the modern languages.

The imperfect has been, to some extent, mixed up with the aorist (luṅ), and both, together with the perfect, lead us into considerations which are of interest only for Pali itself, not having survived or had any influence on modern developments. They may therefore be passed over as immaterial to our present inquiry.

The future, on the contrary, offers many interesting peculiarities, especially, as will be seen hereafter, in reference to Gujarati and some of the rustic dialects of Hindi. The future is a different tense in the modern languages, and every scrap of information which can help to elucidate it deserves special notice. It runs thus in Pali (√ गम् "go")—

Skr. S. 1. गमिष्यामि. 2. °ष्यसि. 3. °ष्यति; P. 1. °ष्यामस्. 2. ष्यथ. 3. ष्यंति.

Pa. S. 1. गमिस्सामि. 2. °स्ससि. 3. °स्सति; P. 1. °स्साम. 2. स्सथ. 3. स्संति.

Here the only noteworthy feature is the change of ष्य into स्स. The Âtmanepada follows the same rule throughout. Although the tendency to keep that form of the root which exists in the present leads to divergences from the Sanskrit future type, yet instances occur in which the Sanskrit type is preserved. These occur in reference to that very troublesome feature in the Sanskrit verb, the intermediate इ, which is sometimes inserted between the root and the termination, and sometimes not. When it is not inserted, the euphonic laws of Sanskrit require that the final consonant of the root be changed to enable it to combine with the initial consonant of the termination. Thus √पच् "cook," when it has to take the future termination स्यति, becomes पक् and पक् + स्यति = पक्ष्यति. Here Pali sticks to the form पच्, because it is used in the present and makes its future पचिस्सति as though there had been (as there probably was in colloquial usage) a Sanskrit future पचिष्यति with the intermediate इ inserted.

In a certain number of verbs, however, it has two forms, one as above retaining the root-form of the present, and the other a phonetic equivalent of the Sanskrit. Kuhn[1] gives the following examples, to which I add the Sanskrit for comparison.

Skr.	√लभ् "get,"	future	लप्स्यते.	Pali	लच्छति	but also	लभिस्सति.
	√वच् "speak,"	,,	वक्ष्यति.	,,	वक्खति.		
	√धा "put,"	,,	धास्यति.	,,	धस्सति.		
	√वस् "dwell,"	,,	वत्स्यति.	,,	वच्छति	but also	वसिस्सति.
	√छिद् "cleave,"	,,	छेत्स्यति.	,,	छेच्छति	,,	छिन्दिस्सति.
	√भुज् "eat,"	,,	भोक्ष्यति.	,,	भोक्खति	,,	भुंजिस्सति.
	√मुच् "loose,"	,,	मोक्ष्यति.	,,	मोक्खति	,,	मुंचिस्सति.
	√श्रु "hear,"	,,	श्रोष्यति.	,,	सोस्सति	,,	सुणिस्सति.

[1] Beiträge, p. 115.

The consonantal changes are in accordance with the treatment of the nexus as explained in Vol. I. p. 304. The striving after uniformity is seen, however, in the retention of the alternative forms having the same type as the present, and it is, moreover, worth observing that the forms which reproduce the type of the Sanskrit without the intermediate इ seem by degrees to have been misunderstood. The illiterate masses, and even those better instructed, seem to have missed the *issati* which so generally indicated to their minds the future tense, and regarded those forms which had not this familiar sound as present tenses. So they made double futures by adding the *issa* to them. Thus from दृश् "to see," future द्रक्ष्यति. Pali made a form *dakkhati*, but the people by degrees took this for a present, and made what to them seemed a more correct future *dakkhissati*. I mention this here as I shall have occasion hereafter to discuss the much-debated question of the origin of the familiar modern stem *dekh* "see" (see § 17). Another instance is

> Skr. √ शक् "be able," future शक्ष्यति. Pa. सक्खति, whence vulgo सक्खिस्सति.

In one case Pali has a future which points back to a Vedic form:

> Skr. √ रुद् "weep." Vedic future रोत्स्यति. Pa. रोच्छति.
> Classic ditto रोदिष्यति. „ रोदिस्सति.

Occasionally the स्स is softened to ह, as in काहति, काहिति from करिस्सति, Skr. करिष्यति. This is noteworthy with reference to Bhojpuri and the eastern Hindi dialects generally.

§ 5. It used to be held that Pali was a descendant of the Māgadhi dialect of Prakrit, but this opinion is now, I believe, exploded. Though the question is not yet set at rest, it would seem to have been fairly established that Mahendra was a native of Ujjayin, and that the language which he carried to Ceylon was the ordinary vernacular of his own province.[1] This dialect was not very different from that of Magadha, and Mahendra may have slightly altered the Mâgadhi sayings of the great master, by his Ujjayini pronunciation, while retaining the name Mâgadhi out of deference to the sacred associations which clustered round the birthplace of Buddha.

Be this as it may, the nearest Indian dialect to Pali seems undoubtedly to be the Prakrit of the Bhâgavatî, a sacred book of the semi-Buddhist sect of Jainas. If Hemachandra, himself a Jain and author of several works on Prakrit, were available for reference, our task would be easier; as yet, however, none of Hemachandra's writings have been printed or edited. Weber's articles on the Bhâgavatî are at present our only source of information.[2]

In the Jaina Prakrit the ten conjugations of the Sanskrit verb are, with *few exceptions*, reduced to the Bhû type. In this respect it goes further than Pali, treating as verbs of the first conjugation many which in Pali retain the type of other conjugations. The fifth, seventh, and ninth conjugations, which in Sanskrit insert न् with certain variations, are all reduced to one head by regarding the न् as part of the root, as is also the case with the य of the fourth class. The *a* inserted between the root and termination of the Bhû class is used throughout, though occasionally weakened to *i*, or changed to *e* from some confusion between this and the *e* = *aya*, which is the type of the tenth class. The following examples will illustrate the above remarks.

[1] Kuhn, Beiträge, p. 7.

[2] Pischel's admirable edition of Hemachandra's Grammar (Orphanage Press, Halle, 1877) has reached me just as this work is going to press, and too late to be of use for this edition, except for a few hasty notes here and there. Mueller's Beiträge zur Grammatik des Jainaprakrit came into my hands about the same time. I find it enables me to add a few illustrations to this section, which, however, was written in the latter part of 1876.

Skr. √ हृ "take," i. हरति — Jaina हरति, हरइ.
√ विद् "know," ii. वेत्ति — „ वेदेइ.
iii. 3 विदन्ति — „ वेदेंति.
√ धा "put," iii. दधाति
with अपि, अपिदधाति — „ पिहेइ "puts on (clothes)" and पिहाइ.
√ सिध् "succeed," iv. सिध्यति — „ सिज्झइ.
but आराध् "propitiate," आराध्यति — „ आराहेइ.
√ आप् "get," v. आप्नोति.
with प्र, प्राप्, प्राप्नोति — „ पाउणइ, the ण being treated as part of the root.
√ चि "gather," v. चिनोति — „ चयति, चयइ, but also चिणाइ, with the same confusion between the नो of v. and ना of viii. as occurs in Pali.
√ श्रु "hear," v. शृणोति
with प्रति, प्रतिशृणोति — „ पडिसुणेइ "promises."
√ छुप् "touch," vi. छुपति — „ छुवेइ.
√ भञ्ज् "break," vii. भनक्ति — „ भंजइ.
√ कृ "do," viii. करोति — „ करइ.
√ ग्रह् "take," ix. गृह्णाति — „ गेण्हइ, here again the ण has passed into the root.
√ ज्ञा "know," ix. जानाति — „ जाणइ.

The tenth class being identical with the first is omitted. It will be seen that the present tense is formed throughout on the model of the first conjugation, the Jain words given above being phonetic modifications of words which would be in Sanskrit respectively *harati, vedati, dhâti, ârâdhati, prâpanati, chayati, snpati, bhanjati, karati, grihnati,* and *jânati,* if all those verbs belonged to the first or Bhû conjugation.

It is not so easy to draw out a full verbal paradigms in this dialect as in Pali, because we have as yet no grammars, and are obliged to fall back on the words that occur in a single text. The range of tenses appears to consist of a present (corresponding to the Sanskrit laṭ), imperative (loṭ), potential (liṅ), imperfect and aorist jumbled together as in Pali, and future (lṛiṭ). The perfect (liṭ) seems to be altogether wanting, as it is in the modern languages.

The present runs thus:—√ नम् "bow."

S. 1. नमामि, 2. नमसि, 3. नमति; P. 1. नमामो, 2. नमह, 3. नमंति.
नमेमि, नमेसि, नमेति; नमेमो, नमेंति.
नमइ; नमिंति.
नमेइ.

Those terminations which contain the vowel *e* have crept into the conjugation of all verbs from the tenth, to which that vowel, as shortened from *aya*, must be held strictly to belong, or to causals. Thus in Bhâg. i. 60, we have *phâḍeti, pâleti, sobheti, threti, pâreti, kiṭṭeti, aṇupâlei, drâhei,* for Sanskrit स्फाटयति, पालयति, शोभयति, तारयति, पूरयति, कीर्तयति, अनुपालयति, आराधयति, respectively. In the last word the causal form becomes the same as the active given above. Of the imperative we have only the S. 2 and P. 2, which are in fact the only persons which an imperative can properly have. The S. 2 takes the ending हि as in Pali with junction vowels *â* and *e*, the P. 2 ends in ह, which, as Weber points out, is from the P. 2 of the present, in Sanskrit थ. Thus—

Skr. √ रुच् "shine," causal रोचय, impr. रोचय. Jaina रोएहि.
श्रद्धा "believe," ,, सद्देहि. ,, सद्दहामि (pres. सद्दहए).
√ बंध् "bind," Impr. P. 2. बन्धेह, ,, बंधह.

The potential, of which only the S. 3 is traceable, resembles Pali in using the termination *eyya* with variant *ejja*.

Skr. √ गम् "go." S. 3. गच्छेत् Jaina गच्छेज्ज, गच्छेज्जा.
√ ग्रह् "take," „ गृह्णीयात् „ गेण्हेज्ज.

But there exist some old simple forms derived by phonetic changes from the corresponding Sanskrit tense, as kujja = kuryât, dajja = dadyât (Mueller, p. 60).

The future resembles that of Pali, thus—

S. 1. भविस्सामि. 2. °इस्ससि. 3. °इस्सइ; P. 1. °इस्सामो. 2. °इस्सह. 3. इस्संति.

It also appears with a termination *ihi* produced by weakening स्स into ह and the following *a* to *i*, thus—

Skr. भविष्यति. Jaina भविहिइ and भविहिति.

Moreover, there is a trace of the double future like Pali *dakkhissati*.

Skr. √ पद् "go," with उप, उपपद् "attain," future उपपत्स्यते. Jaina उववज्जिहिति.

Here उपपत्स्यते would phonetically become उववच्छइ, and by still further softening उववज्जइ, whence, as if from a present, is formed the future उववज्जिस्सइ and उववज्जिहिति.

§ 6. The reduction in the number of tenses necessitates a greatly extended use of participles. This is one great step in the transition from the synthetical to the analytical system. The Sanskrit present active participle takes in that language the characteristics of the ten conjugations, and is declined as a noun in three genders. It ends properly in *ant*, but the nasal is dropped before certain terminations, as

M.	F.	N.
पचन्	पचन्ती	पचत्.
बंधन्	बंधन्ती	बंधत्.

The nasal, however, is retained throughout in Jaina Prakrit, thus—

Skr. पचन् पचन्ती पचत्.
Jaina पयंतो पयंती पयंतं.

This peculiarity is worth remembering; much depends on this retention of the nasal, as will be seen when we come to the modern Sindhi and Panjabi verbs.

Very great interest attaches to the participle of the future passive, which in Sanskrit ends in तव्य. In verbs which do not take intermediate इ, this ending is added directly to the root with the usual Sandhi changes; but as Prakrit prefers to insert the इ in order to preserve the root-form of the present, it comes to pass that the त of the termination stands alone between two vowels, and in consonance with Prakrit phonetics is elided. The hiatus thus produced is in the Jaina writings filled by य. If to this we add the regular mutation of व्य into व्व, we get from तव्य the form यव्व. In its original meaning this participle corresponds to the Latin in *ndus*, as *faciendus*, and expresses that which is to be done, as त्वया गन्तव्यं "by thee it is to be gone," *i.e.* "thou must go." In this sense it occurs frequently in Bhâgavatî, as for instance in § 58:

Jaina एवं देवाणुप्पिया गंतव्वं, चिट्ठियव्वं, णिसीतियव्वं, भुंजियव्वं, etc.
Skr. एवं देवानुप्रिया गन्तव्यं, स्थातव्यं, निषत्तव्यं, भोक्तव्यं, etc.

"Thus, O beloved of the gods, must ye go, must ye stand, must ye sit, must ye eat," where the last two words postulate a Sanskrit form with the इ inserted, such as निषीदितव्यं, भुंजितव्यं.

It is obvious that it would require no great straining of the sense of this participle to make it into an infinitive, and seeing that as early as this Jaina dialect the use of the regular Sanskrit infinitive in तुं has become rare, it follows that recourse should be had to some participial form to supply its place. In this way we find the past passive participle in इत, with the त elided and its place supplied by त्त, employed in a construction where we should expect the infinitive. Thus Bhâg. § 54, इच्छामि पव्वावित्तए, मुंडावित्तए, सेहावित्तए, सिक्खावित्तए (Weber, Bhâg. p. 274): "I wish to wander, to take the tonsure, to practise austerities, to learn," as though from Sanskrit forms प्रव्राजितुं, मुण्डापितुं, सेधापितुं, शिक्षापितुं, the three last being causals formed with *âp*, as is frequently the case with causals in Prakrit, though of course these forms are not found in Sanskrit. In that language the formation of causals by means of प् is restricted to a few stems.

More will be said on this subject in a subsequent chapter, but it is necessary here to note an early instance of this process which takes a much wider development in later times, the infinitive in Gujarati and Oriya and several participial constructions and verbal nouns being derived from it.

§ 7. The scenic Prakrits represent a further step in development. Despite the admittedly artificial character of these dialects, they probably retain forms which were at one time in general use, although that time may not have been the epoch when the dramas were written, and without referring to them, the structure of the modern verb could not be clearly understood. It is expedient to avoid discussing this question, lest attention should be drawn away from the real subject of this work, namely, the *modern* languages. All this part of the present chapter is merely introductory and is only inserted in order to pave the way for a more intelligent appreciation of the origin and growth of Hindi and its fellows.

In the Mâhârâshtrî or principal poetical dialect all conjugations are reduced to the type of the first or Bhû class, and the same holds good for the Çauraseni or chief prose dialect. Only here and there do we find faint traces of the peculiarities of other conjugations. Of the six phases only three remain, active, passive, and causal. The passive differs from the active only in the form of the root, the characteristic य of the

Sanskrit passive having been worked into the stem, and the terminations of the active being added to it. The Âtmanepada and the dual are of course rejected.

Of tenses these dialects have a still more restricted range than the Jaina Prakrits. They have the present, imperative and future, with traces of the potential. The past tense is chiefly formed by the p.p.p. with auxiliary verbs. Thus from √ रुच् "shine,"

Present S. 1. रोचामि. 2. रोचसि. 3. रोचदि.
रोचमि. रोचए.
रोचम्हि.

P. 1. रोचामो. °मु. °म. 2. रोचध. °ह. 3. रोचन्ति.
रोचम. °मु. °म्हो. °म्ह. °त्थ. °धं.
रोचिमो. °मु. °इत्थ.

Here are observable those first indications of a confusion of forms, and uncertainty in their use, which are always characteristic of that period in languages when the synthetical structure is breaking down into the analytical. In these dialects, as in Jaina Prakrit, the practice exists of inserting ए as a junction vowel; thus we have such forms as करेमि "I do," Skr. करोमि, instead of करामि, which would be the regular result of treating कृ as a Bhû verb, गच्छेम्ह for गच्छाम, "let us go." The presence of the म्ह in S. 1 and P. 1 is accounted for by its being confused with that construction in which the present of अस् is used with a past participle; thus we find कदम्हि "I was made" = Sanskrit कृतोऽस्मि, and पेसिदम्हि "I have been sent" = Skr. प्रेषितोऽस्मि.

The imperative has the following forms—

S. 2. रोच 3. रोचदु. P. 2. रोचध 3. रोचंतु.
रोचाहि रोचउ. रोचह.

The S. 2 has also forms रोचस्स, रोचस्सु, pointing to a Sanskrit Âtmane form रोचस्व and P. 2 similarly रोचध्वं = Skr. रोचध्वं, though neither are used in a middle sense, but are equivalents as regards meaning of the Sanskrit active.

The following are a few examples:

पेक्खस्स "look thou!"	Skr.	प्रेक्षस्व.
णमस्स "bow thou!"	"	नमस्व.
सुणध "hear ye."	"	शृणुत.
जाध "go ye."	"	यात.
अवेध "go away."	"	अपेत.
ओसरध "get out of the way!"	"	अपसरत.
करेध "do."	"	कुरुत.
जग्गेध "wake up."	"	जाग्रत.[1]

The future most usually exhibits the form of the Sanskrit present in इष्य = इस्स.

S. 1. रोदिस्सामि. 2. रोदिस्ससि. 3. °इस्सदि.
रोदिस्सं
P. 1. °इस्सामो. 2. °इस्सध. 3. °इस्संति.
etc. °इस्सह.

This form is used indifferently with roots of all classes as in Pali, but here also there still subsist some traces of a future formed without the intermediate इ. Vararuchi (vii. 16, 17) gives the following:—

Skr. √श्रु "hear,"	fut.	श्रोष्यामि.	Pr.	सोच्छं.
√वच् "speak,"	"	वक्ष्यामि.	"	वोच्छं.
√गम् "go,"	"	[गंस्यामि].	"	गच्छं.
√रुद् "weep,"	" Ved.	रोत्स्यामि.	"	रोच्छं.
√विद् "know,"	"	वेत्स्यामि.	"	वेच्छं.

These forms are, however, justly regarded as exceptions; for the rule in scenic, as in other, Prakrits is to retain throughout the root-form of the present. The regular type of the future is that in *issa*-, and the above words have also a future formed in the regular way, सुणिस्सदि, वचिस्सदि, गमिस्सदि, etc. This स्स

[1] Some of these are Mâgadhi Prakrit, but for my present purpose it is not necessary to draw a distinction between Mâgadhi and Çauraseni.

is softened to ह, and the following vowel is weakened to इ, producing as characteristic the syllables *ihi*. Thus—

√ हस् "laugh." S. 1. हसिहिमि. 2. हसिहिसि. 3. हसिहिइ, etc.

By a forgetfulness of the origin of such forms as सोच्छं, the ordinary future terminations may be added to them too, just like *dakkhissati* in Pali (§ 4), so that we find सोच्छिस्सामि, and सोच्छिहिमि.

The various tenses which in Sanskrit indicate past time have already in Pali and the earlier Prakrits been fused down into one. In scenic Prakrit a further step is taken, and the syllables *ia*, erroneously written *ïa* in some MSS., are added to the root for all persons of the past tense (Var. vii. 23, 24. Lassen, Inst. Pr., 353). This is probably the neuter of the p.p.p. in Sanskrit, and its use is due to the frequency of the construction with the instrumental. Instead of saying "I saw, I went, I heard," the people said, "by me seen, gone, heard." This point is one of great importance in modern Hindi and Gujarati.

§ 8. While the Maharashtri and Çauraseni dialects are considered the principal ones in the dramas, there are yet others of great importance, such as the Mágadhi, with its sub-dialects. Among these, however, it is necessary only to notice that called Apabhrança. I do not wish here to touch upon the question whether the dialect called by this name in the dramas really represents the speech of any particular Indian province or not. I assume, for the sake of convenience, that Apabhrança is really a vulgar speech further removed from the classical idiom than Maharashtri or Çauraseni. There may have been half a dozen Apabhranças, probably there were. In this section I am merely seeking to put together examples of verbal forms in a dialect one step nearer to modern times than the principal scenic Prakrits, and having done so, shall go on to my own special subject.

All that we can expect in the way of tenses after what has been said in the preceding sections, is a present, an imperative, and a future. The rest of the verbal work is done by participles.

√प्रछ् "ask." Present S. 1. पुच्छामि. 2. °च्छसि. 3. °च्छइ.
पुच्छमि. छइ.
°च्छिमि °च्छेमि.
P. 1. पुच्छाम. 2. पुच्छह. 3. °च्छंति.
°च्छध.

√कृ "do," Imperative S. 2. करहि. P. 1. करउं. P. 2. करह.
करे.
करि. करहु.
करु. करहु.
कर.

In the future, although the form with the characteristic *issa* is found as कुणरिस्सदि = करिष्यति. Skr. √कृ, yet more commonly we find the form in which स has been softened to ह; thus

S. 1. करिहिमि. 2. करिहिसि. 3. करिहिइ, etc.

The grammarians also give a

P. 1. in उं as करीहाउं = करिष्याम.

The participles resemble in most respects those in other Prakrit dialects, but that in तव्य becomes एवं, as करएवं and करिवं = करिणव्य (कर्तव्य). The gerund ends in पि, पिणु, and a softened form वि; the ordinary Çaurasenī form इय, which will be found in several modern languages, is here also used. To the gerund rather than to the infinitive, as the grammarians would have it, seems to belong the form in एवउं, as करिवउं, the exact genesis of which is doubtful, though, as to the final उं, there is an analogy in the true infinitive करणउं, which very closely approaches to Chaṇḍ's forms, as करएवउं, करएवु.

In addition to the above forms which are found in scenic Apabhrança, others and those more genuine fragments of popular speech are to be picked out from scraps that have been preserved by bards. It is much to be wished that we had more of Hemachandra's works accessible, as in them we should doubtless find a rich mine of such words. Thus for all past tenses there is the participial form in इउ for all three persons, as

मारिउ = मारितं (मारितः).
चलिउ = चलितं.
चढ़िउ = चर्चितं.

It has a plural in आ or या, as:

चाला = चलिताः
मारिया = मारिताः
चढ़िया = चर्चिताः

Sometimes also the *u* of the singular is rejected and *a* substituted, as अखिउ = अखितं. There are other forms to be found in these poems which will be referred to hereafter when the modern forms which they illustrate are under discussion.

As a general result from the preceding brief sketches it may be asserted that Sanskrit, Pali, and the Prakrits taken collectively as the languages of the earlier stage have a common structure, though in different grades. Sanskrit, with its full range of synthetical tenses, yet admits here and there analytical constructions. Pali does the same, though its synthetical tenses are fewer and simpler. The Prakrits reduce the tenses still further, and make greater use of participial constructions. The treatment of the root-syllable also shows a gradually increasing tendency to simplification, for whereas in Sanskrit it is changed in form repeatedly in the various tenses, a practice begins in Pali and grows more common as we go down the stream, of using in all parts of the verb that form of the root which is found in the Sanskrit present.

From the review of these languages given above the passive and causal have been purposely omitted, because the parts which they play in the development of the modern verb are peculiar, and will be better understood when seen side by side with the modern forms. The desiderative and intensive have left few or no traces of their existence, and may be passed over unnoticed.

§ 9. We may now approach the languages of the present day, and the discussion becomes more minute and particular. Though the verb of the new world has ways of its own, yet it stretches out hands across the gulf of centuries to the old world verb, and supports its claim to descent from it by still preserving traces unmistakeable, though often faint and irregular, of the ancient forms and systems.

As in the noun, so also in the verb, the first thing to be considered is the stem. The modern verbal stem undergoes no changes, but remains absolutely the same throughout all moods, tenses and persons. To this rule there is a small though important exception, consisting of some participles of the preterite passive which are derived direct from the Prakrit forms, and are thus early Tadbhavas. The number of these early Tadbhava participles differs in the various languages. They are most numerous, as might be expected, in Sindhi, which has a hundred and forty of them in a total of about two thousand verbs. In Panjabi, Gujarati and Marathi the number is rather less, while in Hindi only five, and in Bengali and Oriya only two exist. They will be found, together with their derivations, in Chapter III. §§ 46, 47, 48.

With this slight exception the verbal stem remains unaltered throughout. Thus, having got, by means hereafter to be explained, the word *sun* for "hear," Hindi simply tacks on to it the terminations; thus *sunnā* to hear, *suntā* hearing, *sunā* heard, *sunūṅ* I hear, *sune* he hears, *suno* hear ye! *sunegā* he will hear, *sunkar* having heard.

Primary stems are almost always monosyllabic, but secondary or derivative stems have often more syllables than one. The latter may be brought under three heads. First, stems derived from Sanskrit roots with which a preposition has already been compounded, principally उत्, नि, प्र, and सं, as *utar* "descend," *nikal* "go out," *pasar* "spread," *sankoch* "distress." Second, stems formed by reduplication, as *jhanjhan* "tinkle," *tharthar* "flutter." Third, stems with an added syllable, as *gaṭak* "swallow," *ghasīṭ* "drag," *karkach*, "bind."

It was seen above that in the old world verb there were six phases, and that two of these, the desiderative and intensive, have since been lost. The modern verb having to provide for active, neuter, passive, causal and other phases, has been obliged to have recourse to processes of its own, by which it arrives at the possession of a much wider range than Sanskrit can boast of, and does it too by far simpler means. Partly this result is obtained by ingenious adaptations of Prakrit forms, partly by modifications of, or additions to, its own stems, and partly by combining two stems together. It will first, therefore, be necessary to examine what phases the modern verb has, and then to proceed to examine the processes by which it has provided itself with the necessary forms for each phase.

§ 10. Those phases which are expressed by one word may be ranged as regards meaning in a regular scale of grades of action, according to the degree and kind of activity they express. In the following scheme we take the neuter as the point of quiescence, and trace degrees which start from it towards a positive pole indicating activity, and a negative pole indicating passivity.

NEGATIVE POLE.	−3	−2	−1	0	+1	+2	+3	+4	POSITIVE POLE.
	Passive Causal.	Passive.	Passive Intransitive.	Neuter.	Active Intransitive.	Active.	Causal.	Double Causal.	

The foregoing table looks, I fear, somewhat fanciful, but I know not how better to express a matter which is a striking and very important feature in the modern Aryan verb. It may be explained by considering each phase separately.

The neuter verb (0) expresses neither action nor passion. It conceives of the subject as in a condition of mere existence, as *being* something, not *doing*, and is therefore the simplest phase of verbal description. Pure neuter verbs are *ho* "be," *rah* "remain."

The next grade is the active intransitive (+1) which conceives of the subject as indeed acting, but acting in such a way that his action does not pass beyond himself to affect an external object, as *soch* "think," *chal* "walk," *phir* "revolve."

The active transitive comes next (+2). In this the subject is considered as acting in such a way that his action affects external objects, as *mâr* "beat," *khâ* "eat," *pî* "drink."

The next grade is the causal (+3), in which the subject acts upon an external object in such a way as to cause it to act in its turn upon a second object, as H. *sunâ* "cause to hear," H. *phirâ* "cause to turn."

In some of the languages there is a yet further grade, the double causal (+4), in which the subject causes the first object to set in motion a second object, so that it affects a third object, as S. *pherâ* "cause to cause to turn," S. *ghârâ* "cause to cause to wound."

Returning now to the neuter or central point, and starting off again in the opposite direction towards the negative pole, we arrive at the passive intransitive (—1). In this phase the subject not only takes no action, but is himself under the influence of exterior agencies. It differs as much from the neuter on one hand as from the passive on the other, and is a sort of middle voice. It is called in Sanskrit grammar *Bhâva-* or *Sahya-bheda*, and is principally used in Gujarati, though existing in the other languages also, as G. *abhadā* "be polluted" (be in a state of pollution), H. *ban* "be built" (be in process of construction).

The passive (−2) is that phase which regards the subject as no longer an agent, but as being acted upon, as S. *dhoija* "be washed."

Lastly comes the passive causal (−3), where the subject causes an object to be acted upon by a second object, as M. *mārwṇ* "cause to be struck."

It must not be supposed that all of these phases are found in every language. On the contrary, in none of the languages are there separate forms for each phase. It is only on reviewing the whole seven in a body that the full range of phases is seen. Generally speaking, the eight phases are represented by six sets of forms:

1. Neuter,	including	0, +1 and −1.
2. Active,	"	+2.
3. Passive,	"	−2.
4. Causal,	"	+3.
5. Passive Causal,	"	−3.
6. Double Causal,	"	+4.

The double causal and passive have separate and distinct forms only in Sindhi. The passive, however, is found in some rustic dialects of Hindi. Generally the use of the passive construction is avoided by having recourse to the passive intransitive (−1) or the neuter (0), the former of which has a distinct form in Gujarati, Old Hindi, and Bengali, and in the construction of sentences in which it is used resembles the active, like *vapulo* in Latin.

Of the above phases the neuter and active are the simplest, the other forms being derived from them by the addition of syllables or internal modifications; the secret of the formation of the modern verb is therefore to be sought for in the neuter and active.

§ 11. Some verbal stems are found only in the neuter form, others, again, only in the active, while a third and somewhat large class has both a neuter and an active form. For convenience, the first two classes may be called single stems, and the last double stems. These double stems arise from the circumstance that two separate but, so to speak, twin verbs, have been made by the moderns out of one old Aryan root, each modern stem being derived from a different part of the old verb, as will be shown further on.

Among single stems, those which are neuter (including active intransitive and passive intransitive) supply the place of an active by employing the causal, thus H. बनना (passive intransitive) "to be made," takes as its corresponding active बनाना "to make," which is really a passive causal, meaning "to cause to be made." Those single stems which are active mostly require no neuter, but should it be necessary to express one, the passive intransitive is used, as कहना "to tell," कहलाना "to be called."

Moreover, in Sanskrit there is a class of verbs derived from nouns, and called denominatives, which express the being in the state described by the parent noun, and sometimes (though more rarely) the action of the subject. Verbs of this sort are common in all languages of the Aryan stock, and notably so in modern English, where a verb may be formed almost at will from any noun; thus we say "to eye," "to mouth," "to beard," "to house oneself," "to shoe a horse," etc. In Sanskrit these verbs take the form of the tenth conjugation, or perhaps it would be more correct to regard them as causals. Examples are Sanskrit *agadyati* "he is in good health," from *agada* "healthy"; *chapaláyate* "he trembles," from *chapala* "tremulous"; *paṇḍitáyate* "he is learned," or "he acts the pedant," from *paṇḍita* "a (so-called) learned man";[1] *yoktrayati* "he yokes," from *yoktram* "a yoke." Probably from this cause it arises that there are in the moderns neuter verbs with a causal termination, as M. कडकावणें "to bang," "crack," H. चकराना "to be amazed," थरथराना "to totter." See § 28.

All these points will be noticed in detail in their proper place, they are cursorily mentioned here as an introduction to the general subject, and to show that there is an interchange and playing to and fro of forms and meanings which is somewhat difficult to unravel, and the more so as in colloquial usage the verbs are *often* very laxly and capriciously employed.

§ 12. Single neuter verbs are to a great extent early Tadbhavas as far as their stems are concerned, and consequently retain the Prakrit type. Thus they exhibit few or no traces of the tenfold classification of the Sanskrit or of the numerous phonetic changes that take place in the interior of the verb, but follow as a rule the form of the root in the present tense of the Bhû class. Here follows a list of some of the simplest and most used stems in the modern languages derived from verbs which in Sanskrit are Bhû. In the dictionaries the modern verbs are generally shown under the infinitive mood, but in the following lists I have thought it better to give only the stem; the reader can add the form of the infinitives if he wishes to refer to them in the dictionaries, as H. ना, P. ना or णा, S. णु, G. वुं, M. णें, O. इबा. In the Bengali dictionaries verbs are given under the stem alone.

Skr. √भू "be," pres. भवति. Pa. भवति and होति. Pr. भोदि, होदि, होइ. H. हो and so in all, except S. हुअ, and in O. होइ is contracted

[1] A *paṇḍit* in the present day in India is an individual who is supposed to be deeply read in all the most useless parts of Sanskrit literature, and is densely ignorant and contemptuous of all other branches of human knowledge.

to है. This verb will be treated at full length further on as the chief auxiliary of these languages (see Chapter IV. § 66).

√चल् "move," चलति. Pa. *id.* Pr. चलइ. H. S. चल. P. चल. G. चाल. चळ. M. चाल, चल, चळ. O. B. चाल.

√लग् "stick," लगति. Pa. लगति and लग्गति. Pr. लग्गइ, where the ग्ग is probably caused by the passive लग्यते or the p.p.p. लग्न. H. लग. P. लग्ग. S. लगु. in the rest लाग. It is neuter in the moderns.

√कम्प् "tremble," कम्पति. Pa. *id.*, Pr. कंपइ. H. कंप, कांप. P. कम्ब, S. कंब, G. M. B. कांप, O. कम्प.

√भ्रम् "wander," Pa. भमति. Pr. भमइ (Vik. iv. *passim*). H. भम, भौं. भंव. P. भरम. भौं or भव. S. भवें. भम. भव, भंव. G. भम, भम. M. भोंव. भोंव.

There is little that is remarkable in the above list, the modern forms being regularly produced by the working of the usual phonetic laws. The verb *sthâ* "stand," being one of the common auxiliaries, demands a fuller notice. Here follow some of the principal tenses in the old languages:

	SKR.	PA.	PR.		
√स्था and ष्ठा 1. S. 3 pres.	तिष्ठति	तिट्ठति ठाति	चिष्ठदि (*Mg.*), चिट्ठदि (*Saur.*), ठाअइ, ठाइ (Var. viii. 25, 26).		
	P. 3. तिष्ठन्ति	तिट्ठन्ति. ठान्ति	चिष्ठन्ति.	चिट्ठन्ति.	ठान्ति.
Impv.	S. 2. तिष्ठ	तिट्ठ	चिष्ठ.	चिट्ठ,	ठाहि.
	S. 3. तिष्ठतु	तिट्ठतु. ठातु	चिष्ठदु,	चिट्ठदु,	ठाउ.
Future	S. 3. स्थास्यति	ठस्सति			ठाहिइ.
Infin.	स्थातुं	ठातुं	चिट्ठिदुं.		
P.p.p.	स्थितं	ठितं	चिट्ठिदं.	ट्ठिदं.	ठिअं.
Gerund	स्थित्वा	ठत्वा. ठत्वान	ठिअ.	ठिअ.	

Of the three forms in Pali that having ठा as its root-syllable has survived to modern times, though in most cases with the dental instead of the cerebral aspirate. In H. there is only a fragment in the shape of a past participle S. था *m.* थी *f.*, P. थे *m.* थीं *f.* S. G. and O. have a whole verb, thus—

		S.	G.	O.
Infinitive		थिअणु "to be."	थवुं (थावुं)	थिबा (थाइबा)
Aorist	S. 1.	थिआं	थाउ	थाएं
(=Skr. pres.)	2.	थिएं, थीं	थाय (थाव)	थाउ
	3.	थिए	थाय (थाव)	थाए
	P. 1.	थिऊं	थइए	थाउं
	2.	थिओ	थाओ	थाअ
	3.	थिअनि	थाय	थान्ति
Present part.		थींदो	थतो	थाउं
Past part.		थिओ	थयो and थयेलो	थिला
Future	S. 3.	थींदो	थशे	थिब
	P. 3.	थींदा	थशे	थिबे

The structure of these forms will be found discussed in Ch. IV. § 60. M. has an old poetical ठेवें "to be," but from the Pr. form थिह there is, as far as I know, only one descendant, and that is the modern Oriya adjective थिरा "standing," which seems to point to Pr. थिट्ठअं, Skr. स्थितं.

It is interesting here to notice the parallel treatment of Sanskrit स्था and Latin *sta* in their respective descendants. Both roots survive, but have almost entirely lost the sense of "standing," and have come to mean "be," "become." In S. G. and O. the above quoted verbs are used as auxiliaries denoting a more special and definite kind of being or becoming, and are thus distinguished from the less definite auxiliaries derived from भू or अस्. Sindhi *hunu* and *thianu*, Gujarati *havuṇ* and *thavuṇ*, Oriya *hoibā* and *thibā*, stand to each other exactly in the same relation as Spanish *ser* from *esse* does to *estar* (from *stare*). Thus *Pedro es enamorado* "Pedro is loving (by disposition)," but *Pedro está enamorado* "Pedro is in love (with some one)." So *el es bueno* "he is good (by nature)," but *el está bueno* "he is well (in health)." In Italian, although *stare* still means "to stand," yet it is constantly and regularly used in the sense of being, thus *sto leggendo* "I am reading," does not imply that the speaker stands while he reads, but merely indicates that he is engaged in reading; just so an Oriya would say *paṛhu thāan*. *Stai bene?* "art thou well?" *sta qui vicino* "he is living close by," would be correctly rendered in O. by the exactly parallel expressions *bhala thāū?* and *ethi nikaṭ thāe*. In French, as in Hindi, the verb has been lost, and a Frenchman has to use the roundabout expression *il se tient debout* for "he is standing," literally "he holds himself on end," just in the same way as the Indian has to say *khaṛā hai* literally "he is propped up," (खड़ा = Pr. खड्डा = Skr. स्तब्ध from √ स्तम्भ to support).

§ 13. **Examples of verbs derived from roots which in Sanskrit belong to other conjugations than the first are now adduced to show how completely all traces of the peculiarities of those conjugations have been abandoned.**

Skr. √ या "go," ii. याति, Pa. *id.*, Pr. जाइ and जाअइ (the latter as if from a Bhû verb जाअति), H. जा, P. M. B. *id.*, G. and O. retain जा in some tenses, but in others shorten it to G. ज, O. जि.

√ स्वप् "sleep," ii. स्वपिति, Pa. सुपति, Pr. सुवइ, सुअइ, सुवेइ, H. सो, P. सौ, S. सुम्हु, G. सू, B. and O. शो.

√ भी "fear," iii. बिभेति, Pa. भायति, Pr. भीअइ, भाअइ, बीहइ (Var. iii. 19), M. भि, S. भे, G. बीह, बीही, बिह (not in the rest).

√ नृत् "dance," iv. नृत्यति, Pa. नच्चति, Pr. णच्चइ, H. नाच, P. नच्च, S. नच, G. M. O. B. नाच्.

√ शक् "be able," v. शक्नोति and iv. शक्यति, Pa. सक्कति, सक्कोति, सक्कुणोति, Pr. सक्कइ, सक्कणोति, and सक्कु°, H. सक, P. सक्क, S. सघ, G. M. शक.

In *nāch*, as in several other verbs derived from Div roots, the characteristic य of the Div class seems to have got mixed up with the root and has thus been preserved. Although in *sak* both Pali and Prakrit retain some traces of the peculiar type of the Su class, the moderns entirely reject them and form as if from a Bhû root, thus H. सकै "he can," postulates a Sanskrit शकति, and so with the other languages.

How the following verb came by its modern form I know not, but all the authorities agree in referring it to √ ब्रू. It is a very common word, and it is just these very common words that are the most difficult to trace. Perhaps ब्रू became ब्रूर, and so ब्रुल and बोल.[1]

Skr. √ ब्रू "speak," H. ब्रवीति and ब्रूते. Pr. बोल्लइ (Mṛichh. 230, end of Act vi.) Old H. बुल्ल (o is short in Pr.), H. बोलना, S. ब्रोलणु, all the rest बोलना.

§ 14. In the above examples the modern verb retains the form of the present tense, but there is a tolerably large class of stems which retain the type of the p.p.p. of Sanskrit as modified by the Prakrits.[2] These verbs express positions of the body, states or conditions whether material or mental, and the possession of qualities. The past participle of the Sanskrit has been treated as an adjective and a new verb formed form it, just as in English we have verbs "to contract," "to respect," "to edit," from the Latin *contractus*, *respectus*, *editus*, the respective past participles of *contrahere*, *respicere* and *edere*.

The modern Romance languages often preserve a long string of nouns derived from a Latin verbal root, while they have lost the verb itself; for instance, French, while it possesses no verb

[1] Since writing the above I see that Hemachandra gives *bollaï* as one of the ten Prakritisms of *kath*; he means it evidently not as derived from *kath*, which is impossible, but as a popular equivalent (Pischel's Hem. iv. 2). In the same place he gives also *sanghaï* for *kath*, in which we see the origin of M. *sângaṇeṃ* "to speak." Hemachandra has also *kahissaï* = kathayishyati (iv. 388), *kahissam* = kathayishyami, *kahijjau* = kathyatām (?), ib. 383. But he gives *bruve* as the equivalent of *brû* in iv. 391, so that the origin of *bol* still remains doubtful.

[2] This process was indicated by me in Vol. I. p. 179. Hoernle afterwards discussed it as if it was his own discovery in Indian Antiquary, vol. I. p. 357. Perhaps he had not then seen my first volume.

directly representing the Latin *sta* "stand," has numerous nouns from that root, as *station*, *étage*, from *statio*, *état* from *status*. From these nouns fresh verbs are derived, as *stationner* and the like. So also the modern Indian languages, while they have lost such roots as *dip*, *kram*, as verbs, have nouns *dīpa*, *dīyā* and derivatives, also *krama* as a noun with numerous secondary formations.

Analogous to this is the practice we are now discussing of forming verbs from Sanskrit participles, a practice which begins as early as Prakrit, and appears to have arisen from the habit mentioned in § 2 of forming a definite preterite by compounding the participle with अस्, as in गतोऽस्मि "I have gone." It was pointed out in § 7 that this practice had been extended in Prakrit so widely that it had resulted in giving a termination in म्हि to the present tense, as in पेक्खम्हि. Examples are:

Skr. √विश् "enter," with उप, उपविश् "take a seat," *i.e.* to pass from a standing to a sitting posture, p.p.p. उपविष्ट "seated." Pa. उपविट्ठो, Pr. उवविट्ठो, and later उवइट्ठो, whence, by rejection of उ, H. बैठ, P. *id.*, M. बैस, where the last consonant is due to a confusion between बैठ् and बस. G. has बेस, which is from Skr. pres. उपविशति. Its p.p.p. is बेठो. S. also विह *by softening of* स to ह, p.p.p. वेठो. With प्र, प्रविश्, "enter," "penetrate," P. पविट्ठो, Pr. पइट्ठो, whence H. पैठ, "to enter" (*generally with the idea of penetrating forcibly*). G. again पेस *from* प्रविशति, p.p.p. पेठो. S. पिह, p.p.p. पेठो.

Skr. √पच् "cook," पचति, p.p.p. पक्व, Pa. Pr. पक्को. H. पक "to be cooked," to be in process of cooking (*if you ask*, "Is dinner ready?" your man answers, पकता "It is being cooked"), *P.* पक्क. G. पाक. M. पिक. It also means "to ripen," "to be in course of growing ripe." B. पाक. There is also a stem *from* the present पचति, as S. पच् "to grow ripe," p.p.p. पचो. H. and all the rest have पच, but in the sense of rotting, decaying.

Skr. √ शुष् "dry," p.p.p. शुष्क, Pa. Pr. सुक्खो, H. सूख "to be dry," P. सुक्ख, S. G. M. सुक, B. O. सुख.

Skr. √ भञ्ज् "break," p.p.p. भग्न, Pa. Pr. भग्गो, H. भाग "to flee" (said originally of an army, "to be broken up and dispersed"), G. भाग, M. भाग, "to yield, give way," also भंज a. "to break," O. भांग. Here again there are stems as if from the present form Bhū भंजति, Pa. भंजति, Pr. भंजइ, H. भंज "to be broken," and भाग. (See § 10.)

Skr. √ गम् "go," with उद्, p.p.p. उद्गत "sprung up," Pr. उग्गओ. H. उग, "to spring up" (as a plant), P. उग्ग, S. G. उग, M. उगव.

It is questionable whether we should here class some words which come from √ सृ with उद्. The present would be उत्सरति, but though the p.p.p. in Sanskrit is उत्सृत, yet in such verbs Prakrit forms the p.p.p. on the model of the present tense, and has उस्सरिओ as if from Skr. उत्सरित, so that the modern verbs उसर, ऊसर, and the like keep the type of the present tense as much as that of the participle.

Another very common word is उठ् "to rise," but in this case Prakrit has already adopted this form for all parts of the verb, as has also Pali; thus from √ उद् + स्था Skr. makes उत्था "to stand up."

		SKR.	PA.	PR.
Present	S. 3.	उत्तिष्ठति	उट्ठहति, उट्ठाति	उट्ठदि, उट्ठेदि, उट्ठेइ
Impv.	S. 2.	उत्तिष्ठ	उट्ठह	उट्ठेहि
	S. 3.	उत्तिष्ठतु	उट्ठहतु	उट्ठेउ
Future	S. 3.	उत्थास्यति	उट्ठहिस्सति	उट्ठिस्सइ
Pres. part.		उत्तिष्ठत्	उट्ठन्तो	उट्ठंतो
P.p.p.		उत्थित	उट्ठितो	उट्ठिदो, उट्ठिओ
Infin.		उत्थातुं	उट्ठातुं	—
Gerund		उत्थाय	उट्ठाय, उट्ठहित्वा	उट्ठिअ

Here, whatever be the form taken in Sanskrit, both Pali and Prakrit assume a stem उट्ठ, and conjugate it as if it were a Bhū verb throughout. It seems as though उठ् being compounded with स्था had lost its final consonant, thereby making a form उथा, whence Prakrit उट्ठ. Sanskrit has adopted the opposite course, and while keeping उद् intact, has sacrificed the स of स्था in the non-conjugational tenses, retaining it in the conjugational ones where it is prevented from coalescing with the preposition by the reduplicated syllable. In the moderns we have H. उठ, P. उट्ठ, S. उथ and उठ, and in all the rest उठ.

The stem रह has undergone a change of meaning which is explainable only by bringing it under this head.

Skr. √रह् "desert," रहति, usually found in Prakrit only in the p.p.p. रहिओ (= रहित) in the sense of "deserted," then almost adverbially, as "without," hence probably the meaning which it bears in the modern languages, "to stop," "stay," "remain," from the idea of being deserted, left behind. It is रह in H. and all except M. राह, G. रेह. It is ancillary in most of the languages as पढ़ी रहो "go on reading." (See § 72, 10).

§ 15. Single active stems exhibit the same method of formation as the single neuter stems given in § 12. A *few* examples are given of roots which in Sanskrit are of the Bhû, or the closely allied Div, Tud, and Chur classes.

Skr. √खाद् "eat," खादति, Pa. *id.*, Pr. खाइ (Var. viii. 27, for खाअइ), H. खा, and so in all. Gipsy *khava*, Kash. *khyun*, Singhalese *kanavā*.[1]

Skr. √चर्व् "chew," चर्वति, Pr. चव्वइ, H. चाब, P. चब्ब, S. चबु, G. M. चाव, O. चोवा, B. चाब.

Skr. √पठ् "read," पठति, Pa. *id.*, Pr. पढइ, H. पढ़ (*paṛh*), P. M. G. *id.*, S. पढ्ह (*which is only their way of writing* पढ़), B. पड़, O. पढ़.

Skr. √प्रछ् "ask," पृच्छति, Pa. पुच्छति, Pr. पुच्छइ, H. पूछ, P. पुच्छ, G. B. *id.*, M. पुस् (*see* Vol. I. p. 218), O. पुछ, पचार.

Skr. √मार्ग् (and मृग्) "seek," I. मार्गति, x. मार्गयति, Pa. मग्गति and मग्गेति, Pr. मग्गइ, H. माँग, P. मंग, S. मङ (*mang*), G. M. माग, B. माँग, O. माग.

[1] Childers, in J.R.A.S. vol. viii. p. 146.

Skr. √ रक्ष् "keep," रक्षति, Pa. रक्खति, Pr. रक्खइ, H. रख "keep," also simply "to put," पोथी को पीढ़ि पर रखो "put the book on the stool." P. रक्ख, S. रख, G. M. B. राख, O. रख, Singh. *rakinawā*.

Skr. √ कथ् "say," कथयति, P. कथेति, Pr. कहइ, कहेइ, H. कह, P. S. B. O. *id.* In M. it is wanting. G. कहे, Singh. *kiyanawā*.

Those roots which belong to other conjugations are almost always reduced to the Bhû type, even if Prakrit retains any of the conjugational peculiarities the moderns do not. They take in most instances the root-form of the present as it occurs in Prakrit, and keep it throughout. Instances are:

Skr. √ ज्ञा "know," ix. जानाति, Pa. *id.*, Pr. जाणादि, also जाणइ (Pr. keeps जाण throughout, but it and Pa. occasionally drop the initial, having आणादि, etc.), H. B. जान, the rest जाण. Gipsy *janaw*, Kash. *zānun*, Singh. *dannawā*.

Skr. √ कृ "do," viii. करोति, Pa. *id.* (see § 1 and § 4), Pr. कुणइ and करइ and the stem कर is adopted in most tenses. The moderns universally reject all forms but कर, which they use throughout except in the p.p.p., which is the phonetic equivalent of Prakrit (see § 48).

Skr. √ श्रु "hear," v. शृणोति, Pa. सुणोति, सुणाति, Pr. सुणइ. H. सुन, and in all सुन or सुण.

Skr. √ आप् "get," v. आप्नोति (but also i. आपति), Pa. आपुणोति, आपुणाति and अप्पोति, Pr. (see § 5) आवइ, seldom used alone. Old H. आपु "to obtain," also used in the sense of giving.

आप मति सरसै सचव ॥

"Having obtained wisdom and the aid of Sarasai (Saraswati)."
—Chand, Pr. R. i. xv.

Also G. आप "to give," which is the ordinary word in that language, may be from this root or from अर्पँ (ऋ). Far more common is the compound with प्र = प्राप. Pa. as above. Pr. पाउणइ and later पावइ. Old H. and P. पाव, H. पाव and पा, S. पा, O. *id.*, G. पाम, M. पाव, B. पावो. In all in the sense of finding, getting, obtaining.

Skr. √ग्रह् "seize," ix. गृह्णाति. The treatment of this root is peculiar. Pa. for the most part takes a form गण्ह्, and Pr. generally गेण्ह्. Some of the principal tenses are given here.

		SKR.	PA.	PR.
Pres.	S. 3.	गृह्णाति	गण्हाति, गण्हति	गेण्हइ
Âtm. Pres.	S. 1.	गृह्णे	" "	गेण्हे
1 Aor.	S. 3.	अग्रहीत्	अग्गहि, अगण्हि	"
Impv.	S. 2.	गृहाण	गण्ह, गण्हाहि	गेण्ह, गेण्हसु
	S. 3.	गृह्णातु	गण्हातु	गेण्हउ
Impv. Âtm.	P. 2.	गृह्णीध्वं	गण्हव्हो	गेण्हह
Fut.	S. 1.	ग्रहीष्यामि	गण्हिस्सं	गेण्हिस्सं
	S. 3.	ग्रहीष्यति	गण्हिस्सति, गहेस्सति	गेण्हिस्सइ
Infin.		ग्रहीतुं	गण्हितुं	गेण्हिउं, गहिउं, घेत्तुं
P.p.p.		गृहीत	गहितो	गहिदो, गिहिदो
Gerund		गृहीत्वा	गण्हित्वा	गेण्हिऊण, घेत्तूण

There are thus two types in Pa. *gaṇh* and *gah*, and three in Pr. *geṇh*, *gah*, and *ghe*. The double *t* in *ghettum* and *ghettûṇa* arises, I fancy, from *e* being short in Pr., and is not an organic part of the word (Var. viii. 15).

In the modern languages H. has गह as an archaic and poetic word. P. also गह्. But M. घे "take," is very much used, as also S. घिनु, and O. घेन. the other languages prefer the stem ले from लभ्. Singh. *gannavâ*, perhaps Gipsy *gelava*, is connected with this root, though it means rather "to bring." (Paspati, p. 241.)

§ 15. Some Sanskrit roots ending in vowels have undergone curious and interesting changes in the modern languages. Such is Skr. √दा "give," iii. ददाति. This is one of the primitive Indo-European race-words, and being such we probably have not got it in its original form in Sanskrit. With the idea of giving is intimately connected that of dividing, or apportioning, and we find in Sanskrit several roots with this meaning, all of which seem to point back to some earlier common root which has been lost. Thus we have √ दा. iii. ददाति "give," √ दा or दो, ii. दाति and iv. द्यति "divide," √ दाय. i. दायते and दे i. दयते. Some grammarians, misunderstanding a rule of Panini's about reduplication, have imagined a √ दद्. i. ददते. but this does not seem to be entitled to a separate existence.[1] It is also to be observed that in some roots in *á* there are traces of a form in *e* or *ai*, which may perhaps be the older form, as गा and गै "to sing," ध्या and ध्यै "to meditate," म्ला and म्लै "to languish," क्षा and क्षै "to wither," त्रा and त्रै "to rescue," मा and मे "to measure." Also roots ending in *á* exhibit in the course of conjugation many forms in which the root-vowel is changed to *i* or *e*. It is not within our scope to do more than hint at all these points, as possibly accounting for the fact that at a very early stage the root दा began to be superseded by दे, and that in the modern languages the univeral form is *DE*. The principal teuses in Sanskrit, Pali and Prakrit are here shown together.

		SKR.	PA.	PR.
Pres.	S. 1.	ददामि	ददामि. देमि. दम्मि दज्जामि	देमि
	S. 3.	ददाति	ददाति. देति. दज्जाति	देइ, दए
	P. 1.	दद्मः	दम्म. देम	देमो
	P. 3.	ददति	देन्ति	देन्ति
Impr.	S. 2.	देहि	देहि	देहि
	S. 3.	ददातु	देतु	देउ
Átm.	P. 2.	दद्ध्वे	देथ. ददाथ	देध
Fut.	S. 3.	दास्यति	दस्सति	दइस्सइ. दाहइ
Infin.		दातुं	दातुं	दाउं. देउं
Pres. Part.		ददत्	ददन्तो. देन्तो	देन्तो (देन्ती *f.*)
P.p.p.		दत्त	दिन्नो	दिन्नो
Gerund		दत्त्वा	दत्वा. दाय. ददित्वा	दाऊण. दत्ता. दइय

[1] Westergaard, Rad. Sanskr. p. 6, note.

Childers thinks the form *deti* has arisen either from Sanskrit *dayate*, or from confusion with the imperative *detu*. The form *dajjati* he, with great probability, considers as a future on the analogy of *dekh* (see § 4). In Çauraseni Prakrit the form दे is used throughout (Var. xii. 4), as also in the moderns. H. दे, P. M. G. *id.*, S. डिअ, B. alone has दा. O. दे, shortened in some tenses to दि. Gipsy *dava*, Kash. *dyun*, Singh. *denava*. This is one of the few irregular verbs in the modern languages; being subjected to numerous contractions, and retaining several early Tadbhava forms.

Further examples are:

Skr. √पा "drink," I. पिबति [Vedic पाति, there is also √पी, iv. पीयते]. Pa. पिवति and पिव°, Pr. पिबइ. H. पी, S. and B. पि, in all the rest पी. Gipsy *piáva*, Kash. *cigun*, perhaps through an old form *pyun*, Singh. *bonava*, p.p.p. *bî*.

Skr. √नी "lead," I. नयति, Pa. नयति, नेति, Pr. नेइ, णेइ (pres. part. णअंतो = Skr. नयन्, fut. णइस्सं = Skr. नेष्यामि, impv. णेहु = Skr. नय). Used in the moderns only in composition, thus—

(*a*) With आ = आनी "bring." Pa. आनेति, Pr. आणेइ. H. आन् "bring," in all the rest आण. Kashm. *anun*, Gipsy *andea*.

(*b*) With परि = परिणी "lead round the sacrificial fire during the marriage ceremony," hence, "to marry," Old-H. परण, परना, P. परणाउ, S. परणं, G. M. परण.

Skr. √डी "fly," with उद् = उड्डी "fly up," I. उड्डयते, iv. उड्डीयते, Pr. उड्डेइ, H. उड (uṛ) "to fly," and so in all. S. has उडिर, probably a diminutive. Kashm. *wudun*, Gipsy *urydua*.

The root या "to go," was mentioned above; with the preposition आ forming आया, it means "to come," and it is from this word that the following are apparently derived:

Skr. आया "come," II. आयाति, Pa. *id.*, Pr. आयाइ, आइ, H. आ "to come," P. *id.*, G. आव, M. ये, Gipsy *avdea*, Kash. *yun*. The B.

आइस. O. आस. S. आव seem to come from आयाति. but both in B. and O. one often hears आय. thus O. *âilâ* or *âilâ*, "he came," and S. makes the imperv. *âo*, so that there is some confusion between the two roots.

In the roots ending in long *î* the modern languages have words descended from compound verbs only, and in them the final vowel of the root has dropped out altogether, while in roots ending in long *û* there is a tendency to soften the final vowel into *i* or *e*.

§ 17. A few words must be given to a verb which has been somewhat hotly discussed of late. In all the modern languages except perhaps M., the idea of seeing is expressed by *dekh*. Kashmiri has *deshun*, Gipsy *dikâva*, and Singhalese *dikanava*. The root is in Sanskrit √दृश्, but the present is not in use; instead of it classical Sanskrit uses पश्यति, from which M. derives its verb पाह. Marathi stands alone in using this stem, instead of *dekh*. From √दृश् comes future द्रक्ष्यति, and it is from this future that Childers derives the Pali दक्खति. He shows[1] that in the earlier Pali writings it is always used in a future sense, and only in later times becomes a present. As I hinted above (§ 4, p. 16), it is very probable that the vulgar, missing in this word the characteristic *issa* of their ordinary future, considered it a present, and made a double future *dakkhissati*. A similar process has been shown to have taken place in several verbs in Prakrit. Pischel draws attention to a fact pointed out in Vol. I. p. 102 of this work, that there is much similarity between *dekh* and the Prakrit *pekkh* from Sanskrit प्रेक्ष. He, however, goes so far as to assume that the word *dekh* was unknown to the authors of the dramas, that they used *pekkh*, which has been changed to *dekkh* by the copy-

[1] In Kuhn's Beiträge zur vergleichenden Sprachforschung. vol vii p. 450. Pischel's article is in the same work.

ists who heard this latter word used round them every day, while they did not know of *pekh*. Unfortunately for this ingenious theory, it happens that the word *pekh* is extremely common in Hindi, Bangali, and Panjabi literature of the middle ages, and is still used in many rustic dialects of Hindi. The idea of a northern Indian scribe not knowing *pekh* is quite untenable. Weber (Prakrit Studien, p. 69) has a long article on this subject, controverting the views of Childers as supported by Pischel. The learned professor would derive *dekkh* from the desiderative of दृश्, which is दिदृक्षते, but I am unable to follow the arguments adduced, or to see how a word meaning "to wish to see" should come to mean "to see." Nor do there appear to be any actual facts in support of this theory, such as texts in which the word occurs in a transitional state of meaning or form. The few desideratives that have left any traces in modern times retain the desiderative meaning, as *piyâsâ* "thirsty," from *pipâsu* (see Vol. II. p. 81). However, I must say to the learned disputants—

"Non nostrum inter vos tantas componere lites."

For my own part the impression I derive from the controversy is that *dekh* is derived through *dekkh* from *dakkh*, which is Sanskrit future द्रक्ष्यति turned into a present by a vulgar error. The idea suggested by me (in Vol. I. p. 161 *et seqq.*) must be modified accordingly. It was not so entirely erroneous as Pischel thinks, for Sanskrit दृश् represents an older दृक्, which seems to be preserved in the future.

§ 18. The examples adduced in the preceding sections will have sufficiently illustrated the most salient peculiarities in the formation of the ordinary single verbs whether neuter or active, and I now pass on to the more difficult subject of the double verbs. As I mentioned before, there is a very large class of these; they appear in two forms, one of which is active and occasionally even causal, the other is neuter or passive intransitive. It is after much consideration that I have come to the conclusion that this is the right way to regard them. It might be said that the forms which are here spoken of as neuters are really passives, and a rule might be laid down that these languages often form their passive by what the Germans call *umlaut* or substitution of weaker vowels. Childers in fact takes this view as regards Singhalese in the article already quoted (J. R. A. S. vol. viii. p. 148). I do not know how the matter may stand in Singhalese, but it is certainly open to much objection as regards the Aryan languages of the Indian continent. The neuters differ from the actives in two ways in the seven languages, either by a change in the final consonant of the stem or by a change in the vowel only. The latter is by far the more frequent. We must not be misled by the accident that many of these neuters can only be translated into English by a passive; that is the peculiarity of our own language, not of the Indian ones. In German or in the Romance languages they can be rendered by the reflexive verb. Thus H. खुलना is "to open," *i.e.* "to open of itself," "to come undone," "to be opened," while खोलना, the corresponding active, is "to open," *i.e.* "to break a thing open," "to undo." Thus द्वार खुलना "the door opens," is in German "die Thür öffnet sich," in French "la porte s'ouvre." While द्वार खोलना "he opens the door," is in German "er öffnet die Thür," in French "il ouvre la porte." So that फिरना is "sich umkehren," while its active फेरना is "umkehren (etwas)." In English we use verbs in a neuter as well as in an active sense, relying upon the context to make our meaning clear.

Moreover, all the languages have a passive, in some a regularly formed derivative from Prakrit, in others a periphrastic arrangement. It is true that, owing to the large number of neuter stems, this regular passive is not very much used; but it is there nevertheless, and would not have been invented had forms which I regard as neuters been true "umlauted" passives.

Of the double verbs, then, as I prefer to call them, some differ only in the vowel, and the difference consists in this that where the vowel of the neuter is always short, as *a*, *i* or *u*, the corresponding active has *ā*, *e* or *o*, occasionally *ī* or *ū*. As types may be taken, H. *kaṭnā*, *n*, and *kāṭnā*, *a*; *phirnā*, *n*, and *phernā*, *a*; *khulnā*, *n*, and *kholnā*, *a*; *lipnā*, *n*, and *līpnā*, *a*; *guthnā*, *n*, and *gūthnā*, *a*. Of the other class, in which the final consonant differs, there are so many varieties, that it will be better to discuss them separately. Sindhi has the largest number of them, and it is with Sindhi therefore that we must begin.

§ 19. Trumpp (Sindhi Gr. p. 252) gives a list of these verbal stems, but it would have been out of place for him to have offered any analysis. The following verbs I take from him, but the explanations are my own. The first group consists of these verbs.

(1.) *Neuter ending in* झ.	*Active ending in* ध.
1. बझणु "to be bound."	बंधणु "to bind."
2. बुझणु "to be heard."	बुधणु "to hear."
3. रझणु "to be cooked."	रंधणु "to cook."

1. Skr. √ बंध्, ix. बध्नाति, Pa. बंधति, Pr. बंधइ, whence S. बंध, H. बाँध, P. बन्ह. In all the rest बाँध a. Skr. passive is बध्यते, whence Pa. बज्झति, Pr. बज्झइ, S. बझ, H. बझ, used as a hunting term "to be caught," also "to stick, adhere," P. बज्झणा. Here, though undoubtedly derived from the passive, the stem बझ is really a neuter or passive intransitive and its conjugation closely resembles the active. There is a regular passive S. बंधिजणु.

2. Skr. √ बुध् "to know," i. बोधति, iv. बुध्यते, from the latter come Pa. बुज्झति and Pr. बुज्झइ, whence S. बुझ, originally "to know," but now meaning "to be heard," H. बूझना "to understand," is active. So also

O. बुझ, B. बूझ, G. बुझ. But M. बुझ is both a and n. The form of the iv. conjugation is identical with the passive, hence S. makes बुझु a neuter and बुंझु is probably due to a false analogy with बंध.

3. Skr. √ रध् or रन्ध् I. रन्धति originally "to destroy," but in moderns always "to cook," Pa. *id.*, Pr. रंधइ. S. रंधु, H. राँध a, and so in all but P. Passive रध्यते, Pa. रज्झति. Pr. रज्झइ, S. रझु, not found in the others.

(2.) Neuter in भ.	Active in ह.
1. लभणु "to be got,"	लहणु "to take."
2. जभणु "stuprari" (de muliere),	जहणु "stuprare" (de viro).
3. दुभणु "to be milked,"	दुहणु "to milk."

1. Skr. √ लभ् "to get," I. लभते. Pa. लभति. Pr. लहइ (भ = ह Vol. I. p. 268), S. लहु, Old H. लहु. H. ले. P. लहि and ले. G. ले, M. घे, O. ले. B. लओ, all a. Pass. लभ्यते. Pa. लब्भति, Pr. लब्भइ, S. लभु, Old H. लब्भ, not in the others.

2. Skr. √ यभ् "coire," I. यभति. Pr. जहइ, S. जहु. Pass. यभ्यते, Pr. जब्भइ, S. जभे. Not in the others, except perhaps M. झवणें, where the aspiration has been thrown back on the ज.

3. Skr. √ दुह्, II. दोग्धि, Pa. दोहति, Pr. दोहइ and दुहइ, S. दुहु. H. दुह and दोह, and so in all a. Pass. दुह्यते, Pa. दुय्हति (Childers writes *duyhati*, which can hardly be expressed in Devanagari letters), Pr. दुब्भइ. From this we should expect S. दुझे. The form दुभे recalls a similar one in Jaina Pr. लिब्भइ for लिज्झइ (Weber, Bhag. 390, 429), Skr. लिह्यते, but this seems to rest upon a doubtful reading of one of those obscure composite characters sometimes found in MSS. written with the thick Indian reed pen. See also Cowell's Var. viii. 50, note.[1] Possibly we have here again a false analogy with लभ्, like बुंझ with बंध.

[1] Hemachandra collects a number of passives in *bbh* from roots ending in *h*, dubbhai, libbhai, vubbhai, rubbhai, from duh, lih, vah, ruh (or rudh?).—Pischel, Hem., iv. 245.

(3.) Neuter in झ.	Active in ह.
डझणु "to be envious,"	डहणु "to torment."

Skr. √ दह् "burn," I. दहति, Pa. डहति, Pr. डहइ, S. डह, H. डाह, दाह. Pass. दह्यते, Pa. डय्हति (Childers *dayhati*), Pr. डज्झइ, S. डझ.

(4.) Neuter in ॼ.	Active in ञ, ञ, ण.
1. भॼणु "to be broken,"	भञणु "to break."
2. भुॼणु "to be fried,"	भुञणु "to fry."
3. छिॼणु "to be plucked,"	छिञणु "to pluck."
4. सुॼणु "to be heard,"	सुणणु "to hear."
5. चॼणु "to be raised,"	चाड़णु "to raise."

1. Skr. √ भंज् "break," vii. भनक्ति, Pa. भंजति, Pr. भंजइ; ञ्ज becomes in S. ञ, hence भञ. Pass. भज्यते, Pr. भज्जइ, S. भॼ (ज्ज = ॼ). H. भंज and भाज.

पुरुषातन भजि किति हाय ॥

"Manliness is broken, fame destroyed."—Chand, Pr. R. i. 172.

P. भज्ज, G. भांज.

2. Skr. √ भ्रस्ज or भृज्, i. भर्जति, vi. भृज्जति, Pa. भज्जति. Pr. would probably be भुजइ. I have not met the word. भुंजइ (Bhāg. 278) is from भुज् "to enjoy." S. भुञ postulates a Pr. भुंज. In the other languages the n occurs. H. भुन "to fry," and भून, P. भुन. G. भुज, M. भाज, but also भुंज, O. भाज, B. *id.*, Pass. भृज्यते, which would give Pr. भुज्जइ, whence S. भुॼ, but the whole stem is somewhat obscure. P. भुज्ज n.

3. Skr. √ छिद् "cleave," vii. छिनत्ति, Pa. छिन्दति, Pr. छिन्दइ (Var. viii. 38), whence S. छिञ by the process न्द = ञ (Vol. I. p. 290). Pass. छिद्यते, Pa. छिज्जति, Pr. छिज्जइ, S. छिॼ.

4. Skr. √ श्रु "hear," which, as already explained, is always सुण in Prakrit and in modern languages. Pass. श्रूयते, Pa. सूयति or सुय्यति, Pr. generally सुणिज्जइ (Var. viii. 57), also सुव्वइ, but a form सुज्जइ is also possible, whence S. सुॼ.

5. Skr. √ खुंद् "rise," I. खुंदति, which would give a Pr. खुंदइ, whence S. खुह, Pass. खुद्यते, Pr. खुज्जइ, S. खुज. This stem does not seem to occur in the other languages, it is peculiar to S., and must not be confounded with खणणु "to dig," from Skr. √ खन्, nor with Skr. खण्ड् "to divide."

(5.) Neuter in स.	Active in ह.
1. कुसणु "to be slain."	कुहणु "to slay."
2. घसणु "to be rubbed."	घहणु "to rub."
3. लूसणु "to be scorched."	लूहणु "to scorch."
4. मुसणु "to suffer loss."	मुहणु "to inflict loss."

1. Skr. √ कष् and कृष् "tear" "drag," I. कृषति, Pr. कुसइ, S. कुह, (स = ह, Vol. I. p. 259), Pass. कृष्यते, Pr. would be कुस्सइ, whence S. कुस, by rejection of one s. Persian كُشتن "to kill."

2. Skr. √ घृष् "rub," I. घर्षति, Pr. घसइ, S. घह, Pass. घृष्यते, Pr. घिस्सइ and घस्सइ, S. घस. The other languages have a different series of stems. H. घस and घिस, n and a, घसीट, a, P. id., G. घस and घसड, a, M. घास, घसड, घांस n and a, O. B. घस.

3. Skr. √ लूष् "burn," I. लूषति, Pr. लूसइ, S. लूह, Pass. लूष्यते, Pr. लूस्सइ, S. लूस.

4. Skr. √ मुष् "rob," I. मुषति, Pa. मुसति, Pr. मुसइ, S. मुह, Pass. मुष्यते, Pr. मुस्सइ, S. मुस.

There are several other pairs of stems which exhibit special types; all, however, are explainable by the above noted process. Thus—

(6.) Neuter in प.	Active in ह.
छुपणु "to be touched,"	छुहणु "to touch."

Skr. √ छुप् "touch," I. छुपति, Pa. id., Pr. छुपइ. प being unsupported goes out and ह is employed to fill up the hiatus, giving S. छुह. Pass. छुप्यते, Pr. छुप्पइ, whence S. छुप, by rejection of one प. In the other languages only the active is found. Old-H. छुह, H. छू, P. छुह and छूह, G. छु, छू, छो, O. छुं, B. id.

§ 20. There is a group of words running through nearly all the seven languages in which the divergence between the two members of each pair is slighter than that just discussed. It consists in the final consonant of the neuter being the surd cerebral ट, while that of the active is the sonant ड; the neuter at the same time has the simple short vowel while the active has the corresponding guna vowel.

The words are in Hindi.

Neuter.	Active.
1. छुट "get loose,"	छोड "set free."
2. टूट (तुट) "fall in pieces,"	तोड (तोड) "break."
3. फट "burst, split,"	फाड "tear."
4. फिट "be discharged,"	फेड "discharged."
5. घुट "be squashed,"	घोड "squash."
6. जुट "be joined,"	जोड "join."

The process in these words differs somewhat from that in the Sindhi stems in the last section, as will be seen from the following remarks.

1. Skr. √ छुट् (also छुड्, छुंट Westergaard, Rad. Skr. p. 128) "to cut," vi. छुटति, but the Bhû type would be छोटति, Pr. छोडइ, H. छोड, and so in all except M., which has सोड, with its usual change of छ to स (Vol. I. p. 218). H., which is pronounced *chhor*, while M. is *sod*, is active, and so is the word in all the other languages. It means "to release, let go, loose." Pass. छुट्यते, *Pr.* छुट्टइ, whence H. छुट, and so in all, but M. सुट. It is neuter and means "to get free, be unloosed, slip out of one's grasp, come untied."

The modern languages appear to have mixed up with this verb one that comes from a totally different root, namely—

Skr. √ छर्द् "vomit," vii. छृणत्ति, also i. छर्दति and x. छर्दयति. Pa. छड्डेति. *Pr.* छड्डइ and छंडइ. Old H. छंड. P. छड्डु. B. छाड. O. *id.*, H. छोड. M. सोड. These words all mean "to reject, abandon," and thus come round to the same meaning as छोड़, with which in consequence B. confuses it. So does Oriya. Even so early as Pali the meaning has passed over from that of vomiting to rejecting, releasing and the like. In modern H., however, छांड़ना retains the meaning of vomiting, and M. सांड means "to spill," with secondary senses of "giving up," "letting go."

2. Skr. √ त्रुट् "break" (a), I. त्रुटति, iv. त्रुट्यति, Pr. तुट्टइ, H. तूट and टूट, with abnormally long u, P. टुट्ट, S. टुटु, B. *id.*, M. तुट. It is neuter in all and means "to be broken, to break itself." Being neuter in Sanskrit, a new process has to be brought into play, namely, causal त्रोटयति, H. तोड़, and so in all but S. टोड़. It is active, meaning "to break in pieces, tear, smash."

3. Skr. √ स्फट् has three forms, each of which has left modern descendants, and there is a different shade of meaning to each of the three groups.

(a) √ स्फट् "split," I. स्फटति, Pa. फटति and फलति (ट = ड = ल), Pr. फट्टइ and फडइ, H. फट (rustic फाट), P. S. फट and फाट, the rest only फाट, neuter.

Causal स्फाटयति, Pr. फाडेइ, H. फाड़ and so in all. This group with stem-vowel A indicates the splitting, cleaving, or rending asunder of rigid objects. Thus we say in H. काठ धूप में फटे "the wood splits, or cracks, in the sun," but काठ को टांगी से फाड़े "he cleaves the wood with an axe."

(b) √ स्फिट् "hurt," x. स्फिटयति, but also vi. स्फिटति, Pr. फिडइ, H. फिट, and so in all but P. फिट्ट, neuter.

Causal स्फेटयति, Pr. फेडइ and फेड्डइ, H. फेट, फेंट and फेंड़, and so in all but B, active. This group, with stem vowel I, implies gently loosing or breaking up into small pieces. It is used for beating up into froth, winding thread, untying; also metaphorically getting out of debt, discharging an obligation, and in P. injuring.

(c) √ स्फुट् "burst open," i. स्फोटति, vi. स्फुटति, Pa. फुटति,

Pr. फुट्टइ or फुडइ (Var. viii. 53), H. फुट and फूट, all the rest फुट, except P. फुट्ट, neuter.

Causal स्फोटयति, Pr. फोडेइ, H. फोड, and so on in all but B. फोड़. Words with the stem vowel U imply the breaking or bursting of soft squashy things, as a ripe fruit, a flower bud, a boil and the like. Only in M. is there some idea of splitting or cracking, but there also the more general idea is that of squashing, as डोळे फुटले "the eyeballs burst."

6. Skr. √जुड or जुट, a somewhat doubtful root, looking like a secondary formation from युज्. It must have had a definite existence in the spoken language as its descendants shew. They appear to have treated it as a neuter pres. जुडति, जुटति. Pa. and Pr. do not appear to know this root, which, however, is very common in the moderns. H. जुड "to be joined," also जुट, and so in all.

Causal जोडयति, H. जोड, and so in all except P. जुड्ड and जुट, meaning "to join two things together."

These instances suffice to exhibit the nature of the parallel that exists between twin verbs of this class, which is a somewhat limited one.

§ 21. More usual is the difference which consists simply in the change of vowel of which I will now give some examples:

1. Skr. √तॄ "cross over," I. तरति, Pa. *id.*, Pr. तरइ, in all तर a "to be crossed over," metaphorically "to be saved."

Causal तारयति "to take one across, save," Pa. तारेति, Pr. तारेइ and तीरेइ (Var. viii. 70). In all तार "to save." The word is one which belongs chiefly to religious poetry, but its compound form with उत् is a word of every-day use; viz.

2. Skr. √उत्तॄ, Pres. उत्तरति "descend," H. उतर, and in all except S. It is a, and is used with a very wide range of meanings all akin to

that of coming down; as alight, descend, fall off, drop down, disembark, abate, decrease.

Causal उत्तारयति "take down," H. उतार, and so in all except G. and O. Active, meaning "pull down, take off, unload, discharge, cast out."

3. Skr. √ मृ "die," vi. म्रियते, Pa. मरति, Pr. मरइ, H. मर, and so in all.

Causal मारयति, Pa. मारापेति, Pr. मारेइ, H. मार in all, but not necessarily meaning "to kill." It rather means "to beat"; the sense of killing is generally expressed by adding to मार the ancillary डाल "throw" (see § 72, 12).

4. Skr. √ सृ "move," i. सरति, Pr. सरइ. In H. सर neuter, means "to be completed," and in all it has the general sense of being settled, getting done. In O. to come to an end, be done with, as से कर्म सरि गला "that affair is done with."

Causal सारयति, Pr. सारेइ, H. सार "to finish," and in all. In O. this verb becomes ancillary (see § 72).

5. Skr. √ हृ "seize," i. हरति, Pa. *id.*, Pr. हरइ. This verb is peculiar. H. हर a. "to seize," so also in G. P. S. In these languages it has the sense of winning a game, a battle, or a lawsuit. In M. हर means first to carry off, then to win. In this sense it is active, as त्याने पहिल्या डावास शंभर रुपये मांडले ते म्यां हरले "In the first game he staked 100 rupees, that I won." When used as a neuter, it means to lose, as मी वाद हरलों "I lost the lawsuit."[1]

Causal हारयति, Pa. हारापेति and हारेति, Pr. हारेइ, H. हार, and so in all but M. n. In these languages it means to lose at play, etc. M. is here also somewhat difficult, and Molesworth admits that हार and हर are sometimes confused. Thus it is active in the sense of

[1] See Molesworth's Marathi Dict. s. v. हर and हार.

winning, as म्यां त्याचे शंभर रुपये हारले "I won from him 100 rupees."

The use of the causal in the sense of losing goes back to Sanskrit times, where the meaning is "to cause to seize," and then "to permit (another) to seize," hence "to lose." So also in Prakrit. In Mṛ. 20, the Samvâhaka says: भावधेअविसमदाए दसमुवण्णअं जूदे हालिदं (Skr. भाग्यधेयविषमतया दशसुवर्णकं द्यूते हारितं sc. मया) "By the untowardness of fortune I lost ten suvarnas at play." From this and similar instances it would appear that in M. it would be etymologically more correct to use हर in the sense of winning, and हार in that of losing; which usage would be more in unison with that of the cognate languages. In Kash. *hârun* is stated to mean both lose and win, but there must be some way of distinguishing the two meanings.

Some more examples may now be given of pairs of words derived from Sanskrit roots ending in a consonant.

1. Skr. √ चर् and स्फुर् "tremble," i. चरति. Pa. चरति. Pr. फुरइ. If I am right in my derivation, there must either have been a third root फिर् (as in चर्, फिर्, स्फुर्), or the moderns have softened *a* to *i*, the former is the more probable. H. फिर = "to turn (oneself)," "to spin round," "revolve," and so in all except G. It is perhaps on the analogy of similar roots, and not directly from a causal of फिर्, that all the moderns have फेर = "to turn (a thing) round," "to make it revolve."

2. Skr. √ घूर्ण् "to move to and fro" (a). Allied to this is घुल्, i. घोलति, apparently unknown in Pali, Pr. घोलइ. H. घुल, P. M. घुळ, B. घुल, meaning to be dissolved by stirring in water, as sugar or similar substances, "to melt."

Causal घोलयति, Pr. घोलेइ, H. घोल, P. घोल and घोळ, G. M. O. घोळ, B. घोला "to dissolve substances in water."

3. Skr. √ पत् "fall," i. पतति, Pa. *id.*, Pr. पडइ (Var. viii. 51), H. पड "to fall," and so in all.

Causal पातयति. Pa. पातेति, Pr. पाडेइ, H. पाड़ "to fell," and so in S. G. M. B., but somewhat rare in all.

4. Skr. √ शद् "decay," I. and vi. शीयते, Pr. सडइ (Var. viii. 51), H. सड़, and in all "to rot."

Causal शादयति, Pr. साडेइ, P. and S. साड़ "to destroy by decomposition." This root is perhaps connected with Sanskrit √ सद् "to be sick," whence सड in Prakrit and the moderns.

5. Skr. √ नम् "bow," I. नमते. It is both Ā and P in Sanskrit, but strictly would be active intransitive, as in the moderns. Pa. नमति. Pr. णमइ, H. नम and नेव, P. नेउ (neu), S. नंवं, B. नु. O. नुइं, नोइं (5) "to bow oneself down," "to prostrate oneself."

Causal नामयति. Pa. नामेति. Pr. णामेइ, H. नाव, ना. P. निवा, S. नंवा, B. नाम, नुया, O. नुआइ "to bow or bend," used as an active with the words "body" or "head" as objects, H. सीस नावना "to incline the head." द्वार आइ पद नायेउ माथा। "Coming to the door, *bowed his head to* (the Guru's) feet."—T. R. Ay-k. 63.

In very common use is the diminutive H. निहुर, P. S. *id.*, but in S. meaning "to bury," "press down." M. uses the compound form from Skr. अवनमति, Pr. ओणवइ (p.p.p. ओणवो = अवनत, Hāla, 9, Mṛ. p. 165), M. ओणव and ओणाव *a* "to stoop." Perhaps S. ओणा "to listen," *a*, is to be referred to this, from the idea of bending the head to listen.

The following word is full of difficulties, and I am not able to elucidate it clearly.

Skr. √ कृष् "drag," I. कर्षति and vi. कृषति, Pa. कड्ढति, Pr. करिसइ, so, at least, says Var. viii. 11, but in Mṛ. 233 occurs कड्ढिद = कर्षित. The Skr. p.p.p is कृष्ट, which would give Pa. and Pr. कट्ठ. *Perhaps this is another instance of a verb derived from p.p.p.*[1] H. काढ़ *a*, "to drag

[1] Hemachandra gives six popular equivalents of kṛsh—kaḍḍhai, sāaḍḍhai, anchai, anachchhai, ayanchai, and āinchai, as well as karisai.—Pischel, Hem. iv. 187. With regard to the four last, see the remarks on *khainch* in § 21.

out," "extract," "to take something out" (from a box, etc.), P. कड्ढ and काढ्ढ. S. कढ, G. B. काढ, M. O. काढ. H. has a corresponding neuter कढ "to be taken out," "to flow forth," "issue," which is perhaps from the p.p.p. Var. viii. 40, gives Pr. वेढइ = Skr. वेष्टति, which affords an analogy for a Pr. कड्ढइ like the Pali, very much used in the compound with निस्: thus—

Skr. निष्कृष्, I. निष्कर्षति, Pa. निक्कड्ढति "to turn out of doors, expel;" as to Pr. in Mr. 334 occurs निक्कस "begone!" and in the line above निक्कड्ढावेहि "turn him out." For the change of ष्ट to ढ, Var. viii. 41 उवेढइ = उद्वेष्टति affords an analogy, as the change in both words occurs only in composition. Several of the moderns have pairs of words, thus: H. निकलना n., "go out," P. निकलणा, S. निकिरु, G. निकळवुं, O. निकिळिबा, and H. निकालना a. "turn out," P. निकालणा, S. निकारु, निकेरु. In the above quoted passages of Mr., the scholiast renders निक्कड्ढावेहि by निष्कासय, erroneously for निष्कर्षय, from निस् and कस्, but this is not the etymological equivalent, for √ कस् with निस् has left a separate set of descendants, whose meaning is, however, almost the same as *nikal* and its group. Thus we find H. निकसना n., "go out," P. निकसणा, O. *id.*, and H. निकासना a., "to turn out," often used in a milder sense, "to bring out," the substantive निकास is frequently used to mean the issue or completion of a business, also as a place of exit, as पानी का निकास नहीं "there is no exit for the water," P. निकास.

§ 22. As exhibiting the phonetic modifications of the root syllable, as well as the treatment of roots in respect to their phase, whether active or neuter, the list which is here inserted will be useful. In the next section will be found some remarks on the deductions to be made from these examples.

Skr. √ तप् "heat," I. तपति, Pa. *id.*, Pr. तवइ. In Sanskrit it is both *a* and *n*, so also in Pali. In the latter the passive तप्पति (Skr. तप्यते) means to be distressed, to suffer, and in this sense Pr. uses तवइ, as in *jaha diṭṭho tavaï khalo*, "as the bad man is distressed when seen" (Hâla, 229). Causal तापयति "to cause to burn," Pa. तापेति "to distress," Pr. तावइ. The moderns take it as a neuter. H. तप n. "to be heated, to glow," and so in all but B. ताप. H. ताव "to heat," P. ताउ, ता. G. ताव, M. *id.*, B. तावा.

Skr. √ लिप् "smear," vi. लिम्पति, Pa. *id.*, Pr. लिम्पइ, लिपइ. H. लीप, लेप. P. लिम्प, लिम्ब, लिम्म. S. लिंब, लिब. G. लिप. M. लेप. B. लेप. O. लिप. Pass. लिप्यते, Pa. लिप्पति, Pr. लिप्पइ, H. लिप "to be smeared with," M. लिप, O. लेप, which is the reverse of the others.

Skr. √ कृत् "cut," vi. कृन्तति, also I. कर्तति, Pa. not given. If the Bhû type be taken, as it generally is, then Pr. should have कट्टइ (on the analogy of वट्टइ = वर्तते). I have not met with it. The Bhû type being Âtmanepada would result in a modern neuter, thus we get H. कट "to be cut," P. कट्टु, S. कट, M. *id.*, B. कट "to wither," become flaccid, O. कट. The causal is कर्तयति, whence G. pass. intrans. (—1) कटा, but if formed on the usual type would give a Pr. काट्टेइ, whence H. काट "to cut," S. M. B. O. *id.*

Skr. √ बध्, बन्ध् "tie," I. बंधति. ix. बध्नाति. Pa. बंधति, बंधेति. Pr. बंधइ. Hence H. G. बांध *a*, "to knot," P. बंध, बज्झ. S. बंध, M. बांध, बांध, both *a* and *n*, O. बांध *a*, B. बांत, बांध, O. बान्ध. Passive बध्यते used in a reflexive sense, whence H. बंध "to be knotted," or बध without anuswara, P. बध. G. बधा (—1). H. has also forms बंध *n*, and बांध *a*, the former from Pr. बंध, Mr. 137.

The p.p.p. ग्रथित appears in Pr. as गुत्थो, perhaps as if from a Skr. गुथित. Hence we have a pair of verbs, H. गुथ "to be threaded (as beads on a string)," P. गुत्थ "to be tightly plaited (as hair), to be strong, well-knit (as limbs)," M. गुंत and गुंथ "to become tangled, to be difficult or involved (as an affair)," O. गुथा, and H. गूथ "to thread," G. गुंथ.

Skr. √ टल् "totter," I. टलति (perhaps connected with √ चल् disturb, see Vol. I. p. 210). I have not found it in Pr.; it is ट in Skr. and thus

H. डल *n.* "to give way, yield, totter," P. G. M. ढळ, S. ढिल, ढर, B. ढल "to slip, stagger." O. ढळ *id.* Causal ढालयति. H. टाल *a.* "to drive away," टेल "to push," P. टाळ, G. M. *id.*, S. टार, B. टाल "to delay, put off, evade." O. टाळ *id.*

Skr. √ तुल्, तूल "raise," "weigh," i. तोलति, x. तुलयति and तोलयति, Pa. तुलेति. Pr. तुलइ. H. तोल, तौल *a.* "to weigh," P. तोल, S. तोर. G. *id.*, M. तुळ, both *a* and *n*. B. तौला and तुल. O. तौल. Pass. तुल्यते, would be Pr. तुल्लइ, H. तुल *n.* "to be weighed, to weigh," *i.e.* to be of a certain weight, P. *id.*, S. तुर, B. O. तुल.

Skr. √ स्तम्भ् "prop," v. स्तभ्नोति, ix. स्तभ्नाति. Pa., the verb is not given in Childers, it would be थंभति, Pr. थंभइ, H. थाम्ह, also spelt थाम and थाँभ *a.* "to prop, support," P. थम्मण or थंमण, S. थंभ, G. थांभ, B. थामा, O. थाम. Pass. स्तभ्यते; there is also an Âtmane conjugation स्तभते. From this latter probably H. थंभ, थम, थँभ *n.*, "to be supported, to be restrained," hence "to stop, cease," P. थंम, S. थम, G. थंभ, M. थम, थाम, थांब. It also means "to stand," especially in G.

The p.p.p. is स्तब्ध, Pr. थड्ढ, whence Old-H. ठाढा "standing," as गोपी सब गोखिन ह्वै चितवति सब ठाढी ॥ "All the Gopis on the terrace standing and looking."—S. S. Bál lila, 47, 14. On the analogy of this the modern colloquial H. खड़ा is probably to be derived from a Pr. खड्ढ, from स्कब्ध, √ स्कम्भ. P. has खड़ा *adj.* "standing," whence a verb खड़ "to stand."

Skr. √ वृत् with नि, निवृत्, i. निवर्तते "to come to an end, be finished," Pr. णिवत्तइ, means "to return," *ṇa ṇiattai jovvaṇam ṇikkantam* = न निवर्तते यौवनं अतिक्रान्तं "Youth when once passed does not return again" (Hála, 231), but we may postulate a form णिवट्टइ, whence H. निबट *n.* "to be finished, to be done with, used up," P. *id.*, S. निबिड or निबिर, B. निबड़, O. *id.* On the analogy of similar words H. निबाड़, निबेड़ *a.* "to finish," P. *id.*, S. निबेर, B. O. निबाड़, it might also come from निपतति = Pr. णिवडइ, but the meaning is less appropriate.

Skr. √ घट् with वि, विघट, 1. विघटते "be destroyed," Pa. विघटति. Pr. विघडइ. With loss of aspiration, H. बिगड़ n., "to become useless, to be spoilt," P. *id.*, S. विगिड़, G. बगड़, M. retains the aspirate बिघड़, B. O. बिगड़. Causal विघटयति, but Pa. विघाटेति, with characteristic long vowel of causal. Pr. I have not found; it would be विघाडेइ. H. बिगाड़ *a.* "to spoil," P. S. G. *id.*, M. बिघाड़.

There are, as might be expected, many verbs, and those often the very commonest, in the modern languages, which cannot be traced back to any Prakrit stem with any degree of certainty. Others, too, though they preserve traces of a Prakrit origin, cannot be connected with any root in use in Sanskrit. These are probably relics of that ancient Aryan folk-speech which has lived on side by side with the sacred language of the Brahmins, without being preserved in it. Sometimes one comes across such a root in the Dhâtupâṭha, but not in literature; and occasionally the cognate Aryan languages of Europe have preserved the word, though it is strangely missing in Sanskrit. An instance in point is the following:

H. लाद् *a.* "to load," P. लद्द, more from analogy than anything else. S. लदु. In all the rest लाद्.

H. लद् *n.*, "to be loaded;" not in the others. Bopp (Comp. Gloss. s. v.) suggests a derivation from √ क्लम्, p.p.p. क्लान्त "tired," or √ ग्लै, p.p.p. ग्लान "tired." This would seem to be confirmed by Russian *klad'* "a load," *klazha* "lading," *na-kladivat'* "to load;" Old-High-German *hladan*, Anglo-Saxon *hladan* "to load," *hlad* "a load," Mod. High-German *laden*. The wide phonetic changes observable between various members of the great Indo-European family so seldom occur between Sanskrit and its daughters, that I am disposed to think that neither Skr. क्लान्त nor ग्लान could well have given rise to a Hindi *lâd*. It seems more probable that this is a primitive Aryan root which has, for some reason unknown to us, been left on one side by classical Sanskrit.

Of doubtful, or only partially traceable, origin, are the following:

H. खोद् and खोदना a. "to dig." P. *id.*, S. खोटे, खोट. G. खोद्. M. खोद. खुद. B. खुद्. And H. खुद्, खुदना "to be dug." With this pair I propose to connect H. खोल a. "to open," P. खोल्ह्, खुल्ह. S. G. M. खोल, B. O. खुल, and H. खुल n. "to come open," P. खुल्ह. S. खुल, G. M. *id.* Pr. has a verb खुड, and this root is also given in the Dhâtupâṭha as existing in Sanskrit, though not apparently found in actual use. The Sanskrit form is probably √ खण्ड् "to divide," with which another root खन् "to dig," has been confused, unless, indeed, the noun खण्ड, "a portion," is formed from √ खन्, and is the origin of √ खण्ड्. The Prakrit occurs in Mr. 346, कूवम्मि खुडिअपासं कणअकलसं व बुड्डन्तं "Like a golden pot with its string *broken*, sinking in a well," where the scholiast renders कूपे खण्डितपाशं, etc. Also in Mr. 210, अद्धुट्ठिदम्मि सूरे गोवालअदारओ खुडिदो, "While the sun was only half risen the cowherd's son *escaped*," i.e. *broke* out. It is probable that the two senses of digging and opening in the two modern pairs of verbs arose from a primitive idea of breaking or dividing.

H. बूड or बुड n. "to dive, be immersed, sink," S. बुड, G. बुड, M. B. O. *id.*, and H. बोड a. "to drown, to immerse," S. *id.*, बोड occurs in M. and S., not as active of बुड, but for ओड (बुंड्) "to share." Apparently, an inverted form of this stem is the more commonly used H. डूब n. "to sink," used in all; it has no corresponding active form. The origin of these words is to be found in Pr. बुड्ड (Var. viii. 68), which appears to be the same as *vuḍḍa* in *daravuḍḍavuḍḍaṇivuḍḍa mahuaro*, "(With) the bee a little dipped, (quite) dipped, undipped" (said of the bee clinging to a kadam branch carried away by a stream).—Hâla, 37.[1] The Sanskrit lexicographers give a √ बुड "to cover," but no instances of its use. The reversed form *ḍubb* is also in use in Prakrit, as in the quotation

[1] Buḍḍaï = masjati.—Pischel, Hem. iv. 101.

from Mṛ. 346, given under भीड़ above, where the speaker is a Chaṇḍâla or man of the lowest caste, who may be held to speak a low form of Apabhrança. It is perhaps another of those Aryan roots which Sanskrit has rejected. The classical language uses instead *majj*, Latin *mergere*.

H. भिड़, भेंट *a*, "to meet" (to join any one), भेड़ *a*, "to close, shut," P. भेड़, S. भेड़ and भीड़, G. भेड़, M. भिड़, both *a* and *n*, B. भेड़, भेड़, O. भेड़; and H. भिड़ "to stand close to, to be crowded," P. *id.*, S. G. *id.*, M. भेड़, B. भिड़ "to approach near to," O. भिड़ "to be tight." The general idea is that of closeness or a crowded state. There is also a substantive भीड़ "a crowd." From the meaning I was led to suppose (Vol. I, p. 176) a derivation from a Sanskrit p.p.p. अभ्यर्ण "near," which, however, has been disputed. The question must for the present be left undecided.

H. मेट "to efface," P. S. *id.*, and more common H. मिट *n*, "to be effaced, to fail, wear out" (as a writing or engraving), and so in all. Of this stem, all that can be said is, that it is probably connected with मृष्ट "rubbed," p.p.p. of √ मृज्, though one would expect a Pr. मिट्ठ or मुट्ठ, and H. मीठ. There are two other stems ending in ट, which present nearly the same difficulty, viz.:

H. पिट "to be beaten," ऐसा करोगे, तो पिटोगे "If you act thus, you will get a beating." P. पिट्ट, M. पिट, both *a* and *n*, B. and O. पिट *a*, and H. पीट *a*, "to beat," not in the others. In Prakrit there is पिट्ट "to beat," पिट्टिअ इदं चेडं णिक्कासेहि "*Having beaten* this slave, turn him out" (Mṛ. 354, again in the mouth of a Chaṇḍâla), and पिट्टिदगद्दहेव्व विअ पुणोवि लोट्टिस्सं "I must roll about again like a *beaten* jackass" (Mṛ. 107). Here, unless this is a non-Sanskritic old Aryan root, we can only refer to पिष्ट "ground, broken," p.p.p. of √ पिष् "to grind," but this is hardly satisfactory, as this root has a descendant, H. पीस "to grind," and पिस *n*, "to be ground."

H. लेट *n*, "to lie," "to be in a recumbent posture," and लिट *n*, "to wallow," P. लेट, लिट, S. लेटु. G. M. *id.* Probably connected with लोट; but there does not appear to be any Prakrit root to which it can be traced. The nearest Sanskrit root is √ शी "to lie down:" loṭṭai = svapiti.—Pischel, Hem. iv. 146.

There is next to be noted a small group of stems ending in च, concerning which also there has been some controversy.

Skr. √ क्री "buy," ix. क्रीणाति and क्रीणीते, Pa. किणाति, Pr. किणइ, H. कीन, S. क्रिणु (is not the ण here due to some confusion with Pr. घेत्तु = ग्रह् "take"?), B. O. किन. This is a single verb, the complications occur in the following compound with वि, विक्री "sell," ix. विक्रीणाति, Pa. विक्किणाति, Pr. विक्किणइ, S. विकिण a, "to sell," O. विक, Gipsy *bikinava*. But in H. बिक is n, "to be sold, to be exposed for sale," as चावल आज सस्ता बिकता "rice is selling cheap to-day." In M. विक is both a and n, as पिकेल तर्हि विकेल "when it is ripe it will sell." So also P. S. विक n, "to be sold." For the active H. has बेच sometimes pronounced बेंच "to sell," as आज चावल बेचता "he is selling rice to-day." P. वेच, G. वेच, B. बेच. When we remember that all verbs are prone to take the forms of the Bhû type, it is intelligible that विक should mean both "to sell" a, and "to be sold" n, for the Parasmai of the Bhû form would be विक्कयति, and the Âtmane विक्कयते, and the final syllable being rejected as in √ भी and √ ली mentioned above, the stem resulting in both cases would be विक. S. and Gipsy have retained the ण of the Pr. विक्किणइ. But whence comes the च in बेच?

H. खैंच, commonly pronounced खींच "to pull, drag," is a similar word. P. खिच and खिंच, G. M. खेंच, B. खेच and खेंच, O. *id.* Also H. खिंच n, "to be dragged," B. खिच, खिंच "to be dragged or distorted (the face), to grin, make faces, writhe," M. खिंच. From the meaning we are led to think of Sanskrit √ कृष् "to drag," and although this root has been shown to have given rise to another pair of verbs *kaṛh* and *kāṛh*, and in composition to *ni-kal* and *ni-kāl*, yet it is not impossible that, used in a different sense, it may have originated another set of words like *khruch* and its congeners.[1]

H. पहुँच "to arrive" n. written in various ways as पहोंच, पहुच, पहूच, P. पहुँच, S. पहुच, G. पोहॉच, पोंच, M. *id.*, B. पहुँच or पहोंच, O. पहुच. In the dialects are some curious forms, as Marwari पूग and पुग, which also occurs in Chand, and in Nepali. Chand uses also a form पहुँ, as दिन दोय मंझ नीके पहुँत ॥ "In two days one easily arrives (there)." Pr. R. i. 175. In Old-Gujarati also there is a verb पहोंच, *e.g.* नळ कहे नारदने वे वचन मन न पहोंचे "Says Nala to Nârada, this story does not arrive at mind" (*i.e.* is not probable).—*Premânand Bhat*, in K. D. ii. 74. S. पहुचणु has p.p.p. पहुतो, which latter looks as if it were from प्र + भूत, but this will not account for the च. Hoernle (Ind. Ant. i. 358) derives this word from the old Hindi adverb पहँ "near," and कर "make," assuming a change of क into च; but though this change occurs in the ancient languages, there are only very few and doubtful traces of its existence in mediæval or modern times, and I do not think we can safely base any argument upon so rare a process. Hoernle goes so far as to consider H. पुकार "to call," as the causal of पुग, which he says was (or must have been) anciently पुक. There is another possible derivation from Skr. प्राघूर्ण "a guest," which becomes in H. पाहुना, but this fails to explain the final च.

Some light may perhaps be thrown on the subject by some stems in the moderns ending in ज, for as ज arises from द् + य, so च arises from त + य (Vol. I. p. 326). Thus:

H. भेज a, "send," P. *id.* Here we have Skr. √ भिद् "cleave," "separate." Causal भेदयति, which would make a passive भेद्यते "he is made to separate," *i.e.* "he is sent away." If we take the active causal as the origin of this word, we must admit an elision of the vowel between *d*

[1] See note to Kṛsh in § 20. The cognate verb [illegible] is also in use in the moderns.

and y; or, taking the simple passive भिज्यते, we may assume that there was a neuter भिज "to be sent," from which the active भेज "to send," has been formed; *bhij*, however, is not found.

H. बजना n. "to sound," P. *id.*, S. बजु and बाजु, G. बाज, M. वाजणें, B. *id.* Also H. बाजना a. "to play (music)," and n. "to sound." Probably from Skr. √ वद् "speak," causal वादयति, Pa. वद्दति and वद्देति, the passive of the causal is Skr. वाद्यते, Pa. वज्जति "to be beaten," *i.e.* "to be caused to speak," as *vajjanti bheriyo* "drums are beaten." Hence the modern *bāj*. The short form *baj* is apparently due to analogy.

§ 23. It is the business of the lexicographer, rather than of the grammarian, to work out the derivations of all the verbs in these languages, and even he would probably find the task one of insuperable difficulty in the present elementary state of our knowledge. It is hoped that the examples and illustrations given above will have enabled the reader to gain some insight into the general principles which have governed the modern languages in the process of forming their verbal stems. To conclude this part of the subject, I will now point out what seem to me to be the laws deducible from the examples above given, and from many others which, to avoid prolixity, I have not cited.

Single neuter stems are derived (i) from the Prakrit present tense of Sanskrit neuter verbs, or (ii) from the Prakrit passive past participle, or (iii) Prakrit has assumed one form for all parts of the verb, which form has been handed down to the modern languages almost, if not entirely, unchanged. Types of these three processes respectively are *ho*, *baith*, and *uth*.

Single active stems are formed from the Prakrit present of active verbs, and in cases where the verb in Sanskrit is not conjugated on the Bhû type, Prakrit usually, and the moderns always, adopt the Bhû type. Here, also, Prakrit has occasionally taken one form of root and used it throughout, and the moderns have followed the Prakrit. Types of these classes are *paṛh*, *kar*, and *ghen*.

In the double verbs two leading processes are observable. Where the root is conjugated actively, or is active in meaning in the ancient languages, the modern active is derived from it, and in that case the modern neuter is derived from the Prakrit form of the Sanskrit passive, as in *lubhaṇu*, *lahaṇu*, or as *chhoṛ*, *chhuṭ*. Where the ancient root is neuter, the modern neuter is derived from it, and in this case the active is derived from the ancient causal, as in *ṭuṭ*, *toṛ*, or *mar*, *mār*.

These rules, if further research should eventually confirm them, do not provide for every modern verbal stem, as there are many whose origin is obscure and doubtful. It is highly probable that as we come to know more about these languages, we shall find out other processes which will throw light upon the method of formation of many now obscure stems.

It should here also be noted that even where the same stem occurs in the same, or nearly the same, *form* in all the languages, it is not used in the same *phase* in all. Marathi and Sindhi have different sets of terminations for neuter and active, so that the fact of the neuter and active stem being the same creates no difficulty, the distinction of meaning being shown by the terminations. Thus in M. गांठ, if treated as a neuter, would be conjugated thus: Present *gāṇṭhato*, Past *gāṇṭhalā* Future *gāṇṭhel*, etc.; but if as an active, thus: Present *gāṇṭhito*, Past *gāṇṭhilā*, Future *gāṇṭhil*. In this language, therefore, we often find a verb used either as active or neuter; while in Hindi, which has one set of terminations for all stems, the difference between active and neuter can only be marked by the stem. In several rustic dialects of Hindi, however, and in the mediæval poets, we often find the neuter verb with a long vowel, but confusion is avoided by giving to the active verb the terminations of the causal, thus बढ़ना "to grow big," "increase," makes its active बढ़ाना "to make big," and rustic and poetical Hindi often uses बाढना for the neuter, as ऐसो देव प्रकट गोवर्द्धन । जाके पूजे बाढै गोधन ॥ "Such a god is manifest in Govardhana, from the worship of whom wealth of cattle *increases*."—S.S. *Govardhanlîlâ*, ii. 15, *et passim*. So also बाढत बेलन मृणालक सूत ॥ "It *grows* like the threads of the lotus."—Padm. This subject will be more fully discussed under the causal.

§ 24. Gujarati, as will have been noticed in the examples given in the last section, often wants the neuter stem with the short vowel, but has in its place a form in which *â* is added to the stem, the included vowel of which is short. This form is not incorrectly treated by some grammarians as the ordinary passive of the language. It should, however, in strictness, be recognized as the passive intransitive (that form marked —1 in the scale, § 10).[1] The rules for its formation are simple, in stems, whether neuter or active, having *â* as the included vowel, it is shortened to *a*, as—

वांच "read,"	वंचा "be read."
पारख "mark, test."	परखा "be tested."
सांभळ "hear,"	संभळा "be heard."

The shortening does not always take place when the included vowel is *î* or *û*, though from the way in which short and long vowels are used indiscriminately in Gujarati, it is not safe to lay down a hard and fast rule on this point, thus—

शीख "learn."	शीखा (शिखा) "be learnt."
सीव "sew,"	सीवा (सिवा) "be sewn."

Where the stem ends in a vowel, व is inserted to prevent hiatus, as—

धो "wash,"	धोवा "be washed."
खा "eat,"	खवा "be eaten."
बिही "fear,"	बिहीवा "be feared."

[1] Van Taylor, Gujarati Grammar, p. 81, from which most of the following remarks are borrowed, though I diverge from him in some points as which his views seem to be open to correction.

With regard to the meaning and method of using this phase, it appears that its construction resembles that of the neuter, while it implies either simple passiveness, habit, or power. As a simple passive, रामखाँ रावणु मराणो "Râvana was killed by Râma," हन खेतर में बी बजाणु "In this field seed has been sown;" as expressing habit, एवं कहिजाणु हे सबं "thus it is correctly said," i.e. "this is the correct way of expressing it;" हो छोकरो मूर्ख सजाणहि "this boy is (usually) thought to be stupid;" as expressing power or fitness, तिणाखाँ चलाणु नहि "he cannot walk," literally "by him it is not walked;" राजा खाँ अन्याउ कराणु नहि "a king cannot (or must not) do injustice;" खूहो अभिटाणो आहे एहुं पाणी पीआणु नहि "the well has become impure, therefore its water is not drunk." Some of the words which take this form are, to all intents and purposes, simple neuters in meaning, like *abhaṭijaṇo* in the sentence just quoted, which means "to be ceremonially impure," and points back to a Sanskrit denominative, as though from अ "not," and भद्र "good," there had been formed a verb अभद्रायते "it is not good." So also वपराणु "to be used," "to be in use," as इक अर्थ में बे प्रत्यय वपराणु हे "two affixes are in use with one meaning," postulates from व्यापार, a denominative व्यापारायते, or perhaps the causal of वि + आ + पृ = व्यापारयति. This seems to be the real origin of this phase, though some would derive it from a form of the Prakrit passive. At any rate, the two stems just quoted (and there are several others of the same kind) look more like denominatives than anything else, though in others this form inclines more to the passive signification, as भीमक सुता जुं वदनु सुधाकर देखीने सोभाणु । चन्द्रमा तो चोख पाणी वादलनि लुकाणु ॥ "Having seen the moon-like face of the daughter of Bhimaka in its beauty—The moon wasted away, having hidden itself in the clouds."—Premânand in K.-D. ii. 74. Here सोभाणु is "to be beautiful," and looks like a denominative, but लुकाणु has more of a passive or reflexive meaning, "to be hidden," "to hide oneself." Again, दमयंती जुं चन्द्र देखी

सुकाणुं सरोवर "Seeing the belly of *Damayanti*, the lake dried up," (*ib.* ii. 75), literally "was dried up." So also घर बाळ्युं ज्यारे कूवो खोदावे छ अग्नि केम ओलवाय। "When the house has caught (fire), he has a well dug, how can this fire be put out?" —K.-D. i. 184.[1] The verb ओसरवुं is also written ओहर°, and is probably the same as O. ओहरिबा "to descend, alight," M. ओहळणें "to trickle, flow down," which I take to be from अप + सृ = अपसरति, Pr. ओसरइ (Mâgadhi), and with change of स to ह = ओहर. It is used in the sense of removing oneself, thus: भाई ते ओसरज "ho there! get out of the way!" (Mr. 210), and causal ओसारियुं मे गाडुं "I have got the cart out of the way," (*ib.* 211) = Skr. अपसारितम्. This phrase is conjugated throughout all the tenses, thus खोवावुं "to be lost." Present खोवाय "he is lost," Future खोवाशे "he will be lost," Preterite खोवायो, खोवायो, or खोवाएलो छे "he has been lost," and in active verbs it is used in the Bhava-prayoga, as a sort of potential, as तेनाथी छोडाय "he can loose," तेनाथी छोडायो "he could loose," तेनाथी छोडाशे "he will be able to loose."

As to the other languages, a similar form is found in the Bhojpuri dialect of Hindi, used as a simple passive, as पकड़ "seize," पकड़ा "be seized," as हम पकड़ाइल बा "I am being seized." In this dialect, however, there are signs, as will be shown further on, of a passive similar to that in use in classical Hindi. In the old Maithil dialect of Bidyâpati, which is transitional between eastern Hindi and Bengali, this form is found; thus, सिकता जल बिहि बरसि सुखायल "As water poured out on the ground *is dried up.*"—Pad. 984. धरणी लोटायल गोकुलचांद। "(He who is) the moon of Gokul *rolled himself* on the earth."—P.K.S. 77. जनु इंदीवर पवने पेलल अलि भरे ओलटायल। "As a lotus pressed down by the wind *is tilted* by the weight of bees" (var. lect. भुरि = by a swarm).—Pad. 1552.

[1] This is equivalent in meaning to our English saying, "When the steed is stolen, shut the stable door."

There seems to be some difficulty in deducing this form from a Prakrit passive. One of the methods in which the passive in Prakrit is formed is by resolving the *y* of Sanskrit into *ia* or *ia*, Skr. वाच्यते = Pr. वाईअदि; and it is supposed that this ई has become इय, and subsequently इज, but no instances of intermediate forms are found; it would seem, therefore, more correct to suppose that this form originates from the causal of Sanskrit in those instances where the causal characteristics are used to form denominatives, and has from them been extended to other verbs. Neither explanation, however, is quite satisfactory, and the question is one which must be left for further research.

§ 25. The regular Passive (phase—2) is found only in Sindhi, Panjabi, and in some rustic dialects of Hindi. It arises from the Prakrit passive in *ijja* (Var. viii. 58, 59). Thus Skr. *çrûyate* = *suṇijjai*, *gamyate* = *gamijjai*, *hasyate* = *hasijjai*. In Sindhi the passive is formed by adding इज or ज to the neuter or active stem.[1] Thus—

पुरणु "to bury." Passive पुरिजणु "to be buried."
घटणु "to lessen," " घटिजणु "to be lessened."

A passive is also made from causal stems, as—

विञाइणु "to lose." Passive विञाइजणु "to be lost."

Here, also, we find denominatives which have no corresponding active form, and have scarcely a passive sense, as उकंडिजणु "to long for," where the causal termination used in Sanskrit for denominatives appears to have been confused with the *ijja* of the passive. Thus Skr. उत्कण्ठा "longing," makes a verb उत्कण्ठयति "to long for," whence the Sindhi *ukhaṇḍijaṇu*. So also अङुरिजणु "to be entangled," which seems to be from Skr. अङ्गुल, or अङ्गुरि "a finger," whence we may suppose a verb

[1] Trumpp, Sindhi Grammar, p. 254.

चहुटबणि "to be intertwined (like the fingers of clasped hands);" डमिर्बणु "to be angry," from डमरु "anger," Skr. डमर "uproar," of which the denominative would be डमरबणि.

In cases where the vowel of the active stem is long in the imperative, but shortened in the infinitive, the passive retains the long vowel. Thus

पीउ "drink thou," पिबणु "to drink," पीबणु "to be drunk."
पुउ "thread thou," पुबणु "to thread," पूरबणु "to be threaded."
धोउ "wash thou," धुबणु "to wash," धोरबणु "to be washed."

A similarly formed passive is used in the Marwâri dialect of Hindi, spoken west of the Aravalli hills towards Jodhpur, and thus not very far from Sindh. Instances are—

करबो "to do." करीजबो "to be done."
खावबो "to eat." खवीजबो "to be eaten."
लेबो "to take." लिरीजबो "to be taken."
देबो "to give." दिरीजबो "to be given."
आवबो "to come." अवीजबो "to be come."

Thus they say मैं सूं अवीजै नहीं = H. मुझ से आया नहीं जाता "by me it is not come," *i.e.* "I am not coming." था सूं खवीजैगो नहीं = H. तुम से नहीं खाया जायगा "by you it will not be eaten," *i.e.* "you will not (be able to) eat it." This passive construction is frequent in the Indian languages, but usually with the negative expressing that the speaker is unable or unwilling to do a thing.[1] The insertion of र instead of ज in ले and दे is peculiar and unaccountable.

Panjabi also has a synthetical passive, though rarely used. It is formed by adding ई to the root, and is probably derived from that form of the Prakrit passive which ends in *ia*, as

[1] I have to thank Mr. Kellogg, of Allahabad, author of the best, if not of the only really good Hindi Grammar, for communicating this form to me in a letter. I was previously unaware of it.

mentioned above. This form of the passive is only used in a few tenses, thus मारना "to beat," Passive present मैं मारीदा "I am beaten." Future मैं मारीवांगा "I shall be beaten." Potential (old present) मैं मारीवां "I may be beaten."

With these exceptions, there is no synthetic form for the passive in the modern languages. This phase is usually formed by an analytical process. It is not much used, the construction of sentences being more frequently reversed, so as to make the verb active. The large number of neuter verbs also renders a passive for the most part unnecessary. It does exist, however, and is formed by adding the verb जा "to go," to the past participle of the passive, जा doing all the conjugational work, and the participle merely varying for number and gender.

Thus from मार "beat," H. Sing. मारा जाना "to be beaten" *m.*, मारी जाना *f.*, Plur. मारे जाना *m.*, मारीं जाना *f.*, P. मारिया जाना *m.*, मारी *f.*, Plur. मारे *m.*, मारीयां *f.* Gujarati also uses this method side by side with the passive intransitive, as मार्यो जवुं "to be beaten," with the participle varied for gender and number as in the others. M. मारिला जावे, B. मारा जाइते, O. मारा जिबा. In these two last the participle does not vary for gender or number.

Occasionally in G. and M. a passive is formed by adding the substantive verb to the past participle, thus M. बैल बांधली होती "the cow was tied," and G. ग्रंथ कर्यो छे "the book is made:" such a construction would in the other languages be incorrect, or, if used at all, would have a different meaning altogether.

The use of जाना "to go," to form a passive, seems somewhat unnatural; होना "to be," would occur as the most fitting verb for this purpose. I am tempted to hazard a conjecture that the use of जाना in this way has arisen from the Prakrit passive form in *ijja*. This, as we have seen above, has given a regular passive to Sindhi and Marwari, and it seems possible that the masses who had quite forgotten, or had never known, the meaning of the added *j*, may unconsciously have glided into the practice of confounding it with the ज of the common word जा, which would lead them to consider the verbal stem preceding it as a passive participle. Thus a form मारिजै "he is beaten," would easily pass into मारा जाइ, as in modern Hindi. The process must, of course, have been unconscious, as all such processes are, but the supposition does not involve a more violent twisting of words and meanings than many others which are better supported by actual facts.

The non-Aryan party have something to say on this head.[1] They point out that the Dravidian languages, like our seven, largely avoid the use of the passive by having recourse to neuter verbs, and that with them, as with us, the neuter is often only another form of the same root as the active. Indeed, the similarity in this respect is very striking, the process is, to a great extent, the same in both groups, though the means employed are different. The passive does not, strictly speaking, occur in the Dravidian languages; a clumsy effort is sometimes made to produce one, by adding the verb *padu* "to happen" (Sanskrit पत्, modern Aryan पड़) to an infinitive or noun of quality. This process, however, is as strained and foreign to elegant speech as the construction with *jâ* is in the Aryan group. It appears, also, that the verb *poyu* "to go," is also used in Tamil to form a passive, as also a verb meaning "to eat," which latter is parallel to our North-Indian expression मार खाना "to eat a beating" = "to be beaten." In this, as in so many other instances of alleged non-Aryan influence, the known facts do not justify us in saying more than that there is a resemblance between the two groups of languages, but that it is not clear which borrowed the process, or whether it was ever

[1] Caldwell, pp. 352, 364 (first edition).

borrowed at all. There is no reason why it should not have grown up simultaneously and naturally in both families.

§ 26. We now come to the Causal, an important and much used phase of the verb. Sanskrit forms the causal by adding the syllable *aya* to the root, which often also takes guṇa or vṛiddhi, √कृ "do," causal कारयति. There is, however, in Sanskrit a small class of verbs which form the causal by inserting प between the root and the characteristic *aya*. These are principally roots ending in a vowel; but in Pali and the Prakrits the form of the causal in प has been extended to a very large number of stems, in fact to nearly every verb in those languages. In Pali, however, its use is optional, thus √पच् "cook," causal *pācheti, pāchayati, pāchāpeti, pāchāpayati*.[1] In Prakrit, also, there are the two processes, by the first of which the *aya* of Sanskrit becomes *e*, thus कारयति = Pr. कारेइ, हासयति = हासेइ (Var. vii. 26), and by the second the inserted प is softened to व, thus giving करावेइ or कारावेइ (*ib.* 27). It is from this form, and not from *aya*, as I erroneously supposed in Vol. I. p. 20, that the modern causal arises. Even in Prakrit the *e* in *kārāvei* is frequently omitted, as it is also in *kārei*, and we find such forms as *kārāī*, *kārai*, side by side with *kārāvei* (Weber, Hāla, p. 60), so that there remains only *āv* for the modern causal.

Among the modern languages Marathi stands alone in respect of its causal, and, as in so many other points, exhibits a hesitation and confusion which confirm the impression of its being a backward language which has not so thoroughly emancipated itself from the Prakrit stage as the others. Whereas those latter have passed through the period in which rival forms conflicted for the mastery, and have definitely settled upon one type to be used universally, the former pre-

[1] Kaccâyana, Senart, Journal Asiatique, vol. xvii. p. 436.

sents us with several alternative suffixes, none of which appears to have obtained undisputed prominence. The authorities for Marathi consist of the classical writers, the one dictionary-maker, Molesworth, and a host of grammarians, all of whom differ among themselves, so that one is driven to ask, "who shall decide when doctors disagree?"

The competing forms are: *ava*, *iva*, *îva*, *avi*, *âva*, *âvi*, and one sees at a glance that they are all derived from one source, the causal with प, modified in Prakrit to व. The difficulty lies in the vowels. Where one authority gives a causal in *ava* to a particular verb, another makes the causal of that same verb by adding *iva*, and so on. Stevenson (Marathi Grammar, p. 67) teaches that *ava* is the ordinary form, as *basaṇeṃ* "to sit," *basavaṇeṃ* "to seat." This type, however, he adds, is peculiar to the Konkan or lowlands along the coast; in the Dakhin or centre table land above the passes the form *iva* is more used, as *karaṇeṃ* "to do," *karivaṇeṃ* "to cause to do." A third form *avi* is said to be "of a middle class," and not characteristic of either dialect, as *karaviṇeṃ*. It is to be noted here that the causal suffix, strictly speaking, ends with the *v*, and the vowels that follow this letter may fairly be regarded as mere junction vowels, used to add the terminations to the stem. In those of the cognate languages which use *â* as the causal suffix, the junction vowel used is either *i*, as B. *karâ-i-te*, O. *karâ-i-bâ*, S. *karâ-i-ṇu*, or *u*, as Old-H. *karâ-u-nâ*, P. *karâ-u-ṇâ*, or hardened to *va*, as G. *karâ-va-vuṃ*. Dismissing, then, the final vowel as unconnected with the suffix, we get for Marathi four types, *av*, *âv*, *iv*, *îv*. Of these four *âv* approaches most closely to the Prakrit, and may therefore be regarded as the original type from which, by a shortening of the vowel, comes *av*, which, all things considered, is perhaps the most common and regular; a further weakening of the vowel produces *iv*; and the fourth form, *îv*, probably owes its long vowel to the Marathi habit of lengthening vowels at the end of a word, or in a syllable, where the stress or accent falls. Thus all four forms may be used, as

करणें "to do," करवणें, करावणें, करिवणें, करोवणें; also करविणें, and करींविणें "to cause to do."[1]

Causals may be formed from every verb in the language, whether neuter, active, active or passive intransitive. The meaning of the causal differs, of course, according to that of the simple verb.

Those formed from simple neuters or active intransitives are generally merely actives in sense, as

बस "sit," बसव "seat."
मिळ "meet," मिळव (junction vowel इ) "mix."
निज "sleep," निजव "put to sleep," "soothe."

Those from actives are causal in meaning, as

मार "strike," मारव "cause to strike."
शिक "teach," शिकव "cause to teach."

Those from passive intransitives are passive causals, as

फिर "turn" (*i.e.* be turned), फिरव "cause to be turned."
कट "be cut," कटव, कटाव "cause to be cut."

Simple roots ending in vowels insert a *v* between the stem and the suffix to avoid hiatus, as

खा "eat," खावव (junction vowel इ) "cause to eat."

So also with roots ending in ह, as

लिह "write," लिहवव "cause to write."

The various forms of the causal suffix in Marathi may be regarded as types of a stage of transition which the other lan-

[1] Godbole's Marathi Grammar, p. 103, § 279.

guages have passed by. The following are examples of the causal in these latter:

लिख "write." H. P. B. O. S. लिखा "cause to write." (H. Pres. *likhātā*, Pret. *likhāyā*, Aor. *likhāe*, or *likhāy*, or *likhāwe*.)

पढ "read," *id.* पढा "cause to read."

सुन "hear." *id.* सुना "cause to hear."

In Hindi, as in the other languages, the causal of a neuter verb is, in effect, nothing more than an active, as

बनना "be made," बनाना "make."

बोलना "speak," बुलाना "call" (*i.e.* "cause to speak.")

चलना "move," चलाना "drive."

जागना "be awake," जगाना "awaken."

उठना "rise," उठाना "raise."

पकना "be cooked," पकाना "cook."

So also in the case of double verbs given in §§ 20, 21, the active form, with long vowel in the stem syllable, may be regarded as a causal. In fact, it might be said, looking at the matter with reference to meaning, that the modern languages have two ways of forming the causal, one in which the short vowel of the stem is lengthened, the other in which *ā* or some other suffix is added. Looking at it in another way with reference to form, the division which I have adopted commends itself, the forms with a long vowel in the stem being regarded as actives, those with the added syllable as causals. In point of derivation, however, both forms are causals. There is a wonderful, though unconscious, economy in our languages; where Prakrit has more types than one for the same phase of a verb, the modern languages retain them all, but give to each a different meaning. For instance, Prakrit has three types for the passive, one in which the final consonant of the stem is doubled by absorption of the य् of Skr. as *gamyate* = *gammai*, a second in *ia*, as *gamyate*=*gamiadi*, and a third in *ijja*, as *gamyate*=*gamijjadi*. The first of these types, having lost whatever might remind the speaker of its passive character, has been adopted in the modern languages as the form of the simple neuter verb, the second survives in the Panjabi passive, as *mârîdâ*=*mârîadi*, the third in the Sindhi and Marwari passive given in § 23. So, also, it seems to me that the two types of the Prakrit causal have been separately utilized; that which corresponds to the Sanskrit type in *aya* with long or guṇa vowel in the stem, has become in the moderns an active verb, as *kârayati*=*kârei*=*kâr*; *troṭayati*=*toṛei*=*toṛ*; while that which takes the प causal is preserved as the ordinary causal of the moderns, as *kârayati* (*karâpayati*)=*karâvei*=*karâ*.

Often, however, both forms exist together, and there is little or no apparent distinction between them; thus from कढ़ना are made both काढ़ना and कढ़ाना, from हटना are made हाटना and हटाना, and so in many other instances.

The causal, properly so called, namely, that with the suffix *â*, *âv*, etc., has always a short vowel in the stem syllable, except in a few instances where the stem vowel is vṛiddhi, in which case it is sometimes retained. Thus in the double verbs the causal suffix may be regarded as added to the neuter form, as in

NEUTER.	ACTIVE.	CAUSAL.
नच	नाच	नचा
घुल	घोल	घुला

In such cases, however, we more commonly find the double or passive causal.

Single verbs with a long or guṇa stem-vowel have causals with the corresponding short or simple vowel, as in the examples घोलना and घुलाना, काढ़ना and कढ़ाना given above.

Verbs whose simple stems end in a vowel insert a semivowel before the termination of the causal, and change the vowel of the stem, if *â*, *î*, or *e*, into *i*, if *û* or *o*, into *u*. The semivowel used is sometimes ल or र, but more commonly व. Thus, लेना "to take," लिवाना "to cause to take," but—

H. देना "give,"	दिलाना "cause to give."
जीना "live,"	जिलाना "cause to live."
पीना "drink,"	पिलाना "give to drink."
खाना "eat,"	खिलाना "feed."
धोना "wash,"	धुलाना "cause to wash."
सोना "sleep,"	सुलाना "put to sleep."
रोना "weep,"	रुलाना "make to weep."

In a few cases of stems ending in ह, or in aspirates, the ल is optionally inserted, as

H. कहना "say,"	कहाना	and	कहलाना "cause to say." "be called."
देखना "see,"	दिखाना	„	दिखलाना "show."
सीखना "learn,"	सिखाना	„	सिखलाना "teach."
बैठना "sit,"	बिठाना (or बै°)	„	बिठलाना (बै°) "seat."

A similar method exists in Sindhi, but with र instead of ल, as is customary with that language, as[1]

डिअणु "give,"	डिआरणु "cause to give."
पुसणु "leak,"	पुसारणु "cause to leak."
विहणु "sit,"	विहारणु "seat."
सिखणु "learn,"	सिखारणु "teach."
उथणु "rise,"	उथारणु "raise."
सुम्हणु "sleep,"	सुम्हारणु "put to sleep."

Here the र is inserted after the causal suffix, and this was probably the method originally in force in Hindi, for we find in the mediæval poets such words as *dikhārnā* "to show," and even in modern colloquial usage *baiṭhālnā* is quite as common

[1] Trumpp, Sindhi Grammar, p. 256.

as *biṭhlánd*. Gujarati forms its causal in an analogous way, but uses ड instead of र, as

धाववुं "suck," धवाडवुं "give suck."
शीववुं "sew," शीवाडवुं "cause to sew."
वागवुं "sound," वगाडवुं "strike" (a bell, etc.)

After words ending in a vowel, the suffix takes व to prevent hiatus, and so also after ह, as

था (थवुं) "be," थवाडवुं "cause to be."
खावुं "eat," खवाडवुं "feed."
देवुं "give," देवाडवुं "cause to give."
सेहवुं "endure," सेहवाडवुं "cause to endure."
कोहवुं "rot," कोहवाडवुं "cause to rot."

This language, like Hindi, also reverses the position of the long vowel of the causal suffix, and uses such forms as *dhavrávr*, *khavrávr*, with change of ड to र.

There is nothing remarkable about the Panjabi causal, which is identical with Old Hindi, merely retaining the junction vowel *u*, as *khilá-u-ná*, *dikhá-u-ná*. In both these languages the old form *áu* has, in a few instances, changed to *o* instead of *á*, as

भिजोणा "to wet," from भीजणा "to be wet."
डुबोणा "to drown," „ डुबणा "to be drowned."

Bengali and Oriya have only the causal form in *á* with junction vowel *i*, as B. *kará-i-le*, O. *kará-i-bá*, and use this form in preference to that with the long stem vowel, even in those causals which are, in meaning, simple actives.

There are thus, independently of the stem with the long or guna vowel, which I prefer to treat as an active, two separate systems of forming the causal in the seven languages: one starting from the Prakrit causal in *áve*, and exhibiting the forms *áw*, *aw*, *iw*, *ew*, *áe*, *áu*, *o*, *á*; the other starting, I know not whence, but probably from a method in use in early Aryan speech, which has only been preserved by the classical language in a few instances, and exhibiting the forms *ár, ád, ál, rá, lá*. Whether these two forms are connected by an interchange between the two semivowels *l* and *r*, is a problem which must remain for future research. Such a connexion is not impossible, and is even, in my opinion, highly probable.

§ 27. The Passive Causal may be also called the double causal. The use of either term depends upon the point of view of the speaker, for whether I say, "I cause Rám to be struck by Shyám," or, "I cause Shyám to strike Rám," the idea is the same. As regards form, the term double causal is more appropriate in some languages. In H. and P. this phrase is constructed by adding to the stem H. वा. P. वाव, in which we should, I think, recognize the syllable *âv* of the single causal shortened, and another *âr* added to it, thus from *sun* "hear," comes causal *suná*, "cause to hear," "tell," double causal *sunvá*,[1] "cause to cause to hear," "cause to tell;" here, as *suná* is from the fuller form *sunâr*, so *sunvá* is from sunâv+âv=sunav+â=*sunvâ*. This double or passive causal is in use mostly with neuter and active intransitive stems, whose single causal is naturally an active, as बनना "be made," बनाना "make," बनवाना "cause to be made." Thus they say, गढ़ बनता "The fort is being built;" थवई गढ़ बनाता "The architect is building the fort;" and राजा थवई के द्वारा गढ़ बनवाता "The king is causing the fort to be built by the architect." In this last sentence, and in all similar phrases, the nature of the construction is such that we can only translate it by the passive causal, we could not render "The king causes the architect to build," etc., by बनवाना in any other way than by putting "architect"

[1] Generally, the semivowel in this form is pronounced softly, almost like the English *w*, so that *sunwâná* would more nearly represent the sound than *sunvâná*. The *v*, however, in all Indian languages is a softer sound than our *v*.

in the ablative with द्वारा or से. When we are told, therefore, that this phase means "to cause to do" (the action of a neuter verb), the assertion, though correctly expressing the form, is incorrect as to the meaning; the dictionary-makers here halt between two opinions. Thus

चढ "rise,"	चाढा "raise" (*i.e.* "cause to rise"),	चढवा "cause to be raised" (*i.e.* "cause A to cause B to rise").
कट "be cut,"	काट "cut,"	कटवा "cause to cut."
खुल "be open,"	खोल "open,"	खुलवा "cause to open."

In double verbs, like those just quoted, however, the single causal in *á* may be used, as कटा "cause to cut." As a general rule, the exact meaning of stems in this phase must be gathered from the sentence in which they are used.

Sindhi makes its double causal by inserting *rá* (Trumpp, 257), as

थिकं "be weary,"	थिकाँ "make weary, tire,"	थिकाँरा "cause to make weary."
घा "wound,"	घारा "cause to wound,"	घारारा "cause to cause to wound, or cause (another) to be wounded."

Stack instances also passive causals formed on the same model as ordinary passives, thus

बर "be on fire," बार "burn," बारा "cause to burn," बाराइज "be caused to be burnt."

One example given by him shows a full range of phases, as धापजु "to be sucked, to issue" (as milk from the breast), neuter; धापु "to suck the breast," active; धापजु "to be sucked," pass.; धाफिवजु "to give suck," neut. pass.; धापारु "to suckle," caus.; धापारजणु "to be suckled," pass. caus.;

धाराराइणु "to cause (another) to suckle," double caus.; धारारारिजणु "to cause to be suckled by another," double pass. caus. The whole of these forms, however, are rarely found in one verbal stem. The double causal is common enough, thus from the causals mentioned in the last section are derived double causals—

सुम्हारणु "to put to sleep," सुम्हाराइणु "to cause to put to sleep."
उथारणु "to raise," उथाराइणु "to cause to raise" (H. उठवाना).

§ 28. Although the suffixed syllables shown in § 26 generally and regularly indicate the causal phase, yet there are numerous verbs having this suffix which are neuter, active intransitive, or passive intransitive. As mentioned in § 11, these stems are probably built on the model of Sanskrit denominatives, and owe their long vowel to the *aya* or *âya* of that form. Hence they come to resemble in form modern causals.

In Sindhi these stems have a development peculiar to that language, and have a corresponding active phase like the double stems mentioned in § 10. Trumpp gives (p. 252, *et seqq.*) the following examples:

NEUTER.	ACTIVE.
उझामणु "to be extinguished."	उझाइणु "to extinguish."
उडामणु "to fly."	उडाइणु "to make fly, to spend."
जापणु, ज़मणु } "to be born."	ज़णणु "to bring forth."
ढ़ापणु "to be satiated."	ढ़ाइणु "to satiate."
ब़ामणु "to be on fire."	ब़ाइणु "to burn."
मापणु, मामणु } "to be contained."	माइणु "to contain."
विहामणु "to be passed, to pass" (as time).	विहाइणु "to pass the time."
घपामणु "to grow less."	घपाइणु "to lessen."

In this group the neuter stems have the type *âpu* and *âwu*, which, if we regard them as derived from the Prakrit type *âbe* of the causal, will appear as respectively a hardening and a softening of the *b* of Prakrit. In some cases the neuter form is clearly derived from the older causal, as in मापणु "to contain," rather, "to go into," Skr. √मा "to measure;" but मापणु, Skr. caus. मापयति "to cause to measure," where, by a natural inversion of the sense, the causal has become neuter. In the case of वापणु the process by which the meaning has been arrived at from Sanskrit √वप् is less clear. The other stems are also obscure, and I possess no data on which to establish any satisfactory explanation.

Sindhi stands alone in respect of this group: Hindi and Panjabi have a number of neuter stems with causal terminations, which stand on a different footing, and recall by their meaning the Sanskrit denominatives, having no corresponding active forms, as—

H. खिसाना "to be abashed," "to shrink away."
छिजाना "to be worn out."
खुजलाना "to itch."
घबराना "to be agitated," "to be in fear" P. घबराउणा.
घमाना "to bask in the sun."
चंचलाना "to tremble," "to be unsteady." P. *id.*
P. नरमाउणा "to grow soft" (a sore).
कुम्हलाना "to wither," to grow flaccid." P. *id.*

In words of this class, also, a syllable इय is often inserted, as

खिसियाना "to grin." P. खिसियाउणा *id.*

This type is evidently closely connected with the passive of Gujarati and other dialects given in § 24, which I have been led by the considerations here mentioned to regard as a passive intransitive. It seems also to be connected with the passive intransitive in B. in such passages as राजपुत्र हवे रूप लक्षणे जानाय । "He must be a king's son, by his appearance and marks (of birth) *it is known*."—Bhârat, B.-S. 378, where *jânáy* = *jânâé*, "it appears," "it is evident," a construction exactly parallel to the Gujarati phrases quoted in § 24.

Marathi has similarly neuters with a causal type, which recall the method of formation of the Sanskrit denominative, inasmuch as they are referred by the grammarians to a nominal origin, thus—

कडका "a cracking or crashing sound;" कडकाविणें "to crack, crash;" कडकावणें "to roar at," "to make a crashing noise."

कमता (from Persian کم) "deficient," कमतावणें "to grow less."

करकर "a grating sound," करकराविणें "to grind the teeth."

कांक्षा (Skr.) "doubt," काकसाविणें "to be doubtful."

—but this may also be formed from the two words का "why?" कसा "how?" and would thus mean "to why-and-how," "to hum and ha;" just as they use in Urdu the phrase لیت ولعل کرنا "to prevaricate," literally to make "would that!" and "perhaps."

A distinction may apparently be drawn in many cases between forms in *âva* and those in *âvi*, the former being rather denominatives, and as such neuter, while the latter are causals. Thus from थोडका "little," "few," थोडकावणें "to grow less," and थोडकाविणें "to make less," but the authorities accessible to me are not agreed about this point, and I therefore hesitate to make any definite assertion on the subject. Molesworth gives, for instance, डरकावणें *n.* "to bellow," "bluster," and डरकाविणें "to frighten by bellowing;" also डरावणी "the act of roaring at," from डराविणें or डरविणें "to intimidate," where the *t* of the infinitive seems to be represented by *a* in the noun.

On the other hand, the close connexion of these neuters with the passive type is seen in S., where the passive characteristic इजु is used, according to Stack, convertibly with the neuter, having the short vowel. Thus ध्रापु or ध्रापजु "to be satiated;" while there are also verbs of two forms, one with the neuter type, the other with the causal type, but both having a neuter sense, as ढिरु and ढिराइु "to grow loose or slack."

Further examples are—

घटु and घटिजणु "to grow less;" also घटाजणु "to decrease."

मुभाइजणु and मुभिजणु "to fade," "tarnish."

माइु and माइजणु "to be contained in."

It is not certain how far later and better scholars like Trumpp would confirm the accuracy of Stack's definition. He seems to be somewhat inaccurate and careless in drawing the distinction between the various phases of the verb.

§ 20. Secondary verbs are not so numerous as secondary nouns, and those that exist have, for the most part, a familiar or trivial meaning. They are formed by the addition of a syllable to the verbal stem, or to a noun. This latter feature is especially common in H. verbs formed from feminine nouns in *aka* (Vol. II. p. 31), thus Behari Lál

छुटी न सिसुता की झलक झलकी जोबन अंग ॥

"The splendour of childhood has not ceased, (yet) youth shines in the limbs."—Sats. 17.

Here the substantive झलक "glitter," "splendour" (probably formed from √ झल), gives rise to a verb झलकना "to shine." Similarly all the nouns quoted in the passage referred to in Vol. II. have verbs formed from them as there stated. It is unnecessary to give a list of them, and it may be here observed that in languages which, like English, have advanced far into the analytical stage, great freedom of formation exists, so that many words may be used either as nouns or verbs. Many nouns have, in common usage, verbal terminations added to them, and thus become verbs. We see constantly in modern English, French, and German, new verbs thus formed, as, for instance, by adding *-ise*, *-iser*, or *-iren*, as *colonise*, *coloniser*, *colonisiren*, several of which have not found their way into dictionaries. The same is the case with our Indian languages, and it is impossible here to follow or set forth all these constantly arising innovations. Those which have received the sanction of literature will be found in the dictionaries, and many more will probably be admitted to the dictionaries of the future, if the authors of those works are wise enough to keep pace with the actual growth of language, and do not permit an overstrained purism to prohibit them from truly recording the language as it exists in their day.

I will content myself with giving a few examples of this class of verbs from Marathi, which, as I have before noticed, is very rich in forms of this kind. This language has secondary stems formed by the addition of अट, अड, आड, अव, अळ, अळ, अर, a series the items of which seem to indicate a progressive softening from some earlier type. Thus—

घासणें "to rub" (Skr. √ घृष्), secondary stems घसटणें "rub," घसरणें "slip," घसपटणें (a potential form) "graze the skin," "be practised in" (an art or science), घसाडणें "scour" (pots), घासटणें a. "rub off, deface," n. "be rubbed," "be despoiled of." Analogous is H. घसीटना "drag."

डुबणें "to sink" (rarely used), डुंबणें, डुंब°, डुम°, "to splash about in the water," डुबकणें *id.*, डुबकाविणें "to plunge into water," (causal) डुबकळणें "to dip."

ठांव "place," ठांभारवें "to arrange."

थाप "pat," थापटवें "to pat," थापवावें "to back water," "to steady a vessel by short strokes of the oars while working the sails."

दंड "stick," दंडवें "to press, punish," दंडपवें "to compress," दंडारवें "to stiffen," compare B. दांडाइते "to stand up."

Materials are, unfortunately, deficient, so that in the present state of research, no thorough analysis can be made. Nor can any definite separation into classes be effected. As so many verbs of this kind, however, are derived from nouns, the course to be pursued would probably be to affiliate each group of verbs to that formation of nouns with which it corresponds, verbs which add ड to the primary stem being regarded as formed from nouns in ड, and so on. In this method no further explanation is required for secondary verbs, as the origin of the afformative syllable has been explained under the noun. Thus the secondary verbs, whose added syllable is *aṭ*, or *vaṭ*, are explained under nouns so ending in Vol. II. p. 65, those having *al*, *aḷ*, or cognate forms, are referable to the nouns in Vol. II. p. 90, and so on.

§ 30. Reduplicated and imitative verbal stems are very common. The former usually express sounds, or motions, while both frequently partake of the denominative character and type.

In Hindi the second syllable usually contains the same consonants and vowels as the first, and the question arises whether the first or the second of the two syllables is the original, in other words, whether reduplication is effected by prefixing or affixing a syllable. The following examples show that the reduplicated syllable, whichever it be, contains, as a rule, the same vowel as the original.

(*a*) with *a*.

खटखटाना "to knock, pat, rap," from खटखट s. *f.* onomatopœa.

खड़खड़ाना "to clatter, rattle, jar," from खड़खड़ n. f. onomatopoea.

खदखदाना "to bubble, simmer," "

गड़गड़ाना "to rumble" (of bowels, Gk. κορκορυγέω, βορβορύζω), onomatop.

धड़धड़ाना "to quiver," probably connected with धर q.v. "to be seized and shaken."

बड़बड़ाना "to mutter, murmur."

झड़झड़ाना "to flap, flop," from झड़ना "to fall off."

झनझनाना "to tinkle, jingle, clank," Skr. झणझण.

झमझमाना "to glitter, glare, throb," Skr. झम्?

फड़फड़ाना "to flutter, twitch," Skr. स्फुट्?

थरथराना "to tremble, quiver," probably onomatop.

(β) with *i*.

खिलखिलाना "to giggle, chuckle, titter," onomatop.

गिड़गिड़ाना "to quiver, waver" (the voice in supplication), dimly traceable to Skr. गै, गीति?

घिनघिनाना "to turn sick at," from घिन "disgust," Skr. घृणा; there are also verbs घिनियाना, घिनौना and घिनाना.

चिचियाना "to squeak," onomatop.

चिनचिनाना *id.* "

झिड़झिड़ाना "to rave, rage, scold."

टिंटिंयाना "to twang," onomatop.

(γ) with *u*.

खुपखुपाना "to envy, be spiteful," perhaps from Skr. क्षुभ् through H. खुभना and खुपना "to pierce."

गुंगुनाना "to mutter."

चुपचुपाना "to be silent, to move about quietly," from चुप "silent."

चुनचुनाना "to itch, tickle."

तुलतुलाना "to be soft or squashy."

फुसफुसाना "to whisper," onomatop.

भुरभुराना "to powder, sprinkle."

The above exhibit the ordinary type of this class, in which both syllables are the same. In some cases, where the root-syllable ends in a nasal, the first syllable of the reduplicated word softens the nasal to anuswâra, as in ठुंठुनाना, धंधनाना "to throb," and even with च, as चंचलाना "to be unsteady," where the reduplication takes place already in Sanskrit चंचल. From the analogy of this last word we may conclude that the latter of the two syllables is the original one, and that reduplication has been effected by prefixing a syllable. There is, however, another class of such words, in which the second syllable differs from the first in the initial consonant, which, for some reason, is generally a labial. Thus side by side with खड़खड़ाना, खलखलाना are found खड़बड़ाना and खलबलाना with the same meaning. So also कुलकुलाना and कुलबुलाना, the latter with the different, though allied, meaning of being restless or fidgety. In other examples there is some slight difference of meaning in the various forms, thus from चर, which has the general sense of moving, come the adjectives चरचरा "talkative," चरपरा "acrid, pungent," चरफरा "active," चरबरा "expert, alert," whence the verbs चरचराना "to crackle, to sputter, to scold," चरपराना "to smart," चरफराना "to shake, swing," चरबराना "to speak plausibly, to wheedle." Other instances are—

छटपटाना "to toss, tumble, flounder."

धुधकाना "to be on fire."

झिलमिलाना "to flicker."

फड़फड़ाना "to flutter."

झिरमिराना "to dazzle, glisten."

लड़खड़ाना "to stagger."

बलबलाना "to stammer, stutter."

In Panjabi, as also to a great extent in other languages, there is a tendency to use a reduplicated substantive with an auxiliary verb, rather than a reduplicated verb itself. These substantives are, to a large extent, imitative or onomatopoetic, as ठाँ ठाँ करना "to bang, to pop," expressing the sound of a gun going off, चुँ चुँ करना "to pipe," as young birds. It has, however, a large number of the same words, as Hindi. Of these, the following may be cited: चिड़चिड़ाउणा "to prate, sputter," चिरचिराउणा "to smart," फुरफुराउणा and फुरफुर- "to flutter," झुनझुनाउणा "to tingle" as the limbs when benumbed.

In Sindhi, also, I find reduplicated nouns, but few, if any, verbs, and the language does not appear to be rich even in these. From भड़भड़ "blaze," comes भड़भड़ाइणु "to blaze;" and a few more may be found, but the large group given in Hindi, to which many more might have been added, is either not existent or not recorded.

Gujarati is fuller in this respect, as खखडवुं and खखडावुं "to rattle," also खडखडवुं; चडपडवुं "to fret," चचरवुं "to throb, smart," खणखणवुं "to clink, clank," also खखणवुं; फफडवुं "to flap, to scold," and फफडावुं; थथरवुं "to shake, rock." In its vocabulary Gujarati agrees in the main with Hindi.

As might be expected from the genius of Marathi, there is a great variety of such verbs, more even than in Hindi. In examining only the first consonant of the alphabet, numerous formations of this kind are observed. Thus from कांत for Skr. क्लान्त "fatigued," by prefixing a shortened form कं, they make कंकांतणें "to be distressed, to starve," and कंकांतवणें "to worry, harass." From the onomatop. कच "brawl," "noise," "row," comes first a reduplicated noun कचकच, and then कचकचणें "to gnash the teeth," कचाकणें "to screech," कचकटणें "to slip, give way with a noise." With a second syllable added, beginning (as we have seen in H.) as such syllables often do with a labial, is the imitative substantive चभचभ expressive of "squashing," "muddling of soft substances," also of "things grating on the ear," or "being gritty in the mouth," whence चभचवै (from चभचभवै) "to dabble with mud," "to stir," "to finger," which, from a sort of remembrance of मळ "dirt," is often changed into चभमळवै "to make a mess by dabbling." Another imitative syllable, which it is not necessary to regard as formally derived from Sanskrit कृत् "cut," or from कष्ट "trouble," though the existence of these words has probably led the native mind in that direction, is कट expressive of "teasing, quarrelling;" whence कटकटवै "to wrangle, tease by squabbling," "to make harsh or cracking sounds." Allied to this is the word कड़कड़ expressive of "the snapping of little things," whence कड़कड़वै, which may be generally rendered "to go kaḍkaḍ," that is, "to crash, crack, peal, to squabble, to hiss and bubble as hot water, oil," etc., also, "to be violently angry." Perhaps connected with this is कड़मड़वै "to be feverish, to glow, ache," which, from some remembrance of मोड़ "breaking," is also pronounced कड़मोड़वै. In these outlying words, the irregular cavalry of language, forms melt into one another, like a cloud of Pandours or Cossacks hovering on the outskirts of an army, bound by no law, and disregarding all the acknowledged tactics. A list here follows:

कसकसवै "to be feverish," from कस and कसुकस "feverishness," "heat and throbbing," "cramp."

करकरवै "to caw" (as a crow), from करकर "cawing" or any other harsh sound.

कळकळवै "to glow with heat, to be qualmish" (as the stomach), from कळकळ a word meaning "all sorts of disorders brought on by heat, or rage," possibly connected with Sanskrit कलह "dispute."

कसकसणें "to ache, shudder, palpitate," from कसकस "pains and aches."

कळमळणें the same as कळवळणें.

कळवळणें "to writhe, yearn."

किचकिचणें "to chatter" (as a monkey), from किचकिच "any gritty or sharp clacking sound."

कुजबुजणें "to whisper, mutter, murmur," from कुजबुज "low, soft murmuring."

Under other letters the following may be quoted:

झटपटणें "to go to work smartly," from झटपट "smartly, quickly," connected with झट, which in all the languages means "quick!" "look sharp!"

झणझणणें "to tinkle, tingle, ring."

लखलखणें "to glitter, sparkle."

झुरझुरणें "to trickle, ooze, pine away."

फरफरणें "to twitch, flutter."

मिरमिरणें "to sting, be pungent."

In Bengali such forms are less common, it is by nature the language of a poor scanty population, and when Bengal became rich and populous, new ideas were expressed by borrowing from Sanskrit, instead of forming new words from the existing resources. There are numerous reduplicated nouns, but these are verbalized rather by adding the verb *kar*, than by making a new verb. Thus, where M. makes a verb jhaṇjhaṇaṇeṅ, B. prefers to say झन झन or झनझन करिते. The following are a few examples:

गुनगुनाइते "to buzz, growl."

झिकमिक करिते "to blaze, glitter."

टनटन क॰ "to throb, ache."

टिपटिपाइते "to fidget, twitch."

ठखाठखि क° "to backbite or quarrel mutually."

ठुकठुका क° "to rap, tap."

झकझक क° "to sparkle, shine."

थुरथुरिते "to quiver, tremble, shake."

भनभनाइते "to buzz, hum."

गुजगुजाइते "to murmur, whisper."

Many of these words are, as it has been seen, onomatopoetic, and in a language so unfixed as Bengali, it is impossible to say how many are really admitted into the proper stock of the language, and how many are mere local or individual peculiarities. Thus Bharat Chandra adorns, or disfigures, his poems by innumerable fanciful words of this sort, which probably no one but he ever used, and which he has merely invented for the occasion, *e.g.*

झनझन कङ्कण रनरन नूपुर।
घुनु घुनु घुंघुर बोले॥

"The bracelets go *jhan jhan!* the anklets go *ran ran!*
Ghunu ghunu goes the girdle of bells."—B.-S. 290.

The remarks made about Bengali apply equally to Oriya, in which there is not any very extended use either of reduplicated or onomatopoetic nouns or verbs.

§ 31. Occasional mention has been made in the foregoing sections of some of the stems used in the Gipsy verb. That strange, wandering, low-caste people has, however, picked up many of its words from Iranian and Slavonic, as well as from non-Aryan sources. But true to the original instincts of its race, it has retained Aryan stems for its most common words, only adopting new words to express the few new ideas which, in spite of its nomad unsociable life, have been forced upon it by circumstances.

Rejection of initial *h* occurs in many words, as *asdra* "to laugh," Skr. √हस्, even when the initial *h* has arisen from an earlier aspirated letter, as in *uváva* "to become," Skr. √भू, Pr. हो. An *a* is also prefixed to roots, as *arakáva* "to guard, to find," Skr. √रख्, H. रखना; and in the impersonal verb *aráttilólar* "it is night," Skr. रात्रि. As might be expected, however, the Prakrit or modern form of verbal stems is that generally adopted. Thus *katáva* "to spin," H. कातना, *keráva* "to do," H. करना, *kináva* "to buy," Skr. √क्री, H. कीनना, *ghosháva* "to clean," Skr. √घृष्, H. घिसाना "to rub," but घृष् might give a Pr. घुस्, whence this word, also pronounced *khosháva*. *Korliováva*, from *korlo uváva*, Skr. कोमल, with हो "to be," "to be soft;" *khanjiováva*, from *khanj uváva*, "to scratch, to itch," Skr. खर्जू "itch," H. खाज, खुजली. *Khásiováva*, also *khasáva*, "to cough," Skr. √कास्, but H. खांसना. *Khanáva* "to dig," Skr. √खन्; *kháva* "to eat," Skr. √खाद्, Pr. खा, H. *id.*, but the nomads of northern Rumelia use a form *khaderáva*, which preserves the *d* of Sanskrit. *Khiniováva* for *khino uváva*, Skr. खिन्न with हो "to be fatigued."

There are three very similar verbs which illustrate the principle of stem-formation in this language well; *ghedáva* "to assemble," *ghelâva* "to bring," *ghenáva* "to count." The last of these three reminds us of Skr. √गण्, H. गिनना, for the *gh* is only so written to secure the *g* being pronounced hard; the p.p. is *ghendo*, Skr. गणित; *ghedáva* is apparently for *ghen dáva*, the latter word meaning "to give," and being added as an ancillary, just as देना is in H., so that *ghen dáva* = H. गिन देना. Its p.p. is *ghedino*, and that of *dáva* is *dino*, Pr. दिण्णो, Old-H. दीन्हा and दीना, which confirms this derivation. Similarly, *ghelâva* is *ghen láva*, where *láva* means "to take," H. लेना. From these two examples, it would appear that the *ghe* of *ghedáva* and *ghelâva* is not connected with *ghenáva*, but is Skr. √ग्रह्, Pr. गेण्ह "to take."

Strange perversions of meaning occur, as might be expected, thus *chalaváva*, Skr. √चल्, H. चलाना, should mean "to cause to move," H. चलाना. It means, however, "to beat," thus *jâ, dik kon chaldeela o vudár*, "Go, see who knocked at the door!" This is singularly close to the Indian languages. We might say in H. *jâ, dekh kon chalâya dwâr ko.* The confusion between the two meanings of Skr. √ चर् is apparent here also. In Skr. चर् and चल् mean "to move," and the former, by a natural transition, is used also of cattle grazing. In H. they are kept apart, चलना meaning "to move," and चरना "to graze." In Gipsy *chardva* "to eat," makes its p.p. *chalo*, the causal *charovâva* is "to lead out cattle to pasture," and a neuter verb *chârlovâva* or *chaliovâva* "to be satiated." Again, *chalardva* "to be satiated with," p.p. *chalardo* "full," "satisfied."

Frequently, as in the Indian languages, a primitive verb is wanting, and its place supplied by a compound, thus they say, *chumí dâva* "to kiss," Skr. √ चुम्ब्, H. चूमना, but the Gipsy is = चूम देना. So, also, *chungár dâva* "to spit," probably to be referred to Skr. √ क्षीव्, and connected with H. छींक, M. शिंक "sneeze."

Under ज् occur words familiar to us in India, as *jandva* "to know," Skr. √ ज्ञा, H. जानना; *jâva* "to go," Skr. √ या, H. जाना, with its old-Tadbhava p.p. *gelo*, B. गेल. H. गिया, गया; *jangâva* "to awaken," Skr. √ जागृ, H. जगाना, and the neuter *jangâvio-vâva*, H. जागृत होना, जागना; *jivâva* "to live," Skr. √ जीव्, H. जीवना, जीना, p.p. *jivdo*, Skr. जीवित.

Under त् we find *tavâva* "to cook," Skr. तप् p.p. *tavdo*, Skr. तापित, also *tatto* "hot," Pr. तत्त, Skr. तप्त, H. तत्ता. Connected with this probably are *tâp dâva, tâv dâva*, "to beat," where Skr. ताप, H. ताव, has passed over from the meaning of heat through that of vexation into that of beating. The neuter is *tabiovâva* or *tapiovâva* "to be burnt," as in *leskeré sheresté tâbiolas shamdâla* "at his head burnt a candle." A more modern form with the characteristic *l* of the p.p. in M. G. B. and O. is *tablo* "hot." A derivative is *tabarâva* (a causal) "to cause to burn."

It is apparent, from these examples, which might be indefinitely increased, that the base of Gipsy verbal stems is the Prakrit, in its earlier as well as its more modern forms; that the phases of the Indian verb are also fairly represented; that the practice of using ancillaries is also not unknown; and that thus this wild and wandering race has carried with it, wherever it has gone on the face of the earth, the principles and sentiments of speech formation which it inherits from the land of its birth, the deserts of the Indus and the Chenab.

CHAPTER II.

THE SIMPLE TENSES.

CONTENTS.—§ 32. Classification of Tenses.—§ 33. The Simple Present or Aorist.—§ 34. The Imperative.—§ 35. The Future in Old Hindi and Gujarati.—§ 36. Type of the Active Verb in Sindhi and Marathi. § 37. Synopsis of the Simple Tenses in all Seven Languages.—§ 38. Simple Tenses in the Gipsy Verb.

§ 32. The preceding Chapter has dealt only with the stem, or that part of the verb which remains unchanged throughout all moods and tenses; we have now to consider the processes used to express the various relations which the idea involved in the stem is capable of undergoing.

The tenses of the modern verb fall naturally into three classes or grades, and it is surprising that so patent a fact has not been noticed by any of the grammar-writers. It is impossible to give, as some writers do, a fixed number for the tenses in any of our languages, for the combinations are almost infinite; but a broad, general classification would, one might suppose, have suggested itself to the most mechanical compiler. The grammar-writers, however, including even authors so superior to the general run as Trumpp and Kellogg, have been, for the most part, led away by giving their attention, in the first place, if not exclusively, to the *meanings* of the various tenses. This practice has led them to lose sight of the primary idea as evolved out of the *structure* of each tense. Had the structure been first considered, it would have been easy to discover which of the many conventional senses of a given tense was its primary and legitimate one, and by adhering to this process, a more simple and natural classification of tenses would have been arrived at.

Kellogg does, indeed, clearly grasp the principles of the structure of the Hindi verb, but he is too metaphysical in his considerations about the meaning of each tense, and has adopted a phraseology which cannot but prove bewildering to the student, and which scientific linguists are not likely to adopt.

In Sindhi Trumpp divides the verb into simple and compound tenses. The simple present is by him called the Potential, though he is well aware of the fact that it is really the old Sanskrit present indicative, and in his philological notes duly recognises the fact. His classification is sufficient for Sindhi, though it would hardly cover all the tenses in the cognate languages. As usual, he is, in this respect, much in advance of all other grammar-writers on the modern languages. In the Grammars of Gujarati, Marathi, and Oriya, the same distinction between simple and compound tenses is preserved, though in many cases erroneously worked out.

It appears to me, however, that for purposes of comparison between all the languages of this group, a finer distinction still is required, and I would suggest a threefold division, which it will be my business in the following pages to substantiate and describe in detail.

First, there are the simple tenses,—exact modern equivalents of corresponding tenses in the Sanskrit and Prakrit verb, whose form is due to the ordinary processes of phonetic change and development, and in which the old synthetic structure, though very much abraded, is still distinctly traceable.

Secondly, the participial tenses, formed from participles of the Sanskrit verb, used either alone, or with fragments of the Sanskrit substantive verb, worked into and amalgamated with them so as to form in each case one word only. In the latter case these tenses have a pseudo-synthetical appearance, though the principle on which they are formed is really analytical.

Thirdly, compound tenses, in which the base is a participle with an auxiliary verb added to it, but not incorporated into it, each person of each tense thus consisting of two words in juxtaposition.

A further development of the analytical system produces the large class of verbs with ancillaries, in which the master-stem, so to call it, remains unchanged, and the ancillary does all the work of conjugation. Each of these classes will now be considered in its turn. The present chapter is devoted to the first class, or simple tenses.

It must here also be noted that the seven languages have but one conjugation each, that is to say, that the terminations and methods of forming tenses in use in any one language are applied without variation to every verb in that language. A partial exception may, at first sight, seem to occur in Sindhi and Marathi, in both of which there is one method for conjugating neuter, and another for active verbs. It will be shown, however, that though at first sight the terminations of the neuter verb seem to differ from those of the active, as in M. मी सुटें "I escape," *n*., but मी सोडीं "I set free," *a*., yet in reality the scheme of terminations is one and the same for both, and the difference is due to a process of preparing the root to receive terminations, and to the abrasion of those terminations, in some cases from euphonic causes, and not to the existence of a double system of conjugation.

§ 33. First among the simple tenses comes, in all the languages, the old Sanskrit present indicative, which, in form, preserves clear traces of its origin, though, as in its abraded condition it now no longer indicates with sufficient clearness present time, it has wandered away into all sorts of meanings, and is given by grammarians under all sorts of titles. Considering the very vague meanings which it now expresses, especially in regard to the note of time, it has seemed to me that the Greek term "aorist" more accurately describes this tense in its modern usage than any other. The fact that it is a present, no matter what additional indefinite meanings may be attached to it, is, however, necessary to be borne in mind, and I think that in modern grammars it should always head the list of tenses, as the simplest and most genuine, and legitimately first in order, of them all. In those languages of this group with which I am personally acquainted, I can assert, from my own experience, that it is far more frequently used in colloquial practice as a present, pure and simple, than our grammar-writers, basing their views too much on the literary aspects of the languages, would have us believe.

The terminations of the aorist in the classical form of each language in the present day are the following. (For the full forms, see the tables at the end of this chapter.)

	SING. 1.	2.	3.	PLUR. 1.	2.	3.
Hindi	ऊं	ए	ए	एं	ओ	एं
Panjabi	आं	एं	ए	ये	ओ	अन्
Sindhi	आं	ईं	ए	ऊं	ओ	अनि
Gujarati	उं	ए	ए	ईये (ये)	ओ	ए
Marathi	ऊं	एस (अस)	ए	ऊं	आं	अत्
Oriya	इं	अ	ए	उं	अ (ओ)	अन्ति
Bengali	इ	इस	ए	इ	अ (ओ)	एन (अन्)

The third person singular is the same in all the languages, ending universally in ए. In Oriya poetry it ends in अइ, and this now somewhat antiquated form is still occasionally heard, as in करइ "he does," अटइ "it is." The form in अइ is in use in the rustic dialects of Hindi and Gujarati, as is also the intermediate form ऐ. It seems certain that this universal ए has been formed from अइ, the termination of this person in

Prakrit, and corresponds to the Sanskrit अति. Thus चलति becomes चलइ, चलै, and चले. The rustic Hindi forms चलयि, चलय, are, I think, to be explained by the Prakrit process of inserting य and व to fill a hiatus; thus चलइ becomes चलयि and चलवि. In the hill dialects of Kumaon and Garhwâl the final vowel is lost, and they say चल for चलै. The same takes place in Nepali.

The third person plural similarly points to the same person in the Sanskrit present. Oriya has here preserved the termination unaltered, as करन्ति "they do," मारन्ति "they beat," though in common conversation there is a tendency to drop the final *i*, and to say *karant, mârant*. P. S. and B. have lost the न, and with it P. and B. have rejected the vowel also, which Sindhi retains. Hindi has softened the nasal consonant to anunâsika, and Gujarati has rejected the nasal altogether, so that the 3 plural is the same in form as 3 singular. This also is the case in the dialects of Hindi spoken in Rajputana, which have मारै "they strike," where classical H. has मारैं. After the rejection of the न, which is a phonetically anomalous, though widely used process, the remaining form would be अंति, as मारंति, closely approximate to which is Garhwâli मारन. The Braj form मारैं is deducible also from मारंति, through an intermediate मारंइ and मारंए. The last-named form is still in use in the Eastern Hindi area, and has in Bhojpuri modulated into मारेँ; while the type मारंइ is preserved in the Oudh and Riwa form मारँइँ, where इ has been substituted for ए, and an inorganic second anunâsika added, concerning which there will be more to say presently.

Marathi stands alone in preserving the *t* of the Sanskrit *anti*. In old Marathi the final vowel is preserved and lengthened, as उठती "they rise;" in the modern language उठत. In the Konkani dialect[1] all three persons of the plural are said to end

[1] Grammatica da Lingua Concani (Goa, 1859), p. 74.

in *â*. Thus in the Portuguese method of transliteration, which is not very accurate, the words are thus written, *amî asati* "we are," *tumî asati* "ye are," *te asati* "they are." We should probably write असति = classical M. असत. The author tells us, however, that one may also say *amî asunî* "we are," which is classical M. first person plural आम्ही असूं, though in Konkani it may be used for all three persons of the plural.

The second person singular ends in ए in H. and G., and is from Skr. असि by elision of स, thus चलसि, चलहि, चलइ, चलै (Braj), चले. In B. it formerly ended in असि, but the final vowel has been rejected, and the *a* weakened to *i*, thus देखिस "thou seest;" this form has been excluded from literature, but is extremely common in speech. In M. also the स has persisted, as सुटेस "thou dost get free," where the *e* is apparently due to the epenthesis of the final *i* of an earlier सुटसि. The *i* may, however, be dropped altogether, without leaving any trace, and one may say सुटस. P. and S. take anunâsika, as करें "thou doest," which is perhaps due to the influence of the स, which has disappeared. The termination इस is often heard among the lower classes in the Hindi area, but always in a past sense, and extended to all persons, as किहिस "he did," कहिस "he said" (also I or thou). The O. termination स for this person is abnormal, and I am at a loss to account for it.

The second person plural in all but M. ends in *o*, for though B. and O. write अ, they pronounce *ŏ*, and when emphasis is used, *ô*. There is no difficulty in affiliating this termination to the corresponding Skr. 2 plural in *tha*, through Pr. *dha* and *ha*, thus चलथ "ye go," where, by elision of *h* and conflation of the two vowels, we should get चलअ and चला. The final *â* has been lengthened to *o*, as in the plural of nouns. Marathi also forms this person on the analogy of its noun, in which the final anuswâra is typical of the plural, so that we get चलां. The process, however, is quite modern, for in the mediaeval poets the second person plural ends in *â* without anuswâra.

There is some obscurity about the first person in both numbers. In H. and G. the singular ends in ऊँ (औं), while the plural ends in एँ (ऐं): but in S. M. and O. it is the plural which ends in ऊँ, while एँ is in M. and O. the termination of the singular. Now if we look to the earlier forms, it would seem more natural to derive चलें from चलामि, where the presence of the final इ accounts easily for the ए, and so the plural चलामः: with its Prakrit representative चलामु would regularly result in ऊँ. Moreover, in many dialects even of Hindi, the plural is still चलाउँ and चलौं, चलूँ, चलाँ. In the Rajputana dialects it is चलां, which agrees with the singular of modern P. and S. For five of the languages Skr. चलामि softened to चलाइँ would become चलाएँ, whence M. and O. चलें "I go," and further shortened, B. चालि *id.*, while the rejection of final इ gives P. चलां, S. चलां "I go." The singular, therefore, in these five is easily understood. So also is the plural, for Skr. चलामः, Pr. चलामु, would become चलाउ and चलाउँ, whence dialectic H. चलां (Rajputana), चलूँ, चलौं, चलौं (in the Himalayan dialects), S. चलूँ, M. *id.*, G. चलूँ. But how are we to account for the singular and plural in H. and G.? It seems as if an inversion of the two persons had taken place. It is probable enough that a form originally plural should have become singular, because natives universally speak of themselves as "we" even when only one person is speaking. In this way the plural form may have passed over into a singular. And this tendency would be further developed by the fact that in H. and G. the languages which make the singular end in ऊँ, the pronoun of the first person was, in mediaeval times, and dialectically still is, हौं, so that it would be natural to say हौं करौं "I do," on account of the identity of sound. In the other languages this pronoun has dropped out of use (see Vol. II. p. 302). Even if this conjecture be disapproved, and if it be thought that the singular चलूँ is derived from Pr. चलामि by loss of the final *i* and softening of the *m* into anuswâra, we are still as far as ever from the origin of the plural in *en*. I think that this might perhaps be accounted for by the form of the third person plural having passed over into the first. That forms belonging to one person or case do often get extended to other persons or cases, is generally admitted. In the Riwa dialect of H. the 1 pl. ends in न, as मारन "we strike," which seems to be connected with the 3 pl. of P. S. and B., and in most of the dialects the 1 pl. is identical with 3 pl. Now the 3 pl. has a right to an *i*, coming as it does from a Skr. *-anti*, and the presence of the *n* in the Riwa, and other eastern Hindi dialects, points to the same source. The inorganic anuswâra in poetic Hindi, as मारहिं "they strike," and dialectic forms, seems to have arisen from a feeling that final anuswâra was the proper type of plurality, and thus depends upon a false analogy with the plural of nouns. The widespread Bhojpuri dialect has मारीं both for 1 pl. and 3 pl., where the ending retains the nasal and the *i*, though the latter is lengthened. We may, however, also suppose that करें 1 pl., "we do," is really the singular, and that the real plural having been used for a singular, the real singular became a plural. For though a native is fond of speaking of himself individually as "we," yet the consciousness of only one person being referred to might lead him to use the singular verb, just as the Muhammadans in Orissa, in their corrupt Urdu, say *ham karûngâ* "I will do," literally "nos facimus," a plural pronoun with a singular verb. So, also, the French peasant says "je faisons," "j'avons;" and the English one "we goes," "he do," "they says."

The above remarks leave this difficult point still far from elucidation. It is surprising that none of the grammarians have observed the existence of the difficulty, or offered any hints towards its solution. It is further complicated by the fact that P. and G. insert *i*, *î*, *ay* or *iy* between the stem and the termination of the 1 pl., thus P. पढ़ये, पढ़िये, G. पढ़ीये, पढ़ये "we read." Here it has been suggested that the Apabhrança form in *imo* is the origin, thus हसिमो "we laugh" became हसिवो and हसिवे, but the change from म to व is unusual.

On the whole, then, the correspondence of the modern forms of this tense with those of the ancient synthetical present is so close that there can be no doubt as to its derivation therefrom. The terminations, however, have been so much worn away, and in some respects confused with one another, that the tense itself no longer indicates present time with sufficient definiteness, and other forms, which will be treated of hereafter, have been called in to supply the place of a present. This tense has thus become vague, and in modern times is often used in both a future and a past sense. In Marathi grammars it is set down as an "Habitual Past," so that मी सुटें means "I used to get loose." In Panjabi it is given as an indefinite future, as मैं घलां "I would send," or, "I am going to send." It bears this meaning also in Hindi. Still, in literature, it is frequently the present, and nothing else, while in Bengali it is used as an "historic present," namely, that tense which is used by historians when, to give vigour to their style, they speak of past events in the present tense, thus *tatpare katak-guli loka giyā pāthara sangraha kare, emana samaye ekakhāni baṛa pāthara khasiyā paṛe*, "After that several people went and collected stones, suddenly a great block of stone slipped and fell;" where *kare* and *paṛe*, though they must be translated by preterites, are really the old synthetic present. This practice is extremely common in modern Bengali, both in the literary and in the colloquial style.[1]

It is unnecessary further to pursue the question of the

[1] In the Gujarati grammars of Leckey and Edalji this tense appears several times over. It is the first present and first habitual past of the Indicative mood, first Aorist of the Subjunctive, first present of the second Potential and the Optative. All this merely means that it is used in the senses which, in a Latin or Greek verb, would be assigned to those tenses: but as the words are the same in all, it would be quite as accurate, and much simpler, to record it once only, and note that it is used in a variety of senses.

various senses in which this tense is now employed, as the point is one which belongs not to the domain of comparative philology, but to the grammar of each individual language. The name "aorist," which I have suggested, has the advantage of being indefinite as to time, and in this way represents fairly the scope of the tense.

§ 34. The next simple tense is the IMPERATIVE, and this, like the aorist, is descended from the imperative of the ancient languages. As might be expected, it closely resembles the aorist or old present, and has the following scheme of endings:

	S. 1.	2.	3.	P. 1.	2.	3.
Hindi	ऊं	√[1]	ए	एं	ओ	एं
Panjabi		√			ओ	
Sindhi		उ			ओ	
Gujarati		√			ओ	
Marathi	ऊं	√	ओ	ऊं	आ	ओत
Oriya	एं	√	उ	उं	अ (ó)	अन्तु
Bengali		√	उक		अ (ŏ)	उन्

In this scheme only the second persons singular and plural have been given for P. S. and G., because the other persons are the same as the aorist. This is also true of H., the aorist being used as a potential in all these languages, the first and third persons of both numbers can only be considered imperatives in so far as the potential is itself imperative, just as in Latin and other Indo-European languages. So we may say in H. *paṛhe* "he reads," or, "let him read." It was shown in §§ 4, 5, etc., that even in Pali and the Prakrits the present and imperative had been confounded together, a practice that has paved the way for the modern system.

It is only in M. O. and B. that the third singular has a

[1] This mark means that the 2 sing. is the simple stem, as *kar* "do thou!" *paṛh* "read thou!"

separate form, which may in all cases be traced back to the Skr. 3 sg. अतु, Pr. अउ, which in M. becomes ओ. In M., however, the termination उ for this tense is also in use. To the same origin may be ascribed the O. उ and B. उक, the final क of which, however, presents considerable difficulty. It will be discussed along with a similar termination in the future.

The third plural in M. O. and B. is parallel to the singular, and is connected with Skr. अन्तु, just as the corresponding person in the aorist is with Skr. अन्ति. In O., owing to the influence of the final *u*, this termination is often written *untu*, as *karuntu* "let them do," *jāuntu* "let them go."

In all but S. the second singular is the bare verbal stem. In M. a final उ is heard, and slightly also in B. and O. In the dialect of Northern Gujarat a उ is sounded after the final consonant, as करुं "do thou," बोलव "speak thou," जाव "go thou."[1] But in the rest this person ends with the final consonant, as *kar* "do," *dekh* "see." In the H. mediæval poets this person often ends in हि, as stated in §§ 4, 5, 7, corresponding to which is a plural in हु, as

गहहु बेगि गहहु बेगि गुन जंपि बोल्ह ।

"Seize ye! seize ye! muttering of war."—Chand, Pr. R. xix. 88.

This form is also found in G., and in Old-M. takes the shape of ईं, as पावें "find thou!" for पावई, from पावहि, with inorganic anuswâra. Sindhi, which causes all its words to end in a vowel, makes this person end in उ, which is apparently only a weakening of the final vowel of the stem. The dialectic forms of H. present few noteworthy peculiarities, in some cases the forms which Kellogg gives as imperatives are really other tenses used imperatively. Thus the form मारब "beat ye!" common in the eastern area, is really a future, "ye shall beat." Often, too, in colloquial Hindi, and in Urdu, in giving an order,

[1] Vide Taylor, Grammar, p. 53.

the future is used, as राम को अपने संग लाओगे "You will bring Râm with you," that is, "bring him with you!" So also the infinitive, as यह सब काम आजही करना "Do all this work to-day," literally, "(Take care) to do," इस रिन को चुका दे तब चले जाना "Pay this debt, and then go away."[1]

Most of the seven languages have, in addition to the ordinary imperative, a respectful form used in addressing a superior, or in entreating and asking a favour. This, in Hindi, ends in Sing. इये. Plur. इयो. In P. this form is seldom employed, and when used, may be considered as borrowed from H. In the other languages are—

Sindhi	Sing. 2. इजे, इजि.	Plur. 2. इजो, इजा.
Gujarati	" जे.	" जो.

In a few stems in H. which end in *e*, ज is inserted between the stem and the termination, the final vowel being changed to *î*, as ले "take," लीजिये, दे "give," दीजिये; the stem कर "do" is in this case changed to की, making कीजिये "be pleased to do." Sindhi sometimes takes in the singular इजु instead of इजे, probably on the analogy of the simple imperative, which ends in *u*; and in the plural, instead of इजो, the forms इजा, इजाउ, इजाहु, इजाऊ are used when great respect is implied, as वञिजा "be pleased to go," बुधिजाउ "be pleased to hear." Many of the rustic dialects of Hindi have also this form; thus Rajputana इजे, इजो, ईजे, or simply जे, as मारिजो, मारीजे, मारजे "be pleased to strike."

Vararuchi (vii. 20, 21, 22) teaches that *jja* and *jjâ* may be optionally substituted for the affixes of the present and future, also for those of the imperative, in verbs which end in a vowel. In Old-Marathi, accordingly, a form with inserted ज is found in present, past, and future, as well as imperative, as करिजेतो "he does," करिजैला "he did," करिजैल "he will do," करिजे "do

[1] Pincott's Sakuntalá, p. 12, a first-rate text-book in admirable idiomatic Hindi.

them," in which the junction vowel between the inserted ज and the termination has been changed to *e*. As, however, the inserted ज is also a type of the passive, this form has occasionally been mistakenly used in a passive sense, as मी मारिजेतो "I am struck." Lassen (p. 357) refers this increment to the Skr. potential, which is confirmed by the Pali forms quoted in § 4, and by the dotted य in S., which usually indicates that a double letter has existed. The य of the Skr., as in पचेत्, is doubled in Pa. पचेय्यासि, and hardened to ज्ज in Pr., whence the modern ज, with lengthening of the preceding vowel in H., and change of *e* to *a* in G. (cf. G. हुज = हैज). As Vararuchi, in extending the use of this increment to present and future, is writing of the Maharashtri dialect, it is not surprising that the modern Marathi should show a wider use thereof than the sister idioms, in which the sense of a potential has passed over into that of a respectful imperative, or, as Trumpp well calls it, precative.

To this tense belong the two M. words म्हणजे and पाहिजे. The former is the precative of म्हण (Skr. √भण्) "to speak," and means literally, "be pleased to say;" in modern times it means "that is to say," "*i.e.*," "videlicet," as अश्व म्हणजे घोडा "*aśwa*, that is to say, a horse." It has also a future form म्हणजेल, meaning "in that case," as पाऊस पडला म्हणजेल पीक होईल "If rain falls, *then* (or, in that case) there will be a crop." The latter, with a plural पाहिजेत, and a future पाहिजेल, is from पाहणे "to see," literally "please to see," and means "it ought," as हे काम केले पाहिजे "this work *ought* to be done," literally "please to see (that) this work is done;" "see" being used in M., as in English, in the sense of "seeing to," "providing for," "taking care for."[1]

Similar to these is the H. चाहिये, lit. "please to wish," but

[1] See Molesworth's Marathi Dictionary under these words; also Godbole's Marathi Grammar, p. 92.

meaning "ought," and, like चाहिये in M., used with the past participle, as वह काम किया चाहिये "this work *ought* to be done." Colloquially, however, and even among good writers, चाहिये is often, like other ancillary verbs, constructed with the oblique form of the infinitive, and it would not be absolutely incorrect to say करने चाहिये. In fact, the construction both in M. and H. with the past participle remounts to a period when the participial character of this form was not yet forgotten. Since, however, the past participle in H. has come to be used simply as a preterite, this construction has lost its significance. Not so in M., where, as will be seen hereafter, the distinction between the preterite and participle still survives.

Gujarati has an analogous formation in the word जोइये "it is wanted," French "il faut," Italian "bisogna." It is from the verb जोवुं "to see," and is used with a dative of the subject, as अमें बीजो वर जोइये नहीं "I want no other blessing," like Latin "mihi necesse est, oportet, decet," etc. It is conjugated throughout the full range of tenses, as सफर मां जे कांइ जोइतुं हतुं "Whatever *was required* for the voyage," जो मारे हरण जोइशे तो "*Should I require* venison, then . . . ."

§ 86. A simple future derived from the old synthetical tense exists only in Gujarati and in Old-Hindi. The tense is as follows, taking the stem *kar* "do," as a type:

	SING. 1.	2.	3.	PL. 1.	2.	3.
Gujarati	करीश	करशे	करशे	करीशुं	करशो	करशे.
Old-H.	करिहौं	करिहै	करिहै	करिहैं	करिहौ	करिहैं.

Kellogg (Gr. p. 238) gives the following interesting transitional type from eastern Rajputana:—

SING. 1.	2.	3.	PL. 1.	2.	3.
करसूं करस्यूं	करसी	करसी	करस्यां	करस्यो	करसी.

There are, in fact, four types of the future in the modern languages, having for their characteristics respectively the letters स, ग, ल, and ब. The *sa* type has a variant *ha*. The *ga*, *la*, and *ba* types belong to the class of participial tenses, and will be discussed under that head. The *sa* type, with its variant *ha*, found in G. and Old-H., with dialectic variations in several of the modern rustic dialects of H., is the only one which is directly derived from the corresponding Sanskrit and Prakrit tense. It is the Sanskrit future in *ishya*, as in *karishyámi*, which, as already pointed out in § 4, becomes in Pali *karissámi*, and retains that form in the higher Prakrits. The transition from this to the eastern Rajput करसूं seems to rest upon the confusion between the first persons of the singular and plural already noticed in H.; for Rajp. करस्यां, though now a plural, represents करिस्सामि better than does करसूं, which latter leads to Pr. plural करिस्सामु, just as does G. करिशुं. The G. 1 sing. करीश has rejected all terminations, and lengthened the preceding vowel; this form is also, in the general confusion, due to the corruption of personal affixes, used for the 2 sing. The second and third persons of both numbers may be traced back to the corresponding persons of the Prakrit just as in the aorist, and the loss of the *i* in the second syllable is probably due to the neglect of vowels in G., where the first plural even is written in three ways, as करीशुं, करिशुं, or करशुं. The orthography of G. is, it will be remembered, still unfixed.

In most of the Prakrits the future has undergone a further weakening, by which the स्स of the higher types has been resolved into ह, so that we get such forms as करिहिमि side by side with करिस्समि. It is from this weakened form that the Hindi type is derived. Thus 3 sing. करिहै represents Pr. करिहइ from करिहिति; 3 pl. करिहैं = करिहंति, and so on. Here also come in the old Purbi forms करिहहि, करिसहि, which are transitional from Pr. to Old-H. In poems in the Braj dialect occur such forms as करैहौं, करैहै, where the *ai* has crept into the second syllable, probably from the analogy of the *ga* type *karsi-gá*. The commonest form is that given above, with short *i* in the second syllable. This is Chand's ordinary future, as

हम नायंत सब जुझिहै ।
राज चंदेल न जाय ।

"We nobles all *will fight*,
(That) the kingdom of the Chandel may not perish."
—Pr. R. xxi. 94.

कै सिर तुमहि समप्पिहौं ।
कै सिर धरिहौं छत्र ।

"Either I *will yield* my head to thee,
Or I *will put* the umbrella on my head."—Pr. R. i. 279.
(*i.e.* I will either die or conquer.)

कनवज लूटि रिधि सब हरिहौं ।
पाछै जुध मोहोबै करिहौं ।

"Having plundered Kanauj, I *will carry off* all your riches,
After that, I *will fight* at Mahoba."—*ib.* xxi. 87.

It is also the ordinary future throughout Tulsi Das's Ramayan, as

सबहि भांति पिय सेवा करिहौं ।
मारग जनित सकल श्रम हरिहौं ।

"In every manner I *will serve* my beloved,
I *will take away* all the fatigue of the journey."
—Ay-k. 399.

Also universally in Kabir, as

ना जानो कब मारिहै का घर का परदेस ।

"Ye know not when he (*i.e.* death) *will strike*, whether at home or abroad."—Ram. xix. 5.

बहुरि न ऐसी पैहौ ठावा ।

"*You will never find* such a place again.—*ib.* xliii. 2.

where पैहौ = पाइहौ 2 pl. fut. of पावा "to find."

When the *ga* future, which is now the ordinary type in Hindi, arose, cannot be clearly defined. It is not in use in the mediæval poets, and, as has been shown above, it has not succeeded in expelling the old synthetical future from the rustic dialects.

§ 36. In M. and S. the terminations of the old present or aorist, and those of the imperative in S., seem at first sight to differ in the active from those in the neuter verb, and some remarks are necessary in explanation of this peculiarity. The neuter सुटणें "to get loose," and the active सोडणें "to set free," are thus conjugated in the present in M.

SING. 1.	2.	3.	PL. 1.	2.	3.
सुटें	सुटेस (°टस)	सुटे	सुटूं	सुटां	सुटत.
सोडीं	सोडीस	सोडी	सोडूं	सोडा	सोडीत.

Similarly in S. the neuter हलणु "to go," and the active छडणु "to give up," conjugate the present thus:—

SING. 1.	2.	3.	PL. 1.	2.	3.
हलां	हलें	हले	हलूं	हलो	हलनि.
छडियां	छडियें	छडे	छडियूं	छडियो	छडीनि.
	छडें				छडिनि.
	छडीं				

On comparing these two sets of forms, it will be seen that the active differs from the neuter by insertion of ई in M., and of इ in S. This inserted vowel has, however, disappeared in some persons, as in M. first and second plural, and in S. third singular, and, optionally, also second singular and third plural. Some writers on Marathi seek to derive the forms of the neuter from those of the Skr. Atmanepada, and the forms of the active from those of the Parasmaipada. There is, however, a fatal objection to this argument in the fact that the Skr. Atmanepada had died out of use so early as the Prakrits, and that the neuter forms of M. agree closely with the forms in use in the other languages, where there is nothing to lead us to look for an origin from the Âtmanepada, inasmuch as the known changes of the Parasmaipada afford a satisfactory explanation, and in those languages the type which in M. is restricted to neuter verbs is used for both neuter and active. A more probable supposition is that which would derive the forms of the active in M. and S. from the Skr. causal, the characteristic *aya* having been changed in Pr. to *e*, and still further shortened in S. to *i*, while in M. the personal terminations have been blended with the य of *aya* into a long vowel; thus M. चोरी presupposes an earlier form चोरयाए or चोरयि, for it must be noted that the termination ए resulting from Skr. आमि, Pr. आए, has been dropped in this word. So in the first sing. S. चोरियां represents an older चोरयामि, and is thus earlier in type than M. चोरीं for चोरयिं, through चोरयाएं. The second singular in which the personal termination is retained also supports this view, for in it the characteristic इ holds the same place in the word as the characteristic *aya* of the Sanskrit causal, namely, *between* the stem and the termination: so it does in Sindhi in all the persons. The value of the comparative method is shown in cases like this where a student, who is guided by the facts of one language only, is liable to be misled, owing to want of the light supplied by the sister languages.

It is only in S. that the imperative differs in the active from that in the neuter. According to strict rule, the second singular of neuter verbs ends in *u*, as मरणु "to die," imperative मरु "die thou;" while in active verbs it ends in इ, as पालणु "to cherish," imperative पालि "cherish thou." Trumpp, however, gives a long list of active verbs whose imperative ends in *u*, while there are others which take both terminations. It is impossible, at present, satisfactorily to account for this irregularity, but it seems probable that active verbs in S. derived from actives in Sanskrit form the imperative in *u*, while those which are derived from S. causals form it in इ. Should this suggestion be confirmed by further research, the इ would appear to be the representative of the Skr. *aya* of the causal. Thus while Skr. भव produces S. भउ, Skr. पाचय produces S. पचि, shortened from पाचें (Pr. पाचेहि). The second plural of neuters ends in *o*, as वञो "go ye!" while that of actives ends in *io* or *yo*, as करिओ or कर्यो. The earlier form in *iho* (Pr. इह) is also in use as करिहो.

In the following list there is no reason why the imperative should not end in *u*, notwithstanding the rule, for the words are derived from simple Sanskrit active verbs of the Bhû conjugation, or, if in Sanskrit of other conjugations, yet reduced to the Bhû type in Prakrit.

```
पढणु "to read," Imp. पढु     Skr. √पठ्      Imp. पठ.
पचणु "are,"      „   पचु      „   पचति       „  पच.
पिसणु "grind,"   „   पिसु     „   √पिष्      „  पिंष, but Pr. पीस
                                                    (Hem. iv. 185).
चरणु "graze,"    „   चरु      „   √चर्       „  चर.
रखणु "keep,"     „   रखु      „   √रक्ष्     „  रक्ष.
कहणु "say,"      „   कहु      „   √कथ्       „  कथय, but Pr. चव
                                                    (Hem. iv. 2).
```

आखणु "to inform," makes आखु and आखि, it is from Skr. आख्या, imperative आख्याहि, from which comes regularly आखि, through a form आखहि, but this verb may be also neuter, as in "tell! tell!" and would thus, by the masses, be formed like neuters, and have आखु. धंवणु "to blow" (with bellows), makes धंवु and धंवि, it is from Skr. ध्मा, imp. धम, whence regularly धंवु. Here the form धंवि, the ordinary form for actives, may have been introduced from forgetfulness of the special reasons for that ending in *u*. As a general result, it may be suggested that each of these peculiar verbs requires to be traced back to its origin, in which case there will generally be found some special reason for the divergence from the normal type.

§ 37. Here follows a table showing the simple tenses in each language. A common verbal stem in each is given to exhibit the method of adding the terminations.

		HINDI.	PANJABI.	SINDHI.	GUJARATI.	MARATHI.	ORIYA.	BANGALI.
		dekh "see."	*mār* "beat."	*hal* "go."	*chhoḍ* "leave."	*suṭ* "escape."	*kar* "do."	*dekh* "see."
AORIST.	S. 1	देखूं	मारां	हलां	छोडुं	सुटें	करे	देखि
	2	देखे	मारें	हलें	छोडे	सुटेस(°टस)	कर	देखिस
	3	देखे	मारे	हले	छोडे	सुटे	करे (करउ)	देखे
	Pl. 1	देखें	मारिये	हलूं	छोडिये	सुटूं	करं	देखि
	2	देखो	मारो	हलो	छोडो	सुटा	कर	देख
	3	देखें	मारन	हलनि	छोडे	सुटत	करन्ति	देखेन
IMPERATIVE.	S. 1	देखूं				सुटूं	करे	देखि
	2	देखू	मार	हलु	छोड	सुट	कर	देख
	3	देखे				सुटो	करु	देखुक
	Pl. 1	देखें				सुटूं	करं	देखि
	2	देखो	मारो	हलो	छोडो	सुटा	कर	देख
	3	देखें				सुटोत	करन्तु	देखुन
FUTURE.		OLD HINDI.	EAST-PANJ.					
	S. 1	देखिहौं	मारसूं (°सां)	*devel*	छोडीश (°शुं)	*devel*	*devel*	*devel*
	2	देखिहै	मारसी	"	छोडशे	"	"	"
	3	देखिहै	मारसी	"	छोडशे	"	"	"
	Pl. 1	देखिहैं	मारसां	"	छोडीशुं	"	"	"
	2	देखिहौ	मारसो	"	छोडशो	"	"	"
	3	देखिहैं	मारसन	"	छोडशे	"	"	"

§ 38. The simple tenses in the Gipsy verb, as given by Paspati and Miklosich, differ very widely from the Indian type, and it is difficult to grasp their forms, so much have contraction and a slurring habit of pronunciation weakened the original terminations. The present among the Rumelian gipsies has the following endings: S. 1. *a*, 2. *sa*, *s*, 3. *l*; Pl. 1. *sa*, *s*, 2. *na*, *n*, 3. *na*, *n*. Thus from *kerása* "to do"—

Sing. 1.	kerávn, or keráv.	Pl. 1.	kerásn, or kerás.
2.	kerása „ kerás.	2.	keréna „ kerén.
3.	keréla „ kerel.	3.	kerena „ kerén.

Of the two forms, those ending with *a* are the fuller and more correct forms, and those ending in the consonant which precedes the *a* are used in ordinary conversation. The S. 2 sounds also kereas, keréa. Here we distinguish two junction-vowels *á* and *e*, as ker-á-sa, ker-é-sa, a peculiarity which recalls the practice in Prakrit by which the *e* originally proper to the tenth conjugation is often used in verbs of the Bhû and other types, and as often omitted in causals; so we have पुच्छामि and पुच्छेमि, रोचामि and रोचेमि, हासइ and हासेइ, करइ and करेइ. But with regard to the terminations, there is much difficulty; we recognise, indeed, the termination *âmi* of S. 1. in Paspati's *âva*, or *âv*, and *asi* in his *âsa*, or *âs*. So also *anti*, Pr. *enti*, reappears in *ena* or *en*. The *ela*, *el* of S. 3. may stand to *ati* in the same relation as the *ila* of O. and M. p.p.p. does to Skr. *ita*; but if so, it is a strange confirmation, and from an unexpected quarter, of what is as yet little more than an unsupported hypothesis. In the P. 2. the *ena*, *en* may have been borrowed from P. 3, for we have seen similar cases in the other languages, but the P. 1, with its ending in *s*, is entirely inexplicable.

The Syrian gipsies have retained a fuller form of the S. 1, as *jâmi* "I go," *âvami* "I come," *sîâmi* "I am," and the following almost pure Prakrit words, *bihemi* "I fear," *chinemi* "I cut," *dámi*, *demi* "I give," *jánámi*, *jánemi* "I know," *anemi* "I bring" (from आनति), *kinimi* "I buy" (क्री), and others (Miklos. ii. 4).

The imperative is the only other simple tense, it has the forms *ker* "do thou," *kerén*, do ye," *me kerel* "let him do," *me keren* "let them do." The meaning and origin of this prefix *me* is not explained by Paspati, and I am not aware of anything in the Indian languages with which it can be connected. It is probably a construction borrowed from modern Greek, or Turkish, or some of the languages spoken in or near Rumelia. The imperative is, in its general form, precisely analogous to the languages of our group, but there is nothing specially noteworthy about it.

CHAPTER III.

THE PARTICIPIAL TENSES.

CONTENTS.—§ 39. Definition of the Participial Tenses.—§ 40. The Participle Active.—§ 41. Tenses formed therefrom—the Sindhi Future.—§ 42. Marathi Indicative and Conditional Present.—§ 43. Bengali and Oriya Conditional.—§ 44. Hindi, Panjabi, and Gujarati Present.—§ 45. The Past Participle Passive.—§ 46. Early Tadbhava Participles in Sindhi and Panjabi.—§ 47. The same in Gujarati and Marathi.—§ 48. The same in Old and New Hindi.—§ 49. Tenses formed from the Past Participle.—§ 50. The *Prayogas*.—§ 51. The Future Participle Passive.—§ 52. Tenses formed from it in Sindhi, Gujarati, and Marathi.—§ 53. The Future in Oriya, Bengali, and Eastern Hindi.—§ 54. The Hindi and Panjabi Future.—§ 55. Marathi Future compared with that in certain Hindi Dialects.—§ 56. Synopsis of the Participial Tenses in all Seven Languages.—§ 57. Participial Tenses in the Gipsy Verb.

§ 39. So widely has the modern verb diverged from its parent, that the simple tenses, in which there still remain traces of the ancient synthetic structure, are, as we have just seen, extremely few. Far more numerous in all the languages are those tenses which are formed by the aid of a participle derived directly from the Prakrit. These tenses may be divided into two classes, (1) consisting either of a participle alone, as in H. *chaltā* "he moves," which is really "moving (he is)," or of a participle, to which are attached much-worn fragments of the old Sanskrit substantive verb, as in M. *hasatos* "thou laughest," which is really "laughing thou art," Pr. *hasanto 'si* (whether the remnant of the substantive verb still appear, or whether it have entirely dropped out, in either case the principle underlying the formation is the same, and words like H. *chalâ*, and M. *hasatos*, belong, therefore, to the same category): (2) consisting of a participle, to which is subjoined a substantive verb, the two words standing separate, but forming one phrase, as in H. *dekhtâ hai* "he sees," *i.e.* "he is seeing," M. *lihit âhe* "he is writing."

Between these two classes there is this fundamental difference, that in the former the traces of the substantive verb which do exist are still in the Prakrit stage of development, whereas in the latter the substantive verb, which is combined with the participle, is not in the Prakrit shape, but is a later form, evolved by the languages out of the Prakrit.

The first of these two classes I propose to call "participial tenses," and they will be treated of in this chapter; the second I shall call, following the example of the grammarians, "compound tenses," and shall reserve their discussion for another chapter.

The participle used in the formation of tenses may be traced back to the Prakrit equivalents of the following Sanskrit participles.

1. The present Active (Parasmai.), as in पचन् *m.*, पचन्ती *f.*, पचत् *n.*

2. The past Passive (with inserted इ), as in चलितः *m.*, चलिता *f.*, चलितं *n.* (Pr. चलिदो etc.).

3. The future participle Passive or verbal adjective, as in कर्तव्यः *m.*, °व्या *f.*, °व्यं *n.*

To these must be added certain much abraded forms of special past participles, which are used in a peculiar way in three of the languages, as will be shown hereafter, and it must be borne in mind that, especially in the case of the past participle passive (noted as p.p.p.), it is the Prakrit forms that are to be looked to, rather than those which occur in classical Sanskrit. The classical language does not prefer to insert the intermediate इ in the p.p.p., but the popular languages do prefer it to a very great extent, so much so, that it has almost become the rule to insert it, and the cases where it is omitted may be classed as exceptions.

§ 40. The participle of the present active in Pali and the Prakrit takes the forms of the *a*-stem of nouns, and retains the nasal throughout; thus चलंतो *m.*, चलंती *f.*, चलंतं *n.* The variations introduced by the conjugational peculiarities of the Sanskrit verb are neglected, and all roots take this one form.

Sindhi reproduces this universal Prakrit form with softening of त into द, and declines it for gender and number thus (*hal* "go")—

Sing. हलंदो *m.*, हलंदी *f.* Pl. हलंदा *m.*, हलंदियूं *f.*, "going."

In active verbs, with which must be reckoned causals, the characteristic *i* appears (§ 36), but here lengthened to *í*, as (*bhar* "fill")—

Sing. भरींदो *m.*, भरींदी *f.* Pl. भरींदा *m.*, भरींदियूं *f.* "filling."

There are some minor exceptions and contractions which may be learnt from the special grammar of the language, but the forms given above are the regular types.

Panjabi retains the nasal in verbs ending in vowels, as *já* "go," जांदा "going," *ho* "be," हुंदा "being," *sev* "serve," सेवंदा "serving." In some of the rustic dialects the nasal is retained also after stems ending in a consonant, thus I have heard मारंदा or मरिंदा "beating." In the classical dialect, however, the nasal is omitted after a consonant, as singular मारदा *m.*, मारदी *f.*; plural मारदे *m.*, मारदीआं *f.* Not unfrequently the द is dropped, and we hear जाआ, हुआ for जांदा, हुंदा.

Hindi has two sets of forms; one indeclinable originally ended in *ant*, and still exists in several rustic dialects with the termination *at*. Chand inserts or omits the nasal at pleasure, to suit his metre, as चरन तीन धरंत "*possessing* three feet"

(Pr. R. i. 61); श्रवन सुनत होत भंग। "the ear *hearing*, it is broken" (*ib.* i. 150); दपंत "shining," सजंत "arraying," सुभंत "being beautiful," कटंत "being cut," etc. (*ib.* vi. 18), but बजत "playing (music)," चढत "mounting (a horse)" (xix. 3). Tulsi Das chiefly uses the latter form, as जात "going" (Râm. S.-k. 7); गुंजत "humming" (*ib.* 9); ध्यावत "meditating," पावत "finding," भावत "being pleased," गावत "singing" (all in Ay-k. 1); and this is also common in most mediæval poets, thus Bihari Lall धरत "placing" (Sat. 6), परत (पड़त) "falling" (*ib.*), सोहत "being beautiful," लखत "appearing," चितवत "looking" (*ib.* 7, 9, etc.). Kabir जियत "living" (Râm. 30, 5); बंधत "being bound" (*ib.* 31, 3). It survives in all the dialects of the eastern Hindi area, in Oudh, Riwa, and Bhojpur, and even in the Gangetic Doab.

The other form ends in a vowel, and is in use in classical Hindi, as sing. मारता *m.*, मारती *f.*; pl. मारते *m.*, मारतीं *f.* "beating." In the Braj dialect it takes the forms मारतु *m.*, मारति *f.*; pl. मारत *m. f.* The Garhwali dialect preserves the older form, as मारदो, but has also, as have the Rajputana dialects, मारतो. Kellogg gives also a Kumaon form मारदु, which probably arises from मारदो, just as Panjabi जावा from जांदा.

It would seem that, to account for the co-existence of these two forms, one ending in a consonant, and the other in *â* (=o), we must have recourse to Hoernle's theory of the *ka-* affix, and derive करंत, करत from Pr. करन्तो, while we derive करता, करता from a Pr. करन्तओ. The *ka-* theory, however, thus begins to assume rather formidable dimensions, and will, ere long, require a whole treatise to itself.

Gujarati has also two forms, one indeclinable ending in तां, as छोडतां "loosing," the other declinable, as sing. छोडतो *m.*, ती *f.*, तुं *n.*; pl. छोडता *m.*, ती *f.*, तां *n.* The terminations are those of the adjective in this language (Vol. II. p. 150). There is also a form of the indeclinable participle in ते, as छोडते, which, like the Bengali, is apparently the locative singular, while that in तां has the ending of the old nom. pl. neuter, though, in sense, it approaches more to the locative, as मारा बंधनें छोडतां तारा दांत भांगे "If *in loosing* my bonds thy teeth should break."[1] Vans Taylor, however, distinguishes two separate words with this ending, one of which he would derive from the locative singular of Sanskrit feminines, as बंधनायाम्, the other he would derive from the Skr. infin., as कर्तुं. The first form he assumes to have been the origin of such phrases as मारे आवतां "on my coming," the second, of such as करतां शिखवेछे "he teaches to do." This, however, is very doubtful.[2]

Two forms are also observable in Marathi, or rather two sets of forms. The indeclinable ends in त, तां, and तांना, as सुटत, सुटतां, सुटतांना. The first of these agrees with Hindi, the second with Gujarati, and the third is merely the second with an enclitic particle ना added for emphasis. In active verbs the characteristic *i* appears, as सोडीत, सोडीतां, सोडीतांना "loosing." There is also a declinable form, which, however, is not now used as a participle, but appears in the third person of the present tense, thus sing. सुटता *m.*, सुटती *f.*, सुटतें *n.*; pl. सुटते *m.*, सुटत्या *f.*, सुटतीं *n.*

Oriya has only one form for the present participle. It is indeclinable, ending in उ or उं, as देखु, देखुं "seeing." Of these two forms, that with the nasal is the older, though now less used, and probably comes from the Pr. neuter in अं, though the intermediate steps are not easily traced.

Even in the earliest writings in Bengali there is no regular present participle, but a form derived from the locative of the Prakrit is in use. It ends in इते, as देखिते, and is now used as an infinitive, meaning "to see." Literally, it means "in seeing," and is used in this sense by Bidyâpati, and the older poets. Thus केश निङाडिते बहे जल धारा । "*In wringing* (or

[1] Leckey, Grammar, p. 179. [2] Grammar, p. 112.

from wringing) her hair there flows a stream of water" (Pr. K.-S. 13, 15); हेराइते हृदये हानल पाँचबाण । "*On seeing* (her), love smote him in the heart." (*ib.* 15, 7). Even here, however, it becomes almost an infinitive, as जाइते पेखलु नाहए गोरी । "I saw the fair one *go* to bathe (*i.e. in going, or while going*)" (*ib.* 13, 13); कानु हेराइते सुखे भेल परमाद । "*In seeing* (or *to see*) Kānh, there has been new delight" (*ib.* 20, 10). So Bhārat शुनाइते शुनिते पाइब समाचार "*By causing to hear*, and *by hearing*, I shall obtain news" (Bidya S. 247).

§ 41. Having thus given the *forms* of the present participle, we next proceed to exhibit the tenses constructed therefrom, either with or without the addition of fragments of the old substantive verb, and it will be seen that there is great variety in the practice of the respective languages, though all the variations are sufficiently alike to justify their being classed generally as structurally present tenses. In some cases the sense of present time is more clear and definite than that afforded by the old present of the synthetic system, or, as we now call it, the aorist, while in others it has wandered away in different directions.

Sindhi,[1] to begin with, makes this participle into a future. In the third person of both numbers the participle is used without any addition, thus

Sing. हलंदो *m.*, हलंदी *f.* Pl. हलंदा *m.*, हलंदियूं *f.* "he, she, etc., will go."

The second person, however, retains traces of the substantive verb अहु "to be," though much abraded and indistinct, it runs

Sing. हलंदें *m.*, हलंदिअं *f.* Pl. हलंदउ *m.*, हलंदिऊं *f.* "thou, ye, etc., will go."

The singular masculine ends in एं, just as does the corre-

[1] This section follows, for the most part, Trumpp, pp. 280, 291, etc.

sponding person of the aorist, and we may resolve it thus, *halando asi* = *haland' asi* = *haland' ai* = *halandē*. The anuswâra is here, probably, as in the aorist, put in to fill up the hiatus caused by loss of *s*, and first stood over the *a* of *ai*; when these two syllables were contracted into one, it took its place over that one. In the singular feminine we start from *halandī asi*, where the final long *ī* of the participle is shortened, and *asi* = *ai* = *ē*, giving *halandiē*, a form still in use, though Trumpp gives as the classical type the still further contracted *halandiē*. The plural masculine arises from *halandā atha*, where *atha* has become *tha*, and then *ha*; the *h* being dropped, we get *halandāa* = *halando*, subsequently resolved into its present form *halandau*. The plural feminine is merely the feminine of the participle, there is no trace of the substantive verb.

In the same way may be explained the first person of both numbers.

Sing. हलंदुसि *m.*, हलंदियसि *f.* Pl. हलंदासीं *m.*, हलंदियसीं *f.*

Here, again, we meet an instance of the curious change of स्म into स, which we observed in the Panjabi and Sindhi pronouns of the first person plural असीं and असां (Vol. II. p. 308). Thus *halando asmi* becomes *halando asi*, then *halandu 'si*, the final *o* being shortened to *u*. In the feminine, however, the elision of the *a* of *asmi* cannot take place by the old laws of Sandhi; instead, the *ī* of the participle changes to its semivowel, producing *halandy asi*, which the Sindhians in the present day write either as above, or हलंदसि. or even हलंदियसि. As to the termination सीं of the plural, I am disposed to regard it as formed by analogy from a singular सि, rather than, with Trumpp, as a derivative of Skr. स्मः, which, if the म be rejected, would yield सो or सु, but not, according to any known processes, सीं.

§ 42. Closely analogous to the Sindhi future is the definite present in Marathi. In this tense, as in the S. future, the third person preserves no trace of the substantive verb, and in this respect curiously resembles the periphrastic future of Sanskrit (*bodhitâsmi*, *bodhitâsi*, but *bodhitâ*).

The participial form which enters into the composition of this tense is, apparently, not used alone in a participial sense. करितो or करिता would always imply "he does," never "doing." For the purely participial sense the indeclinable participles given in the last section are used.

There is much more difficulty in tracing out the Marathi persons than those of Sindhi, not only because the remains of the substantive verb are more abraded, but because in the second and third persons there are two sets of terminations, one of which is used when the sense is that of the indicative present, the other when it is conditional.

Beginning with the third person, we have these forms (*sut* "escape"):

Indicative. Sing. सुटतो *m.*, ती *f.*, तें *n.* Pl. सुटतात *m.*, *f.*, *n.*, "he, she, etc., escapes."

Conditional. Sing. सुटता *m.*, ती *f.*, तें *n.* Pl. सुटते *m.*, त्या *f.*, तीं *n.*, "were he, etc., to escape."

Here the indicative strikes us at once as the older type; adjectives do not now in M. end in *o* in the masculine singular, though they did so in Maharashtri Prakrit; the *to* of the indicative therefore preserves the earlier form. So also in the plural there is but one form for all three persons which contains the verb *asti*, in Old-M. changed to *âti*, just as in the third plural of the aorist, but with disregard of the varying terminations for gender of the modern participle. The conditional, on the other hand, is simply the modern participle, with its full range of endings for number and gender.

The second person runs thus:

Indicative. Sing. सुटतोस *m.*, तीस *f.*, तेंस *n.* Pl. सुटतां *m.*, *f.*, *n.*

Conditional. Sing. सुटतास *m.*, तीस *f.*, तेंस *n.*, Pl. सुटतां *m.*, *f.*, *n.*

Again, in the indicative, the older ending in *o*, *suṭaton*=*suṭato* *'si (asi)*; while in the conditional, *suṭatās* = *suṭatā asi*, with the modern ending in *ā*. The plural, however, is the same in both, and agrees in termination with the aorist. The first person is the same in both indicative and conditional, and is—

Sing. सुटतों m., तें f., तों n. Pl. सुटतों m. f. n.

Final anuswâra here represents probably Pr. sing. *amhi*, pl. *amho*; but the *sandhi* is irregular, as *f. suṭatẽ*=*suṭati amhi*; the variant *suṭatyẽ*, used in the Konkan, is more regular for *suṭaty amhi*. The pl. *suṭatõ* = *suṭatā amho*, where, again, the steps of transition to *suṭatõ* are difficult to work out.

§ 43. A similar use of the participle, in a conditional sense, occurs in Bengali and Oriya. In the former, the present tense is made up by using an auxiliary, and it will come under discussion in the next chapter, but the conditional has traces of the old Pr. form of the verb, and therefore belongs to this place. The tense is (*dekh* "see")—

Sing. 1. देखिताम. 2. देखितिस. 3. देखित. Pl. 1. देखिताम, 2. देखिता. 3. देखितेन.

The participle here has lost its terminations for gender, as the Bengali adjective has (Vol. II. p. 147): *dekhitām* therefore =*dekhita asmi*=*dakhita amhi* in the sing., and *dekhita amho* in the pl., lit. "seeing I am;" *dekhitis*=*dekhita asi*, where, on the analogy of the aorist, the *i* has crept into the penultimate (now ultimate) syllable; *dekhitā* similarly=*dekhita stha*, whence *dekhita tha* = *dekhitaha* = *dekhitā*. So, also, *dekhiten* = *dekhita (s)anti*, with the same treatment of the verb as in the aorist. The third singular is the simple participle.

In Oriya this tense runs thus:

Sing. 1. देखंति, 2. देखंतु. 3. देखंता. Pl. 1. देखंतु (ऊं). 2. देखंत. 3. देखंते.

In this tense is preserved the older form of the participle Pr. *dekhanto*, O. *dekhantā*, which, as usual, appears unchanged in the third sing., as also the pl. Pr. *dekhante* preserved in the 3 pl. The other persons exhibit only slight modifications of the terminations of the aorist, which are those of the Sanskrit present *ami*, *asi*, etc.

In B. and O. this tense is used with यदि (जदि) "if," prefixed, "*if I were to do*," etc.; when used alone, it means "I might or should do," and in B. narrative it occasionally appears as an habitual past, "*I used to do*."

It should also be mentioned that just as the Bengali pandits have banished the old singular of the pronoun and declared it vulgar, so they have branded the singular number of all their tenses as low, and those grammarians who write under pandit influence gravely assure us that "the singular and plural are the same in Bengali verbs, and it is the nominative case before them which determines whether they are singular or plural" (Yates's Gr., ed. Wenger, p. 43). When they come to the real old singular, their agitation is extreme, they are too honest to leave it out, and too fastidious to put it in. So they preface it thus, "*If a person speaks with the greatest humility of himself, or with the greatest contempt of another, he employs this form*: but it is not found in good composition. We should have been happy to pass it over entirely; but to enable the student to understand what he will *but too often* hear (alas! yes, far too often, in the mouths of ninety-nine out of every hundred persons in Bengal), it seems necessary to give one example" (*ib.* p. 47).

The best Bengali poets had not discovered that these forms of their mother-tongue were low or vulgar down to the beginning of the present century. In a page opened at random in the Mahabarat of Kasiram Das occur रहिल "he remained," बलिला "he said," जिज्ञासिला "he asked," दियाछे "he has given," होइबे "he shall be." Kabi Kankan uses पडिलि "thou shalt fall," मरिलि "thou diedst," आछिलु "I was;" and Bharat Chandra, कैलि "thou hast done," पालु "I found," and innumerable other forms, which would be classed as vulgar by the purists of the present day.

§ 44. In the remaining languages, Hindi, Panjabi, and Gujarati, both forms of the present participle are used as an indefinite present tense, without any trace of the old substantive verb. The indeclinable form occurs constantly in Chand, thus कातिक न्हात पहुकर सनान । गोकन्न महातम सुनत कान ॥ "In Kartik he *performs* ablutions at Puhkar, and *hears* with his ears the glories of Gokarn."—Pr. R. i. 108. The long list of words of this form in vi. 39, describing the fight at the darbâr, may be construed either as participles or present tenses. It is one of those scarcely translateable jingles of which Chand is so fond घुकंत धार धार सौं । धकंत मार मार सौं ॥ झुकंत धार धार सौं । तकंत धार धार सौं ॥ and so on for fifty lines. Perhaps the meaning may be thus roughly paraphrased—

They thrust with sword-edge biting,
They shout the shout of smiting;
They crouch from weapons sweeping,
They watch the steel blade leaping.

The meaning is clearer in other places. बहत पवन पावक समान । तपकत दुखाय मन । सुकत सरोवर मचत कीच । तलफत मीन तन ॥ (Pr. R. ix. 17), "The wind *blows* like to fire, distressing the mind (as if with) penance, the tanks *dry up*, the mud *is stirred up*, the fishes' bodies *pant*." So in Bihari Lal, मकराकृत गोपाल के कुंडल सोहत कान । धस्यौ मनो हिय घर समर ड्योढ़ी लसत निसान ॥ "The dolphin-shaped earring *shines* (sohat) in the ear of Gopal, as the flag of love *appears* (lasat) at the threshold while he enters the heart" (Sat. vi.). He constantly uses the feminine Braj form in ति both as a participle and a present. बहुति न हेरत की कुपत कुमतिय कबहु करति ॥ पंचर

सत संभारु तिय मुख नहिं कुवचनि जानि ॥ "The virtuous wife *does not repeat* the bad words of her husband's younger brother, *fearing* (ḍaratī) a quarrel, but *dries up* with fear, like a parrot when a cat approaches its cage" (Sat. xv.).

In classical Hindi both *forms* are used as a present tense, it is unnecessary to give instances, as the practice is universal. The same is the case in P., where मैं घल्लदा "I send," is the ordinary indefinite present. शक्कर दी रोड़ी मुंडे कुड़ी दे मुंह पाउंदे "They put a lump of sugar in the mouth of the boy and girl."[1]

Classical Hindi also uses this participle, with "if" prefixed as a past conditional; thus they say यदि मैं जानता तो कबहीं नहीं जाता "Had I known, I never would have gone,"—a similar practice to that of O. and B. mentioned in the last section.

The declinable participle is used in G. as a past habitual, or as a subjunctive aorist, according to the grammarians, so that हुं छोडतो means "I used to loose," or, "I should loose." In the former sense it *is* employed in the same way as the old present or aorist हुं छोडुं. The example given is तमे बराबर भाग राखता (pl. masc.) नहीं "you used not to keep a fair share."[2] Most commonly, however, it is used with an auxiliary verb in a variety of meanings, this language being very fertile in the production of compound tenses.

§ 45. The passive past participle in Sanskrit has many forms; the simplest, though *least* widely used, in the classical language, is, however, that in *ita* (*itas*, *itā*, *itam*), as पतित "fallen." The त of the affix, as would be expected, becomes in the higher Prakrits द, and in the more common dialects falls out altogether; thus we have हारिदं = हारितं "lost," मुसिदो = मुषितः "robbed," गहिदं = गृहीतं "taken," and many others.

But Var. vii. 32 admits even in Maharashtri the form from

[1] "Panjab Customs," in Appendix to Panjabi Grammar, Loodhiana, p. 91.
[2] Leckey, Grammar, p. 100.

which the इ has entirely dropped, and instances हसिअ for हसिद "laughed," पढिअ for पढिद "recited," and this form has become the type of most modern languages. In Old-Hindi this participle regularly ends in sing. यौ *m.*, ई *f.*, pl. ए *m.*, ईं *f.*, as जर्यौ *m.*, जरी *f.*, etc., "burnt." Here the य represents the इ of the Prakrit, hardened into a semivowel before the final vowel. In the feminine it is merged in the ई of the affix, and in the plural lost altogether, for जर्ये easily passes into जरे.

Chand uses this form throughout, as तन रह्यौ जोति गय देव धाम। "his body *remained* bright, he *went to* the abode of the gods" (i. 299); कर्यौ "done," गयौ "gone," etc. It is, however, more frequently used as a tense than as a participle, and further illustrations will be given in a following section.

The form in यौ lasts all through the mediæval poets, and is still in use in the dialects of Rajputana and in Braj. In the former a slight change has occurred, sing. मार्यौ, pl. मार्या, while in Kumaon the form is sing. मारियो, pl. मारिया.

Modern classical Hindi has sing. मारा *m.*, मारी *f.*; pl. मारे *m.*, मारीं *f.*, "struck."

Panjabi retains the इ of the Prakrit, and has sing. मारिआ *m.*, मारी *f.*; pl. मारे *m.*, मारीआं *f.*, "struck;" so also does Sindhi, sing. हसियो or हस्यो *m.*, हसी *f.*; pl. हस्या *m.*, हसियूं *f.* Trumpp seems to be here in error in saying that the य has been inserted to fill the hiatus caused by the elision of the इ. It is rather the इ of इदो hardened to a semivowel, as in Old-H. and P.

Oriya has rejected the final syllable, just as it has in its present participle, and has an indeclinable past participle in *i*, as *dekhī*. This is never used alone, but only in composition, with an auxiliary forming a tense. The past participle used to form the passive ends in *ā*, like H., as *dekhā jibā* "to be seen."

The same form is found in Gujarati, as sing. छोड्यो (chhoḍyo) *m.*, छोडी *f.*, छोड्युं (chhoḍyũ) *n.*; pl. छोड्या *m.*, छोडी *f.*, छोड्यां *n.*

G., however, in common with M. B. and O., has another

form of this participle ending in an affix, whose special type is ल. The forms may be brought together for comparison—

G. Sing.	छोडेलो *m.*,	छोडेली *f.*,	छोडेलुं *n.*
M. (neuter) Sing.	सुटला *m.*,	सुटली *f.*,	सुटलें *n.*
„ (active) „	सोडिला *m.*,	सोडिली *f.*,	सोडिलें *n.*
G. Pl.	छोडेला *m.*,	छोडेली *f.*,	छोडेलां *n.*
M. (neuter) Pl.	सुटले *m.*,	सुटल्या *f.*,	सुटलीं *n.*
„ (active) „	सोडिले *m.*,	सोडिल्या *f.*,	सोडिलीं *n.*

B. देखिल, in Old-B. देखिला (only used as a tense combined with *as*). देखिले "having seen."

O. देखिल (the same), देखिले *id.*

The Bhojpuri dialect of Hindi has also an indeclinable past participle मारल, in some districts also मारिला, from which it forms a tense.

Here the junction vowel varies much. In B. O. and the active of M. it is इ. In G., on the other hand, it is ए, while in the neuter of M. it is *a*. M. has a long string of verbs, both active and neuter, with the junction vowel *â*; some of these are causals by origin, as पळ "flee," p.p. पळाला, for *paḷâ-ilâ* (as in B. and O. पळाइल). Others, again, owe the long vowel to a Skr. *ay*, as उड "fly," p.p. उडाला, Skr. उड्डयित √ उद् + डी. Others are denominatives, as दीप "be dazzled," दीपाला, Skr. दीपयित: there are, however, some which I am not able to explain on any of the above grounds. The list comprises about thirty verbs only, and in twenty-five of them participles, with the junction vowel *a*, are also in use.

The usual explanation of this form in *l* is that it is derived from the Skr. p.p.p. in *ita*, through Pr. *ido*, by change of द to ड, and thence to ल. The change is undoubtedly possible as far as ड and ल are concerned, or as far as त and द are concerned; but the change from द to ड is a great stumbling-block. The great authority of Lassen (p. 303) is usually quoted in support of this view, but even he cannot avoid being struck by the coincidence between this and the Slavonic preterites in *l*.

As regards the change from ड to ल, it is observable that it only occurs in those Skr. preterites which contain a cerebral. Thus कृत becomes in Magadhi कडे (Mr. 270). Here, however, there was evidently a form कर्तं = कट = कड, so that there is no question of a ड at all. So also in वावड for व्यापृत = वावर्त = °वट = °वड (Mr. 227). The only other instance known to me is मडे for मृत (Mr. 270), but here we may fairly assume a false analogy with कडे = कृत. So widespread a form as the modern participle in *l* must rest upon some firmer proof than the rare examples given above.

I am disposed to think that we have in this participle the survival of an ancient form which has not been preserved in classical Sanskrit, nor in the written Prakrits. Perhaps (but here I tread on ground somewhat beyond my own domain) that type of the passive past in Skr. which ends in न or ण may be the classical representative of this ancient form; thus we have from √लू "cut," लूनः, from √भिद् "cleave," भिन्नः, and in some roots both forms, that in त and that in न, stand side by side, thus √पॄ "fill," makes पूर्णः and पूर्तः, √नुद् "push," नुन्नः and नुत्तः

Even in the Slavonic languages, however, the characteristic *l* of the preterite is thought to have arisen from an original *d*, and that again from *t*.[1] If this be so, we have here an ancient change which took place before the separation of the various members of the Indo-European family, and not a mere local corruption confined to Indian ground. In Russian the preterite is a participle with forms for gender, thus from *dielat'* "to make," pret. sing. dielal' *m.*, dielala, dielalo *n.*, pl. dielali *omn.*[2] In Servian the same form occurs, *trés* "to shake," has—

Sing. trésao *m.*, trésla *f.*, tréslo *n.*
Pl. trésli *m.*, trésle *f.*, trésla *n.*

[1] Rapp, Verbal-organismus, vol. i. p. 99.
[2] Reiff, Russ. Grammar, p. 97; Rapp, vol. i. 137.

Compare Marathi—

Sing. *trâsalâ*, *trâsalî*, *trâsalẽ*.
Pl. *trâsale*, *trâsalyâ*, *trâsalîṅ*

from त्रासणें "to trouble." The similarity is striking, and seems to be more than a mere accidental coincidence. Moreover, the connection between this Slavonic *l* and *n* is shown in more than one instance. Thus, the Russian verb has from *nes* "to drag" a pret. past sing. *nesén m.*, *neséna f.*, *nesono n.*, pl. *neseny*. The same form occurs in the Czech.

But we are getting beyond bounds. The comparison is attractive, and, if there were time to study the Slavonic languages as well as the Indian, might perhaps be worked out to some conclusive result. All that can be said at present is that two groups of the same family have a preterite in *l*, and that there may be some connection between the two; while, on the other hand, the derivation of this preterite from a past participle in *t* seems strained and ill-supported as regards the Indian group, and if true for the Slavonic group, must have occurred a long while ago, before the separation of the families, and has strangely failed to leave any traces of itself in the most important language of the Indian group in its most cultivated stage.

§ 40. Let us turn to matters more within our scope. The passive past participle is the only part of the modern verb which affords an exception to the general rule of the unchangeableness of the stem-syllable. Each one of the modern languages has a few such participles, which, being derived from the Prakrit developments of the Skr. p.p.p., differ from their respective verbal stems, which latter are derived generally from the form of the root used in the present tense. These early Tadbhava participles, as they may justly be called, are most numerous in Sindhi. Trumpp gives (p. 273) a list of no less than 140 of them, a number which far exceeds that to be found in any other of the languages. They owe their existence chiefly to the omission in Skr. of the intermediate इ, so that the affix त of the p.p.p. is added directly to the root, and when this root ends in a consonant, there arises a strong or mixed nexus, which in Prakrit has to be dealt with according to the ordinary phonetic laws. Sometimes, as we saw in § 14, the stem of the verb itself is entirely borrowed from the p.p.p., and in that case the modern participle does not differ from the rest of the verb: but when the ordinary stem is derived from the older present, and only the participle from the old p.p.p., the two differ so much that it is difficult at first sight to recognize the connection between them.

The verbs given in § 19 have mostly old Tadbhava participles, and it is through these participles that the clue is found to the derivation of the verb. Thus—

SINDH.	SKR.	P.P.P.	SKR.	PR.
बझु "be bound" / बंधु "bind"	√बंध्	बधो (quasi बंधित / बधो	बंधो). / बद्ध	
बुझु "be heard" / बुधु "hear"	√बुध्	बुधो	बुद्ध	
रझु "be cooked" / रंधु "cook"	√रंध्	रधो	रद्ध	
लहु "get" / लभु "be got"	√लभ्	लधो	लब्ध	लद्धो
डुझु "be milked" / डुहु "milk"	√दुह्	डुधो	दुग्ध	दुद्धो
डहु "torment"	√दह्	डधो	दग्ध	दद्धो
भजु "be broken" / भञु "break"	√भञ्ज्	भगो	भग्न	भग्गो
भुजु "be fried" / भुञु "fry"	√भ्रस्ज्	भुगो	भुट्ठ	भुट्ठ (analogy of भग्ग)

STEM.	SKR.	P.P.P.	SKR.	PR.
छिजु "be broken" / छिनु "break"	√छिद्	छिनो	छिन्न	
सुजु "be heard" / सुणु "hear"	√श्रु	सुणो	सुत	
		सुणियो	(regular modern form)	
वधु "raise"	√वर्द्ध	वधो	वृद्ध	वधियो
कुहु "kill" / कुसु "be killed"	√कुष्	कुठो	कुष्ट	कुट्ठो
गहु "rub" / गसु "be rubbed"	√घृष्	गठो	घृष्ट	घिट्ठो, घट्ठो
छुहु "touch" / छुपु "be touched"	√छुप्	छुतो	छुप्त	छुत्तो

The exact coincidence of these participles with the Sanskrit and Prakrit confirms the derivation of the verbal stems given in § 19. There are many others equally instructive as retaining the Prakrit form; thus, for instance, we can explain the following:

S.	SKR.	S. P.P.P.	SKR.	PR.
लिंबु "smear,"	√लिप्	लितो	लिप्त	लित्तो
तपु "warm,"	√तप्	ततो	तप्त	तत्तो
सुम्हु "sleep,"	√स्वप्	सुतो	सुप्त	सुत्तो
पा "get,"	√आप्	पातो	आप्त	पात्तो [?]
आणु "bring,"	√आनी	आंदो	आनीत	
रु "weep,"	√रुद्	रुनो	रुदित	रुण्णो

So also the origin of उघु "wipe out," is obscure, till we look at the p.p.p. उघठो, which leads to Skr. उद्घृष, and then we see that *ughaṇu* is for *ugahaṇu*=*udgharshaṇam*. The participles in *ṭho* similarly explain themselves, as

S.	SKR.	S. P.P.P.	SKR.	PR.
डिसु "see,"	√दृश्	डिठो	दृष्ट	दिट्ठो
वसु "rain,"	√वृष्	वठो, वुठो, वठो	वृष्ट	वुट्ठो

S.	SKR.	S. P.P.P.	SKR.	PR.
पिह, पेह "enter,"	√प्रविश्	पेठो	प्रविष्ट	पविट्ठो (H. पैठ)
विह "sit,"	√उपविश्	वेठो	उपविष्ट	उवविट्ठो (H. बैठ)
पीस "grind,"	√पिष्	पीठो	पिष्ट	पिट्ठो
तुस "be pleased,"	√तुष्	तुठो	तुष्ट	तुट्ठो

The next three words have old Tadbhava participles in almost all the languages of this group:

डिअणु "give," p.p.p. डिनो. Pr. दिण्णो.
करणु "do," ,, कीतो. किओ. कयो. Skr. कृत. Pr. किओ. see under H.
मरणु "die," ,, मो. मुओ. Skr. मृत. Pr. मुओ.

Another class is composed of denominatives or neuter verbs with the causal type *âm* (§ 28). These are

Infin.	उभामणु "to boil over,"	p.p.p	उभाणो
,,	उझामणु "to be extinguished,"	,,	उझाणो
,,	उडामणु "to fly,"	,,	उडाणो
,,	खपामणु "to decrease,"	,,	खपाणो
,,	बामणु "to be burnt,"	,,	बाणो
,,	विसामणु "to be extinguished,"	,,	विसाणो
,,	विकामणु "to be sold,"	,,	विकाणो

There is, as already mentioned, considerable obscurity as to the derivation of these words: *uḍâmaṇu* is, however, certainly from Skr. *ud-ḍî*, p.p.p. *ḍîna*; *ujhâmaṇu* perhaps from Skr. *ut-kshi*, p.p.p. *kshîṇa*; *vikâmaṇu* from Skr. *vikrî*, p.p.p., however, not *krîṇa*, but *krîta*. On the analogy of those verbs whose p.p.p. ended in *na*, may have been formed the modified p.p. in *ṇo* for all verbs of the class, regardless of the fact that in the classical language the causal p.p. would end in *âpita*, e.g. *sthâpita*. In

Hindi, also, stems ending in *ā* take this p.p. in *yo* in the poets as बिसरा, p.p. बिसरायो, or apocopated *n*, as दिखा p.p. दिखाय.

The above remarks explain nearly half the words in Trumpp's list, for the rest the uncertainty is too great to admit of satisfactory explanation. Trumpp, for instance, would derive ध्रापणु "to satisfy," and ध्रापजणु "to be satisfied," from Skr. √तृप्, तर्पति, but the p.p.p. ध्रापो can hardly represent तृप्त. Others again there are whose p.p. is intelligible, while the infinitive is not. जुटो "engaged" (in work) explains itself by Skr. युक्त, Pr. जुत्तो, clearly enough, but its infinitive should be *jujaṇu* or *junjaṇu* (Pr. जुज्जइ). Whence then comes it that the infinitive is *junbaṇu*? So also *ruḍho* "busily employed" is clearly Skr. रुद्ध (रुध्), one form of the infinitive *rujhaṇu* is regularly derived from Skr. रुध्यते, but what are we to say to another form *rumbhaṇu* or *rubhaṇu*?

Panjabi has several of the same early Tadbhava participles as Sindhi, and a few of its own. The total number, however, is much smaller than in Sindhi. The commonest are

	P.P.	SKR.
करना "do,"	कीता	कृत (dialectically also कीहा).
जाणा "go,"	गिया, गइआ	गत (also जाता = Skr. यात).
जाणना "know,"	जाता	ज्ञात.
देखणा "see,"	डिट्ठा	दृष्ट (also डिठा *more Sindhico*).
देणा "give,"	दित्ता, दिता	दत्त.
लैणा "take,"	लीता, लिया	लभित, instead of classical लब्ध.
वरसणा "rain,"	वुट्ठा	वृष्ट.
खाणा "eat,"	खाधा	खादित.
पैणा "fall,"	पिया	पतित, Sindhi *id.* through पइओ.
बंन्हणा "bind,"	बद्धा	बद्ध.
पछाणना "recognize,"	पछाता	परिज्ञात? *H.* पहिचानना.
सिउणा "sew,"	सीता	सीवित.
सौणा "sleep,"	सुत्ता	सुप्त.

	P.P.	SKR.
पहुंचणा "arrive,"	पहुतो, पुज्जो	?
रिंन्हणा "cook,"	रिद्धा	रद्ध.
विवाहुणा "marry,"	विवाहुतो	विवाहित.
कहिणा "say,"	किहा	कथित.
रहिणा "remain,"	रिहा	रहित.

In the two last the ह has leapt over into the preceding syllable, and *kihá*, *rihá*, are for *kahiá*, *rahiá*, respectively. The above list nearly, if not quite, exhausts the early Tadbhava participles of Panjabi, and Hindi influence is already at work in favour of the ordinary type.

§ 47. Gujarati has, like Panjabi, a smaller number of these participles than Sindhi.

INFIN.		SKR.	PR.
करवुं "do"	कर्यो, कीधो	कृत	करियो
लेवुं "take"	लीधो	लब्ध	
पोहोंचवुं "arrive"	पोहोंच्यो, पोहोतो	?	
देखवुं "see"	दिठो, दीठो	दृष्ट	
बीहीवुं "fear"	बीहीनो, बीहीधो	भीत	बिहिद्दो (§ 13)
खावुं "eat"	खाधो	खादित	
उपजवुं "produce"	उपन्यो °न्नो	उत्पन्न (present *utpadyate*)	
नीपजवुं "	नीपन्यो °न्नो	निष्पन्न (pres. *nishpadyate*)	
पीवुं "drink"	पीधो	पीत	
सुवुं "sleep"	सुतो	सुप्त	
मरवुं "die"	मुओ	मृत	
देवुं "give"	दीधो	दत्त	
बेसवुं "sit"	बेठो	उपविष्ट	
पेसवुं "enter"	पेठो	प्रविष्ट	
नासवुं "flee"	नाठो	नष्ट (present *naśyati*)	
जवुं "go"	गयो	गत	

In the instances of *kidho*, *bhidho*, *khadho*, *pidho*, and *didho*, we have probably formations based on the analogy of *lidho*, for the exception of *bhidho*, which may owe its *dh* to a combination of the *h* and *d* of Pr. *rihido*, there is no older form which would yield *dh*. The origin of these forms will be more fully inquired into under Hindi, where they are well illustrated.

So far does the original meaning of these participles appear to have been obscured, that from them a participle ending in *elo* is also formed, and they say *kidhelo*, *didhelo*, and the like, where the participial element occurs twice. The ordinary verb having two forms of participle, one in *yo*, the other in *elo*, the verbs in the above list were bound to have them also, and instead of adding *elo* to the stem, and making *karelo*, *lelo*, it has been added to the already formed early Tadbhava participle.

There appears to be a slight difference in meaning between the two forms of the Gujarati past participle, that in *elo* being somewhat more emphatic than that in *yo*. Thus हुं आव्यो छुं "I am come," but हुं आवेलो छुं "I *am* come," (emphatically).

Marathi has early Tadbhava participles, and it has others, which are accounted irregular by the grammarians from other causes. The former are not numerous, and are chiefly found in the same stems as in the other languages. Thus we have—

जा "go,"	p.p.p.	गेला
ये "come,"	,,	आला
मर् "die,"	,,	मेला
घे "take" (wear),	,,	घातला
कर् "do,"	,,	केला

Stems ending in ण exhibit ट in the participle, as

खण "dig,"	p.p.p.	खटला
म्हण "speak,"	"	म्हटला
हाण "slay,"	"	हाटला

The explanation of these words is apparently to be found in a contraction of syllables; thus Skr. √ खन् "dig" forms regularly p.p.p. खात, but the न being changed to ण in Prakrit, a p.p.p. खणित would be legitimately formed, whence खण्ट, to which, forgetful of the fact that this is already a participle, M. adds its own participial termination ला, and by rejection of the nasal arrives at खटला. So also √मन्, p.p.p. मणित, whence मण्ट and म्हट + ला. Skr. हन् has p.p.p. हत, but a Pr. form हणित would be, and is, used, whence हण्ट, and the stem-vowel having been lengthened, हाट + ला.

To a similar retention of the त of the Skr. p.p.p. may be attributed the following, though the etymology is in some cases very obscure:

घे "take,"	घेतला "taken."
धू "washed,"	धुतला "washed."
बघ "see,"	बघितला "seen."
माग "ask,"	मागितला "asked."
सांग "tell,"	सांगितला "told."
घाल "put,"	घातला "put."
खा "eat,"	खाल्ला "eaten."

In § 15 it was shown that Pr. inserts त in forms like *ghettum*, *ghettūna*, which may be a retention of त in *grihīta*. In the next four words on the list there seems to be a double participle, as in G. *kidhelo*, etc. The origin of घाल is unknown to me, it looks like an early causal of घे take. In खा the p.p. is apparently a contraction of खादिला, Skr. खादित.

§ 48. Hindi has very few of these participles. In the classical language only the following are in use:

करना "do," किया "done."
मरना "die," मुआ "dead."
लेना "take," लिया "taken."
देना "give," दिया "given."
जाना "go," गया "gone."

All the other verbs in the language form this participle from the common stem used in all the other tenses, though in the mediæval poets some of the old Tadbhava participles are found, as *diṭṭhau* "seen," *tuṭṭhau* "pleased," (*tushṭu*) in Chand. The three verbs *kar*, *le*, and *de*, however, have several peculiar forms in Old-H., and in the mediæval poets, which are still heard in some of the rustic dialects. There are three parallel forms:

कर् has i. कीयौ or कियौ. ii. कीनौ or किन्नौ. iii. कीधौ or किद्धौ.
दे " i. दीयौ or दियौ. ii. दीनौ or दिन्नौ. iii. दीधौ or दिद्धौ.
ले " i. लीयौ or लियौ. ii. लीनौ or लिन्नौ. iii. लीधौ or लिद्धौ.

The curious thing about these three verbs is that every two of them have borrowed a form peculiar to the third. For *kiyau* is properly the participle of *kar*, Skr. कृत, Pr. कियो and किदो. It has been borrowed by *le* and *de*. So *dīnau* belongs to *de*, Skr. दत्त, Pa. and Pr. दिन्नो, and has been borrowed by *kar* and *le*. Also *līdhau* belongs to *le*, Skr. लब्ध, Pa. and Pr. लद्धो, and has been borrowed by *kar* and *de*. We cannot get *kīnau* or *kīdhau* phonetically from √ कृ, nor *dīyau* and *dīdhau* from √ दा, nor *līyau* and *līnau* from √ लभ्, without forcing etymology. These three verbs are so constantly used together, and fall in so conveniently for rhymes in the poets, that it is not surprising that, in the general decay and confusion of forms out of which the modern languages sprung, they should have borrowed from one another. To begin with our oldest author, Chand, कियौ, कीयौ, and किय्यौ, all occur frequently, with the first vowel both long and short, and the final vowel occasionally cut off if it happens to be in the way of the metre. कन्या कियौ चहौर ॥ "The girl *made* lamentation" (Pr. R. i. 171). It is long in

कीयौ तब चित चिहुँ दिस ॥
"He then *made* reflection on all sides."—xx. 20.

कीयौ चलन कौ साज ॥
"He *made* preparation for going."—xx. 28.

Apocopated, as दीय and कीय in

गढ़ पतिस गढ़ भार दीय ॥
पूरब दिस तब गमन कीय ॥
"He *entrusted* the fort to the castellan,
Made a going to the eastern country."—xx. 29.

करिये सब घोषित संब बज्जिय ॥
"*Took* all shouting and playing on drums."—*ib.*

A form with *n* occurs for *le* and *de* only, as लीनौ विप्र गुर बोल ॥ "*Took* Brahmins and gurus, saying" (*ib.* 20), and दई सु कन्या वचन वर ॥ "When the maiden *gave* her troth to the bridegroom" (*ib.* 22).

Commonest by far is the second form with either long or short vowel, in the latter case generally with doubling of the following consonant, and very frequently with the last vowel apocopated. Of these types that with the double consonant is nearest to the Prakrit, and thus presumably the oldest, the rejection of one consonant and lengthening of the preceding vowel is a later feature. In Chand, however, there is no distinction between the two; so that one rhymes with the other, as in

भैर महल पिथिराज रमी रमना रस रमिय ॥
कुसुम पटा सिर पाग बाघ कंद्रप रस कीयव ॥
"In his private apartments Prithiraj dallied with his wives and attendants,
In saffron robes and turbaned head he made the sport of love."
—[illegible] 22.

So also लुट्टि धरत्ती लिद्धि लिच्छव "having plundered the land, he has taken treasure" (xxi. 30). In this passage the preceding line ends with सिद्धव. (In Hindi *av* = *au*, so *kinnav* is to be read *kinnau*, etc.)

विहसित वरं वचन लियौ नरिंद ॥

"Smiling the king accepted the espousal."—xx. 23.

सहस घटु सिव उपर कीनौ ॥
तीन उपास नेम तब कीनौ ॥

"He poured (gave) a thousand jars over Siva,
Then he took a vow to fast three (days)."—i. 189.

See also the quotation at p. 268 of Vol. II.

Instances of the apocopated form occur chiefly at the end of a line; as

दस कोस जाय मुकाम कीन ॥
बिच गाम नगर पुर लूट कीन ॥

"Having gone ten *kos* he made a halt,
Villages and towns between he plundered."—i. 208.

परिमाल जुद्ध पर हुकम दीन ॥

"Parimal gave the order for fighting."—xxi. 5.

The third form is more frequently found with *de*, to which it least of all belongs, and has an additional termination *iya* sometimes attached to it, as

दान मान बहु दिद्धिय

"He gave gifts and honours abundant."—i. 342.

In this passage it rhymes with कद्धिय, which ought perhaps to be read लिद्धिय "having taken."

There is an instance of the natural change into the palatal in

सगरी नाव जाय थंभ लिज्जिय ॥
आल्हा ऊदल उतरन न दिज्जिय ॥

"Carts and boats he went and stopped;
Âlhâ and Ûdal he suffered not to alight."—xxi. 66.

for किन्ही and दिन्ही respectively. This latter occurs frequently, in a slightly altered shape—

भट ढोंढी दुआ नरिंद ॥
"Dhundhá gave a blessing to the king."—i. 306.

प्रिथिराज ताहि दी देस दिव ॥
"Prithiráj gave him two provinces."—*ib.* 307.

All three types may be found repeatedly throughout the poem. In later times, as in Tulsi Das and in Braj poetry generally, these verbs take the forms कीन्ही, लीन्ही, and दीन्ही, and the last syllable is occasionally apocopated as in Chand. Thus Tulsi Das—

इहि बिधि दाह क्रिया सब कीन्ही ।
बिधिवत न्हाइ तिलांजुलि दीन्ही ॥
"In this way he performed all the ceremony of cremation,
Having duly bathed, he presented the offering of sesamum."
—Ay-k. 994.

मोहि उपदेस दीन्ह गुरु नीका ।
"The *guru* hath given me good advice."—*ib.* 928.

तौ कत कीन्ह संग कटकाई ॥
"Then why has he taken an army with him?"—*ib.* 982.

The above examples may suffice for these special types, which have no analogy with other preterites in H. Oriya and Bengali have few such forms, for O. मला and कला are merely contractions of मरिला and करिला, from मर "die," and कर "do," respectively. From जा "go," O. गला, B. गेल, is about the only real old Tadbhava in those two languages.

§ 40. The participial tenses formed from the past participle are analogous to those from the present. In ordinary Hindi the participle itself is used as a past tense, without any relic of the substantive verb; it will have been noticed that in all the passages quoted in the last section, the participle must be translated as a preterite, and this is the case in the modern language.

both for active and neuter verbs, as *bolá* "he said," *kiyá* "he did." In the mediæval poets, however, and to this day in the rustic dialects of Oudh and the eastern Hindi area, there exists a preterite with terminations retaining traces of the incorporation of the old substantive verb. Before these terminations the long *á* and *í* of the p.p. masculine and feminine are shortened, and the vowel of the masculine is often replaced by *e*. Thus we have (*már* "strike")—

	sing. 1.	2.	3.	pl. 1.	2.	3.
m.	मारउँ	मारउ	मारउ	मारेन्हि	मारेहु	मारेन्हि
f.	मारिउँ	मारिउ	मारिउ	मारिन्हि	मारिहु	मारिन्हि

Also in *m.* मारेउँ, *etc.* In the sing. 2, 3, the syllable सि is often added, as मारेसि, and variated into हि, as मारेहि *m.*, मारिसि, मारिहि *f.* Thus चलेउ हरषि हिय धरि रघुनाथा "he went rejoicing, holding in his heart Raghunátha" (Tulsi Das, Ram. Sund-k. 4), देखेउँ नयन राम कर दूता "I have seen with my eyes the messenger of Ram" (*ib.* 12). Tulsi does not observe the gender very closely, if at all,—पुनि परिहरेउ सुखानेउ परना । "Again *she gave up* even dry leaves" (Bal-k. 165), पूछेसि लोगन्ह काह उछाहू । "She asked the people, why is this rejoicing?" (Ay-k. 87). But the feminine is kept in सिखवनिहि दीन्हेउ तोहि । "The flatteress has given instruction to (has prompted) thee" (Ay-k. 101). The type ending in *si*, though used for both 2 and 3 sing., more strictly belongs, I think, to 2 sing. from Skr. *asi*; but in this tense the traces of the substantive verb are so much abraded that it is difficult to speak with certainty about them. The following handful of instances, taken at hazard from one page of the Sundara-káṇḍa of Tulsi's work, will show the various senses in which this affix is used: खाएसि फल अरु बिटप उपारे "He *eats* the fruit, and tears up the bushes" (S-k. 40), कछु मारेसि कछु मर्देसि कछुक मिलाएसि धूरि । "Some he *slew*, some he *trampled* under foot, some he caused to mix with the dust," कह कपिस बचन है

कीन्हा । केहि के बल घालेसि बन खीसा । कीधौं श्रवन सुनेसि नहिं मोहि । . . . . मारेसि निसिचर केहि अपराधा । "Saith the lord of Lanka, who art thou, and what? By whose strength *hast thou torn* to pieces the forest, *hast thou* never *heard* of my fame, . . . for what fault *hast thou killed* the demons?" (*ib.*) Panjabi throws no light on the subject, as it does not use this form, but employs the participle simply as a tense, as *main*, *tū*, *uh mārid*, "I, thou, he, smote." Indeed, to such an extent in H. and P. has this custom of using the bare participle as a preterite tense prevailed, that it cannot now be used in any other sense, and if we wish to say "smitten," we must not use H. *mārā* or P. *mārid* alone, but must add the participle of the modern substantive verb, and say H. *mārā hūā*, P. *mārid hoā*. The only trace in P. of the old substantive verb is to be found in a dialectic form which I have often heard, though it does not seem to be used in writing, as कीतोस "he did," which is probably to be referred to S. कृतोऽस्ति. The grammarians, however, suppose that *kītos* is in some way a metathesis of *us ne kīta*, so that *kītā* + *us* = *kītos*. The instrumental, however, of *uh* "he," is not *us ne*, but *un*; *us ne* is Hindi, and would hardly have been resorted to in the formation of a pure dialectic type like this. Moreover, in the 1 plural we have such expressions as खांदेसां, which is evidently *khānde* + *'sā*, for *sā* = *smah*.

Different from modern, but strikingly similar to mediæval, Hindi in this respect is Sindhi, which does not employ the participle singly as a preterite, but, except in the 3 sing. and pl., has relics of the substantive verb incorporated with it, thus (*hal* "go")—

	SING. 1.	2.	3.	PL. 1.	2.	3.
m.	हलिअसि	हलिएं	हलिओ	हलिआसीं	हलिअउ	हलिआ
f.	हलिअसि	हलिएं	हली	हलिअंसीं	हलिउं	हलिउं

By comparing these terminations with those of the S. future, which is based upon the present participle (§ 41), it will be seen that they are absolutely identical, thus:

halandu -si	corresponds to	haliu -si.
halandia -si	,,	halia -si.
halandā -sī	,,	haliā -sī.
halandiū -sī	,,	haliū -sī.
etc.		etc.

and the terminations may, in the case of the preterite, therefore, as well as in that of the future, be referred to the old Skr. verb *as* in various degrees of decay.

Marathi exhibits the same analogy between the present and the preterite; to its p.p. in ला *m.*, ली *f.*, लें *n.*, etc., it adds the same terminations as to the present p. in ता *m.*, ती *f.*, तें *n.*, etc. Thus

Sing.	1. कुटलों *m.*,	कुटलें *f.*,	कुटलों *n.*
	2. कुटलास *m.*,	°लीस *f.*,	°लेंस *n.*
	3. कुटला *m.*,	°ली *f.*,	°लें *n.*
Pl.	1. कुटलों *m. f. n.*		
	2. कुटलां *id.*		
	3. कुटले *m.*	°ल्या *f.*	°लीं *n.*

The forms exactly agree with those of the present, as will be seen by turning to § 42. There is no conditional as in the present. When it desires to use this form in an adjectival sense, M., having apparently forgotten its originally participial nature, adds another इला, thus we get मेलेलें जनावर "a dead animal," केलेला पुरुष "a made (*i.e.* experienced) man." The fact so well established for S. and M. may help us to understand, if we cannot fully explain, the preterites of O. and B., which are formed in the same way. From a p.p. देखिल, O. constructs a preterite, thus—

Sing.	1. देखिलि	2. देखिलु	3. देखिला.
Pl.	1. देखिलु	2. देखिल	3. देखिले.

where the terminations correspond exactly with those of the conditional, which is similarly formed from the present participle.

Bengali does the same (*pace* the Pandits), as—

Sing. 1. देखिनु 2. देखिलि 3. देखिल.
Pl. 1. देखिलाम 2. देखिला 3. देखिलेन.

Here the 3 sing. has also देखिलेक with a final क, as in the imperative and future, concerning which see § 53. The 1 sing. in *nu* is frequently heard in speaking, and is very common in the old poets, as अपरूप पेखनु रामा "*I saw* the fair one looking woe-begone" (Bidyapati, vii. 1), where some read पेखिनु.

In Gujarati the participle is used alone as a preterite in both forms, that in *yo* and that in *elo*, but more frequently a modern substantive verb is added for greater clearness. This language has no traces of the old incorporated Sanskrit *as*.

§ 60. In the past tenses of all but B. and O. the *prayogas* or constructions mentioned in Vol. II. p. 264, are employed. In most of the languages, indeed, their use is restricted to the past tenses. The direct or *kartá prayoga* is used with neuter verbs, and requires the subject to be in the nominative case, while the participle, which does duty for a preterite, changes with the gender of the speaker. Thus

H. वह बोला "he spoke." वे बोले "these men spoke."
वह बोली "she spoke." वे बोलीं "these women spoke."

So, also, in P. S. and G. In M. the principle is the same, though there is more variety of forms:

तो म्हटला "he said." ते म्हटले "illi dixerunt."
ती म्हटली "she said." त्या म्हटल्या "illae dixerunt."
तें म्हटलें "it said." तीं म्हटलीं "illa dixerunt."

And so through all the persons except 1 and 2 plural, where no distinction of gender is necessary, as the speaker is known. In the active verb, however, the *karma* or objective construction is used, where the subject is put in the instrumental, the verb agreeing in number and gender with the object. Thus, H. मैं ने तुम से बड़े कठोर वचन कहे हैं "I have spoken very harsh words to you" (Sak. 33). Here the subject *maĩ ne* is in the Instrumental, the verb *kahe haĩ* is masc. plural, to agree with the object *vachan*. दैव ने ऐसा ही जोग मिला दिया (*ib.* 39) "Destiny has joined just such a joining" (has brought about such a marriage).

So also in M. the p.p. is declined for all three genders in both numbers so as to agree with the object, as त्याने पोथी वाचिली "he read the book," where *vāchilī* is fem. sing., to agree with *pothī*. In M. and S. many verbs are both active and neuter, in which case the preterite has a double construction, direct or *kartā* when the verb is used as a neuter, objective or *karma* when it is used as an active. So also in G. The distinction appertains to syntax, and not to formlore, and need not be more than mentioned here.

There is also a third or impersonal construction technically known as *bhāva*, in which the object is not expressed, and the verb, therefore, remains always in the neuter. In M., however, this construction is used even when the object is expressed, as त्याने त्याला मारिलें "he beat him," literally "by him to him beaten."

§ 51. The participle of the future passive, which in Sanskrit ends in तव्य, plays an important part in the modern verb in some languages. It does not, like the two previously noticed participles, form modern participles, but rather various kinds of verbal nouns, such as in Latin grammar we are familiar with under the names of gerunds and supines, also the infinitive. The Latin gerund itself is, however, closely allied to the participle of the future passive, for *amandi*, *amando*, *amandum*, are respectively the genitive, dative, and accusative of *amandus*. There is, therefore, a participial nature inherent in these forms which justifies their inclusion in the present chapter. The Skr. *tavya* becomes in Pr. *davya*, and with elision of the *d*, *avva*. Thus Skr. चोरयितव्य, Pr. चोरिदव्व, चोरिअव्व. So also Pr. करिदव्व, करिअव्व, which must be referred to a Sanskrit form करितव्य rather than to the classical form कर्तव्य, for Prakrit, as mentioned before, generally takes no heed of Sanskrit subtleties about inserting or omitting the intermediate इ, but treats all verbs alike, as if that letter were inserted, and it naturally gives the type to its modern descendants in all cases.

The treatment of the form so inherited from the Prakrit differs in the various languages, both in form and meaning.

Sindhi uses it as a present passive participle ending in *ibo*, Pr. करिअव्वो, losing the *a* and the first *v* of the suffix, becomes करिबो, meaning "being done." The transition from the original sense of "that which is to be (or must be) done," into "that which is being done," is simple and natural. Examples are—

घुमाटणु "to choke,"	घुमाटिबो "being choked."
ठगणु "to cheat,"	ठगिबो "being cheated."
झलणु "to seize."	झलिबो "being seized."[1]

Gujarati differs from Sindhi in rejecting the इ and retaining the व, thus making करवो "being done," as छोडवो *m.*, वी *f.*, वुं *n.*, etc., "being loosed;" लाववो, however, means "bringing," where the sense has become active. The neuter of this form does duty as an infinitive, as जवुं "to go," of which more hereafter.

In Marathi the vowel preceding the *v* is lengthened, and one *v* rejected, giving a form करावें, which is the same for active and neuter verbs. The meaning, to judge by the

[1] Trumpp, p. 56.

examples quoted, has also changed, for although properly the same as in the older languages, "that which has to be done," it is used in constructions where it implies "the doing" of a thing only. It takes all three genders, and is commonly used also in the genitive and dative cases करावयाचें and करावयास, or करायास. Thus तें मी करावयास सिद्ध आहें "I am ready to do that" (*i.e.* "to the doing of"), आपणाशीं कांहीं बोलावयाचें आहे "I have something to say to you," *i.e.* "with you something of that which must be said I am." Thus it approximates somewhat to the infinitive of G., as in the following passage:

न करावा संग । वाटे दुरावावें जन ॥
सेवावा एकांत । वाटे न बोलावी मात ॥
जन धन तन । वाटे लेखावें वमन ॥

"It is proper not to associate, to be separated from the world;
It is proper to preserve solitude, not to speak at all;
People, wealth, self it is proper to consider as vomit."

—Tukaram. Abh. 1555.

Here *vāṭe* (Skr. वर्तते) means "it seems," *i.e.* "it seems proper," like Latin decet, oportet, licet, used impersonally, and the participle agrees with the object. Thus *saṅga* and *ekānta* being masc., the participles are masc. *karāvā* and *sevāvā*; *māt* (Skr. वार्ता) being fem., *bolāvī* is fem. also; *jan*, *vaman* neut., hence *durāvāveṃ*, *lekhāveṃ* neut. The original meaning of a passive participle may be exhibited by supposing the sentence to be "society is not to be made . . . this seems proper," which is easily inverted into the rendering given above.

When used in the genitive or dative case, the व sometimes drops out, and they say, for instance, आम्हास देशांतरीं जायाचें पडेल "We shall have to go to another country," for जावया. literally "to us in another country *of going* it will fall." Latin would here use the corresponding passive participle, Nobis eundum erit, or Skr. *gantavyam asti*.

Panjabi has apparently no trace left of this participle, nor has classical Hindi, but in rustic Hindi, especially in the eastern parts of its area, as well as in Bengali and Oriya, this participle exists. In Bhojpuri it ends in बे or बै, without any junction-vowel, and means the doing of anything, as सुनबे न कैलन *sunbe na kailan*, "they did not make *a hearing*," i.e. "they would not listen," मानिबै न करिहैं *mānab na karihai*, "they will not make *an obeying*," i.e. "they will not obey."[1] It is more emphatic than a simple preterite or future, and implies that the persons referred to obstinately refused to hear or obey.

In B. and O. it is a simple infinitive, but as a noun is declined in all cases, thus B. O. देखिबा "to see," genitive देखिबार "of seeing," etc. As a noun, it also implies the act of doing anything, as O. अश्लील गीत शुणिबा दोष अटे गाइबा त पाप "the hearing of, or listening to, obscene songs, is a fault, the singing (of them) is a crime" (see § 74).

§ 52. The tenses formed from this participle come next to be considered. In Sindhi the old substantive verb is incorporated, just as in the tenses derived from the present and past participles, but it is used to form a future passive from active verbs only, as (*chhaḍ* "abandon"), "I shall be abandoned," etc.

Sing.	m.	1. छडिबुसि	2. छडिबें	3. छडिबो
	f.	1. छडिबिअसि	2. छडिबिअं	3. छडिबी
Pl.	m.	1. छडिबासीं	2. छडिबउ	3. छडिबा
	f.	1. छडिबिअसीं	2. छडिबिअउं	3. छडिबिअं

Here the terminations are precisely identical in every respect with those of the active future and preterite, exhibited in the preceding sections.

In Gujarati this participle used alone, and inflected for

[1] Kellogg, Grammar, p. 231.

gender, constitutes what the grammar-writers are pleased to call the second present of the second potential mood. It is, however, really a construction of the objective, or *karma*, kind, in which the verb agrees with its object, and the subject or agent is in the instrumental or (as usual in G. in this construction) in the dative; thus they say मारे or मैं छोडवो "I ought to release," *i.e.* "by me it is to be released." तारे or तैं विश्वास करवो "you ought to have confidence," *i.e.* "by thee trust is to be made," Skr. त्वया विश्वासः कर्तव्यः.

The genitive case also, oddly enough, forms a tense of its own, also with no trace of the old substantive verb, as छोडवानो *m.*, नी *f.*, नुं *n.* The meaning seems hardly, if at all, distinguishable from that of the nominative, and the construction is objective, as in that tense; thus जे काम अमारे करवानुं "the work which we ought to do." I am not altogether satisfied, however, with the explanation of this tense as the genitive of the above participle, and would suggest that it may possibly be derived from the Âtmane. pres. part. in *mâna*, like *bhavamâna*. It is possible, I think, that though the Âtmanepada has dropped out of use at an early epoch, yet that this participle, not being specially recognized as belonging to that phase of the verb, may, in some dialects, have held its own. From the want of documents of the intermediate period, however, the question is one which must remain, for the present at least, obscure.

Marathi combines the terminations used by it in the indicative present and past, with this participle also, but, from a memory of its origin, employs the tense so formed somewhat in the same way as G., namely, as indicating that a thing ought to be or should be done. From this strict and primary sense other subsidiary meanings branch out, as might be expected. The neuter verb uses the direct or *kartâ* construction, also the *bhâva* or impersonal; the active uses the *karma* and *bhâva*. As it is only in the direct construction that the verb is conjugated for person, it is only in the neuter verb that the verbal terminations occur. Thus (*sut* "escape")—

Sing. m.	1. सुटावा	2. ०वास	3. ०वा	Pl. 1. ०वे	2. ०वेत	3. ०वे
f.	सुटावी	०वीस	०वी	०व्या	०व्यात	०व्या
n.	सुटावें	०वेंस	०वें	०वीं	०वींत	०वीं

The 2 plural here differs from the other tenses in preserving a separate form for all three genders, in which the final *t* recalls the termination of the 2 plural of the Sanskrit optative.

In the active verb with the *karma* construction, the participle is declined for all three genders of both numbers, but in the nominative case only, and the agent is in the instrumental, thus म्यां, तूं or त्याणें सोडावा -वी -वें, etc., "I, thou, he, should loose." In both neuter and active, when the *bhâva* construction is used, the verb stands in the neuter singular with all persons, as सुटावें or सोडावें.

Stevenson (p. 101) distinguishes no less than fourteen different senses of this tense, but the distinctions seem somewhat too finely drawn, and belong rather to the department of conventional usage than to that which deals with the organism and structure of the language.

With a short *a* preceding the characteristic व, which is all that remains of the participial ending, M. forms a whole potential mood, which may even be looked upon as a separate phase of the verb. Thus (*sod* "loose")—

Aorist (Past habitual)	मला सोडवे	"I used to be able to loose" (*rare*),
Present	,,	सोडवतें "I can loose,"
Preterite	,,	सोडवलें "I could loose" (*rare*),
Future	,,	सोडवेल "I shall be able to loose,"
Imperfect	,,	सोडवत होतें "I could have loosed,"
Pluperfect	,,	सोडवलें होतें "I had been able to have loosed,"

and so on, through all the range of compound tenses. The construction is the Bhâva or impersonal throughout, showing that the form originates from the participle, and is to be literally rendered "by me to be loosed it is, or was," which accounts for the neuter form being used.

§ 53. It is to this place that I would now refer the *ba* type of the future as used in B. and O., and in the Bhojpuri dialect of Hindi. It has been usual to compare these tenses with the Latin future in *bo*, as *amabo*, and the comparison is tempting, but, as I now think, delusive. It rests upon the supposition that the *b* of the termination represents the substantive verb *bhû*; but to this there are the seemingly fatal objections that *bhû*, in its modified form of *bhava*, had from very early times become *ho*, losing its labial element altogether, and that the present tense *bhavâmi*, etc., though much changed and worn away in modern times, always retains its characteristic vowel *o*, sometimes shortened to *u* or resolved into *ua*. It is only when an *i* follows the *o*, that the combination *oi* is at times shortened to *e*, as in O. *hebâ* = hoibâ.

Judging by the analogy of the cognate languages, it seems that we ought now to see in the B. and O. future the Skr. participle in *tavya*, in combination with the present tense of √*as*. The forms are (*dekh*, "see")—

B.	Sing.	1. देखिब	2. देखिबि	3. देखिबे ०बेक
O.	,,	1. देखिबि	2. देखिबु	3. देखिब
Bhojpuri.	,,	1. देखब्	2. देखब	3. देखी
B.	Pl.	1. देखिब	2. देखिबा ०बे	3. देखिबेन
O.	,,	1. देखिबु ०बा	2. देखिब	3. देखिबे
Bhojpuri.	,,	1. देखब्	2. देखब	3. देखिहैं

The 3 sing. and 3 pl. of Bhojpuri may be excluded from this

group, as they belong to the *sa* or *ba* type of the future (§ 35). The dialect of Riwâ has some forms of the *ba* type, as 2 sing. मारिबेस, 1 pl. मारिब, मारब, and मारिबे, 2 pl. मारिबा. The dialect of Oudh (Avadhî) has 1 sing. मारबू, 2 मारबेस, मारबे, 1 pl. मारब, 2 मारबो, and in the old Purbi dialect मारब *mârab* is used for all three persons of both numbers.

There is thus apparent a general tendency to the use of the *ba* type of future throughout the eastern area of the Aryan territory in India, and it will be seen by comparing either B. or O. terminations of the future with those of the tenses formed by those languages from the present and past participles respectively, that they are almost, if not quite identical. Thus O.—

		PRESENT.	PAST.	FUTURE.
Sing.	1.	dekhant -*i*	dekhil -*i*	dekhib -*i*
	2.	dekhant -*u*	dekhil -*u*	dekhib -*u*
	3.	dekhant -*á*	dekhil -*á*	dekhib -*á*
Pl.	1.	dekhant -*ũ*	dekhil -*ũ*	dekhib -*ũ*
	2.	dekhant -*a*	dekhil -*a*	dekhib -*a*
	3.	dekhant -*e*	dekhil -*e*	dekhib -*e*

As the analogy of the other languages compels us to see in these terminations abraded fragments of the present tense of *as*, when combined with the present and past participles, the same process of reasoning leads us to see the same element in combination with the future participle, and the 2 sing. of the Riwâ and Avadhi dialects further confirms this view by having preserved, like Marathi, the characteristic *s* of the Skr. 2 sing. *asi*. There is the same agreement of the final vowel in these three tenses of the B. verb, though it is not so accurately preserved as in the more archaic Oriya. Thus B. *dekhib-e* does not correspond with *dekhit-des*, and *dekhil-dm*. So, also, B. *dekhit-is* differs from *dekhil-i* and *dekhib-i*. There is, however, sufficient general similarity, and the differences consist mostly in this, that one tense has preserved a more archaic form than the other, thus *dekhildm* preserves Skr. *asmi*, Pr. *amhi*, better than *dekhibo*, *dekhilis* preserves the *s* of *asi*, while *dekhili* and *dekhibi* have rejected it. Thus, while the abrasion of the substantive verb has been carried to so great a pitch in those two languages as almost to obliterate all traces of it, yet, from the general analogy of cognate forms, there is little doubt that we have in the *be* future the Skr. participle in *tavya*. The final *k* in the 3 sing. of B. is a phenomenon for which I have in vain sought an explanation; the most probable one is, I think, that which considers it merely as a *tag*, or meaningless addition, but why a tag should have been added to this person merely, and not to others also, remains to be explained.

§ 54. The two remaining types of the future may appropriately be introduced here. They are certainly participial tenses, though not participial in the same sense or on the same plan as the other tenses discussed in this chapter; they are, in fact, exactly the reverse. Whereas, in the other participial tenses, it is the modern stem which is the participle, and the ancient verbal additions are a present tense, in the two types of future, which we shall now examine, the modern stem is a present tense, and the ancient verbal addition is a participle.

The first of the two is the *ga* type. This consists in adding H. sing. गा *m.*, गी *f.*, pl. गे *m.*, गीं *f.*, to the aorist, and the same in P. except the pl. *f.*, which is गीआं. In the pl. *f.* H. also ordinarily drops the anuswâra. This type is only found in H. and P. The tense runs thus (*sun* "hear"), "I will hear," etc.

H. Sing.	1. सुनूंगा	2. सुनेगा	3. सुनेगा
" Pl.	1. सुनेंगे	2. सुनोगे	3. सुनेंगे
P. Sing.	1. सुनांगा	2. सुनेंगा	3. सुनेगा
" Pl.	1. सुनांगे	2. सुनोगे	3. सुनणगे

If the reader will compare this example with that of the *aorist* in § 33, it will be at once apparent that this tense is formed by adding the syllables *gá, gí*, etc., to that tense. Among the Mahomedans of Delhi and other large cities, this form is used even as a present, and one frequently hears such a word as *haigá*, for *hai* "it is." There can be little doubt that this *gá* is the Skr. p.p. गत, Pr. गदो, गओ, गयो. In H., as mentioned in § 48, the p.p. of *jáná* "to go," is *gayá m.*, and this in the mediæval poets is often shortened to *gá*. The *f.* is गई *gai*, which easily becomes गी, so also pl. *m.* गए becomes गे. The meaning of the tense is thus, "I have gone (that) I may do," a construction which recalls our English idiom "I am going to do," and French "je vais faire." The participial nature of the affix is shown by its being inflected for gender and number in concord with the agent.

This type seems to be of late origin. It is not much, if at all, known or used by the early writers, who, except when they use the future of the *ba* type, generally express a future sense by the aorist only. As this method grew by degrees to be felt insufficient, the participle was added to give greater distinctness.

§ 55. The second type is that which has *l* for its characteristic. Among the classical dialects Marathi only employs this form, and there has been much speculation about the Marathi future by those who only looked to the language itself. It had, however, long been known that a future with this type existed in the Marwári dialect, belonging to the Hindi area, and spoken over a large extent of country in Western Rajputana. The able researches of Kellogg have recently placed us in possession of two more instances of a future of this type spoken in Nepal and by the mountaineers of Garhwál, and Kumaon in the Himalayas, who are by origin Rajputs from the plains. Thus, the Marathi future now no longer stands alone, and we are in a position to compare the whole group of futures of the *la* type (*paṛ* "fall," *mār* "strike," *ho* "be," *suṭ*, *soḍ*).

SINGULAR.

Marwari.	1. पडूंलो	2. पडैलो	3. पडैलो
Garhwali.	1. मारलो	2. मारिलो	3. मारलो
Kumaoni.	1. मारूंलो	2. मारैलो	3. मारलो
Nepali.	1. हुंला	2. होलास	3. होला
Marathi neuter.	1. सुटेन	2. सुटशील	3. सुटेल
Marathi active.	1. सोडीन	2. सोडिशील	3. सोडील

PLURAL.

Marwari.	1. पडांला	2. पडौला	3. पडैला
Garhwali.	1. मारला	2. मारिला	3. मारला
Kumaoni.	1. मारूंला	2. मारला	3. मारला
Nepali.	1. हौंला	2. होला	3. हुनन्
Marathi neuter.	1. सुटूं	2. सुटाल	3. सुटतील
Marathi active.	1. सोडूं	2. सोडाल	3. सोडितील

In these dialects the aorist has had added to it a form लो sing. and ला pl., which does not appear to be inflected for gender, but has only sing. and pl. masc. So far as it goes, however, it directly corresponds to H. and P. *gā*, *ge*, etc., and like them points to a participial origin. In Marathi the inflectional terminations have been dropped, and in some cases even the *la* itself. The 1 sing. of the neuter aorist is सुटें, and adding ल to this, we get सुटेंल, which, being difficult to pronounce, has glided into सुटेन. In the 1 pl., however, the ल has simply been rejected, so that it is the same as the aorist. In the 2 sing. the aorist has सुटस, but, as has already been shown, this is a contraction from सुटसि, and सुटसि + ल =

करसील, from the Marathi habit of lengthening the vowel of a final syllable. In the 2 pl. aorist करा, the ल has neither been fused with the anuswára into न, as in the 1 sing., nor has it altogether dropped out, as in the 1 pl.; but there is no trace of the anuswára; the reason of this is that the anuswára in this person is not organic; the older language has simply á, as करा, and it is to this that the ल has been added, and not to the modern form. The third person singular and plural is still simpler; aor. करे + ल = करेल, and (archaic) करती + ल = करतील. The same process is followed by the active verb exactly.

I look upon this ल as the shortened form of a sing. लो *m.*, ली *f.*, pl. ला *m.*, ली *f.*, of which the feminine is apparently not in use, and I derive it from Skr. √लग्, p.p.p. लग्न, Pr. लग्गो, of which the *gg* has been reduced to *g* according to ordinary practice, and the single *g* has then dropped out, leaving लओ, shortened into लो. This derivation is confirmed by the fact that in all the languages this verb is used in the sense of beginning to do any thing, as in H. करने लगा, "he began to do." In M. especially it is used in a very wide range of applications, and करेल appropriately means "he begins (that) he may do," in other words "he is about to do," "he will do."

§ 56. I give here, for convenience of comparison, a tabular view

I.—Present Par-

Sanskrit पचन् *m.*, पचन्ती *f.*, पचत् *n.*

		Hindi.	Panjabi.	Sindhi.	
				Neuter.	*Active.*
Participle.		देखता °ती	1. जांदा °दी °दे °दीयां	हलंदो °दी	मरींदो °दी
(*a*) declinable.		°ते °तीं	2. मारदा °दी, etc.	°दा °दिउं	°दा °दिउं
(*b*) indeclinable.		देखत देखते	"	"	"
Present (Future, etc.) Tense.	S. 1.			हलंदुसि °दिअसि	मरींदुसि, etc.
	2.	देखता °ती	मारदा °दी	हलंदें °दियें	मरींदें °दियें
	3.			हलंदो °दी	मरींदो °दी
	Pl. 1.			हलंदासीं °दियूं	मरींदासीं, etc.
	2.	देखते °तीं	मारदे °दीयां	हलंदउ °दूं	मरींदउ °दूं
	3.			हलंदा °दूं	मरींदा °दूं

[1] On account of the multiplicity of forms in Marathi, the masculines

of the participles and the participial tenses derived from them.

TICIPLE ACTIVE.

Prakrit चलंतो *m.*, °ती *f.*, °तं *n.*

GUJARATI.	MARATHI.		ORIYA.	BANGALI.
	Neuter.	*Active.*		
छोडतो °ती °तुं	बुडता °ती °तें	सोडिता °ती °तें		
°ता °ती °तां	°ते °त्या °तीं	°ते °त्या °तीं	,,	,,
छोडता °ते	बुडत °तां °तांना	सोडीत °तां °तांना	देखु °न्तु	देखिते
	बुडतों[1]	सोडितों	देखन्ति	देखिताम
छोडतो °ती °तुं	बुडतोस बुडतास	सोडितोस सोडितास	देखन्तु	देखितिस
	बुडतो बुडता	सोडितो सोडिता	देखन्ता	देखित
	बुडतों	सोडितों	देखन्तु	देखिताम
छोडता °ती °तां	बुडतां	सोडितां	देखन्त	देखिता
	बुडतात बुडतें	सोडितात सोडिते	देखन्ते	देखितेन

…ruly of the indicative and conditional are given in this table.

II.—Past Participle Passive.

Sanskrit कृतः *m.*, कृता *f.*, कृतं *n.* Prakrit करिओ *m.*, करी *f.*, करिअं *n.*

		Hindi.	Panjabi.	Sindhi.	Gujarati.	Marathi.		Oriya.	Bangali.
Participle.		मारा -री -रे -री	मारिया -री -रे -रीयां	हणो -णी -णा -णूं	बोल्यो -ली -लुं -ल्या -ली -ल्यां and बोलेलो, etc.	सुटला -ली -ले -ले -ल्या -ली	बोलिला -ली -ले -ले -ल्या -ली	देखिल	देखिल
Past Tense.	S. 1.	मारा -री	मारिया -ई	हणिओमि -यमि	बोल्यो -ली -लुं	सुटलों -लें -लों	बोलिला -ली -लें	देखिलि	देखिनु
	2.			हणिएं -एं	बोलेलो -ली -लुं	सुटलास -लीस -लेस		देखिलु	देखिलि
	3.			हणो -ई		सुटला -ली -लें		देखिला	देखिल
	Pl. 1.	मारे -री	मारे -रीआं	हणिआसीं, etc.	बोल्या -ली -ल्यां	सुटलों	बोलिले -ल्या -ली	देखिलु	देखिलाम
	2.			हणिआउ -यूं	बोलेला -ली -लां	सुटलां		देखिल	देखिला
	3.			हणिआ -यूं		सुटले -ल्या -लीं		देखिले	देखिलेन

III.—Future Participle Passive.

Sanskrit बोधितव्यस् *m.*, ॰व्या *f.*, ॰व्यं *n.* Prakrit बोधिअव्वअ, बोधिअव्वं.

	HINDI.	SINDHI.	GUJARATI.	MARATHI.		ORIYA.	BANGALI.
Participle (Infinitive, etc.).	सुनबे मारिबे	छडणो ॰णी ॰णा ॰णूं	छोडवो ॰वी ॰वुं ॰वा ॰वी ॰वां	सुटावा ॰वी ॰वें ॰वे ॰व्या ॰वीं	सोडावा ॰वी ॰वें ॰वे ॰व्या ॰वीं	देखिबा	देखिबा
	(Bhojpuri.)						
S. 1.	देखब्[1]	छडिंदुसि[1]		सुटावा[2]		देखिबि	देखिब
2.	देखब	छडिंदें		सुटावास		देखिबु	देखिबि
3.	*deest*	छडिंदो	छोडवो, etc.	सुटावा	सोडावा ॰वी ॰वें	देखिब	देखिबे ॰बाह
Pl. 1.	देखब्	छडिंदासीं	छोडवानो, etc.	सुटावे		देखिबु ॰आ	देखिब
2.	देखब	छडिंदउ		सुटावे त		देखिब	देखिबा ॰बे
3.	*deest*	छडिंदा		सुटावे		देखिबे	देखिबेन

[1] See other dialectic forms in § 83.

[2] Only the masculine is given from want of space.

§ 57. The only participial tenses in the Gipsy verb are those formed from the past participle. This participle is sometimes regularly formed from the modern verbal root, and sometimes, as in the other languages, is an early Tadbhava, perpetuating the type of the Prakrit participle.

There are, as in the other languages, three types of this participle ending in (1) *to* or *do*, (2) *lo*, (3) *no*. Examples of the first type are—

andva "to carry,"	ando,	Skr. ânî,	p.p.p.	ânîta, S. ândo.
jivdva "to live,	jivdo,	,, jîv,	,,	jîvita.
kerdva "to do,"	kerdo,	,, kṛi,	,,	kṛita, Pers. karda.
nashdva "to depart,"	nashto,	,, naç,	,,	nashṭa.
chindva "to cut,"	chindo,	,, chhid,	,,	chhinna.

Of the second type—

avdva "to come,"	alo,	,, âyâ,	,,	âyâta, M. âlâ, B. O. âlla.
jâva "to go,"	gelo,	,, yâ,	,,	yâta, M. galâ, B. gela, O. galâ.
dikâva "to see,"	diklo,			B. dekhila, O. dekhilâ.

Of the third type—

dâva "to give,"	dino,	,, dâ,	,,	datta, Pr. dinno, O.-H. dinnâ, dinâ.
lâva "to take,"	lino,	,, labh,	,,	labdha, O.-H. linnâ, linâ.
rovdva "to weep,"	rovno,	,, rud,	,,	rudita, Pr. ruṇṇo, S. runo.
uryâva "to fly,"	uryano,	,, uḍḍî,	,,	uḍḍîna, S. uḍâṇo.

The Aorist is formed by adding the terminations of the old substantive verb, thus from *lino* "taken"—

Sing. 1. linom, 2. linân, 3. linâs,
Pl. 1. linân, 2. linân, 3. linâs "I took," etc.

So from *kerdo* "done," comes

Sing. 1. kerdom, 2. kerdân, 3. kerdâs,
Pl. 1. kerdâm, 2. kerdân, 3. kerdâs "I did," etc.

And from *muklo* "abandoned" (Skr. mukta)—

Sing. 1. muklom, 2. muklân, 3. muklâs,
Pl. 1. muklâm, 2. muklân, 3. muklâs "I left," etc.

This proceeding is strictly analogous in principle to the method employed in Sindhi, to which, of all the Indian languages, that of the Gipsies bears the closest relation.

The future is formed by prefixing to the present tense the word kâma, Skr. kâm "desire," and thus means "I wish to do," etc. Thus kerâva "I do," kamakerâva "I will do," *i.e.* "I wish to do." The prefixed word does not vary for number or person. This method of forming the future is, as Paspati (p. 101) points out, borrowed from modern Greek, in which θέλω contracted to θὲ and θὰ, is used in this way, as θὰ ὑπάγω "I will go." There is nothing strictly analogous to this method in our seven languages, though the futures of the *ga* and *la* types are formed on a not very dissimilar principle.

CHAPTER IV.

THE COMPOUND TENSES.

CONTENTS.—§ 58. Definition of the Compound Tenses and Auxiliary Verbs.—§ 59. The Root AS, Present Tense.—§ 60. Imperfect in Panjabi and Gipsy.—§ 61. AS with a Negative.—§ 62. Compound Tenses formed with AS.—§ 63. The Root ACHH: Discussion as to its Origin.—§ 64. Tenses derived therefrom.—§ 65. Compound Tenses formed therewith.—§ 66. BHÛ;—the Simple Tenses.—§ 67. HÛ;—the Participial Tenses.—§ 68. Compound Tenses formed therewith.—§ 69. STHÂ.—§ 70. VÂ.—§ 71. Ancillary Verbs Defined.—§ 72. Examples of Ancillaries.

§ 58. Further removed from the old synthetical type than either of the preceding classes of tenses is that class which now comes under discussion. It is by means of this class that the seven modern languages, after having rejected the numerous and complicated formations of the Sanskrit verb, have secured for themselves the machinery necessary for the expression of very delicate shades of meaning. So numerous, indeed, are these shades of meaning, and so fine are the distinctions between them, that it is very difficult for a foreigner to catch them.

The tenses in question are constructed by adding to the participles already mentioned various tenses of certain auxiliary verbs, and in a few instances by adding these auxiliaries to the simple present, or aorist. The auxiliaries themselves are modern formations capable of being used alone, and are traceable to well-known Sanskrit roots through processes partly Prakritic and partly post-Prakritic. Pali and the Prakrits carry the verbs in question through certain grades of change.

and the modern languages either preserve the Prakrit form unchanged, or subject it to further changes of their own, such changes being often governed by laws unknown to the Prakrit stage of development.

The roots so employed are √अस्, √भू, √स्था, √या, and another, whose origin is somewhat obscure in Sanskrit, but which appears in Prakrit under the form अच्छ. It will be necessary first to examine each of these roots and draw out the modern forms to be affiliated to each, after which the tenses formed by them may be arranged in order.

§ 59. *As.* This root means "to be," and is the simple copula like Latin *esse* (see under *sthā* in § 12). Only the present tense can be clearly traced in the modern languages, though there are some detached fragments here and there which may possibly represent other tenses. These will be noted further on. In Sanskrit the root belongs to the second or *ad* conjugation, in which the terminations are added direct to the root, thus giving rise to various euphonic changes in accordance with the laws of Sandhi. Pali and the scenic Prakrits, in contradiction to their usual practice of employing the *bhū* type for all roots, retain in this verb the *ad* type. Omitting the dual, the tense runs—

Skr.	Sing.	1. asmi,	2. asi,	3. asti.
"	Pl.	1. smaḥ,	2. stha,	3. santi.
Pa. and Pr.	Sing.	1. asmi, amhi.	2. asi,	3. atthi.
"	Pl.	1. asma, amha.	2. attha,	3. santi.

In Prakrit the initial vowel is often elided as *'mhi, 'mha.* These forms, however, belong to the scenic Prakrit, which, as Pischel has shown, is really almost as artificial a language as Sanskrit, and on comparing the corresponding tense in the modern languages, it seems difficult, if not impossible, to derive it from the scenic forms. We are not justified in assuming that the modern tense was derived, according to different phonetic laws, from those which have guided and effected the transformations of other words in these languages. On the contrary, in the absence of a continuous chain of documents exhibiting the gradual changes that have taken place, we have nothing to guide us but the general principles of phonetic evolution, which we have been able to formulate for ourselves from undoubted instances. We have numerous well-established cases in which the Prakrit, followed by the moderns, has conjugated a verb according to the *bhû* type, though in classical Sanskrit it follows some other conjugation; indeed, it may, I think, be considered as proved that the forms of the *bhû* conjugation have swallowed up all other conjugational types, just as much as those of the *a* stem in nouns have driven out all other declensional forms. In this view there would be strong reasons for postulating the existence of a present tense of √अस् conjugated after the *bhû* type, thus—

Sing. 1. asâmi, 2. asasi, 3. asati.
Pl. 1. asâmaḥ, 2. asatha, 3. asanti.

It is only from such a form as this, the existence of which, though I am not aware of any text in which it is found, may fairly be inferred from analogy, that the modern forms can, in accordance with the ordinary laws of development, be derived.

Beginning with Sindhi as the most archaic, or nearly so, this tense runs thus—

Sing. 1. आंहियां. 2. आंहिं, आंहीं. 3. आहे.
Pl. 1. आंहियूं. 2. आंहियो. 3. आंहिनि.

Now, barring the troublesome superfluity of anunâsikas which the Sindhians have seen fit to bestow on this aorist, the forms are strikingly similar to those of the Sanskrit tense postulated above. The 3 sing. *âhe* is contracted from *ahai*, which, again, is good Prakrit for *asati*, but it could hardly be deduced from *asti*, which, as we have seen, naturally results in

Prakrit *atthi*. The terminations of the other persons agree with those of the aorist of the active verb given in § 33, and those are obviously and admittedly derived from the terminations of the *bhá* type. I am unable to account for the peculiarity of this tense using the forms of the active verb, where we should naturally have expected those of the neuter, आहां, etc. like हुआं, etc. Trumpp does not notice this point, and as I am not in possession of any documents in mediæval Sindhi, I have no materials on which to form an opinion. It is to be hoped that the learned author, in the next edition of his very valuable grammar, will furnish some elucidation of this curious anomaly. This tense is all that remains to us in Sindhi of the Sanskrit substantive verb *as*.

Only the aorist, also, has survived in Marathi, which has—

Sing.	1. आहें,	2. आहेस	3. आहे.
Pl.	1. आहों	2. आहां,	3. आहेत.

These are the regular terminations of the aorist in the neuter verb, only the 1 plural differs slightly, having ओं instead of ऊं. In M., as in S., the initial vowel is lengthened, the reason for which is not obvious, as there has been no loss of consonants requiring compensatory lengthening. M., like S., has only this one tense from *as*. No traces of it are found in G. or O., except in a negative form, which will be treated of in the next section.

Hindi and Panjabi agree very closely in the aorist. Classical Hindi represents, however, a modern development of this tense. In the mediæval writers, and in the present dialects of the eastern and central Hindi area, the older form is preserved thus—

	Singular.		
Old-H.	1. अहउं	2. अहहि	3. अहहि
Avadhi.	1. अहेउँ	2. अहेउ	3. अहै
Bhoj.	1. हूँ, बाँ	2. है	3. है, बा

PLURAL.

Old-H.	1. अहहिं	2. अहहु	3. अहहिं
Avadhi.	1. अही	2. अहौ, अहो	3. अहैं
Riwai.	1. हैं	2. अहिन, हौ	3. अहैन आहीं आ.

The 3 singular in the poets is sometimes written with, and sometimes without, the last *h*, as in Kabir तिहिमा सुभ मारग एक अहइ "There *is* one line of duty in the world" (Ram. lvi. 1), or written as a disyllabic word, as राम नाम अहि निज सारू ॥ "The name of Ram *is* itself the true one" (*ib.* lxiv. 5), or with long *i*, metri gratia, धर्म कहै सब पानी अहई ॥ "Religion, he saith, *is* all (one like) water" (*ib.* lxxiii. 5). The 1 singular occurs in ठहरु सँभारि राम बिचारि कहत अहौं (for अहउँ) जो पुकारि हौ ॥ "Pause and attend, ponder on Ram, thus *I am* calling aloud, oh!" (*ib.* Kah. 7). So also in Tulsi Das, असि मति फिरी अहइ जसि भावी ॥ "Thus her mind *is* changed as fate decrees" (Ay-k. 117), राम चराचर नायक अहहीं ॥ "Ram *is* lord of things moveable and immoveable" (*ib.* 445), बिधि धरम उलटे सब अहहीं "The laws of duty *are* all reversed" (*ib.* 617), सुगम सकल मग तुम्ह कहँ अहहीं "All roads *are* easy to thee" (*ib.* 574).

By aphæresis of the initial *a* we get the ordinary classical Hindi tense—

Sing. 1. हौं, हूँ, 2. है, 3. है. Pl. 1. हैं, 2. हौ, 3. हैं.

The classical language uses हूँ in the 1 sing., but हौं is used in the poets, in Braj, and in the rustic dialects. Between हौं, used as a singular, and हैं, used as a plural, there is the same confusion as in the same persons of the aorist in the ordinary verb (§ 33). The form हौं seems to belong more naturally to a Pr. *ahâmu*, and हैं to *ahâmi*, and we are led to suspect that an inversion of the two words has taken place. Avadhi 2 sing. *ahes* has, like M., a variant *ahas*, both of which lead back to an older *ahasi*, just as 3 sing. *ahai* does to *ahati*. It is obvious that had √*as* not been treated as a *bhû* verb, there would have arisen no such types as *ahai* and *hai*; for *asti* goes into *atthi*, which would have led to something very different.

Panjabi closely follows H., having—

Sing. 1. हां. 2. हैं. 3. है. Pl. 1. हां. 2. हो. 3. हन.

It has also, as noticed in § 54, a form of this tense with the participial addition गा *m.*, गी *f.*, etc., as—

Sing. 1. हांगा. 2. हैंगा. 3. हैगा.
Pl. 1. हांगे. 2. होगे. 3. हनगे "I am," etc.,

where the type of the future is mixed up with that of the present. I have heard this form used mostly at the end of a sentence, where the speaker seems to hesitate, as if he felt the want of something more to say, and ultimately adds a *gá*. It is also used doubtingly, as when you suggest a possible explanation of some difficulty, and your companion answers "well, perhaps it is so"—हैगा.

The same form occurs in the Kanauji dialect of Hindi.

The present of this verb in the dialect of the Rumilian Gipsies (Paspati, p. 80) adheres more closely to the Sanskrit. It runs thus—

Sing. 1. isóm, 2. isán, 3. isi.
Pl. 1. isám, 2. isán, 3. isi.

§ 60. Panjabi has also an imperfect in a great many forms which must apparently be affiliated to this root. First there is a purely participial form—

Sing. 1, 2, 3, सा *m.*, सी *f.*
Pl. से *m.*, सीआं *f.* "I, thou, he was," etc.

Then गा is added as in the present, giving सागा, सीगी, सेगे, सीआंगीआं. I do not remember ever to have heard this form, but it is given in the Ludhiana grammar. One often hears सी, which is properly feminine singular, used for the masculine singular, and plural also. Moreover, there is a defective form having only some of the persons, which looks somewhat inflectional. The singular 2 and 3, and plural 2, are supplied by parts of था.

Sing. 1. आं. Pl. 1. आं. 3. अस, हैस.

To this, also, is added था, thus

Sing. 1. आंथा *m.*, आंथी *f.*

Pl. 1. आंथे *m.*, आंथीयां *f.* 3. असथे *m.*, असथीयां *f.*

Yet another and extremely common form in colloquial usage prefixes है to this type—

Sing. 1. हैआं. 2, 3. हैसी.

Pl. 1, 2. हैथे *m.*, हैथीयां *f.* 3. हैअस.

Most of these forms are dialectic, and, as such, in use only in certain parts of the country. The participial form given first is probably the original; seeing how much the past tenses of the Sanskrit verb had fallen out of use at an early period, we are, perhaps, hardly justified in looking for anything but a participial origin for a modern past tense, and in this view we might postulate a p.p.p. *asita*. On the other hand, however, it so happens that the imperfect of *as* is one of the few imperfects of Skr. verbs, which did live on into the Pali and Prakrit, and the inflectional form of this tense can be phonetically derived therefrom, thus—

Skr. Sing. 1. आसं. 2. आसीः. 3. आसीत्.

Pl. 1. आस्म. 2. आस्त. 3. आसन्.

Pr. Sing. 1. आं. 2. सी. 3. सी.

Pl. 1. आं. — 3. अस.

If we take this view it would seem that the tense was originally inflectional, but that all other verbs in the language having a participial construction, this also was, by the common process of mistaken analogy, considered participial also, and ई being the ordinary termination of the feminine, थी was erroneously taken for a feminine, and a masculine था was invented to suit it, together with the plurals थे and थीं. This reasoning will account also for the fact that थी is often used for the masculine singular. Whether the origin of this multiform tense be participial or inflectional, it is abundantly clear that the present usage of the language presents a mass of confused forms, which, their origin having been forgotten, have become mixed together in great variety.

Here, I would provisionally refer the imperfect in the Braj dialect of Hindi, which is participial in form, and does not vary for person. It is sing. हो *m.*, ही *f.*, pl. हे *m.*, हीं *f.* A variation of this form in Western Rajputana (Márwár) has sing. हो, pl. हा. I think we must see in this form a p.p.p. of *as*, with loss of the initial vowel, and change of स into ह.

So, also, here would, on the same principle, come in two preterites or rather imperfects—

Kanauji. Sing. हतो *m.*, हती *f.*
Pl. हते *m.*, हतीं *f.*, "I, etc., was."
Gujarati. Sing. हतो *m.*, हती *f.*, हतुं *n.*
Pl. हता *m.*, हती *f.*, हतां *n.* *id.*

which appear to come from Pr. present participle संतो "being." The change of meaning from a present to an imperfect has an analogy in the treatment of the corresponding tense of the verb *ho* (§ 67).

The Gipsy language has retained an imperfect of this root, not directly derived from the Skr. imperfect, but formed by the addition of the syllable *as* to the present.[1]

Sing. 1. isómas, 2. isánas, 3. isás (isí + as).
Pl. 1. isámas, 2. isánas, 3. isás.

[1] Paspati, p. 80. Miklosich, vol. II. p. 16, has a long dissertation on the subject, which, however, is very confused and bewildering to read.

This language uniformly makes an imperfect from every root by adding *as* to the present, but the process is so foreign to our Indian languages as to have no interest for us in the present inquiry.

§ 61. The derivatives of *as* in the present tense are in some languages curiously bound up with the negative into a tense which exists in those languages in which there is no trace of the positive form. Thus Oriya, which has no positive present *as*, has a complete negative present, "I am not, etc."

Sing. 1. नुहें. 2. नुह. 3. नुहे.
Pl. 1. नाहुं. 2. नाहु. 3. नाहान्ति.

Here the *u* in the first syllable of the singular is due to some confusion with the tense of *bhû*, to be noted hereafter; but though this form is common in writing, the peasantry often say simply नहे, "he is not." The insertion of this *u* is accounted for by supposing it to have slipped over from the following syllable, thus, *nuhe* would be for *na hue*, and *nuhanti* for *na huanti*. *Nuanti*, and not *nāhānti*, is the older form, as in—

दयला हृदय नुहन्ति निर्दय ।

"Merciful-hearted *they are not*, but pitiless."—Rasak. vi. 18.

There being in O. no positive present from *as*, the survival of the negative present has naturally been accounted for by referring it to the only positive present remaining, namely, that from *bhû*; but this seems to be a false analogy, because, as will be shown later on, in many constructions the negative is used without the *u*, and is generally so used by the rustic classes.

G. has नथी for all persons of both tenses, they say हुं नथी "I am not," तुं नथी "thou art not," ते नथी "he is not." This is a case of forgetfulness of the origin of a word leading to its use being extended to cases where it has no right to be, for

नाहीं is clearly derived from नास्ति, the Pr. form of अस्ति with न prefixed, and thus, strictly speaking, belongs only to the 3 sing.

The negative of *as* is kept distinct from that of *bhû* in Marathi, the former runs thus—

Sing. 1. नाहीं. 2. नाहींस. 3. नाहीं. Pl. 1, 2. नाहीं, 3. नाहींत.

In Hindi नहि and नहीं are used to mean simply "not," and if they ever had any verbal meaning, have now quite lost it. In Sindhi the negative prefixed merely coalesces with it, without in any way influencing it, or bringing about any change in its form; thus नाहे or नआहे "he is not."

§ 62. The present tense from *as* is added to the simple and participial tenses of the neuter, active, or causal stem, to form a class of compound tenses, having significations somewhat more definite than the participial tenses when used alone. In some cases, however, no additional strength of meaning seems to be gained. In the following examples it will suffice to quote the 3 singular in each tense, from which the reader can form the rest for himself.

Hindi adds the present of *as* to the present and past participles of the ordinary verb, to form a definite present and definite preterite respectively, as—

Def. Present देखता है "he is seeing."
Def. Preterite देखा है "he has seen."

Colloquially, also, one sometimes hears a tense formed from the aorist of the verb, and that of the auxiliary, as आवे है "he comes." This usage prevails more in the Western Hindi area, where the language is transitional to Gujarati, and is not approved of in classical speech.[1]

[1] Kellogg, p. 206.

Panjabi has the following:—

Def. Present जांदा है "he is going."

Def. Imperfect जांदा सा "he was going."

Def. Preterite गिया है "he has gone."

Pluperfect गिया सा "he had gone."

Sindhi has, like Hindi, the two definite tenses:—

Def. Present वञंदो आहे "he is going."

Def. Preterite वञियो आहे "he has gone."

Marathi has a wider range; it forms two separate tenses, one from the indeclinable, another from the declinable form of its present participle, a definite perfect from its past participle, and a sort of future with its noun of agency (§ 75). In the last-named instance, however, we have hardly a tense, but rather a participial construction—

Def. Present लिहित आहे "he is writing."

„ (Emphatic) लिहितो आहे "he is writing."

Def. Preterite लिहिला आहे "he has written."

Future लिहिणार आहे "he is about to write."

The other languages having no traces of this auxiliary, naturally have no tenses formed by it.

§ 63. *ACHH.*—This root must be taken next, in order to preserve the natural sequence of tenses in the modern verbs. It has been customary hitherto to accept without inquiry the assumption that the auxiliaries of this form are derived from *as*; but there are considerable difficulties in the way of admitting this view, which appears, as far as I can trace it back, to have arisen from Vararuchi, xii. 19 (*Śauraseni*), *asterachchha*. But the next sûtra gives *tipatthi*, as far as we can see from the very corrupt state of the text, and the parallel passage from the Sankshipta Sâra (Lassen, App. p. 51) gives only *atthi*, though fragments of a present tense *achchhai*, etc., are quoted by LASSEN (p. 340) from the latter authority. By his reference to p. 260, the author would seem to favour a derivation from *asti* by inversion *atsi*, as *ts* we know (Vol. I. p. 317) migrates into च्छ, but this will not account for the other persons of the tense.

It does not, however, follow that Vararuchi, in quoting *achchh* as an equivalent for *as*, ever meant that the former was phonetically evolved from the latter. He is merely giving us the popular equivalent of the classical word. Just in the same way he tells us (viii. 68) that *vuḍḍa* and *khuppa* are used for Skr. *majj*, but no one supposes that *vuḍḍa* can, by any known process of phonetic change, be *derived* from *majj*. It is simply a popular word used instead of a refined one. So, also, when he tells us that *achchh* is used instead of *as*, we are not bound to believe that he means to say that the former is derived from the latter, but simply that it is in use side by side with it. Hemachandra, in the same way, gives many popular equivalents of Skr. roots, which are not derivatives from those roots.

Weber, Hala, p. 41, rejects, and with justice, the idea of any connection between the two words, and suggests that *acch* is a form of *gach* (√ gam), "to go." This view is supported by citations from the Bhâgavati (i. 411, etc.), as e.g. *acchejja vâ ciṭṭhejja vâ nisîeyya vâ uyaṭṭejja*, "Let him go, or stand, or sit down, or rise up." In the examples quoted from the Saptaśatakam, however, the word bears more often the opposite meaning of standing still; and often may be rendered by either one or the other; thus—

> tuppâṇaṇâ kino ac-
> chasi tti ia pucchiâi vahuâi.—Sapt. 291.

Here Weber translates, "Why *goest* thou with anointed face?" but the scholiast has *kiṃ tiṣṭhasi*, "why *standest* thou?" The general meaning of the passage is merely "why *art thou*" thus, *i.e.* "why have you got your face anointed?" So in 344, *osamattamanorahaiṃ acchanti mithunaiṃ*, it must be rendered, "They *are* (or stand) with their desires unfulfilled." In another passage, 169, it has still more unmistakeably the meaning of *stay*:

> acchaü tâva maṇaharaṃ
> piyâi muhadaṃsaṇaṃ aimahagghaṃ
> taggâmachettasîmâ
> vi jhatti diṭṭha suhâvei,

literally, "Let stand (or let be) the heart-entrancing, very precious sight of the *face* of my love, even the boundary of the fields of her village, when seen, straightway delights." He means a sort of hyperbole, as we might say, "Her face delights, said I? not her face merely—(or, let alone her face)—why even the sight of the village where she lives delights." Here *acchaü* is 3 singular imperative; the idiom is in common use in modern speech; thus in O. they would say *tâku dekhibâ thâü, tâhâr grâm sîmâ madhya dekhibâ ânand ate*, "Let the seeing of her stand aside, the seeing of her village boundary merely is delight." It is like the use of the word *âstâm* in Sanskrit. Parallel to the use of O. थाउ in this construction is that of थाकुक in B. Thus, Bhârat Chandra—

> उपोषे उपोषे लोक हैल मृत प्राय ।
> थाकुक आहार कथा जल नाहि पाय ॥

> "From long fasting the folk were nearly dead,
> *Let alone* food, they could not (even) get water."—Mânsingh, 440.

Literally, "Let the matter of food *stand* (aside)," see § 60. In the Chingana or Gipsy also *ach* means "to remain," "to stand." Thus, *opré pirende achâva*, "I stand on my feet," or simply, "I stand," Paspati "se tenir debout;" *achilo korkoro* "he remained alone," *ate achilom* "here I am," literally "here I have remained;" *achen devlésa* "remain with God," "good-bye" (*i.e.* "God be with ye"). Pasp. "Salutation très-commune parmi les Tchinguianés."

Not to multiply examples, the use of this verb in a sense which, whatever its original meaning, has become almost equivalent to that of "being," is well established in the Jaina Prakrit and in Hâla. The aphæresis of an initial consonant is rare. In scenic Prakrit it is confined almost entirely to the root ज्ञ (*jñâ*), as in *âṇâi* = *jâṇâi*, *âṇabedi* = *âjñâpayati*, etc. Also in *uṇo* = *punaḥ*, and a few other words.

But I would suggest that this word may after all be nothing more than a form of Skr. √अक्ष् *aksh*, "to appear." This root seems to have borne in Skr. rather the meaning of "to reach, pervade" (see Williams's Dict. s.v.), but if we are to connect with it अक्षि "eye," as seems probable, the meaning of "to see," or "to appear," would be natural to it. It will be shown presently that the various languages have forms ending in छ, च, and ख, and all these three forms phonetically point to an earlier क्ष.[1]

Leaving Prakrit scholars to decide whence comes this stem अच्छ् or अछ् (Weber writes it in both ways), we may, I think, start from the fact that there is such a stem in Prakrit, and we have the opinion of a high authority for disputing its connection with अक्ष्. Indeed, as has already been shown, अक्ष् so regularly passes into अख् in the moderns, that it is difficult to conceive by what process it could ever have become अच्छ्. I

[1] Hemachandra's evidence seems conclusive against any connection between *acch* and *gam*, for he has a sûtra to the effect that words of the class *gam* take the termination *chha*; the list consists of the four words *gacchai* (*gam*), *icchai* (*ish*), *jacchai* (*yam*), and *acchai* (?).—Pischel, Hem., iv. 215. If *acchai* were only *gacchai*, with loss of the initial consonant, it would hardly be given as a separate instance of the rule. In another passage occurs a use of this word exactly similar to that from Hala quoted above—

jâmahim visamî kajjagaî jîvâṇam majjhe ei
tâmahim acchaü iaru jaṇu suaṇu vi antaraṃ dei,

"As long as [your] circumstances in life go badly (literally 'as long as a difficult condition of affairs goes in life'), so long, let alone (acchaü) the base man, even the good man keeps aloof (literally 'gives an interval')." "Tempora si fuerint nubila, solus eris." Kajjagaî = kâryagati, iaru = itara.

have preferred to treat it as a separate stem altogether, and I think this treatment will be found to be to a very great extent justified by the examples from the modern languages which I shall now adduce.

§ 64. Classical Hindi, Panjabi, and Sindhi, do not retain any traces of this root. M. has, however, a complete verb बस्, which we should refer, I think, to this root, resting on the well-known peculiarity of M., by which it changes च, especially when derived from an earlier त्स, into स (Vol. I. p. 218). The Sanskrit √*as* having in M. become *âhe*, an affiliation concerning which there can be no doubt, we are driven to seek for a different origin for M. *bas*, and we find it appropriately and in full accordance with known phonetic processes in वच्छ्. M. has the following tenses:—

1. Aorist—

Sing.	1. बसें,	2. बसस,	3. बसे.
Pl.	1. बसूं,	2. बसां,	3. बसत.

where the terminations exactly correspond with those of the aorist in the ordinary verb.

2. Simple imperative—

Sing.	1. बसूं,	2. बस, बैस,	3. बसो.
Pl.	1. बसूं,	2. बसा,	3. बसोत.

3. Simple future—

Sing.	1. बसेन,	2. बससील,	3. बसेल.
Pl.	1. बसूं,	2. बसाल,	3. बसतील.

4. Present formed with present participle and Sanskrit substantive verb—

Masc. Sing.	1. बसतों,	2. बसतोस,	3. बसतो.
Pl.	1. बसतों,	2. बसतां,	3. बसतात.

5. Conditional similarly formed. Sing. 3 masc. असता, etc., as in the ordinary verb.

6. Preterite formed with p.p.p. similar to conditional. Sing. 3 masc. असला, etc.

7. Subjunctive formed with future p.p. Sing. 3 masc. असावा, etc.

Oriya comes next, with an aorist of old simple present only, which is thus conjugated—

Sing.	1. अछि.	2. अछु.	3. अछि.
Pl.	1. अछुं.	2. अछ.	3. अछन्ति.

There being no formation from √as in O., this tense does duty for the simple "I am, thou art," etc. With lengthening of the first vowel, in accordance with its usual practice, Bengali has a present, and an imperfect; but in modern times the initial long vowel of the latter has been entirely dropped, so that we now have—

Present	Sing.	1. आछि,	2. आछिस,	3. आछे "I am," etc.
	Pl.	1. आछि.	2. आछ,	3. आछेन.
Imperfect	Sing.	1. छिनु.	2. छिलि,	3. छिल "I was," etc.
	Pl.	1. छिलाम,	2. छिला.	3. छिलेन.

Though used as an imperfect, this latter tense is in form a preterite, corresponding to *dekhinu*, etc., of the regular verb. The loss of the initial *â* is comparatively recent, for it is retained in so late a poet as Bhârat Chandra (A.D. 1711–1755). आछिल किशर डाल मदन मदैते "She was (*i.e.* had been) very wanton in her youth" (Bidya-S. 246). It is common enough, also, in the other Bengali poets, कि नाना वैलाथ फिर आछिल तोमार "What vicissitudes were experienced by you" (Kasi-M. 284), and the poets of the present day freely permit themselves the use of this form as a poetic licence when their metre requires it.

Passing westwards from Bengal, we come to the extreme

eastern limits of Hindi, in the Maithila province (Tirhut, Purnia, etc.), where the rustic dialect has the following present:

Sing. 1. छूं. 2. छु. 3. छै. Pl. 1. छूं. 2. छ. 3. छै.

It has also a feminine singular छी, plural छीं, uninflected for person.

Close to the Bengali frontier, near the junction of the Mahanandâ and Kankai rivers, they speak a curious sort of mixture of Hindi and Bengali, and have a present—

Sing. 1. छि. 2. छिस. 3. छए. Pl. 1. छि. 2. छे. 3. छै.

Further west, in the same district, one hears—

Sing. 1. छौं. 2. छं. 3. छए. Pl. 1. छि. 2. छौ. 3. छाए.

In Bhojpuri, for the present is often heard खे, which is unchanged throughout both persons. This widely-used form seems to confirm the supposition of the derivation from अक्ष्, for क्ष changes both to छ and to ख.

From the Himalayan districts of Kumâon and Garhwâl, Kellogg (p. 201) gives a present of this verb, and it is in use in Eastern Rajputana. It is also the ordinary substantive verb in Gujarati—

SINGULAR.

Kumâon.	1. छौं, छूं	2. छै	3. छ.
Garhwâl.	1. छौं	2. छ, छै	3. छ.
E. Rajputana.	1. छूं	2. छै	3. छै.
Gujarati.	1. छुं	2. छे	3. छे.

PLURAL.

Kumâon.	1. छूं, छौं	2. छा	3. छन, छौं.
Garhwâl.	1. छौं, छवाऊं	2. छव, छवाई	3. छन.
E. Rajputana.	1. छां	2. छो	3. छै.
Gujarati.	1. छइये	2. छो	3. छे.

The first and third of these have also a preterite participle in type like most of the preterites. Thus in Kumaon they say sing. छियो, pl. छिया or छ्या, which seems to point to a Skr. p.p.p. चक्षित = Pr. चच्छिओ. In Eastern Rajputana there is sing. छो, pl. छा.

Although modern classical Hindi does not use this root, yet it is found with the initial vowel in the shape of an indeclinable present participle in the old poets, as in Tulsi's Ramayan—

आपु अछत जुबराज पद रामहि देहु नरेसु

"Thyself remaining, give the heir-apparentship to Ram, O king!"
—Ay-k. 11.

That is, "during thy lifetime," literally "thou being." The dictionary-writers erroneously give this as a Tadbhava from अक्षत, with which it has nothing to do.

It is worthy of consideration whether the forms of the imperfect in P. given in § 60 should not be referred to this root rather than to *as*. The change of छ into ह so characteristic of M. would thus find a parallel in Panjabi.

Gujarati has also a present participle indeclinable छतां and छते "(in) being," and declinable छतो *m.*, ती *f.*, तुं *n.*; pl. छता *m.*, ती *f.*, तां *n.* "being."

§ 65. The compound tenses formed by the addition of this auxiliary are most numerous, as might be expected, in Marathi, that language having a larger range of tenses of the auxiliary itself than the sister-tongues. First, a present habitual is formed by adding the present of the auxiliary to the present participle of the verb, as राहत असतो "he is living," *i.e.* "he habitually resides," लिहीत असतों "I am (always employed in) writing."

Next, a past habitual, by adding the aorist of the auxiliary to the present tense, as बसत असे "he was in the habit of sitting." It will be remembered that in M. the aorist has the sense of a past habitual in modern times. This compound tense seems to differ very little in meaning from the simple tense.

There is also a compound present of the conditional, wherein the leading verb is in the present participle and the auxiliary in the conditional present. It is used with अर "if" prefixed, either expressed or understood, as अर काम करीत असता "If he *were doing* the work," पाऊस पडत असता "(If) rain were to fall (as it is now falling)." The same tense of the auxiliary, when used with the past participle, serves as a conditional preterite, as पडला असता "he would have fallen (if, etc.)."

With the preterite of the auxiliary and the present participle of the leading verb is constructed a present dubitative, as तो जात असला तर हें काम त्याला सोंपा "If he *should be going*, then entrust this affair to him." Similarly, with the same part of the auxiliary and the past participle of the leading verb is made a past dubitative or pluperfect, as तो आला असला तर "Should he have arrived, then, etc."

So, also, with the future participle and the past auxiliary, as अर तो जाणार असला तर मला सांग "Should he be about to go, then tell me."

The future of the auxiliary also forms three tenses with the present, past, and future participles of the leading verb respectively. It is difficult to give these tenses any definite name; the senses in which they are employed will be seen from the following examples:—

1. Present participle of verb + future of auxiliary—

   तुझा बाप तुझी वाट पाहत असेल "Your father *will be waiting* for you" (*i.e.* is probably now expecting you: *vāṭa pāhat*="looks at the road," idiomatic for "expects").

2. Past participle of verb + future of auxiliary—

   तो आला असेल "He will have come" (*i.e.* "has probably arrived by this time").

3. Future participle of verb + future of auxiliary—

मी लिहिणार असेन "I may be now going to write" (*i.e.* "I shall probably be writing presently").

The above is a fair illustration of the remark which I have frequently made before, that the modern verb, while throwing aside all the intricacies of the synthetical system of tenses, still manages to lose nothing of its power of expressing minute shades of meaning. On the contrary, by its almost unlimited power of forming compound tenses, it obtains a fullness and delicacy of expression, which even the synthetic verb cannot rival. Indeed, this fullness is at times somewhat embarrassing, for the subtle distinctions between one tense and another are very difficult to grasp, and, as might be expected, careless or uneducated speakers are unable to observe them accurately. The minute analysis of these various tenses belongs to the domain of syntax rather than to that of formlore, and a very long dissertation might be written upon the numerous shades of meaning involved in each one of them. The selection, for instance, of the different parts of the leading verb and auxiliary depends, to a great extent, upon the method of reasoning employed unconsciously by the speaker. These compound tenses are, in fact, rather phrases than tenses, and much depends upon whether the speaker regards the action as already past, or as actually being done with reference to the rest of the sentence. When we translate one of these phrases into English, or any other language, we do not really translate, but substitute our own way of expressing the idea for the native way. A literal word-for-word translation would be almost unintelligible. Thus, in the sentence above, *Rám ját asalá, tar tẽ kám tyálá sángá*, the words are actually, "Ram going was, then that affair to him tell," where the speaker, as it were, pictures to himself that his messenger, after receiving orders, goes to Ram and finds that he was just going, and therefore tells him the affair. Complicated and of course unconscious undercurrents of thought like this underlie much of the elaborate mechanism of the compound tenses in all our seven languages, and we often find natives of India who can speak English composing in our language elaborate sentences of this sort, to the entire disregard of our English idioms, because they think in Hindi or Marathi, and then translate the idea into English. This fact, which all observant Englishmen who have lived long in India must have noticed, lies at the root of much of the difficulty which our countrymen experience in making themselves understood by natives. They think in English, and render word for word into Hindi or Marathi; thus probably producing a sentence which means something widely different from what they intended. It is the same with all foreign languages; until a man learns to *think* in the foreign language, and utter his thoughts in the shape that they have in his mind, he can never hope to speak idiomatically. In seeking to explain the compound tenses of the modern Indian verb, therefore, it is necessary to analyze the connection and sequence of mental impressions to which they owe their origin, a task for the metaphysician, and not for the student of comparative philology.

Gujarati has also a plethora of compound tenses, but they are less complicated than Marathi, perhaps because the language has been less cultivated. In the simpler languages delicate nuances of expression do not exist, and if one wishes to translate any such phrases into one of these simple languages, it must be done by a long string of sentences. Thus, in trying to exact from a wild forester of the Orissa hills an answer to the question, "Did you know that Ram had run away before you went home or afterwards?" one has to go to work in this way, "Ram fled?" Answer, *ho!* (Yes). "You know that fact?" *ho!* "You went home?" *ho!* "When you reached home they told you 'Ram is fled,' thus?" answer *nā! nā!* (No! No!).

"When you did not go home, before that, they told you?" *ho!* So to get out the meaning of the Marathi sentence quoted above, "If he should be going, then entrust this affair to him," one would have to say, "Near him you having gone, he 'I am now going' having said, this word having heard this matter to him you will tell." Perhaps in citing an Orissa wild man of the woods, I am taking an extreme case; but the remarks will hold good, more or less, for all the peasantry and lower classes all over India, and it must be remembered that the expression "lower classes" means in India eight-tenths of the whole population.

The compound tenses formed with the auxiliary छे in G. are the following :—

1. Definite present; aorist of verb + aorist of auxiliary, as करे छे "he does."

Sometimes both verb and auxiliary lose their final vowel, as कर छ for करे छे "thou dost," करे छ "he does." करो छ for करो "ye do," etc.

2. Definite preterite; p.p. of verb + aorist of auxiliary, as आप्यो छे "he has given," active used in *karma* construction with instrumental of subject. तेणे काम बजाव्युं छे "he has performed the work:" neuter in *kartá*, as हुं चढ्यो छुं "I have ascended."

3. Another definite preterite with the second form of the p.p. in *elo*, as चडेलो छुं "I have ascended." There seems to be no great difference of meaning between this and the last.

4. Definite future; future participle of verb + aorist of auxiliary, as खानारो छे "he is about to eat."

5. Another tense with the second form of the fut. part. in *váno*, as हुं करवानो छुं "I am going to do." The uninflected form of the future participle in *ár* may also be used, as तुं शुं करनार छे "What art thou going to do?" These definite futures differ from the simple future in implying intention and

definite purpose, much as in German *er will thun* differs from *er wird thun*.

The auxiliary है is sometimes also used after another auxiliary derived from *bhû*, as छोड़ती होत है "he is (now) loosing." Of the tenses so formed more will be said further on.

It seems from comparing the examples given of these tenses that there is not for each one of them a distinct special meaning, but that they are used somewhat vaguely, the auxiliary being added or omitted at pleasure. This is certainly the case in Hindi, as will be seen below; and in the poets, who are our only guides for the mediæval period, metrical necessities, rather than any desire to bring out a particular shade of meaning, appear to determine which form shall be used.

Those dialects of Hindi which possess tenses from this root, use them also as auxiliaries.[1] Eastern Rajputana has the definite present formed by the two aorists, that of the verb and that of the auxiliary, मारूं छूं "I am beating," also a preterite composed of the p.p. of the verb and aorist of auxiliary, as मारयो छै "I have beaten." There seems to be some anomaly in this latter, for in the preterite of the active verb छै is added to all six persons, whereas, when used with the substantive verb छौ "be," the auxiliary is participial sing. छो, pl. छा. Perhaps we hardly know enough of these rustic forms as yet to be able to draw accurate distinctions.

Garhwali forms its definite present from the present participle and the aorist मारदो (or मारदू) छौं "I am beating;" and its preterite in the same way from the p.p. and aorist मारे छ "he has beaten," मारा छन "they have beaten." So does Kumaoni, present मारनु छूं, preterite मारो छु; but in these, also, there is still room for more accurate analysis, and a wider range of observations requires to be made in remote and little known parts of the country.

[1] Kellogg, Grammar, p. 240.

Bengali has four well-defined tenses. The definite present and imperfect are formed respectively by incorporating the aorist and imperfect of the auxiliary into one word with the locative case of the present participle, thus—

Def. Present দেখিতেছি "I am seeing" (dekhite + âchhi).
Def. Imperfect দেখিতেছিনু "I was seeing" (dekhite + [â]chhinu).

In the latter of these tenses the 1 pl. has in ordinary speech to a great extent usurped the place of the 1 sing., and we more frequently hear—

দেখিতেছিলাম "I was seeing" (dekhite + [â]chhilâm).

By incorporating the same tenses of the auxiliary into one word with the conjunctive participle (see § 73), it forms a definite preterite and a pluperfect, as

Def. Preterite দেখিয়াছি "I have seen" (dekhiyâ + âchhi).
Pluperfect দেখিয়াছিনু "I had seen" (dekhiyâ + âchhinu).

Here, also, দেখিয়াছিলাম is common for 1 sing. Wonderful corruptions occur in pronunciation in these tenses: ছ loses its aspirate and becomes চ, so that we hear for করিতেছে a word that sounds *kŏrche*, and may be written কর্চে, for হইতেছে "is" vulgo *hŏche* (হচ্চে), for দেখিয়াছে *dekhiche* (দেখিচে), and for দেখিয়াছিলাম *dekhichilĕm*, or *dekh'chilĕm* (দেখিচিলেম ?). So also for চলিতেছে "goes" *chalŏche* (চলচে). These forms are freely used in conversation by educated persons, and some recent authors of comic novels and plays introduce them into the mouths of their characters. The same remark applies to all tenses of the verb, and it is a curious subject for speculation, whether the growth of literature will arrest the development of these forms, or whether they will succeed in forcing their way into the written language, and displace the longer and fuller forms now in use. If the latter event takes place, we shall see enacted before our eyes the process of simplification which has been so fertile a cause of the formation of the present types in the whole neo-Aryan group. I anticipate, however, that the purists, aided by the conservative influence of a literature already copious, will ultimately carry the day against the colloquial forms.

Oriya has the four tenses corresponding to Bengali, but only two of them are formed with the auxiliary we are now discussing, the definite present and the definite preterite—

Def. Present करु अछि "I am doing" (pres. part. *karu* "doing").

Def. Preterite करि अछि "I have done" (p.p. *kari* "done").

Here, also, colloquially, the auxiliary is generally incorporated with the verb, and they say करुछि and करिछि respectively. In the south of the province, also, the older form of the present participle in न्ते prevails, and one hears करन्ति "he is doing," and contracted अन्ति "he is."

§ 60. *BHU*. This widely-used root took as early as the Pali and Prakrit period the form *HO*; and in that form it has come down to modern times. As the ordinary substantive verb "to be," it has a full range of tenses in all the languages, and it not only serves as an auxiliary, but takes to itself the tenses of the other auxiliaries like any other verb. In the latter capacity it need not here be discussed, as the remarks which have been made concerning the ordinary verbs will apply to this verb also.

Although *ho* is the general form of this root in all the Indian languages, yet there are one or two exceptions in which the initial *bh* is retained. In Pali, both *bhavati* and *hoti* are found for 3 sing. pres., *abhavâ* and *ahuvâ* impf., *bhavatu* and *hotu* impt., and in Sauraseni Prakrit we find *bhodu*=*bhavatu*, *bhavia* =*bhûtvâ*, and the like. Distinct traces of the retention of the *bh* are still in existence in some rustic dialects of Hindi, and in the old poets. In the latter, a p.p.p. sing. भयौ *m.*, भई *f.*, pl. भए, is extremely common, used alone as a preterite, or with the verbal endings, as भयेउ, भयउ, etc. It is also contracted into भौ; and in the modern form भया "was," may be heard commonly in the mouths of the lower orders all over the Hindi area of the present time. This form presupposes a Pr. भविओ = a Skr. भवित, with elision of the व, and य called in to fill up the hiatus. I give from Kellogg the dialectic forms (Gr. p. 230)—

SINGULAR.

Kanauji.[1]	1. 2. 3. भयो *m.*, भई *f.*		
Braj.	*id.* भयौ *m.*, *id.*		
Old-Pūrbī.	1. भयउँ *m.*, भा, भइउँ *f.*	2. भयउ *m.* भइ *f.*	3. भयउ *m.*, भा भइ *f.*
Avadhī.	1. भयेउँ *m.*, भया, भयिउँ *f.*	2. भयेस *m.* भयिसि *f.*	3. भवा, भया *m.* भइ, भै *f.*
Riwāī.	1. 2. 3. भा, भ.		
Bhojpurī.	1. भोइलों, भैलों,	2. भैल,	3. भैलस, भैल.

PLURAL.

Kanaujī.[1]	1. 2. 3. भए *m.*, भईं *f.* (also भये *m.*).		
Braj.	*id.*		
Old-Pūrbī.	1. भये, भै *m.* भईं *f.*	2. भये, भयेउ *m.* भई, भइउ *f.*	3. भये, भै *m.* भईं *f.*
Avadhī.	1. भये *m.* भै *f.*	2. भये *m.* भयिउ *f.*	3. भयें *m.* भयेनि *f.*
Riwāī.	1. 2. 3. भयेन, भयेन्ह.		
Bhojpurī.	1. भोइलीं, भैलीं.	2. भैलह,	3. भैलन.

The verbal affixes are the same as those in the ordinary verb explained at § 33. Chand uses the same form as in Braj and

[1] Kanauji may be taken to mean the speech of the country between the Ganges and Jumna, the heart of the Hindi land; Braj, that of the right bank of the Jumna; Old-Pūrbī, of the country north of the Ganges from the Gandak river eastwards; Avadhī, that of Oudh (Avadh); Riwāī, of the country south of the Ganges and between the Chambal and the Son rivers. Braj and Old-Pūrbī are the dialects in use in the mediæval poets generally.

Kanauji, thus भयौ कोपि तामस तोम ॥ "He *became* violently disturbed with anger" (Pr. R. i. 48), अनंगपाल भयौ राय ॥ "Anangpál *became* King" (iii. 17), पुब्ब कथा ज्यौं भई । सो कहौं अद्भुत ॥ "How the former matter *happened*, listen while I tell the wonderful tale" (iii. 15), पुत्र होत भई मृत्त ॥ "While the son was being (born), she *became* dead" (i. 170), भए आदि अंत कवित्त जिते । "As many poems as *have* *been* (written) first and last" (i. 10), भए विकल घाइल घ(ा)यल ॥ "The folk *became* distressed, (being) wounded and beaten!" (xxi. 5). Contracted मन भौ हास बहुरि पुनि आइय ॥ "Laughter *became* (arose) in her mind, then after pity came" (iii. 19). The use of this tense is so common in Chand as to supersede the other form of the preterite हुआ to a great extent.

A few examples may be added from Kabir: दुतिया नाम पारवति भयऊ । तप करता संकर को दयऊ ॥ "Her second name *was* Párvati, the ascetic (*i.e.* Daksha) gave her to Śankara" (Ram. 20, 5). एकै पुरुष एकहै नारी । तातें खानि चार भौ चारी ॥ "One male (energy), one female, from them *were* *produced* four kinds of living beings" (*ib.* 6), एक अंड ओंकार तें यह सब जग भयौ पसार "From one egg, the word *Om*, all this world *has* *been* created" (*ib.* 8). In these three quotations all three forms of the participle are used side by side.

Tulsi Das does not confine himself to Old-Pûrbi forms, but uses, also, those classed above under Braj, as भर्यौ बहोरि भयौ तेहि खारा "It filled again and thus *became* salt (*i.e.* the sea)" (Lanka-k. 3), सेतुबंध भइ भीर अति । "The Setubandh *became* very crowded" (*ib.* 10). But the Pûrbi form is more common, as in माथ नाइ पूछत अस भयऊ "Bowing his head, thus he *was* asking" (Kis-k. 2), करि दंडवत कहत अस भयऊ "Making salutation, thus he *was* saying" (Ar-k. 259). The contracted form is also very common, as भे मन मुदित पाइ प्रिय साथू । "He became (or was) enraptured at meeting with the beloved" (Ay-k. 441).

Closely connected with the Bhojpuri भैल is the form भेल, used by the half-Bengali half-Maithil poet Bidyapati, as in सून भेल मन्दिर सून भेल नगरी ।, सून भेल दशदिश सून भेल सगरी ॥ "Empty *has become* the temple, empty has become the city, empty have become the ten regions, empty has become everything!" (Pr. K.S. 118), कोकिल कलरवे मति भेल भोरा । "From the sound of the koil's notes my mind has become distracted" (*ib.* 120). It does not vary for gender or person.

I am not aware of the existence in any of the other languages of this type with the initial *bh*. It is, as far as I have been able to ascertain, confined to the rustic Hindi dialects mentioned above. In all other respects Hindi keeps to the type *ho*, like the cognate languages.

The aorist has the following forms:—

	SINGULAR.			PLURAL.		
Hindi.	1. होऊं	2. होए	3. होए.	1. होएं	2. होओ	3. होएं.
P.	1. होवां	2. होवें	3. होवे.	1. होवीए	2. होवो	3. होवन.
S.	1. हुआं	2. हुएं	3. हुए.	1. हूं	2. हुओ	3. हुअनि.
G.	1. होउं	2. होय	3. होय.	1. होइये	2. होओ	3. होय.
M.	1. होईं	2. होईस	3. होई.	1. होऊं	2. व्हा	3. होतील.
O.	1. होइं	2. हेउ	3. हुए.	1. हेउं	2. हुअ	3. हुअंति.
B.	1. हइ	2. हओ	3. हय.	1. हइ	2. हओ	3. हन.

In Hindi this tense, as mentioned before, is frequently used as a potential in all verbs, and especially so in *ho*, where, owing to the existence of an aorist with signification of "I am," etc., from *as*, the tense derived from *ho* is more usually employed to mean "I may be." The Pàrbatia or Nepali dialect also uses this tense as a potential, thus—

Sing. 1. हुँ. 2. होस. 3. हो. Pl. 1. हुँ. 2. हौ. 3. हुन.

Several peculiarities call for notice in this tense. In classical Hindi there is the usual diversity of practice always observed in stems ending in *á* or *o*, as regards the method of joining the terminations. Thus we have for 1 sing. हौं in addition to होवुं; 2 and 3 sing. are written होय, होय, होवै, and है; 1 and 3 pl. होवं, होय, होवैं, हैं; 2 pl. हौ as well as होवौ, which makes it identical with the same person in the aorist of *as*.

Dialectically the chief peculiarity, which, like most dialectic forms, is merely an archaism preserved to modern times, consists in the hardening of the final *o* of *ho* into *e*. This is observable in the Rajputana dialects, and partially also in that of Riwâ (Kellogg, p. 233).

	SINGULAR.			PLURAL.		
Rajp.	1. हैजं	2. है	3. है	1. हैवां	2. हैवो	3. है.
Riwâ.		2. हास	3. हाय.		2. हाव	3. हांय.

This peculiarity is more marked in the simple future noted below. It also occurs in M., where the aorist, as shown above, when used as a past habitual = "I used to be," takes the terminations of the active verb; but when used as a simple present, those of the neuter, as—

Sing. 1. होय 2. होस 3. होय. Pl. 1. हों 2. हां 3. होत.

The same combination occurs throughout this tense when used negatively = "I am not," as—

Sing. 1. नव्हे 2. नव्हेस 3. नव्हे.
Pl. 1. नव्हों 2. नव्हां 3. नव्हेत (नव्हत).

and in other parts of the verb affirmative and negative.

In Sindhi this root is throughout shortened to *ho*, and when the vowel is lengthened by the influence of affixes, it becomes *hâ*, rarely *ho*, except in poetry, where 3 sing. होइ is met instead of अहे. The *j*, which in some forms of Prakrit is inserted between the stem and its termination, appears here also, as—

Sing. 1. आजां 2. आजें 3. आजे. Pl. 1. आजूं 2. आजो 3. आजनि.

Oriya sometimes shortens *o* to *u*, but in that language the distinction in pronunciation between these two vowels is so slight that in writing also the people often confuse the two. In a great part of this verb, however, the *o* is changed to a very short *e*. This is generally, but not always, due to a following *i*, where, from the shortness and indistinctness of the *o*-sound, *o* + *i* = a + i = ai = e. Thus 2 sing. is in full हेउ, though generally pronounced *ho*. In Bengali the *o* is generally written *a*, that vowel having in B. usually the sound of short, harsh *o*, like the *o* in English *not*, *rock*, etc. Thus it comes to pass that हुअ and हुन may be regarded, either as shortened from होअ and होन respectively, and thus derivable from *ho*, or as equivalents of H. है and हैं, and so to be referred to *as*. In practice, certainly, the meaning in which they are used favours the latter hypothesis.

The imperative in H. is the same as the aorist, except 2 sing., which is simply हो "be thou." In the Rajput dialects the 2 sing. is हू, 2 pl. होवो; the former occurs also in Chand as a 3 sing. in सब बोलि कही हू सिद्धि सिद्धि। "All speaking, said, 'May there be success, success!'" (i. 178) The Riwa dialect has 2 sing. हाउ, 2 pl. हाव, like the present.

P. 2 sing. हो, 2 pl. होवो. S. has 2 sing. हो and होउ, 2 pl. हो and हवो. G. for 2 sing. and 2 pl. both हो.

M.	Sing.	1. होऊं	2. हो	3. होवो, होव.
O.	„	1. हउं	2. हो	3. हेउ.
B.	„		2. होउ, हुअ	3. हउक.
M.	Pl.	1. होऊं	2. हो	3. होवोस, होअस.
O.	„	1. हेंअ	2. हव	3. हेंतु.
B.	„		2. हुअ	3. हउन्.

The respectful form of the imperative follows that of the other verbs in the various languages. H. here inserts ज, making होजिये "be pleased to be," G. होवजे.

Nepali has somewhat abnormally 2 sing. हुन, 2 pl. होअ.

The simple future in G. is formed according to the usual

rule; but here again we meet the tendency so common in B. and O., to express the *o* sound by *a*, so that side by side with the regular forms होइहउँ, होइहि, etc., we have also sing. 1. हुइहउँ, 2. हुइहै, 3. हुइहै; pl. 1. हुइहुँ, 2. हुइहौ, 3. हुइहैं, which we must apparently pronounce *hôiah*, *hôihe*, etc.

The simple future in old and rustic Hindi is regularly formed, as होइहौं "I shall become," etc.; but in this tense the employment of the type हैं is very common, both in the poets and among the peasantry of the western area. Thus—

	SINGULAR.			PLURAL.		
Braj.	1. हैहौं	2. हैहै	3. हैहै.	1. हैहैं	2. हैहौ	3. हैहैं.
West Rajp.	1. हैस्यूं	2. हैसी	3. हैसी.	1. हैस्यां	2. हैस्यो	3. हैसी.

We have also the curious transitional form of East Rajputana which approaches so closely to G.—

Sing.	1. हैस्यूं, हैसूं	2. हैसी	3. हैसी.
Pl.	1. हैस्यां, हैसां	2. हैस्यो, हैसो	3. हैसी.

Further details of these dialectic forms will be found in Kellogg's admirable grammar. When the wilder parts of the country, at present little known to Europeans, shall have been more fully explored, we may expect to obtain many finer gradations of transition; for all over India the Gujarati proverb holds true, "Every twelve *kos* language changes, as the leaves change on the trees."

The Braj form is interesting to students from the fact of this dialect having become at an early date the traditional literary vehicle of the Krishna-*cultus*, and thus to a certain extent a cultivated classical language. Its forms, however, are found in Chand long before the revival of Vaishnavism. He uses the full form होइहै, a shortened form होहि, and the Braj हैहै. Also occasionally होइ in a future sense, which is probably a form of the 3 sing. aorist for होय (भवतु). Examples are मनो होइहै निम वंसह। "His race *shall become* extinct" (Pr.-R. iii.

20). होहि जदवनि सपुतह ॥ "The Jadavani *shall be* with child" (i. 240). दिवस पंच के अंतरे । होइ सु दिल्ली पत्ति ॥ "In the space of five days, he *shall become* lord of Dilli" (iii. 411). हुआ न होइ हुवै न होइ । "There has not been, and there *shall not be*, any (like him)" (i. 331).

To Tulsi Das, Kabir, Bihari Lal, and all the mediæval poets होइही, होइहि, होहि, and होई are the forms of the ordinary regular future; होगा is very rarely met in their pages, if at all. Instances are, भये जे अहहिं जे होइहिं आगे । "They who have been, are, and shall be hereafter" (Tulsi, Ram. Bal-K. 30). होइहि यही कल्यान अब । "Now this good fortune will be (will happen)" (*ib.* 82), अब तें रति तव नाथ कर होइहि नाम अनंग । "Henceforth, Rati, the name of thy lord shall be Ananga" (*ib.* 96). The form हुवै does not appear to be used by Tulsi Das, though in Bihari Lal the participle हू is common; this latter poet's subject does not give much occasion for the use of the future. बहुरि जनम न होइही ताकी "There shall not again be birth to him (he shall escape the pain of a second birth)" (Kabir, Ram. 57). In the majority of the poets the forms *hvai* and *hoi* seem to be regarded as virtually the same, and they use indifferently the one or the other as it suits their metre. There is unfortunately as yet no critically prepared or corrected edition of the texts of any of them, and owing to the mistaken policy of the Government, by which artificial works written to order have been prescribed as examination texts, the genuine native authors have been entirely neglected.

§ 67. The participial tenses are formed as in the ordinary verb. The present participle is in Old-H. हुवंत, as in Chand हसत हुवंत निवारि "Laughing *being* prevented" (Pr.-R. i. 6). In modern H. the classical form is होता *m.*, होती *f.*, Braj होतु; and in most of the rustic dialects simply होत indeclinable. In the Rajputana dialects the form हुतौ is found. The other languages have P. हुंदा, S. हुंदो, G. होतो, M. होत, होता.

होतांना. O. हेब. B. होइते, though really the locative of a present participle is used as an infinitive.

The past participle is in H. one of the old Tadbhava class mentioned in §§ 46, 47, and as such takes its type from Skr. भूत, H. हुआ. The vowel of the stem is in the present day commonly pronounced short हुआ, and this practice is not uncommon in the poets. P. होइआ, S. हुओ, G. हुयो, होयो, होयलो.

M. has a strange participle झाला, which may be explained as phonetically resulting from an older form ह्याला, shortened from होयाला. I can trace nothing similar in any of the cognate languages, though the change from ह्य to झ is perfectly regular. In the poets a form जाला is found, and even जाहाला. These types have led some writers to regard this participle as derived from the root जा. This, however, is very doubtful. Tukaram always uses जा°, as आजि पुरले नवस । धन्य जाला हा दिवस ॥ "To-day our vows are heard, blessed *has become* (is) this day" (Abh. 508).

O. होइ, हेला. B. होइया, हइया.

The future participle is in M. व्हावा. O. हेब, B. हइब, contracted to हब (hŏbŏ).

These participles serve as tenses, either with or without the remains of the old substantive verb, just as in the regular verb, and need not be more particularly illustrated.

One point, however, deserves a passing notice. The present participle in M. forms with the aid of the substantive verb as a regular present, as 3 sing. होतो *m.* होती *f.* होतें *n.* But the slightly different form of this tense, which in the ordinary verb (§ 42) expresses the conditional present, is in the case of *ho* employed as an imperfect. Thus, while the form just given, *hoto*, etc., means "he becomes," the conditional form *hotā*, etc., means "he was." This usage is analogous to that of the G. *hato*, etc., mentioned in § 59, and agrees with a form of preterite used in Braj Hindi, sing. हतो *m.*, हती *f.* etc. It has been suggested that this latter is derived from Skr. भूत; but against such a derivation must be set the fact that *bhûta* had at a very early epoch lost its *t* and become in Pr. *hûam*, *hoium*, and the like; also that in Chand the *anuswâra* of the present participle is still preserved, as in दुज हंतो दुजविय मोर। (Pr.-R. i. 40), "Brahman *became* to Brahman hostile;" and a few lines further on in the same passage इक हंतो सिंगिय रिख "There was one Śringa Rishi."

§ 68. The tenses of the regular verb formed by the additions of parts of the verb *ho* are numerous, but vary in the different languages. In Hindi we have mostly tenses with a general sense of doubt or contingency, in which those compounded with the present participle run parallel to those formed with the past participle. Thus with गिरता "falling," and गिरा "fallen" (*gir* "to fall")—

1. गिरता होवे (aorist of *ho*) "I may be falling," which may be called a definite present subjunctive or contingent; as in answer to a question हमारे घर को जाते "Are you going to my house?" one might answer जाता होवे "I may be going (but am not sure)."

2. गिरता होगा (future of *ho* shortened from होवेगा) "I shall or must be falling," a future contingent, or doubtful; as in asking राम अबही आता है "Is Ram coming now?" the reply is, हां आता होगा "Yes, he will be coming," or, "he must be coming," *i.e.* "I suppose he is now on his way here."

3. गिरता होता "(If) I were falling," conditional present definite. This is very rarely used, but it seems to denote a phase of action which could not, when occasion requires, be otherwise expressed. It may be illustrated thus: राम यदि भागता होता तो मैं उसको रोकता "If Ram were now running away, I would stop him" (but as he is not, there is no need for me to do so). It is the present participle of the auxiliary used in a conditional sense, as in the simple verb.

4. गिरा होऊं "I may have fallen." Also somewhat rare. In answer to तुम ने उसके नाम कबहीं सुना "Have you ever heard his name?" one might say सुना होऊं "I may have heard it" (but have now forgotten it).

5. गिरा होगा "I must or shall have fallen." This is a very commonly used tense. Thus हुआ होगा is a frequent answer where a person is not sure, or does not care; and is almost equivalent to "I dare say," "very likely," "I shouldn't wonder." Also, it indicates some degree of certainty, as राम ने संवाद पाया है "Has Ram received the news?" Answer, पाया होगा "He will have received it," meaning "Oh yes, of course he has," or with a different inflection of voice, "I dare say he has."

6. गिरा होता "(If) I had fallen." Hardly ever used, except in a negative sentence. I do not remember to have heard it in conversation; though an analogous form with the participle of रह may be heard in eastern Hindi, as तुम यदि कल्ह आए रहते "If you had come yesterday." The only instance Kellogg gives is apparently from a translation of the Bible (John xv. 22) जो मैं न आया होता उन का पाप न होता "If I had not come . . . they had not had sin."

Panjabi makes a somewhat different use of the tenses of *ho*. In this language *ho*, when used as an auxiliary, has rather the sense of continuance in an act, than that of doubt or contingency. Thus we find the ordinary definite present जांदा है "He is going," side by side with a continuative present with *ho*, जांदा होंदा है "He kept on going:" also, "He is in the habit of going." So, also, there is a continuative imperfect जांदा होंदा था "He kept on going," "He was always going." Similarly, there are two forms of the future, one with the simple future of *ho* (like No. 2 in Hindi given above) जांदा होवेगा "He will probably be going," and a continuative form containing *ho* twice over, जांदा होंदा होवेगा "He will probably be always going." Thus, to the question वह किसथाऊ फिर चले

रहिंदा होवेगा "How long will he be stopping there?" the answer might be, उथे उह दा घर है उह ता सदा रहन्दा उथे रहिंदा अंदा होवेगा "His home is there, he will probably always be stopping there." With जे "if" prefixed, the tense जांदा अंदा means "If I were in the habit of going."

Parallel to the above are two tenses with the aorist of *ho*: जांदा होवां "I may be going," and with "if" prefixed, "If I should be going;" and जांदा अंदा होवां "I may be constantly going," "If I should be always going."

With the past participle they combine the present participle of *ho*, as रखिया अंदा "I would have put," and conditionally, जे मैं रखिया अंदा "If I had put," "If I should have put;" as in उह जे रुपईआ बपारीए दे हत्थ दित्ता अंदा तां सानूं मिलिया अंदा "If he had given the money into the care (lit. hand) of the merchant, then we should have got it."

There is also a combination of the past tense with the aorist of *ho*, as गिया होवे "He may have gone," or, "If he has (perchance) gone."

Colloquially, they *frequently* also insert होइआ pleonastically in phrases where it is difficult to attach to it any definite meaning. Thus उस भेजिया है "he has sent," and भेजिया होइआ है "he is having sent." In this latter phrase there is, perhaps, implied the idea of the action having been performed some time ago, and being still in force, so that it harmonizes with the generally continuative meaning of *ho* as an auxiliary in Panjabi. Also, though it is not noticed in the grammar, I remember having heard frequently this word *hoiâ*, repeated probably for emphasis, as मारिआ होइआ होइआ "beaten" (repeatedly, or very much indeed).

In Sindhi the present and past participle are both compounded with the aorist of *ho* to form potentials, thus—1. वेंदो अहे "he may be going;" 2. वियो अहे "he may have gone." There does not appear to be in this language so strong a sense of doubt, or of continuance, in these combinations, as in

H. and P., probably because *ho* plays a more important part in S. than does *as*, which is represented by only one tense, or *achh*, which is not represented at all.

3. वञंदो हो "he was going." This is the present participle of the verb with the preterite of *ho*.

4. वञिओ हो "he had gone." The past participle with the same. These two are exactly parallel.

5. वञंदो हूंदो "he will be going." Definite future, made up of present participle with future of *ho*.

6. वञिओ हूंदो "he will have gone." Past future, the past participle with the same. These two are also exactly parallel.

In the passive phase of active verbs there are also six tenses formed by the same process, whereof 2, 4, and 6 are the same as in the active, or, in other words, these two tenses may be construed either actively or passively, according to the structure of the sentence. Trumpp gives them twice over, probably for this reason:

1. छडिबो हुए "he may be being released." Future participle passive (§ 51) with aorist of *ho*.

3. छडिबो हो "he was being released." The same with preterite of *ho*.

5. छडिबो हूंदो "he will be being released." The same with future of *ho*.

Gujarati employs *ho* in the following tenses (Taylor, p. 92), mostly dubitative (*chaḍ* "ascend"):

1. Present participle + aorist, चडतो होय "he is ascending." Definite present.

2. The same + future, चडतो हशे "he may be ascending." Contingent present.

3. The same + pres. part. indeclinable, चडतो होत "(if) he were ascending." Subjunctive present.

A parallel group with past participle:

1. Past p. + aorist, चड्यो होय "he has ascended." Definite preterite.

2. The same + future, चढ्यो हशे "he may have ascended." Contingent preterite.

3. The same + pres. p. ind., चढ्यो होत "(if) he had ascended." Subjunctive preterite.

The same combinations may be formed with the p.p. in *elo*, as चढेलो होत, but there does not seem to be any very great difference in the meaning.

Also a group with future participle; in the form *vâno* (see § 52)—

1. Fut. p. + aorist, चढवानो होय "he is about to ascend." Definite future.

2. The same + future, चढवानो हशे "he may be about to ascend." Contingent future.

3. The same + pres. p. ind., चढवानो होत "(if) he were about to ascend." Subjunctive future.

An example of the use of the last of these tenses is जो मने छोडवानो होत तो छोडत "If he were going to (or had intended to) release me, he would have released me (long ago)." Three similar tenses are formed by combining the three above parts of the auxiliary with the participle in *âr* or *âro*, which, as in Marathi, is rather the noun of the agent, and will be discussed further on (§ 75).

Compound tenses in Marathi are formed so largely by the auxiliaries derived from *as* and *achh*, that there is comparatively little left for *ho* to do. It is used in the following tenses:

Imperfect, made up of present part. and imperfect of *ho*, as ते येत होता "he was coming."

"Incepto-continuative" imperfect, as the grammar-writers call it, made from the present part. and the preterite of *ho*, as तो बोलता झाला "he began to speak." This is rarely used.

Future preterite formed by the future participle and imperfect of *ho*, as मी लिहिणार होतों "I was to have written," *i.e.* "It had been arranged that I was to write under certain circumstances." The example given is मी काल बापाचा कडे येणार

होतों पण शरीरास विकृति झाल्यामुळें घरींच राहिलों "*I was to have called* (yeṇár hotãṇ) on you yesterday, but in my body illness having been (*i.e.* feeling unwell), I stayed at home."

Future continuative composed of the present participle and future of *ho*, as तो बोलता होईल "he will begin to speak (and go on speaking)."

Imperfect subjunctive, from the subjunctive (future pass. part.) and imperfect of *ho* used in the *Karma prayoga*, as त्वां सांगावें होतें "you should have told," lit. "by you to be told it was." This may also be expressed by using पाहिजे "ought," as म्यां चालावें पाहिजे होतें "I ought to have walked."

Another preterite phrase is formed by adding the imperfect of *ho* to the neuter genitive of the future pass. part., as म्यां चालायाचें होतें "I had to walk," *i.e.* "I was obliged to walk."

It will be seen that all these instances of the use of *ho* as an auxiliary are rather elaborate verbal phrases than tenses, ingenious and successful attempts at filling up the gap caused by the loss of a large range of synthetical tenses and participles from the earlier stage of language.

This verb is not used as an auxiliary in O. or B., though it is used as an ancillary to form a pedantic sort of passive with Tatsama p.p. participles, as B. प्रेरित होइबे, O. प्रेरित हेबा "to be sent." This, however, forms no part of the actual living languages of either Orissa or Bengal, and may be passed over with just this much notice.

§ 69. *STHÁ.* The Pali and Prakrit forms of the various tenses of this verb were given in § 12, where also the principal parts of the verb in S. G. and O. were given. In Hindi there is only one part of this verb in use as an auxiliary, namely, the participial tense *thá* "was," sing. था *m.*, थी *f.*; pl. थे *m.*, थीं *f.*[1]

[1] I had formerly connected this tense *thá* with O. and Braj *hato* and been thus led to refer it to *as*; but further research, aided by the dialectic forms brought to light by Kellogg and others, has led me to abandon that view, and to adopt that given in the text,—*dies diem docet.*

This form is, I believe, shortened from थियो, and that again from the Skr. p.p.p. स्थित. It is therefore analogous to the shortened forms of other p.p. participles so largely employed in the modern languages. We saw in Vol. II. p. 275, how the genitive postposition *kâ* had been evolved by a long and varied process from Skr. *kṛita*; so, also, *gâ* in the H. and P. future from *gata*, *hâ* in Old-Hindi from *bhûta*, *lâ* and *lo* in M., and other futures from *lagna*; and in exact parallelism to these is *thâ* from *sthita*.

The Kanauji Hindi has sing. थो *m.*, थी *f.*; pl. थे *m.*, थीं *f.*; but the Garhwali still preserves a fuller type in sing. थयो *m.*, थई *f.*; pl. थया *m.* Nearer still to *sthita*, and with incorporation of the Skr. root *as*, so as to make a regular imperfect, is the Nepali "I was," etc.—

Sing. 1. थियां 2. थियस् 3. थिया. Pl. 1. थियुं 2. थियौ 3. थिया.

Nepali is not an independent language, but merely a dialect of Hindi. The people who speak it call it Pârbatiya or mountain Hindi; it may therefore appropriately be taken into consideration in arguing as to the origin of Hindi forms. था is used in Hindi in two tenses only.

1. With present participle, बोलता था "was speaking." Imperfect.

2. With past participle, बोला था "had spoken." Pluperfect.

In P. था is occasionally used, though सा, in its numerous forms, is far more common. This verb is also used with a full range of tenses in Sindhi. Trumpp[1] calls it an auxiliary, but I can find no instances of its being used to form tenses of the ordinary neuter or active verb like *as* or *hô*, and it takes parts of the latter to form its own compound tenses. There are, however, two parts of *sthâ* in use as auxiliaries in Sindhi, the former of which थो probably = स्थितः *nom.*, and the latter

[1] Grammar, p. 303.

थे = थिले *loc.* थो agrees with the subject in gender, and is used to form with the aorist an indefinite present—

Sing. 1. हलां थो *m.* हलां थी *f.*

Pl. 1. हलूं था *m.* हलूं थिऊं *f.*, "I go," etc.

This auxiliary differs from all others in the seven languages, in that it may be put *before* the principal verb. थे has the same peculiarity, and is used to make a continuative imperfect with the past participle of the principal verb; it does not vary for gender or person. Thus—

Sing. 1. हुलिअसि थे 2. हुलिएं थे.

Pl. 1. हुलिआसीं थे, etc., "I used to go," or simply "I was going."

Examples are—

ब जालूं बार हि बार थे विढ़ियूं "Two women were quarrelling (*the rifahyiu*) about a child."

हिकिड़ा ब जणा परे परदेहि थे विआ "Two men were going (*the bid*) to a foreign country."[1]

Here the auxiliary precedes, and with reference to the suggested origin of this auxiliary from the locative *sthite*, it is more natural that it should do so, for the verb, whether in a simple or compound tense, naturally comes last in the sentence, so that the phrase "I am (in the act or condition of) having gone," is rendered "in having been, I am gone."

G. has also the full verb in all its tenses, and it may apparently be used as an auxiliary just as *ho*. As regards meaning, रहु is more powerful than थीउ; the latter also, is more powerful than छे. There are thus three grades of substantive verb. छे "he is," is merely the copula; थीए "he is, or becomes," is a definite expression of existence; रहे "he remains," is positive and prolonged existence. The distinction,

[1] Stack, Grammar, pp. 134, 135.

as pointed out before, is analogous to that between *ser* and *estar* in Spanish.

वञु forms compound tenses by taking parts of होणु as auxiliaries, just as the ordinary verb, thus—

Imperfect वञी हुती, as in सा लड़ाई वञी हुती "That fight was going on."

Preterite वञो होय हे, as in तिंहुं जो मन कठन वञु होय हे "His heart has become hard."

Dubitative present वञो हुजे, as in सो हुजे पछतायो वञो हुजे "Therefore you may now be regretting," and so on.[1]

In Oriya this verb plays a somewhat different part. It is there used not as a second auxiliary side by side with *ho*, but to the exclusion of it, and forms, with the participles of the principal verb, a range of well-defined tenses, which cannot be expressed otherwise.

1. With the present participle (*kar* "do") करु "doing"—

a. Aorist of *thâ* करु थाए, karu thâe, "he is (or was) doing." Continuative present.

b. Preterite ,, करु थिला, karu thilâ, "he was doing." Imperfect.

c. Future ,, करु थिब, karu thibě, "he will be doing." Continuative future.

2. With the past participle करि "done"—

a. Aorist of *thâ* करि थाए "he has (usually) done." Habitual preterite.

b. Preterite ,, करि थिला "he had done." Pluperfect.

c. Future ,, करि थिब "he will have done." Future perf.

The difference between 1*a* and 2*a* is very delicate, and rather difficult to seize. *Karu thâe* implies that a person habitually

[1] The examples are from Lackey, Grammar, pp. 76, 81.

does an act, and thus that he was doing it at the time mentioned, according to his usual custom. Thus, to a question से हाटरे बसु थिला "Was he sitting in the market?" the answer might be हाँ सेठि बसु थाए "Yes, *he always sits* there;" and thus it is implied that he was sitting there at the time referred to. So again, कबिराज जेबे बेळे आसिला मुं भलहेउ थाए "When the doctor came, *I was getting* well," implying that I had been improving before he came, and continued to do so. *Kari thāe*, on the other hand, literally, "He remains having done," implies a habit which is not necessarily in force at the time referred to, as भारजा प्रति ताहार बड राग होइ थाए "He is always very angry with his wife," not implying that he is actually angry at the moment of speaking. It is also used of an action which lasted some time, but has now ceased, as से समयरे मोर बड कास होइ थाए[1] "At that time I had a bad cough," implying that he had a cough which lasted a long while, but from which he has now recovered. Both tenses thus imply continuity, but the *former* indicates continuity still existing, the latter continuity in past time, which has now ceased.

There are similarly two imperatives formed respectively with the present and past participles—

a. करु था "Remain thou doing."

b. करि था "Remain thou having done."

Here, also, the same fine distinction is drawn as in the other tenses. गोबिंद से काम करु थाउ "Let Gobind go on doing that work." But, as Hallam well remarks (Grammar, p. 153), "The Oriya very often uses a past participle in his mode of thought, where we should use the present."[2] He illustrates this tense

[1] Hallam, Oriya Grammar, p. 78.

[2] I had the advantage of assisting Mr. Hallam when he was writing his grammar, and the definition of this tense was a source of much difficulty and discussion. He consulted a large number of natives, both educated and uneducated, the former as to the *rationale*, and the latter as to the practice. The latter, without knowing the reason why, often corrected *karu thāi* into *kari thāi* instinctively, and a large range of observations led to his adopting the definition in which I have followed him.

thus: "Suppose a person should say to another, 'Do that work *so*,' and the person addressed should reply, 'I have done it *so*,' and the first speaker should then say, 'Well, always do it so,' or, 'Continue to do it so,' this last phrase would be expressed by this tense." Ex. gr.:—

तुमे सेहि काम सेमति कर "Do that work so."

Answer मु सेमति करिछि कि "I have done it so," or, "as (you order) so I have done."

Rejoinder भला सेमति करि था "Well, always do so," literally, "thus having done, remain."

Here, if we used *karu thá*, we should imply that the person addressed was actually doing the work while we were speaking, while *kari thá* is used when he is not actually working.

Lastly, there is a pair of tenses with the conditional—

करु थांता "he might be doing," or, "if he were doing."

करि थांता "he might have done," or, "if he had done."

These explain themselves.

Bengali does not employ the primary form of this auxiliary, but has instead a secondary stem derived from it. This is थाक्, which is conjugated throughout in the sense of remaining, and partakes of the combined senses of continuity and doubt peculiar to this verb. There are, strictly speaking, no compound tenses formed by this verb, and the method of its employment is rather that of an ancillary verb.

§ 70. *Yá*. This root takes the form जा, and is used in H. P. M., occasionally in G. and B., and usually in O., to form the passive voice. G. having a passive intransitive of its own (§ 24), does not often have recourse to this verb, and S. having a regularly derived synthetical passive (§ 25), dispenses with it altogether. When used as in H. P. and M. to form a passive, it is compounded with the past participle of the principal verb, as (*dekh* "see")—

H. Aorist	देखा जाए "he is seen."	P. डिठा जावे.
Imperfect	देखा जाओ "be ye seen."	डिठा जावो.
Future	देखा जाएगा "he will be seen."	डिठा जावेगा.

So also in M. and O. The various tenses of जा are formed in the same manner as other verbs. When compounded with any other part of the verb than the past participle, *jā* is ancillary, and is used in various other senses.

There has been, in former times, much discussion about this form of the passive, some writers declaring it inelegant, others considering it unusual and opposed to the genius of the Indian languages, while some have even gone so far as to deny its existence altogether. The most discerning inquirers, however, admit it as a form in actual use, though they point out certain circumstances which obviate the necessity for recourse to it. Such are the existence of a large class of neuter verbs, the practice of changing the object into a subject, and figurative expressions like "to eat a beating," *mār khānā*, "it comes into seeing," *dekhne meṅ ātā*, and the like. Speaking as one who has lived in daily and hourly intercourse with natives of India for nearly twenty years, I can testify to the use of this form by speakers of Hindi, Panjabi, Bengali, and Oriya frequently, and even habitually. Idiomatically, many other ways of expressing the passive idea undoubtedly exist, and in some languages, as Bengali and Marathi, *ho* may be used to form a passive. There are phrases and occasions, however, where it would be more idiomatic to use the passive *jā* than any other construction, and we may conclude that, though its use is somewhat restricted, it is erroneous to describe it as always inelegant and unidiomatic, and still more so to deny its existence altogether.

§ 71. By using the expression "compound tense" in a wider sense than that in which it has been employed in the former part of this chapter, we may legitimately include under it that large and varied class of phrases in which two verbal stems are used together to express one idea. In such a combination the first verb remains unchanged, and all the work of conjugation is performed by the second, which acts, so to speak, as a handmaid to the first. For this second verb I have thought it advisable to employ the term "ancillary," as expressing more clearly than any other that occurs to me, the actual relation between the two. The ancillary verb differs from the auxiliary, in that the former runs through all the tenses of the verb, and the principal verb on which it waits remains unchanged, while the latter only forms certain specified tenses in composition with several parts of the principal verb, being attached now to the present, now to the past or future participle. Thus, the tenses formed by the aid of auxiliaries are integral portions of the primary simple verb. In the case of the ancillary, on the other hand, it, together with the principal verb, forms, in fact, a new verb, which, though consisting of two elements, must be regarded for conjugational purposes as essentially one throughout. Thus, the elements *már* "strike," and *ḍál* "throw," combine into the compound verb *már ḍálná* "to kill," which is conjugated through the whole range of simple, participial, and compound tenses of *ḍálná*, *már* remaining unchanged.

Grammarians have invented many strange names for these verbs with ancillaries, calling them Frequentatives, Inceptives, Permissives, Acquisitives, and many other -ives. It would, perhaps, be simpler not to seek to invent names for all, or any of them, but merely to note the combinations that exist with their meanings. Indeed, it is hardly possible to group them into classes, because, in practice, some ancillaries may be combined with any verb in the language, while others again can only be combined with one or two specific verbs. Moreover, there are exceptions to the general rule that a verb with an ancillary runs through the whole range of tenses, for some ancillaries are only employed in one tense, or in two tenses; thus *lag*, in Hindi, is usually only employed in the past tense, as *kahne lagā* "he began to say." Some again are formed in only one tense in one language, while they may be used in several tenses in another language.

The subject is a very wide one, for the number of primary verbal stems in the seven languages being small, they are driven to express complicated ideas by combining two of them together. They have also lost the facility of expressing such ideas which is possessed by most original Aryan languages, through the *upasargas*, or prepositions, and can no longer develope from one simple root a variety of meanings by prefixing *pra*, *abhi*, *upa*, or *sam*. Under such circumstances they have taken a number of their commonest verbs and tacked them on to other verbs, in order to imply that the action expressed by the principal verb is performed under the conditions expressed by the added, or, as we may call it, the ancillary verb. As might be expected, however, while the principle is the same in all seven languages, the method of its application, and the particular ancillaries used, differ, to some extent, in the several languages. It will be better to take each ancillary separately, exhibiting the general effect of each as combined with different parts of the principal verb.

§ 72. Ancillaries may be attached not only to other verbs, but even to themselves; the verb to which they are attached is placed in the conjunctive participle, and remains in that form throughout. Another class, however, exists, in which the principal verb is in the infinitive mood, which, as Kellogg justly observes, is not strictly a case of a compound verb, but that of one verb governing another, and in this view would more properly be regarded as a matter of syntax. Inasmuch, however, as certain well-known and constantly-used phrases of this kind have grown up in all the languages, whose use, to a great extent, supplies the want of regular tenses, it will be better to give them all here, so as to complete the survey of the modern verb in all its aspects. It must be noted, also, that in Hindi, and occasionally in P., M. and G., the conjunctive participle loses its final syllable, and thus appears in the form of the simple stem; that it is the participle, and not the stem, is shown by the analogy of the other languages, and by isolated instances of the preservation of the participial form even in Hindi.

1. दे "give," and ले "take," are in H. widely used as ancillaries, and the meanings which are obtained by their use are somewhat varied. In a general way, it may be said that *de* is added to verbs to express the idea that the action passes away from the subject towards the object, while *le* implies that the action proceeds towards the subject. Thus *de* can, strictly speaking, be used only with actives and causals; and in some cases adds so little to the meaning of the principal verb, that it appears to be a mere expletive. With active verbs examples are—

फेंकना "to throw," फेंक देना "to throw away."

निकालना "to take out," निकाल देना "to turn out, eject."

Thus घर से भात निकाला "he took the rice out of the house," where the idea is, that the man being outside went in and brought out the rice; but in मुझ को घर से निकाल दिया है "he has turned me out of the house," it would be understood that the speaker had been forcibly ejected.

रखना "to put," रख देना "to put away, lay by."

मारना "to strike," मार देना "to beat off."

With causals it is used very frequently, and with scarcely any perceptible change of meaning—

समझाना and समझा देना "to explain."

गिराना .. गिरा देना "to cause to fall, or to throw down."

बैठाना .. बैठा देना "to seat, or to put into a seat."

Perhaps one can sometimes trace in the form with दे a sense of the action having been done with some force, while in the simple verb the idea of force is wanting, but in the majority of instances no such distinction could be traced. There is occasionally some additional emphasis, as in the common phrases दे दो "give," and ले लो "take," where the ancillary is added to itself, but these expressions belong more particularly to the Urdū side of the language.

When attached to the infinitive of another verb, *de* implies permission, as जाने दो "let (him) go," हम को बैठने दीजिये "please let me sit down."

P. uses *de* in the same way as H., but it does not appear to be so used in Sindhi. In G. it is added to the conjunctive participle of another verb to give emphasis, it also expresses impatience, but, in both cases, like H., with a general idea of the action being from the speaker towards the object. Thus छडणु "to abandon," छडी देयो "let (it) alone!" "let go!" फाकणु "to throw," फाकी देयो "throw (it) away!" But as in H., with the infinitive it implies permission, वञणु "to go," वञण देणु "to allow to go," पवण देणु "to let fall," लिखण देणु "to permit to write."

M. has the same usage of दे; when added to the conjunctive participle it has the same senses as in H., as लिहून देणें "to write," खणून देणें "to dig;" in both of which phrases there is only a little additional emphasis implied, or perhaps an idea of finishing and having done with, as "write it off," "dig it up and have done with it," as in टाकून दे "throw it away."

With the infinitive it implies permission, as मला जाऊं दे "suffer me to go," वारा लिहूं देत नाहीं "the wind will not let me write."

Precisely similar is the usage in O. and B., as O. फिटाइ दिअ "break it open," literally, "having caused to open, give;" but with the infinitive मते आसिबाकु देला नाहीं "he would not let me come."

Bengali uses this verb with the conjunctive to imply completeness or emphasis, as पुस्तक देखिया दियाछि "I have seen the book," that is, "I have examined or perused it." With the infinitive it, like the rest, signifies permission, as आमाके पडिते दिलेन ना "They did not allow me to read."

2. ले is in all respects used similarly to दे, but with exactly the opposite meaning, namely, that of the action being directed *towards* the speaker, or the subject. In this construction its meaning is often very slightly different from that of the simple verb. Thus we may say, पीता "he drinks," and पी लेता "he drinks up," or "drinks down," in the latter case implying a more complete action. With causals it is used when the action is towards the subject, as राम को हमारे पास बुला लो "call Ram to me," where the simple verb बुलाना merely means "to call." The distinction between the use of *de* and *le* is well shown when added to रखना "to put:" thus रख लो means "put it away (for your own use)," but रख दो "put it down (and leave it)." There is, as Kellogg has shown, a sense of appropriating a thing to oneself involved in *le*.

P. follows the usage of H., but has less frequent recourse to this auxiliary. S. uses निअणु, which is the same word as *le*, in the sense of "taking away," which in H. is expressed by ले जाना, as in सांढ़ोर समुंडु खे निहोरे निया "In crossing the ocean they were forcibly carried off" (Trumpp, p. 340). In another instance, however, the meaning is more that of simple taking. मोटाए निअणु "to bring back," literally, "having caused to return, to take."

In G., the meaning is the same as in H., acquisition, or action towards the speaker or subject, as in समजी लेवुं "to understand," *i.e.* "to make oneself acquainted with," शीखी लेवो "learn (this)," *i.e.* "acquire this knowledge."

M., as before remarked, uses घे, where its sisters have ले. It is used *freely* in all combinations involving the idea of taking, and seems, like many other ancillaries, to be often used pleonastically. Perhaps, however, we ought to make allowance for the trains of thought which, in the minds of native speakers, underlie the expressions which they use, and, in this view, to admit that an idea of taking may be present to their minds in expressions which, in our mode of thought, would not involve such an idea. It is difficult to get a native to concentrate his mind upon what he is actually saying or doing, he will always mix up with his present speech strange undercurrents of nebulous fancies as to what he did or said last, or what he is going to do or say next, and this habit influences his speech and produces phrases which, to the practical European mind, seem unnecessary and confusing. Thus Molesworth (s.v. घे) reckons as pleonastic the use of this ancillary in लवकर स्नान करून घ्या "quickly having bathed take." Here the word "take" is probably inserted from a feeling that the person addressed is wanted again after he has had his bath. Thus, if you were about to send a man on an errand, and he asked (as a native usually does) to be allowed to bathe and eat first, you might use the above sentence. In Hindi one would use *âna* "to come," in the same way, as झट स्नान करके आओ. If you did not use some ancillary or other, it might be understood that you did not want the man's services after he had bathed. In another phrase पोरानें हात पोळून घेतला "The child burnt his hand." judging from the analogy of similar phrases in the cognate languages, I feel that if घेतला were not used, the person addressed would be capable of supposing that the child burnt the whole of his hand up, whereas, what is really meant is, that the child got a burn on his hand.

The O. verb नेबा is used as in H., as कागज पत्र बुझि नेबुं "I will take charge of the papers and accounts," where he means that he will take them and study them, it is literally "having understood I will take."

So also with B. लओ, as चिठी पड़ाइया लइलेन "they took and read the letter."

3. आ "come," जा "go," as also the cognate stems in the other languages, when used as ancillaries, stand to each other in the same contrast as *le* and *de*. H. आ is not very widely used, and principally with neuter verbs; it implies doing a thing and coming back after having done, and thus has a certain sense of completing an action. Thus बनना "to be made," बन आना, or sometimes colloquially, बने आना "to be completely done, successfully accomplished," खेत को देख आया हूं "Having seen the field, I am come," *i.e.* "I have been and looked at the field," and he implies, "I have examined it, and am now ready to make terms for the rent of it." The usage is similar in P., though rarely heard.

The equivalent of *á* in S. is अचणु, pres. part. ईंदो "coming," p.p. आयो "come." It is used with the infinitive to mean beginning to do, and this usage is thus different from that of H. and P. Thus वसण अचणु "to come to rain," or, as we should say, "to come on to rain," as—

विजूं वसण आईयूं आयो वरिसो वेस ।

"The lightnings have begun to rain, the rainy season has ascended (his) couch."—Trumpp, p. 344.

G. आव is used in the sense of coming into action, or into use, becoming, and is used with the present participle, as बगड़तुं आवतुं "to become spoilt." But far more frequently आवी, the conjunctive participle, takes other ancillaries after it.

ये in M. is also used in a potential sense, but generally, as far as I can learn, with the indeclinable form of the present participle, and with the subject in the dative case; thus it literally means "to me, to you, etc., it comes to do," as मला जातां येतो "I can go," lit. "to me going comes." Similar to this is the use of *ānā* in H. as an independent verb, chiefly in negative sentences, as उसको लिखापढ़ी आती नहीं "He does not know how to read and write," lit. "To him reading-writing comes not." So also in O. and B.

4. जा "go," is used more frequently, and in a wider sense than *ā*. In H. it implies completeness or finality, as खाना "eat," खा जाना "eat up," चले जाना "go away," where the principal verb preserves the termination of the conjunctive participle. In the familiar compound हो जाना "to become," the ancillary adds a little distinctness to the idea of the principal. So, also, in कह, or कहि, जाना; thus, if a man is hesitating or fumbling over a story or message, you say कहि जाओ, *i.e.* "Speak out!" or "Out with it!"

When added to neuter verbs (especially the double verbs mentioned in § 18), it seems to add no special meaning, and one may say टूटना or टूट जाना "to be broken;" मिलना or मिल जाना "to meet" or "be obtained." Colloquially, and especially in the past tense, the form with *jānā* is far more commonly heard than that without it; thus, for "it is broken," one hears टूट गया twenty times for once of टूटा. This practice seems to confirm what was conjecturally advanced in § 25, concerning the origin of the use of जाना to form a passive, as compared with the Sindhi passive in *ija*.

Sindhi uses, in a similar way, its stem वञणु "go" (impt. वञु, p.p. वियो, pres. p. वींदो, वेंदो), from Skr. √व्रज्, Pr. वच. Thus, लही वञणु "to take off," मरी वञणु "to be dead," *i.e.* "to go, having died." चढी वञणु "to ascend," *i.e.* "to go, having ascended." There is also a phrase in which it is added to खणणु "to lift," as खणी वञु "be off!" "go away!" The general effect of this ancillary may thus be taken to be that of completeness. Trumpp gives the following examples (p. 340): सो वधिहिं वडो तडिहिं मरी वियो "When he was grown up, then he died" (say "died off"). सुकाणि जी सलाह वठु त वोरिट वंञे वधि "Take the advice of the pilots that thou mayst *pass over* (or pass through and escape from) the flood tide."

Completion or finality is also indicated by *jā* in G., attached to the conjunctive participle, as in H. and P.; when added to the present participle, it implies continuance, as लखतो जा "go on writing."

In M. B. and O., this stem is not used as an ancillary.

5. सक "be able," is attached to the stem-form or apocopated conjunctive participle of all verbs in H. to imply power, as चल सकता "he is able to walk," कर सकेगा "he will be able to do." It is rarely, if ever, used alone in correct speaking, though one sometimes, in the eastern Hindi area, hears such an expression as हम सकेंगे नहीं "I shall not be able." This, however, is probably to be regarded merely as an elliptical phrase for हम कर सकेंगे नहीं "I shall not be able *to do*."

In P. also it is used always as an ancillary, as पढ़ सकदा है "he is able to read," and is conjugated throughout the verb. In S. the corresponding verb सघणु is used with the conjunctive participle in the same sense, as करे सघणु "to be able to do."

In all these three languages this verb may be added to the inflected form of the infinitive, though in H. and P. this construction is avoided by those who desire to speak elegantly. Still one often hears it, as जाने सकता नहीं "he cannot go," and in the eastern Hindi area it is very common, as well as in the Urdu spoken by Musulmans in all parts of India. Among these latter, indeed, *karne saktā* is much commoner than *kar saktā*.

It is used in G. as in H., and may also be used in M., but in this latter language the existence of another method of expressing potentiality (§ 54) renders its use less frequent.

B. and O. do not know this ancillary. In its place they use पार् in B. with the infinitive, as करिते पारि "I can do," in O. with the past participle, and generally with the future of the ancillary, as करि पारिबि "I shall be able to do," where we should use the present. Thus in asking, "Can you tell me his name?" one would say तांहार नाम कहि पारिब, literally, "Shall you be able to say his name?"

6. लग "begin" (see § 13). In H. and P. with the infinitive, as देखने लगना "he began to see." The ancillary is mostly used in the preterite, indeed almost exclusively so; for देखने लगता "he begins to see," would be inelegant, and, I believe, quite unidiomatic. S. uses the same construction, as रुअण लगिओ "he began to cry." So also G., as मारवा लागवुं "to begin to strike," and M. with infinitive of the principal verb, as मारूं लागला "he began to strike," but also with the dative of the future passive participle, as करावयास लागला "he began to do." B. the same, as करिते लागिल "he began to do." O. करिबाकु लागिला.

7. चुक "fail," hence "leave off, cease to do." In H. added to the conjunctive part. in the sense of having already finished, as खा चुका "he has done eating," जब खा चुकेगा "when he shall have done eating." P. does not use this verb in this sense. S. uses चुक, as in करे चुकणु "to have finished doing;" but it has also other ways of expressing this idea, as by रहणु "to remain," वठणु "to take," निबिरणु "to be ended," करि रहणु *id.* G. करी चुकवुं "to have finished doing." B. the same, as दिया चुकियाछि "I have done giving." O. uses सार, as खाइ सारिछि "I have done eating," से कर्म होइ सारिला "That business is quite finished." B. also uses फेल "throw," in this sense, as बलिया फेलिलेन "They have done speaking."

8. Marathi has two verbs not used in the other languages, ठेवणें and टाकणें, which are employed in many senses, and the distinction between which appears to be, at times, hard to draw.

The illustrations given, however, show that each word is faithful to its original meaning; ठेवणें = स्थापय, and consequently means "put," while टाकणें = त्याज, and means "throw away." These two words stand to each other in the same contrast as ले and दे in H., thus हें कापड घडी करून ठेव "Fold up this cloth and lay it by," ती गाय बांधून ठेव "Tie up that cow" (having tied, put), but त्याची पोथी त्याला देऊन टाक "Give him up his book" (*i.e.* "give it him and let him go"), तें झाड उपटून टाक "Root up that tree" (*i.e.* "uproot and throw away").

9. कर "do," is used in the sense of repetition or continuance. In H. with the perfect part., as आया करता "he always comes," तुम क्यों ऐसा किया करते हो "Why do you keep on doing so?" In Sindhi this sense is obtained by repeating the verb in the required tense after itself in the conjunctive participle, as सोई सो ख़तु पढ़िओई सो पढां "Even that, that letter I read over and over again" (Trumpp, p. 343), where the participle has the emphatic *i* added to it. G., like H., uses करवुं with the inflected form of the p.p., as कर्या करवुं "to keep on doing," वांच्या करवुं "to keep on reading." The various uses of *karnā* in forming compounds both with nouns and verbs are so numerous and peculiar, that they cannot be inserted here, but must be sought for in the dictionaries of the respective languages, and, still better, by those who have the opportunity, from the mouth of the people.

10. रह "remain," differs from कर, in that it implies continuance in a state, while कर implies repetition of an action. In H. and P., with the conjunctive participle, as बैठ रहना "to remain sitting," खेल रहते हैं "They are going on with their play;" also with the present participle, as नदी बहती रहती "The river flows on continually," *labitur et labetur.* There is a curious phrase in Hindi, जाता रहना (literally, "to remain going") used for "to be lost and gone," as an euphemism for death; thus मेरा बाप जाता रहा है "My father is dead (has passed

away);" also for loss of things, as उसका सब धन जाता रहा "All his property is gone." I do not find this idiom in the sister languages.

Sindhi uses रहणु in the sense of continuance, as वीदो रहंदो फिर्दो मिसिर शाम "He goes on travelling in fatigue from Egypt and Syria" (Trumpp, p. 344). The same sense is produced by वतणु "to turn, wander," as बीजलु घोड़ा चारींदो वते "Bijalu goes on grazing the horses" (*ib.*). In both cases the principal verb is in the present participle.

G. employs रेह, which is its version of रह with conjunctive participle for continuance, as करी रेहेवुं "to remain doing," and with the present participle in the sense of completion, as चढ़तो रेहे "he ascends completely."

This ancillary is truer to its original meaning in M., where it implies leaving off, refraining, with the genitive of the future participle, as मारावयाचा राहिला "he left off beating." This sense recalls that of Skr. रहित = "deprived of."

B. and O. do not use this verb as an ancillary. B. substitutes for it थाक, and O. था.

11. पड़ "fall," implies generally accident, as in H. जानना "to know," जान पड़ना "to be found out" (*i.e.* "to be known by an accident"), as उस का दोष जो जान पड़े तो हम भी नहीं बचेंगे "If his fault should be found out, then we, too, shall not escape." So also in G., as वळगवुं "to stick to," वळगी पड़वुं "to become attached to, to get caught in." M. uses it with the dative of the future participle, as तू ज्वरयुक्त झाल्यामुळें मला येथें वाटावाट पडतें "On account of your being attacked with fever, I *have to* waste my time in travelling," literally, "to me the throwing away of journeys falls." Here the sense is that of necessity, as also in बायको केली तर घर बांधाबांध पडेल "If you marry a wife, you will have to set up house." The same idea is expressed in H. by adding पड़ to the infinitive, as तुम को जाने पड़ेगा "You will have to go (whether

you like it or not);" so also in B. बाइते पड़िब, where it also implies subjection, or falling into a state, as धरा पड़िब "he got caught," as सुन्दर पड़ेछे धरा शुनि विद्या पड़े धरा "Hearing that Sundar had been caught, Bidya falls to the ground" (Bhârat B.-S. 350, where there is a pun on the double use of the phrase), घुमिया पड़िब "he fell asleep," मारा पड़िब "he caught a threshing." The same in O., as धरा पड़िछि (for पड़ि अछि) "he has been caught."

This verb sometimes precedes the principal verb in the sense of doing a thing accidentally, and is then put in the past participle. In this sense I would explain the sentence quoted by Kellogg (p. 195) एक बाघ पड़ा फिरता था "A tiger happened to be prowling about," literally, "a tiger fallen was prowling," the word "fallen" being used to express accidentally arriving. In P. the verb takes the form पइणा (= पड़ना), and the p.p. is पिया; thus they say वह पिया खांदा है "He is engaged in eating," where the sense is rather that of continuance: when put after the principal verb, it implies setting to work at a thing, as तुरणा "to walk," तुर पइणा "to set out on a journey." So also in Sindhi, where the verb has the form पवणु, the conjunctive participle पई or पेई precedes another verb with the sense of emphasis or energy, as वखर सो विहाइ जो पई पुराणो न थिए "Buy those goods which do not grow old" (Trumpp, p. 341); here पई न थिए means rather "do not happen to become," "are not likely to become." खणी, the conjunctive of खणणु "to lift," is used in the same way, but the two verbs appear to be contrasted much as *le* and *de* in H., *khaṇī* being used where activity, *paī* where receptiveness or accident is implied. Thus खणी लिखणु "to set to work writing," खणी वजाए "he sets himself to play (music)." The past participle पियो is also prefixed with much the same effect, as तंहिं में तजिया विजिलियूं वांगे पिया पिसजनि "In it flashes like lightnings are found" (or "take place," or "appear;" Trumpp, *ib.*).

12. The above are the principal, if not the whole, of the

ancillaries in general use. There are, indeed, a few others, but their use is restricted to one or other of the languages. Thus पाना "to find," is used with an infinitive in Hindi in the sense of being able, or being permitted, to do a thing. The verb in this construction is neuter, as मैं उसको देखने नहीं पाया "I was not allowed to see him," तुम घर के भीतर जाने नहीं पाओगे "You will not be permitted to go inside the house;" so also in B. पड़िते पाइ ना "I am not able to read," that is, not because I do not know how to read, but because I cannot find leisure, or cannot get the book.

डालना "to throw," is used in H. with verbs implying injury to show that force also was used, as—

मारना "to strike," मार डालना "to kill."
तोड़ना "to break," तोड़ डालना "to dash in pieces."
काटना "to cut," काट डालना "to cut down, hack, hew."

There are, besides, numerous combinations of two verbs, in which the latter of the two does all the work, the former remaining unchanged; but for these the reader is referred to the Dictionary, though, as far as I have seen, Molesworth's Marathi dictionary is the only one where they will be found fully treated.

CHAPTER V.

OTHER VERBAL FORMS.

CONTENTS.—§ 73. The Conjunctive Participle.—§ 74. The Infinitive.—§ 75. The Agent.—§ 76. Sindhi Verbs with Pronominal Suffixes.—§ 77. Conjugation of Stems Ending in Vowels in Hindi, Panjabi, and Sindhi.—§ 78. The same in Marathi.—§ 79. The same in Bangali and Oriya.

§ 73. The participles of the present, past, and future, being used in the formation of tenses, it has been found necessary to depart from the natural order of the verb, and to discuss them in Chapter III. There remains, however, a very widely used and important participle, which is not employed to form a tense. From the fact that it is used to connect one clause with another, and thus helps the native speaker or writer to build up those interminable sentences of which he is so fond, it has been called, very appropriately, the Conjunctive Participle. It implies "having done," and the sense of the clause in which it is used remains incomplete until another clause containing a finite verb is added; thus, instead of saying, "Next morning he woke and arose, bathed, ate, dressed, collected his goods, loaded them on his camel, bade farewell to his friend, and started on his journey," the Indian languages would say, "Having woken, having risen, having bathed, having eaten, having dressed, having collected his goods, having loaded them on his camel, having bidden farewell to his friend, having started on his journey, he went."

Sanskrit has two forms of this participle, one in त्वा, as भूत्वा "having been," the other in य, as संभूय "having met." Each of these forms has left descendants in the modern languages, and although the form in *ya* is, in classical Sanskrit, restricted, for the most part, to compound verbs, yet this peculiarity has been overlooked in the spoken languages, and simple verbs, as well as compound ones, are treated as having this form also.

Thus in Prakrit we find **सुणिऊण** = Skr. **श्रुत्वा** "having heard," as well as **णिक्कमिअ** = **निष्क्रम्य** "having gone out." So also **दइअ** = **दत्वा** "having given," **चोरिअ** = **चोरयित्वा** "having stolen," **गदुअ** = **गत्वा** "having gone," **सिंचिअ** = **सिक्त्वा** "having sprinkled," **गेण्हिअ** = **गृहीत्वा** "having taken."

In Old-Hindi this participle ends in *i*, as **करि** "having done," **चलि** "having gone," which is apparently the Prakrit form with loss of the final *a*, thus—

सुनि कग्गर पुथराज मनु । भौ आनन्द सुभाए ।

"Having heard the paper, King Prithiraj was glad, being pleased."
—Pr. R. xii. 62.

Chand, however, in his more archaic passages, uses a form in *ya*, and one in *nya*, as—

भुगति भूमि किय क्यार ।
वेद सिंचिय जल पूरन ।
बीज सबन धव मध्य ।
ज्ञान अंकूर अकूरन ।

"Taking possession of the earth, like a garden plot,
Irrigating it with the fullness of the Veda, as with water,
Having placed good seed in its midst,
Up sprung the shoot of knowledge."—Pr. R. i. 4.

Here **किय** "having made," and **भुगति किय** = mod. **भोग करके** "having made (or taken) possession," **सिंचिय** "having watered," **धव** = **धरिअ** "having placed."

Mediaeval Hindi has regularly the form ending in **इ**, as **राम वचन मृदु गूढ़ सुनि** "*Having heard* the gentle mystic speech of Rama" (*Tulsi*, *Rām. Bālk.* 113), **पंडित भूले पढ़ि गुनवेदा ।** "Sages *having read* the Veda erred as to its qualities" (Kabir, Ram.

34, 1). भक्ति विमुख जो धर्म सु सब अधर्म करि गायो । "The religion that is opposed to devotion (bhakti), all that *having made* (i.e. having declared), irreligion he sang" (Bhaktamál, Múl. 30).

From the habitual neglect of final short vowels, it results that this participle often appears in the form of the bare stem, as in the verbs with ancillaries given above, and this form, appearing to be not sufficiently distinct, a secondary form has arisen, which is now the ordinary one in modern Hindi. This consists of adding कै, कर, करके, करकर, and even करकरके to the stem, namely, the conjunctive participle of करना "to do;" as देख कर "having seen," जाकर "having gone." The first of these forms के is softened from कै, which, again, is from करि, the older form of the conjunctive part. of करना, and is used in the mediæval poets and in Braj and the rustic dialects to this day. Thus Kabir बहु बिधि के चित्र बनाइकै हरि रच्यो क्रीडा रास । "*Having made* many kinds of appearances (*máyá*), Hari has arranged the sport and pastime (of the world;" Hindola, 16). It having thus become customary to add the participle of कर to all verbs, it has been added to कर itself, thus making करके and करकर, and this reduplicated form again is added to other verbs. In all the dialects we find such forms as मारिकै, मारकै, मार, मारि, and even apocopated as Garhwali मारिक and मारीक "having beaten." Kumaoni has a curious compound form मारिबेर "having beaten," which is probably the old form मारि with बेर "time" (Skr. वेला), literally, "at the time of beating."

In the case of the common verb *ho*, the conjunctive participle, like the future, takes in Old-Hindi the forms होय and ह्वै, especially the latter, as गुरु भक्ति एक न्यारी नहीं ह्वै सकै । "Guru-bhakti alone could not remain apart" (*sak* ancillary with conjunctive of *ho* = "could be;" Bhaktamál, 116, 1), रजनी अंध कूप ह्वै जाइ "The night becomes as dark as a well" (Kabir, Ram. 16, 4), मानुष बडे बडे ह्वै आये "Very great men came" (lit. "having become very great;" *ib.* 17, 6).

P. is the same as H., and with the latter closely agrees O., which forms this participle by short *i*, as देखि "having seen." This form also appearing too indefinite, in ordinary conversation they add करि, often pronounced किरि, as देखिकरि "having seen." O. has also another, and in the classical speech the only admissible, form in *ile*, as मारिले "having beaten," which is also used in B., and in both appears to be the old locative case of the past participle, and is thus literally "in having beaten." The old form of the locative case having in O. fallen into disuse, the same has taken place in the participle; thus arise the forms देखिकारे "in having seen," and देखिकारु "from having seen," which are respectively the locative and ablative, formed after the modern fashion by adding ठारे and ठारु, the initial syllable of which is rejected (Vol. II. p. 274).

B. has, besides the form in *ile*, one in *iyā*, which approaches closer to the Prakrit, as पड़िया "having fallen," बसिया "having sat," धरिया "having seized." This latter form is that which is used to string together long sentences, in preference to the form in *ile*, which is used more in short sentences. Thus Bhârat—

आर जन पुनः चाहे फिरिया फिरिया ।
पिंजरेर पाखि मत बेड़ाय घुरिया ॥

"Another craftily looks, repeatedly turning round,
Like a bird in a cage walks round and round."

—Bidyā-S. 245.

literally, "having turned, having turned, looks," and "having twisted round, walks."

S. has four forms for this participle. Neuter verbs take the ending *î*, as मुड़ी "having returned;" active and causal verbs have *e*, as मले "having rubbed," both of which correspond to the Pr. ending *ia*. Less widely used is a form in *io* or *yo*, as मोटियो "having returned," धोतो "having washed," which is identical with the p.p.p. Thirdly, the inserted *jja* of Prakrit reappears here, as from उखणु "to lift," उखिजे "having lifted."

Lastly, S. follows the example of H., and adds करे, the conjunctive of करणु "to do," as वरी करे "having returned."

G. resembles S., having its conjunctive in *î*, as होई "having become." Ordinarily it puts this participle in the objective case, adding the postposition ने, often dropping the anuswâra, as करीनें or करीने "having done," देईने "having given." As G. makes no distinction between *i* and *î*, this is often written with short *i*, as देइने.

M. stands quite alone, having its conjunctive in ऊन, as जाऊन "having gone," होऊन "having been." This is sometimes written ओन, and in the poets takes an increment, and appears as ऊनियां, ओनियां, as तुम्हांपाशीं यावें येऊनियां काय ॥ (Tuk. Abh. 1888) "What is the good of my going to you?" (literally, "I near you *having come*, what?") देखोनियां बरें भूषणांचिं जन । तत्काळ मरण येतें मज ॥ "*Having seen* men in fine clothes and ornaments, I am ready to die at once" (*ib.*).

This form is the old Maharashtri Pr. form in ऊण, shortened from तूण, Skr. त्वानं, accusative of त्वा (Lassen, p. 367), and has undergone singularly little change. I see in this a confirmation of the belief that modern Marathi is really the representative of the Maharashtri Prakrit, for it is only in Maharashtri that the conjunctive in *ûṇa*, *tûṇa*, is found. All the prose dialects without distinction take forms of the conjunctive derived from the Skr. *-ya*; this consideration seems to be fatal to the theory (Trumpp, p. 283; V. Taylor, p. 114, § 250) which would derive the G. conjunctive in *îne* from M. *ûṇa*. Setting aside the absence of any analogy for a change from *û* to *î* in such a connection, there is abundant evidence that G. is, by origin, a Rajput dialect belonging to that large group of dialects which we roughly class under the name of Hindi, and Śastri Vrajlâl (G. Bh. It. p. 3) points out the great gulf that exists between G. and M., as also the close connection of G. with the northern dialects. We have therefore strong reasons for not looking to M. for the origin of any G. form. The latter has, like the rest of the eastern Hindi group, Sauraseni for its parent, and the form in *-ise*, when compared with that in *l* in the same language, points clearly to the Sauraseni conjunctive in *is* with a modern case-postposition *se* or *sen* added.

§ 74. The Infinitive is, in all the languages, a verbal noun declined throughout all the cases of the noun. Its numerous forms may all be grouped under two general types, which may be called the *Ba*, and the *Na* types respectively.

The *Ba* type is found in the rustic dialects of Hindi, in Bangali, Oriya, and Gujarati, and is declined as a noun. It occurs in the oldest Hindi poems. Chand has it in—

जो बिलंब करि रहै। सो मारि हनिबे कों आवै॥

"If any one makes delay, he comes to strike him."—Pr. R. i. 196.

उठि जुरिबे कों धावौ॥

"Rising up, rushed to fight."—*ib.* i. 254.

It takes the junction-vowel *i*, and in these passages is in the accusative case. It may be rendered "*to or for* the purpose of fighting." This form does not once occur in the Ramaini (रमैनी) of Kabir, and only rarely in his other works. I have noted तरिबे कौ "to cross over," चलैबो (चलाइबो) "to urge on," in the Rekhtas. It is more common in Braj, and in Tulsi Das's Ramâyan, where, besides the form with junction-vowel *i*, as तोरिबे "to break," occurs also a shorter form in *ab*, as फिरब "to return." In the dialects (Kellogg, p. 241) occur the following (*mâr* "strike") :—

Braj मारिबौ. East Rajput मारबौ. West Rajp. *id.* Old-Purbi मारब. Avadhi, and Riwai *id.*

In Gujarati, this is the only form of the infinitive. It is declined as an adjective for all three genders, thus—

Sing. लाववो *m.*, लाववी *f.*, लाववुं *n.*

Pl. लाववा *m.*, °वी *f.*, °वां *n.* "to bring" or "the act of bringing."

and agrees with the object, as mentioned in § 52, where it is used to constitute a tense. In the neuter singular it performs the functions of a simple infinitive, as गावुं "to sing," करवुं "to do."

In Oriya it is the ordinary infinitive, as बसिबा "to sit," and, though without gender, is declined for case, as—

Gen.	बसिबार "of sitting."	एहि बसिबार जागा "this is a place of sitting," *i.e.* "a fit place to sit in."
Loc.	बसिबारे "in sitting."	बसिबारे किछि हेब नाहीं "in sitting nothing will become," *i.e.* "you will do no good by sitting still."
Acc.	बसिबाकु "to *or* for sitting."	बसिबाकु हेब "*for sitting it will become*," *i.e.* "you will have to, *or* must, sit."
		देखिबाकु आसिला "he came to see."
Abl.	बसिबारु "from sitting."	सेठि बसिबारु जरही धारिब "*from sitting* there a chill will attack," *i.e.* "if you sit there, you will catch cold."

Bengali does not use this *form* as its ordinary infinitive, having utilized for that purpose the locative of the present participle, as हइते "to be" (lit. "in being"), थाकिते "to remain," याइते "to go;" but it is used in the genitive case to form a sort of gerund or verbal noun, as बीज बपिबार काल आछे "It is the time of sowing, *or* for sowing, seed." More common still is its employment with जन्ये, कारण or निमित्ते "for the sake of," as देखिबार जन्ये "for the sake of seeing," करिबार निमित्ते "for the sake of doing."

The infinitive of the Gipsies ends in *den*, and probably belongs to this group. Paspati writes *kerden* "to do," *lden* "to take," *dden* "to give," *sovden* "to sleep," *mangden* "to ask," *rovden* "to weep," which may be transliterated perhaps करदेन, लेन, देन, सोवदेन, मंगदेन, रुदेन respectively. These are words of the Chinganes or Turkish Gipsies. Those in Bohemia apparently drop the final *a* and shorten the *á*, as *chorav* "to steal" (चोरव), *kerav* "to do" (करव), *chinnav* "to tear" (छिनव). Those in Wallachia appear to pronounce the termination as *ao* (अवौ or आवौ?), as *jao* "to go" (जावौ), *khao* "to eat" (खावौ), *pio* "to drink" (पीवौ).[1]

In all these languages the idea of an infinitive glides off imperceptibly into that of a verbal noun, and the *Ba* form thus reveals its origin from the Sanskrit future passive participle in तव्य, from which, as we have seen in Ch. III. § 51, many tenses are formed.

The *Na* type occurs in Hindi, as also in P. S. M. It has two forms in H., one archaic and poetical ending in *anu*, the other modern and classical in *nā*. The first of these two forms I would derive from the Sanskrit verbal noun in *anam*, as करणं "doing," पतनं "falling." It is in frequent use, uninflected, throughout the poets, thus—

पुरुषातन तिन बंधन विचारि ।
"Having plotted *to stop* his virility."—Pr. R. i. 178.

कियौ चलन की साज ।
"He made preparation *to go*."—*ib.* xx. 28.

बंध जुरन काढ़िय जुझार ।
"*To join* battle a terrible warrior."—*ib.* xx. 31.

सत्य कहौं मोहि जान दे माई ।
"I speak truth, suffer me *to go*, mother."—Tulsi-Ram. S.-k. 7.

राम सैल बन देखन जाहीं ।
"They go *to see* the hill and forest of Rám."—*ib.* Ay-k. 91.

It is unnecessary to give more instances of this very common form. It still survives in Kanauji, as मारन "to strike." The other form in ना was anciently written नौ, and is always so written in Braj, as मारनौ "to strike," आवनौ "to come." This form I now agree with Hoernle in deriving from the Sanskrit

[1] Miklosich, Zigeuner Europa's, part ii. p. 8.

future participle in *anîya*, so that from करणीयं, through Pr. करणीअं and करणअं, would come Old-H. करनौं, M. करणें, and P. करना. I, however, would refer the S. करणु to the verbal noun in *anam*, because the final vowel is short, and, as in all similar nouns, reproduces the final *o* = *u* of the *a*-stem (see Hoernle's essay in J.A.S.B. vol. 42, p. 59, etc.). The two forms of the infinitive are thus analogous in respect of their derivation, and the fact of the existence side by side of two sets of forms with precisely similar meaning is explained by that of there being two participles of similar meaning in Sanskrit, both of which have left descendants.

Under these altered lights I must withdraw the opinion formerly held by me as to the origin of the infinitive in *nd*. That in *ana* is now obsolete, except in Kanauji, and the *nd* form is declined as a noun in *â*, making its oblique in *e*, as *karne kâ* "of doing," *karne meŋ* "in doing." In M. the infinitive is also declined as a noun of the sixth declension (Vol. II. p. 192), thus gen. *karaṇyâ châ* "of doing," dat. *karaṇyâ lâ* "to doing." In Sindhi, however, the infinitive vindicates its claim to be considered as a descendant of the verbal noun in *anam* by exhibiting the declension of masculines (*i.e.* neuters) in *u*; the oblique ends consequently in *a*, as *ginhaṇa jo* "of buying," *ginhaṇa meŋ* "in buying," etc. This would not be the case were the S. infinitive derived from the participle in *anîya*.

M. has an infinitive peculiar to itself ending in ऊं, as मरूं "to die," which is comparatively little used, and only with the present tense. I am unable to suggest any thoroughly satisfactory explanation of this form which does not appear to have any analogy in the cognate languages. It may be the only descendant of the Skr. infinitive in *tum*, with elision of the *t*, but this is somewhat doubtful. To this place must also be referred the B. infinitive or verbal noun in *â*, as करा "to do," or "the act of doing," which, after stems ending in a vowel, appears as या, the *y* of which is not pronounced; thus खोया

pronounced "hôwâ," देवोवा "dewâ." The origin of this form is not clear to me, but it is probably connected with the participle in नव.

§ 75. On the basis of the infinitive in *nâ* is formed the agent. This, in Hindi, is made by adding to the oblique of the infinitive the words वाला, हारा; as करनेवाला "a doer," देखनेहारा "a seer." Of these the former is apparently Skr. पालक "protector, keeper." Thus Skr. गोपालक "cowherd," becomes H. ग्वाला; as to the latter there is some difference of opinion, some would derive it from Skr. धारक "holder," others from कारक "doer." I myself incline to the latter view; the क would be elided when it ceased to be initial, and its place supplied by ह, which is often used to fill an hiatus. This is Trumpp's opinion (Grammar, p. 75), who shows that in S. this form of the agent exists as *kâro* or *kâru* = respectively *kâraka* and *kâra*, as in—

सिरजणु "to create,"	सिरजणहारो (रु) "creator,"
लिखणु "to write,"	लिखणहारो (रु) "writer,"

also in its original form of *kâro* or *kâru*, with nouns, as झेड़ो "quarrel," झेड़ाकारु "quarreller."

Kellogg (p. 245) refers to the phrase कारन कारनं in Chand's first verse as confirming the derivation from कारक; but this identification rests on a translation of that verse very confidently put forward by a writer whose high estimate of himself as a translator of Hindi has not yet been confirmed by the opinion of scholars in general. The translation in this particular instance is extremely uncertain, and no argument can be based on it.

Hindi has also an agent in ऐया, as करैया "a doer," रखैया "a keeper," which is shortened from वारिया, a dialectic form of वाला. It is confined almost to rustic speech, though the shorter form वारा is not uncommon in the poets. H. वाला may be added also to nouns, to imply the doer of an action, or the person who takes care of a thing, in which latter respect the original meaning of *pálaka* is well preserved. Thus घोड़ेवाला "one who takes care of a horse." So also in P. घरवाला "husband," *i.e.* one who takes care of or maintains the house, and still more frequently घरवाली *f.* "wife." Sindhi changes ल to र *more suo*, and has वारो, as घरवारो "householder," from घरु "house," and डिअणवारो "giver," from डिअणु "to give," H. देनेवाला.

Chand uses the form in हार, shortened from हारा, to make a sort of future participle, in the verb हो "be." Thus—

होइ होनहार सीता हरन ॥

"The rape of Sita, *which was to be*, takes place."—Pr. R. iii. 27.

Also—

तैं कछु होनहार पहचानिय ॥

"Thou knowing something of *futurity*."—*ib.* xxi. 92.

इमहार एही कही । कही जु आल्ह उपाय ॥

"It is written thus as *destined to be*, the plan which Alha has spoken."
—*ib.* xxi. 94.

Probably, also, to this place belongs the affix वारी in words like पटवारी "a village accountant," the व being an indication of a lost क, from कारी (कारिन्) "doer."

In M. and G. this form loses its initial consonant, and appears simply as *ára*. In G. it is incorporated into one word with the verbal noun in *aṇu*, of which, except in this conjunction, no traces remain. Thus from होवुं "to be," comes होणार "one who is." But, just as in the Old-H. होनहार, the sense of futurity has usurped the place of the original idea of agency, and *honár* now means "he who, or that which, is to be," as सची होणार ते होय । सत विना बीजुं नही कोय ॥ "That which in truth is (destined) to be, comes to pass, except truth there is nothing else" (Samaldas, Leckey, p. 64). It also takes the long *o*, as थणार or थणारो "that which is about to become," from थवुं "to become," शकणार "that which is able," from

सकवुं "to be able;" and is in practice used simply as a remote future tense, less immediate in its action than the simple future of the *as* type, but equally common. Thus एटला माटेज अमे तने मारनार "For this very reason we are *about to kill* thee;" पोतानो धर्मने कदी छोडनार नथी "He *will* never *forsake* his religion," in other words, "he is not a forsaker (H. छोडनेवारो) of, or one who is likely to forsake, his religion;" हुं बीजाने मारीने सुख भोगवनारो हतो "Having killed another, *I was about to enjoy* happiness," literally, "I was becoming an enjoyer" (Leckey, p. 161).

It is probably owing to the absence of any derivative of the verbal noun in *ana* that the grammar-writers have failed to understand the true origin of this form, and have supposed it to be composed of the verbal stem and a suffix *nār* or *nāro*, so that *chhoḍanāro* is by them divided *chhoḍa-nāro*, instead of *chhoḍan(a)-(h)āro*.

A similar misapprehension has occurred in M. In that language, also, *ār*, *ārā*, are used, added to the infinitive in णें, to make, not a noun of the agent, but a future participle, so far, at least, as the meaning goes. Thus from करणें come करणार "a doer," and करणारा, obl. करणारे. But these are used in the sense of "one who is about to do," as in G. So येणारे लोक is "the people who are coming," i.e. "who are expected to come." Godbol, at p. 109 of his excellent Marathi Grammar, indicates rightly the origin of this tense, and illustrates it by such nouns as Skr. कुम्भकार, Pr. कुम्भआर, M. कुंभार. Other grammarians, however, still speak of "the participle in णारा."

This noun, used, as above explained, participially, is employed to form compound tenses, § 62. In H. and P. the noun in *wālā* (not *vālā*) is used in a future sense, as वुह जानेवाला था "he was just about to go." This is not perhaps a classical phrase, but it is one which one hears a dozen times a day from the mouths of people of all classes.

In O. one also hears a form in *wālā* added to the infinitive, as पाद्‌वाचीयाणा "a receiver." I suspect, however, that this is a recent introduction from the Hindi. There is no व in Oriya, and in trying to express the sound, they imitate the Bengalis, and put that form of य which it has as the last member of a nexus (the *ya-phala* as they call it), behind an ओ. They pronounce this extraordinary combination *we*, and not *oya*, as it should be. The natural genius of the language has no form for the agent; instead of saying "the speaker," they would say, "he who speaks," or, if educated, would use the Sanskrit agent in तृ.

B. had, in its original state, apparently no noun of the agent. In modern times, recourse has been had to Sanskrit agents, which have been used whenever required, but colloquially it is easy to do without a *nomen agentis*, by slightly varying the arrangement of the sentence, and this is generally the course pursued. Such forms as कर्ता "doer," दाता "giver," used in literature, are, of course, Sanskrit pure and simple, and as such do not concern our present inquiry.

§ 76. The pronominal suffixes which are peculiar to Sindhi among the languages of the Indian group are also affixed to verbs, and, indeed, much more copiously used in that connection than with nouns. At Vol. II. p. 334, these suffixes, as applied to nouns, were briefly treated; they require more elaborate handling under verbs. It was mentioned, at the place cited above, that in this respect Sindhi allied itself with the neighbouring Aryan group of the Iranian languages, especially with Persian and Pashtu. I am not in a position to analyse the Persian and Pashtu analogies, and with respect to the latter language, though Trumpp has shown (Zeitschrift d. D. M. G. vol. xxiii. p. 1) that it is in many respects more closely allied to the Indian than to the Iranian group, yet it is so evidently a border language, transitional between the two, that to admit it to the present work would carry me beyond the limits of my undertaking. It will suffice merely to notice, without attempting to discuss, the suffixes of that language as they occur in analogy with Sindhi.

These suffixes are used to bring the object of the verb's action into one word with it, and may be thus considered as datives, accusatives, or whatever case expresses the nature of the action of any particular verb. They are the same in form as those attached to nouns, and stand thus in comparison with Persian and Pashto:

	SINGULAR.			PLURAL.		
Sindhi	1. मि	2. इ	3. सि.	1. ऊं, अं	2. व	3. नि, नु.
Persian	1. أم	2. أت	3. أش.	1. مَا	2. تَمَا	3. كان.
Pashto	1. me	2. de	3. e.	1. mu, um	2. mu	3. e.

Taking the aorist of the active verb as the simplest tense, we find the suffix simply added without effecting any phonetic changes in the termination of the verb. Thus—

Sing. 1. मांखे छडिआं "I let go," with suff. of 2 sing. छडिआइ "I let thee go," छडिआंसि "I let him go," with suff. of 2 pl. छडिआंव "I let you go," छडिआंनि "I let them go."

Sing. 2. तूं छडिएं "thou lettest go," with suff. of 1 sing. छडिएंमि "thou lettest me go," and so on.

Pl. 3. उन छडिनि "they let go," with suff. of 3 sing. छडिनिसि "they let him go," and so on.

The imperative is treated exactly in the same way. The respectful form takes इजां in the singular in this connection, not इजे, as छडिजांमि "Please to let me go," छडिजांसि "Please to let him go."

In the participial tenses a still greater variety of forms results from the change of the termination for gender in the third person singular and plural. The first person, however, also undergoes changes. Thus, in the present participle used as a future, हुंदुसि "I shall be," *m.*, becomes हुंदोसां, and हुंदियसि "I shall be," *f.*, becomes हुंदीसां. So that we get forms—

m. हुंदोसांइ "I shall be to thee," हुंदोसांसि "I shall be to him."
f. हुंदीसांव "I shall be to you." हुंदीसांनि "I shall be to them."

So, also, the plurals हुंदासीं *m.*, and हुंदियूंसीं "we shall be," become respectively हुंदासूं and हुंदियूंसूं. The second person remains unchanged, merely affixing the personal suffixes. In the third person *m.* हुंदो is shortened to हुंदु, and *f.* हुंदी to हुंदय or हुंद: pl. *m.* हुंदा becomes हुंद, except with the suffix of the first person plural, as हुंदासूं "they shall be to us," but हुंदव "they shall be to you:" pl. *f.* remains unchanged.

The past participle used as a perfect tense undergoes analogous changes. Thus—

1 Sing. *m.* होसि "I was," becomes होसां, as होसांइ "I was to thee."
" *f.* हुयसि " " हुईसां, " हुईसांसि "I was to him."
1 Pl. *m.* हुआसीं "we were," " हुआसूं, " हुआसूंनि "we were to them."
" *f.* हुयूंसीं " " " हुयूंसूं, " हुयूंसूंव "we were to you."

The second and third persons remain almost unchanged. In active verbs, however, where only the 3 sing. is used, owing to the objective construction, a somewhat different system prevails. The subject, which in other languages is put in the instrumental, may in S. be indicated by a suffix, and the object being also shown by a suffix, it arises that the verb may have two suffixes at the same time. Thus "I forsook thee," would be in H. मैं ने तुझ को छोड़ा, lit. "by me thee forsaken," where the subject is in the instrumental, and the object in the accusative case, the verb (*i.e.* participle) being left in the masc. singular, because there is no neuter in H. In M., which has a neuter, the Bhâva or impersonal construction is used, as मूं तुभा छोड़िओ "by me to thee released," as though it were *a me tibi relictum* (est). Sindhi expresses this sentence by one word छडिओमाइ, *i.e. chhaḍio-māṇ-i* = "forsaken-by me-thee." Thus there arises a long string of forms for every possible combination of the agent and the object. A few may be given as examples; a full range will be found by those who desire to pursue the question further in Trumpp (p. 371):

छडिओमासि "I have forsaken him."

छडिआईसि "he has forsaken him."

विहारिआईसि "he caused him to sit."

चिआऊसि "they said to her."

चिआईनि "she said to them."

The suffixes denoting the agent are ई sing. and ऊं pl., which Trumpp considers to be shortened from इन "by him," instr. of हो "this," and उनि "by them," instr. pl. of ऊ "that," respectively.

A curious proof of the antiquity of these complicated forms with suffixes is afforded by the fact, that in connection with them the 3 sing. aorist of √अस् appears still in its old Pr. form of अथ (अस्ति), § 59. This form exists only in combination with the pronominal suffixes, whereas the ordinary form आहे is used both with and without suffixes. Thus they say आहेमि and अथमि "there is to me," as in the line—

मुझो अथमि गाल्हड़ी आउ वीझ तां चोरीआं ।

"*There is to me* a secret matter, come near, then I will tell it."

—Trumpp, p. 340.

It is used just as in Latin "est mihi," in the sense of "I have," as अथमि "I have," अथी (for अथइ) "thou hast," अथसि "he has," अथूं (for अथऊं) "we have," अथव "ye have," अथनि "they have." It is incorrect to say with Trumpp (*loc. cit.*)

that *sīho* has in S. "been transferred to the plural." The verb remains in the 3 sing. throughout, and takes suffixes of both numbers and all three persons.

In the compound tenses the suffixes are attached to the auxiliaries, leaving the principal verb unchanged. Both single and double suffixes are used in this way, just as with the simple and participial tenses. Thus किथी होए "thou hadst made." जंहिं खिद्मतगार (خدمتگار) खे अगे सेखारिओ हुआईं (for हुआई) तंहिं डे निहारिआईं "He looked towards that servant whom he had previously instructed," literally, "Which servant previously by him instructed, to that (one) by him looked" (Trumpp, p. 379).

It is tempting to look for the origin of this habit of using suffixes to the Semitic languages, which, from the early conquests of the Arabs in Persia and Sindh, may have had an influence upon the speech of those countries. On the other hand, however, the presence of a precisely similar habit in Italian and Spanish, seems to show that there exists a tendency to such constructions even in the Aryan family; for I suppose that even if we see in the Spanish forms a trace of Arab influence, no such motive power can be argued for any part of Italy, unless it be Sicily.

In Italian there are separate forms for the suffixed personal pronouns, and when used with a verb in the imperative or infinitive, these suffixed forms are incorporated into the verb; thus they say risponde*temi* "answer *me*," parlate*gli* "speak *to him*," date*le* "give *her*," imaginar*lo* "to imagine *it*," offrite*ci* "offer *us*." Double suffixes are also used, as assicurate*mene* "assure *me of it*," date*glielo* "give *it to him*," mandate*glieli* "send them to him."

So also in Spanish, vino á ver*me* "he came to see *me*," vengo á soccorrer*te* "I come to help *thee*," quiero castigar*os* "I will punish *you*," deja*me* "let me go," pasando*me* "*as I was* passing," escribe*le* "write *to him*," di*les* "tell them." Here, also, double suffixes may be used, as decir*telo* "to tell *it thee*," mostrar*nosla* "show her to us."

It is noticeable, however, that this habit in Italian and Spanish is modern, and does not exist in Latin, any more than it does in Sanskrit. Is it, then, a result of the confusion of forms that sprung into existence simultaneously with the decay of the old synthetic system, or is it an adoption of a Semitic principle? Diez finds the origin of the suffixed pronouns in shortened forms of the dative and accusative of Latin, which were already in use in the classical period.[1] It remains, however, to be explained how this peculiarity arose in the Romance group, in one member of the Iranian, and two members of the Indian group, only, and nowhere else in all the wide range of the Indo-European family.

§ 77. Having now gone through all the forms of the modern Indian verb, the subject may be closed by some remarks on the way in which the terminations are added to those verbal stems which end in a vowel. So many of these terminations begin with vowels, that a hiatus necessarily ensues, and the modern languages, though they do not, as a rule, object to a hiatus, do in this particular make occasional efforts to avoid it.

Hindi stems end only in long vowels—*â, î, û, e, o*. Some grammarians call those stems which end in a long vowel *open* roots, and those which end in a consonant *close* roots. This terminology has nothing to recommend it, and there is no advantage in retaining it. The tenses whose terminations begin with vowels are the aorist, future, imperative, and past participle.

Before terminations beginning with *î* or *o*, no attempt is made to soften the hiatus, but before *â* and *e* there is sometimes inserted a य् or व्. As types may be taken the stems जा "go,"

[1] Gramm. d. Romanischen Sprachen, vol. ii, p. 93, *et seqq.*

पी "drink," छू "touch," दे "give," and बो "sow." The aorist of these five is as follows:—

SINGULAR.

1. आऊं	2. आए, आवे, आव	3. *id.*
1. पीऊं	2. पीए, पीवे	3. *id.*
1. छूऊं	2. छूए	3. *id.*
1. देऊं, दूं	2. देवे, दे	3. *id.*
1. बोऊं	2. बोए, बोवे	3. *id.*

PLURAL.

1. आएं, आवें, आव	2. आओ	3. आएं, आवें, आव
1. पीएं, पीवें	2. पीओ	3. पीएं, पीवें
1. छूएं	2. छूओ	3. छूएं
1. देवें, दें	2. देओ, दो	3. देवें, दें
1. बोवें, बोएं	2. बोओ	3. बोवें, बोएं

The common stems *de* and *le* usually suffer contraction by the elision of their final vowel, and one more commonly hears *do* "give!" *lo* "take!" *dūngā* "I will give," *lūngā* "I will take," than the full forms.

The future and imperative follow the same rule as the aorist. In the past participle of stems ending in *ā*, य् is inserted before the *ā* of the termination, as आ "come," p.p.p. आ-य्-आ (आया), पा "find," पाया, खा "eat," खाया. But in the poets, especially in Tulsi Dās, instead of य् we find व् commonly inserted. Thus, यहि बिधि राम सबहि समुझावा "In this way Rām explained to all" (Ay-k. 457). आवा "came," बनावा "made," पावा "found," गावा "sung," for आया, बनाया, पाया, गाया respectively. Kabir uses both forms indifferently. Thus in Ram. 48, i. पढ़ावा "caused to read," पावा "found," but in the next, Ram. 49, पाया and आया. In the *fem.* sing., however, and in the pl. m. and f., the junction-letter य is not used, thus आई "she came," बनाई "she made," fem. sing., आये, पाये masc. pl. As all causals end in *á*, these forms are of frequent occurrence, and sometimes even an इ is inserted, as बनाइया. In the old *ha* future, the á of the stem and the initial *i* of the termination frequently coalesce into ऐ, as—

कछुक दिवस जननी धरु धीरा ।
कपिन्ह सहित ऐहैं रघुबीरा ।
निसिचर मारि तुमहि लै जैहैं ।
तिहुं पुर नारदादि जस गैहैं ।

"For a few days, mother, sustain thy courage,
Raghubir *will come* with the monkeys,
Slaying the demons, *will carry* thee *off*;
The three worlds, Nárada and all *shall sing* his praise."

—*Tulsi, Ram.*, S.-k. 25.

where ऐहैं = आइहैं, जैहैं = जाइहैं, and गैहैं = गाइहैं; so also we find पैहैं "they will find," for पाइहैं, mod. पावेंगे (Tulsi, Ram., S.-k. 10). In other places, however, we find the junction-letter व, as पावहिं, आवहिं, etc.

In Panjabi the junction-letter for the aorist, imperative, and future is regularly व, as जावे "he goes," जावेगा "he will go," but before *o* it is omitted, as जाओ "go ye," जाओगे "ye will go." For the past participle it is इ, as होइआ "been," masc. sing., and is omitted before *e*, as होए "been," masc. pl. In the three first-named tenses the व is regularly inserted in pure P., but in speaking it is now sometimes, under the influence of Hindi, omitted, and होगा is heard instead of the more characteristic होवेगा.

In Sindhi all verbal stems end in a vowel, those stems, which in other languages end in a consonant, having in that language a short *a* or *i*. In this class of stems, before the neuter infinitive in अणु, a व is inserted, as प "fall," infin. पवणु; नि "bow," infin. निवणु. Before the active infinitive in इणु no junction-letter is employed, as म "measure," infin. मइणु.

Stems, whether active or neuter, ending in *í* and *ú*, and sometimes those ending in *o*, shorten those vowels in the infinitive, as—

पी "drink," infin. पिअणु
पू "string," " पुअणु
धो "wash," " धुअणु
रो "weep," " रुअणु
हो "be," " हुअणु

but, on the other hand, ढो "carry," has infin. ढोअणु; and stems in *á*, including causals, retain the long vowel, as—

गाल्हा "speak," infin. गाल्हाइणु
फेरा "cause to turn," " फेराइणु.

The aorist follows generally the type of the infinitive, retaining the short vowel. In the persons व is inserted as in P., except before *ú* or *o*; thus पवां "I fall," is declined—

Sing. 1. पवां 2. पवें 3. पवे. Pl. 1. पऊं 2. पवो 3. पवनि.

The व may be dropped before 2 and 3 sing., as चए "thou sayest," or "he says." The common verb डिअणु "to give," undergoes contraction in this, as in all the other languages; thus 2 sing. डीं "thou givest," not डिएं, 3 pl. डीनि, not डिअनि.

Verbs ending in *á* insert य before *á*, *ú*, and *o*, as बुढायां "I grow old," बुढायूं "we grow old," बुढायो "ye grow old."

The imperative and other tenses follow the general rule, which may, for Sindhi, and, to a great extent, for the other languages also, be thus stated; the junction-letters are य and व. व is omitted before vowels of its own organ, as *u* and *o*, and य is omitted before *i* and *e*; before *á* both are employed, but preferentially य after short vowels, and व after long ones.

Thus, in the present participle, which is used as a future, य is either inserted or omitted, as—

पवणु "to fall," पवंदो "falling."

पिअणु "to drink," पिअंदो "drinking."

धुअणु "to wash," धुअंदो "washing."

Contraction also occurs, as चवणु "to speak," चूंदो (चवंदो) हुअणु "to be," हूंदो (हुअंदो) डिअणु "to give," डींदो (डिअंदो). The past participle regularly ends in इओ or यो, and the inserted व is naturally dropped before it, thus—

चवणु makes चयो, not चव्यो.

पवणु „ पयो „ पव्यो (Old-H. पायउ).

If the stem ends in a palatal vowel or consonant, the *i* of the termination is dropped, as—

थिअणु "to become," थियो, not थीयो = थि + इयो.

चुअणु "to speak," चुयो.

पुछणु "to inquire," पुछ्यो.

Passives naturally drop the euphonic व of the active infinitive before their palatal junction-vowel, as—

चवणु "speak," imperfect चउ, Passive चइजणु "to be spoken."

पवणु "fall," „ पउ, „ पइजणु "to be fallen."

The stems quoted above, as shortening their radical long vowel before the termination of the infinitive active, naturally retain the long vowel in the passive, as—

पी "drink," पीजणु "to be drunk."

पू "string," पूजणु "to be strung."

धो "wash," धोइजणु "be washed."

There is very little to notice, in this respect, about G. The orthography of that language is still in so unfixed a state, that it is impossible to seize upon any principles as to junction-letters. One writer will insert them, while another omits them, or the same writer will insert them on one page and omit them on the next. Thus we find होए, होवे, होय, होव written indifferently, also कइबे and कइए. Until the natives of that province make up their minds as to how their language ought to be spelt, it is impossible for foreigners to evolve any laws or rules on the subject.

§ 78. Marathi is slightly more sensitive to hiatus, and has a greater fondness for the य-sound than the other languages. There exists, consequently, in some persons of certain tenses, a system of Sandhi for Tadbhava words and forms, which differs in its general principles from that prevailing in Sanskrit. The grammar-writers, unfortunately, either omit entirely or only casually note these important combinations. The following remarks are offered as a contribution to the subject.[1]

The tenses of the M. verb, whose terminations begin with a vowel, are the aorist, imperative, future, and subjunctive, also the participles present and past, the conjunctive and infinitive. These are for the neuter verb; in the active verb the ई, which is inserted between the stem and termination, causes a collision of two vowels in the other tenses also. Verbal stems ending in all the vowels except *a* have here to be considered (khâ "eat," pî "drink," ghe "take").

Aorist, (in modern usage past habitual)—

SINGULAR.			PLURAL.		
1. खाईं	2. खाईस	3. खाई.	1. खाऊं	2. खा	3. खात.
1. पीईं	2. पीईस	3. पीई.	1. पीऊं	2. प्या	3. पीत.
1. घेईं	2. घेईस	3. घेई.	1. घेऊं	2. घ्या	3. घेत.

But in the 3 sing. घे, पी are used, so also खास, घेस in 2 sing., and in the 3 pl. the final ई is elided. In 2 sing. both ई and ए are changed to the palatal semivowel before â, though not before û, so that we have प्या, घ्या side by side with पीऊं (not प्यूं), घेऊं (not घ्यूं).

[1] For the illustrations to this section I have to thank Captain G. A. Jacob, Inspector of Schools, Punâ, who kindly furnished me with details which are wanting from most of the grammars.

In the future there is similarly in 2 pl. खाल, प्याल, द्याल, and so also in the imperative 2 pl. खा, प्या; ये "come," makes aorist 2 pl. या, future याल, and occasionally one hears ये aorist 3 sing. for the more regular येई.

In the subjunctive the semivowel occurs again, as खावा, प्यावा, but यावा simply from ये. This last verb should, by analogy, form य्यावा, but the double *y* in such a position would be unpronounceable, and a single *y* is therefore exhibited. It must not be supposed that the *e* of ये has simply been dropped.

For the potential the termination of the present वतें might have been expected to be simply added to the verbal stem, as no hiatus would thus be caused. But the origin of this form from the Skr. part. in तव्य renders this course impossible. The त of तव्य having suffered elision, there naturally results an hiatus. Thus from खादितव्यं, Pr. खाइअव्वं gives खावव, the first व supplying the place of the lost इ, so that in the potential we get not खावतें, but खाववतें. Similarly पीववतें, देववतें, घेववतें, and even in stems ending in ह, as लिह "write," लिहववतें.

Stems ending in *u* preserve the hiatus almost throughout, thus *dhu* "wash"—

Aor. धुई, धुइस, धुई; धुऊं, धुवा (but धुत).
Fut. धुईन, धुईल, धुऊं; धुवाल, धुतील.
Subj. धुवावा or धुयावा.
Pot. धुववतें.

In the present participle only त is added, not ईत or वत, as खात, पीत, देत, घेत, धुत, and in the past participle the semivowel is generally used, as—

खा p.p. खाला "eaten."
ले „ ल्याला "put on."
भी „ भ्याला "feared."
वि „ व्याला "brought forth."
पी „ प्याला or पिला "drunk."

Some stems avoid the hiatus by insertion of त, as घेतला, धुतला (see § 47), which is also used in some stems ending with a consonant.

The conjunctive is खाऊन, पीऊन, घेऊन, देऊन. These are all the forms in which an initial vowel of a termination comes in contact with a final stem-vowel, and it will be observed that the change of the latter into a semivowel occurs generally before *a* or *â*, but not before *i* or *û*. When the stem-vowel is *u* or *e*, the semivowel is added to, not substituted for, the vowel, as in धुवावा, not ध्वावा. From this and other instances in word-building, and in the formation of the case of the noun, it would appear that the labial and palatal vowels are more permanent and less liable to change in Marathi than the guttural vowel.

It is somewhat difficult to follow the author of the Portuguese grammar of the Konkani dialect, in consequence of the peculiarity of the system of transliteration which he uses, and only half explains, but there would appear to be several forms peculiar to that dialect. Thus he tells us that ये makes its past part. *yelo* or *ailo*, which latter he calls "marattismo," as if all Konkani were not Marathi. घे makes *gheilo* (perhaps घेइला), as well as *ghetlo* (घेतला). *Ghalā* (घा) makes *ghelo* (घेला) "outros dizem *ghailo*" (घाइला), he adds, "ambos irregulares," though the latter, from a Marathi point of view, would be more normal than the actually used घातला. Perhaps the author would call it a "marattismo." Generally speaking, it would appear from the specimens of Konkani given by Burnell,[1] that the termination of the p.p. consists of लो, ली, लें, etc., added to the stem without an intermediate vowel, as बसलो "sat" (M. बसला), पडलॆं "fell" (M. पडला), राव्ली "remained" (M. राहिली), and the like.

The differences between Konkani and Marathi do not, I

[1] Specimens of South Indian Dialects (Mangalore, 1872).

think, entitle the former to be considered a distinct member of the Aryan group, but rather a dialect of the latter, which has been subjected very largely to Dravidian influences. Parallel to it, on the opposite coast of India, is the Oriya spoken in Ganjam and Vizagapatam, which, though radically Oriya, has, nevertheless, been much Dravidianized by the influence of the Telugu which surrounds it. Both Ganjam Oriya and Konkani Marathi show traces of this influence not only in pronunciation, but even in structure. There is much to be said on this subject, were this the proper place for it, and, from the known results in languages under our own eyes of Dravidian influences on Aryan speech, we might base considerations as to the probable extent and nature of those influences in former times. The subject would require a whole treatise to itself.

§ 79. In Bangali no attempt is made to avoid hiatus, the verbs ending in vowels simply add the terminations without any change. Thus जा "go" (pronounced *jā*), makes—

	SINGULAR.			PLURAL.		
Aorist.	1. जाइ	2. जाइस	3. जाय.	1. जाइ	2. जाओ	3. जान.

Present जाइतेछि, subjunctive जाइताम, and so on.

Contraction, however, takes place in the 3 pl. of the aorist, as in जान for जाइन, हन (hōnō) for होइन, and in the familiar verb दे "give," almost throughout; thus we have—

	SINGULAR.			PLURAL.		
Aor.	1. दि	2. दिस	3. देय.	1. दि	2. देओ	3. देन
Pres.	1. दितेछि, etc.					
Pret.	1. दिनु	2. दिलि	3. दिल.	1. दिलाम	2. दिले	3. दिलेन
Fut.	1. दिब	2. दिबि	3. दिबे.	1. दिब	2. दिबा ०बे	3. दिबेन.

contracted from देइ, देइतेछि, देइनु, देइब, etc., respectively. As a rule, however, though in ordinary speech many of the forms of stems in vowels are very much contracted, yet in writing the full forms are always used. It is only in a few very familiar words that the contractions are admitted into the written style of the present day. The old poets, however, writing more freely and naturally, employ them frequently. Thus Bhârat Chandra, मजुन्दारे सङ्गे लिया घोडा चढाइया "He *took* Majumdâr along with him, having mounted him on a horse" (Mansingh, 417), where लिया is for लइया, from लइते "to take." So he constantly uses कय for कहे "says," as कोटाल हासिया कय। कहिते लाज ना हय। "The Kotwal laughing, says, Are you not ashamed to say so?" (Bidyâ-S. 356), also कब for कहिब, as हाय हाय कि कब विधिरे "Alas! alas! what shall I say to fate?" (*ib.* 360), and दिल for दइल aorist 3 sing., as आगे दिया कतदुख मध्ये दिल कतसुख "First having given how much pain, they give in between how much pleasure" (*ib.* 359).

The contractions admitted in Oriya are similar to those in Bangali, but the language does not avoid the hiatus in any way; and in both O. and B. the terminations are almost universally preceded by short *i*, which does not combine with the preceding vowel, but in pronunciation often disappears altogether. Thus they say, O. खाउ "wilt thou eat?" for खाइउ. In a few words the vowel of the root has gone out, thus from जा "go," we have जिबि "I will go," for जाइबि: from था "remain," infin. थिबा for थाइबा; पा "find," however, retains its vowel, as पाइलि, पाइबि, पाइबा. Also जा and था retain their vowels everywhere except in the preterite, future, and infinitive.

CHAPTER VI.

THE PARTICLE.

CONTENTS.—§ 80. ADVERBS NOMINAL AND PRONOMINAL.—§ 81. PRONOMINAL ADVERBS OF TIME, PLACE, AND MANNER.—§ 82. ADVERBS DERIVED FROM NOUNS AND VERBS.—§ 83. CONJUNCTIONS.—§ 84. INTERJECTIONS.—§ 85. POSTPOSITIONS.—§ 86. CONCLUSION.

§ 80. THE seven languages are rich in adverbs, and have a specially symmetrical range of pronominal adverbs, corresponding to the several classes of pronouns. The forms were given in Vol. II. pp. 326–38, in order to show their analogy to the pronouns, but nothing was said in that place about their origin; it will now be necessary to consider them more closely. The pronominal adverbs may be at once assumed to have sprung from the pronouns to which they respectively correspond, by the incorporation of some noun indicative of time, place, manner, and the like. On the other hand, the adverbs which have no pronominal meaning are clearly derived from various cases of nouns, whether substantives or adjectives. Participles, also, in virtue of their seminominal character, are used adverbially, either in their original form, or with certain modifications. Adverbs, therefore, may be divided into two classes, nominal and pronominal, with reference to their origin, and into three general categories of time, place, and manner, with reference to their meaning. To these must be added adverbs of confirmation and negation, and certain little helping words which are more adverbial in their nature than anything else. It is also to be noted that, while on the one hand simple nouns are often used adverbially, on the other hand, adverbs are capable of being used as nouns with postpositions after them, as in H. तब की बात, lit. "the word of then," *i.e.* "the matter that took place then," अब के राजा लोग "the kings of now," *i.e.* "those of the present day."

§81. (1). *Pronominal adverbs of time.*—The near demonstrative is H. अब, G. हवे, M. हल्लीं, O. एबे. All these hang together, and are apparently compounds of the Skr. वेला "time," with the type of the demonstrative अ, ए, or इ. The fuller form in O. shows this, it is एते बेळे, which is clearly the locative case of a masculine बेळ, literally, "in so much time." G. has prefixed a ह, but many words in G. may be indifferently written with ह or अ; there is, therefore, nothing organic about this letter when met with in this connection. In M. हल्लीं also the ह seems to be somewhat anomalous. There are also, however, many other forms for "now" in the various languages, which appear to be unconnected with वेला.

Hindi is mostly, however, faithful to the type in अ; thus in Braj अबै, Marwari अबि, and still more clearly Bhojpuri एबेर, which approaches to the O. एबे. The same type runs through all the pronominal forms, as जब "whenever," तब "then," कब "when." Bhojpuri जबेर, तबेर, कबेर, Braj जबै, तबै, कबै. The Skr. forms यदा, तदा, कदा appear in H. जद, तद, कद, and in the dialectic forms, जदि, जदो, जदू, जदां, जधां; as also तदि, etc., कदि, etc.; the forms with the palatal and labial vowels have, I think, arisen from the incorporation of the affirmative particle ही or हु "indeed," of which more further on.

Panjabi हुण, G. S. हाणे, B. एखन, and a dialectic form in O. एखुण, all meaning "now," are to be referred, as the B. form clearly shows, to the Skr. क्षण "instant, moment." For the rest of the series P. has जद, तद, कद. S., however, has another type हिंअर, हेर "now," in which we may, perhaps, see the Skr. वार "time," combined with the pronoun हिअ "this;"

for the other members of the series it has जॾहीं "whenever," तॾहीं "then," कॾहीं "when?" which arise from the Skr. यदा, etc., with the emphatic ही, which has changed the preceding vowel into the *i* which is so common in S. They also write जॾीं and जॾहिं as dialectic variations; also जां, तां (but not कां), where the द of यदा has suffered elision.

G. has, besides हवे, also हमणां, हवडां, and for the rest जेवारे, तेवारे, केवारे, commonly contracted into ज्यारे, etc., in which we see the Skr. वार "time." Owing to the G. peculiarity in respect of initial ह, we have also अमणां, and with a modernised form of Skr. अत्र "here," अबारे (अब वारे) "at this time," "now."

M. is consistent throughout एव्हां, जेव्हां, तेव्हां, केव्हां. In Old-M. forms जेधवां, etc., occur, showing that the modern व्ह *vh* is an inversion from ह्व *hv*. The suggested origin from Skr. यदा, by aspirating the द and adding वां, the termination of the locative (Godbol, p. 75), is unsatisfactory. M. has also a series जंव, etc., meaning "while," "as long as," which recalls H. जब with inorganic anunásika.

O. has the fuller forms, जेबे जेबेळे, etc., and जेबे explained above; the former is quite as frequently used as the latter, if not more so. "Time is made for slaves," and not for Oriyas.

B. जखन, तखन, etc., uniformly, pronounced *jókhon* or *jókhono*, etc. H. adds constantly ही for emphasis, as अभी "now" (अबही), कभी "sometimes" (कबही), and with the negative कभी नहीं "never."

For the indefinite pronominal adverb "ever," "sometimes," the other languages have, P. कदी (कदही), कदीं, कदे, S. कॾहीं, G. कदी, M. कधीं, B. कखन, O. केबे, केबेहिं. All these are repeated to signify "sometimes," as P. कदी कदी, M. कधीं कधीं.

The above express definite or quiescent time; for progressive time, whether past, as "since," or future "until," the adverbs above given are used as nouns with case-affixes. Thus H. अब से "from now," "henceforth," तब से "thenceforth," कब से

"since when?" जब से "from the time when," or with the older affix तें in the poets, as in जब तें राम ब्याहि घर आये। "From the time when Ram married and came home" (Tulsi-Rám. Ay-k. 6). P. जदों. S. जडिहाको, जडिहोको, जडिहाकर; where को is probably a shortened form of कर, an oblique from कर, which we may connect with काल "time," as in हिणर "now." The long á or o of *jaḍiká, jaḍiko*, as contrasted with the *i* of जडिहीं, seems to indicate an oblique form. G. हमणाथी "henceforth," जमारथी, and apparently also मारथी, and the rest of the series. They also say जमार पछी "henceforth." M. uses मग or मागें, which are not pronominal. Neither B. nor O. have special forms for this idea.

To express "until" in Old-H. लगि, लौं, लौ, in modern H. तक, तलक, and लग, are affixed to the pronominal adverb, as in Chand—

तब लगि कष्ट दरिद्र तन।
तब लगि लघु सुचि गात।
जब लगि हौं आयौ नहीं।
तौ पाइ न सेवात॥

"Till then, pain and poverty of body,
Till then, my limbs were light (*i.e.* mean),
So long as I came not to thee,
And worshipped not at thy feet.—Pr.-R. i. 276.

Here, as always in H., the negative has to be inserted, and we must translate जब लगि by "so long as." This idiom is not peculiar to H., but is found in many other languages. In modern Hindi जब तक राम घर को नहीं आवे "So long as Rām comes not home," *i.e.* "until he comes," and the same in P.

S. has हितीं or इथीताईं "up to this time," जोतीं or जोतीताईं "up to that time," where ताईं, as explained in Vol. II. p. 298, is Skr. स्थाने, which, from meaning "in the place," has grown to mean "up to." तीं, I suppose, is a contraction of समय "time."

(2). Pronominal adverbs of place.—See list in Vol. II. p. 336.

The Hindi series यहां, वहां, जहां, तहां, कहां, is composed of the pronominal bases with हां, which we are justified in referring to Skr. स्थाने; thus तहां = तस्थाने. The dental is preserved in several dialectic forms (Kellogg, p. 265), as Marwari अठै, अठो, ऐठै "here," उठै, etc., "there," Avadhi यहठियां, वोहठियां, Bhojpuri एठां, एठाईं. But the Braj इतै, इत, is, I think, by Kellogg rightly referred to the Skr. series अत्र, तत्र, etc. The Bundelkhandi form हान्नी is probably only another way of pronouncing हाँ, as we find in Old-Bengali such words as कहाणि for कहाँई (modern कहाइया). To *sthâne*, also, are to be ascribed the P. forms इत्थे, उत्थे, etc. S. has not only इति, जिति, etc., which may come from अत्र, यत्र, but इत्थे, which agrees with P., and हिते, which is, I suspect, like हिक्को "one," an instance of a ह being put on to the front of a word without any etymological cause.

G. has various forms अहीं, आहां, ह्यां, अहींआं "here," and the same variety through all the series. The adverbial part agrees with H. Shortened forms ह्यां, त्यां, क्यां, and even आं, तां, कां, are also in use.

M. agrees closely with P. and S. in its series येथें, तेथें, etc., where the final anuswâra, like that of Bhojpuri एठाईं, preserves the *n* of *sthâne*. But कोठें "where," has the cerebral.

O. having first made *sthâna* into ठा, proceeds with the declension through its own affixes, and has thus a modern locative ठारे, in एठारे, सेठारे. The final रे is often dropped, and एठा, सेठा, or even shortened एठि, सेठि are used. B. uses थाने, which seems to come from स्थाने on the analogy of थंभो = स्तंभ (Var. iii. 14) and थाणु = स्थाणु (*ib.* iii. 15). For "where," however, it has a more regular form कोथा, in older Bengali कोथाय, as तार मत तपस्विनी पाइब कोथाय "Where shall I find a female saint like her?" (Bharat, Bidyá-S. 399), where the final य for ए is a relic of the *e* of *sthâne*. We also find हेथा and हेथाय "here," etc.

In the case of the adverbs of this group, as in those of time, the case-affixes are used, as H. कहाँ से "from where?" "whence?" G. आहाँ थी "hence," P. किधरों "whence?" But this practice is only in force to imply motion *from* a place. To express motion *towards* a place a separate set is used.

In classical H. the adverbial element is धर, as इधर "hither," उधर "thither." The dialectic forms are very various. Bhojpuri has इन्हर, उन्हर, as also इमे, उमे, etc.; in eastern Behar one hears इम्हर, हेवर, and many others. Kellogg quotes also a curious form from Rîwâ इहै मेर, इहै कवीन, or इहै मुंह. If we take the original of all these forms to be धर, that is a word of many meanings both in Skr. and H.; but I am disposed to connect the series with M. म्होर "face," G. मोहडुं *id.*, a diminutive from Skr. मुख, so that the older adverbial element would be म्हर, as in Bhojpuri, whence म्ह, which would, by a natural process, glide into हर and धर. For the Rîwâ form I can suggest no origin.

The S. and M. forms seem to be connected, and with them I would associate the common O. expressions ए आड़े "in this direction," "hither" (से आड़े, सो आड़े, etc.), which are locatives, and ए आड़ु, etc., "from this place," "hence," which are ablatives. The Sindhi adverb, as usual in that language, is written in a dozen ways, but the simplest form is हिडे "hither," and हिडां "hence," which, like O., are respectively locative and ablative. Marathi has what is apparently a fuller form इकडे "hither," locative, where the adverbial portion is कड "a side," said to be from Skr. कट "hip, loin." It has also an ablative series इकडून "hence." May we not here throw out a crumb for our Non-Aryan brethren? There is a long string of words in our seven languages of the type *aḍḍa*, and our Sanskrit dictionaries give √अड्ड "to join," also "to stop." On the other hand, Telugu has *ikkaḍa* "here," *ikkaḍiki* "hither," which looks very like M. *ikaḍe*. So, also, in Telugu *akkaḍa* "there." All the Dravidian languages have a root *aḍḍ*, which, in various forms, has a range of meanings such as "to be near," "close," "to cross," "to stop," and the like. They may have borrowed from the Aryans, or the Aryans from them. It by no means follows, as the opposite party always assume, that when a word is common to both groups, it must have been originally Dravidian. In the O. expression बाट is a noun meaning "direction," and is used in that sense independently of its adverbial employment with the pronoun.

(8). Pronominal adverbs of manner.—The Hindi series यों, ज्यों, त्यों, etc., and for the near demonstrative and interrogative respectively softened forms यूं and क्यूं, vary very little in the dialects. Marwari has यं, इसो "thus," and, together with Braj and Mewari, has the far demonstrative, which is wanting in the classical dialect, वौं or वूं. Mewari adds यार and या, as ईयार, ईया "thus," which Kellogg looks on as from Skr. इ and मत respectively, and rightly so; for even in classical H. we have क्यूंकर "how?" and in Chand and the poets करि or कर (कि) are added to all this pronominal series at will.

The older form of this group is still preserved in the Purbi form इम or इमि, जिमि, तिमि. Chand has both this series and the modern one in यौं, as यौं मयौ रिखि चयधुन । "*Thus* the Rishi was absorbed in thought" (Pr.-R. i. 48), यौं इह कथ्य प्रमानं । यौं जानि कोविद जाने । "*Thus* this story is proved, its learned folk know" (*ib.* xiii. 5), पद्मावती इम ले चल्यौ । हरषि राज प्रथिराज । "King Prithiraj, rejoicing, thus (*ima*) led away Padmâvati" (*ib.* xx. 35), तहां सु कैसे किम्मी जाय । "*How* can one go there?" (*ib.* i. 90). Tulsi Das has इमि, जिमि, etc., as in तन पसेउ कदली जिमि कांपी "Her body was in a sweat, she trembled *as* a plantain-tree (trembles)."—Ram. Ay-k. 131.

M. may be excluded, as it has no series of this type, but merely the neuter of the adjective pronoun, as असें, कसें, तसें. All the other languages have closely allied words. B. एमन, एमन, एमने, एमते, "thus," केमन, etc.; the first two are nominatives, the last two locatives. O. एमन्ति, केमन्ति, locatives; also

इ पहि, the pronominal type, with a postposition. G. एम, केम, where the termination has been lost, also for demonstrative आम. This series is sometimes written एवम, केवम, जेवम, but केम is the more common, as in कीर्ति चढ़ नळ नी विस्तरी जेम सूरज ना पसरे किर्ण । "The fame of Naḷa was spread abroad, as spread the rays of the sun" (PremAnand in H.-D. ii. 71).

Next in order comes the Old-Purbi H. इमि, etc., and, with the nasal weakened, probably through an intermediate form इंव, and change of the semivowel to its vowel, P. इउं and जिउं *wiũ*, and the full series जिवें, तिवें, किवें, as well as one without the *i*, जवें, तवें, etc., to which is allied H. ज्यौं, etc., for जिवें. S. rejects the labial element in हेंव, जींव, केंव, and the rest of the series.

In this instance B. and O. preserve the fuller forms, and the other languages fall away by degrees, in the order given above. The whole group points, in my opinion, clearly to a type in मत् or वत्. This is still more clearly seen by comparing the pronominal adjective of quality in B. and O. जेमन, तेमन, for मन्तो is the regular Prakrit form of the masc. मत्, just as वन्तो is of वत् in Skr. It is true that the existing Skr. series means rather quantity than manner, thus—

इयान्, इयती, इयत् "so much,"
कियत् "how much?"
एतावान्, °वती, °वत् "so much,"
यावत् "as much as."

But the affixes *mat* and *vat* imply possession, and thus naturally pass over into the idea of manner. It seems that we have in the modern group this affix added to the ordinary range of pronominal types, and thus a *formation* of a later kind, rather than a direct derivation from the Skr. Kellogg's suggestion of a derivation from a Skr. series in *tha*, of which only *ittham* and *katham* are extant in the classical writings, fails to account for the Old-Purbi and G. forms, as well as for those in B. and O. Also the S. form हिंथ seems to be more naturally referred to an earlier *smama*, through *sam*, than to *itthaṁ*, unless, indeed, we regard the anuswára as inserted to fill the hiatus left by elision of *tth*. S. does, undoubtedly, insert anuswára to fill a hiatus; but as the cognate languages have a थ just where the anuswára in S. occurs, it is more natural to regard the one as a weakening of the other, and the final anuswára in H. and P. as the same, pushed one syllable forwards, so that H. यहीं would be for an older form यहिंथ. As the change, whatever it was, was completed before our earliest writer Chand's days, there is no actual proof forthcoming.

§ 82. Adverbs derived from nouns and verbs.—Under this head may be classed certain words such as those given in Vol. II. p. 298, which are either postpositions or adverbs, according to the connection in which they are used. In either case they are, by derivation, locative cases of nouns. Some are peculiar to one or two languages, while others are common, in one form or another, to the whole group. I do not, of course, undertake to give them all, but only a selection of those most commonly used, so as to show the practice of the languages in this respect. There are, for instance, H. आगे "before," and पीछे "behind," which are used adverbially in the sense of "formerly" and "afterwards" respectively, that is, with reference to time, and in this sense take, like the pronominal adverbs, the case-affixes, as आगे की बात "the former matter," lit. "the matter of formerly," पीछे के दुख मैं कहूंगा नहीं "I will not tell the suffering that followed," lit. "the suffering of afterwards." So also with नीचे "below," and the other words given at Vol. II. p. 298.

Strictly referring to time definite are H. आज "to-day," P. अज्ज, S. अजु, etc. (Vol. I. p. 327), from Skr. अद्य; also H. कल from Skr. कल्य "dawn." This word has two meanings, it is used for both "yesterday" and "to-day." In rustic H. we have the forms काल्ह, कालि, कालह, and कल्ह (see Vol. I. p. 350). As the Skr. means only "dawn" in general, it is used in the moderns in the double sense, but in cases where the meaning might not be clear from the context, a word meaning past is employed when "yesterday" is intended, and a word meaning future when "to-morrow" is implied. It also takes case-affixes, as कल की लड़ाई में घायल हुआ "He was wounded in *yesterday's* battle," but कल की लड़ाई में यदि घायल हूंगा "If I shall be wounded in *to-morrow's* battle." G. काले. S. कल्ह, कालह. M. काल.

So also are used the following :—Skr. परश्वस् "the day after to-morrow." In the moderns it has also the sense "the day before yesterday," as H. परसों, and dialects परसौं, परहीं, परौं. P. परसों, S. परिहं, परिहंको, seem to be used only in the first meaning. G. परम, M. परवा. O. has पर always in combination with दिन, and where the sentence does not of itself sufficiently indicate the meaning, they add the words "gone" and "coming" to express it more clearly, गत पर दिन "the day before yesterday," and आसंता पर दिन "the day after to-morrow."

H. goes a step further still, and has नरसों "three days ago," or "three days hence," where the first syllable is probably Skr. त्रि "three." Similarly S. टरिहं, but also with rejection of initial ट, अरिहं. Kellogg quotes dialectic forms in H. अतरसों, नरौं, नरौं. In H. we have even a still further अतरसों "four days ago," which is rarely, however, used, and the initial of which, I conjecture, comes from अन्य, as though it were for अन्य नरसों "another day (besides) three days ago."

H. सबेर "early," "betimes," and अबेर, or more usually अबेर "late," are Skr. स and अ, compounded with वेला respectively. S. सवेर and अवेर, also अवेल, besides the adjectivally used forms सवेरो and अवारो, as well as अवेरो. In this sense is also used H. सकारे, सकारे, O. and B. *id.*; in O. it is frequently used in the sense of "early in the morning," also "early *to-morrow* morning," as आजि बाट पारिबु नाहिं सकाळे जिबु "To-day we shall not be able to go, we will go early to-morrow morning." H. here uses तड़के, conjunctive participle of तड़कना "to break," as we should say "at break of day;" also भोर "dawn" is used in H. and O., भोरे in B. for "at dawn;" where G. has पाहांटे, M. उषा (Skr. उदय "sunrise"). Common also is Skr. प्रभाते, B. *id.*, G. परभाते, of which the Oriyas make पाहान्ते "at dawn;" in Eastern Bengal one hears पाहाट. The H. भोर is probably connected with the Skr. √भा in some way not very clear. G. has a curious word मळसके "at dawn," probably connected with मळवुं "to meet," and, like Skr. सन्ध्या, indicating the meeting of darkness and light.

"Rapidly," "quickly," "at once."—This idea is expressed by derivatives of the Skr. √त्वर्, principally from the p.p.p. त्वरितम्, which is used adverbially already in Skr. The forms are: H. तुरंत, M. तुर्त, G. तुरत, तरत, त्वरीत, S. तुर्त, O. B. तुरंत, त्वरित. M. has a peculiar word लवकर "at once, quickly," Skr. लव (√लू "to cut") "a minute," M. लवणें "to flash, twitch, move quickly." It is not found in any other language. Commoner, however, is H. झट "quick!" reduplicated झटपट, M. झटकन्, S. झटिपटि and फटिपटि, O. झट, झटपट, B. झटि, from Skr. झटिति. "Immediately" is also expressed in M. by तत्काळ, O. and B. तत् क्षणात्, but these are pedantic. H. P. M. and S. have also a word अचानक; H. also अचांचक "suddenly," "unexpectedly," corresponding to which is G. अचानचेत, ओचिंतो, pointing to a derivation from अ and √चिन्त् "to think," though I am disposed also to remember Skr. चमत्कार, H. चौंक, in this connection. O. and B. use हठात्, literally ablative of Skr. हठ, meaning "by force." It is used generally of sudden and forcible action, but also in sentences where no force, only surprise, or a sudden fright, occurs. Similarly in H. and G. एकाएक "all of a sudden," M. एकाएकीं, are used.

Among adverbs of place, considerable divergences exist, each language having a large stock of words peculiar to itself, in addition to those which are common to the whole group. Sindhi is rich in words of this class, most of which are of somewhat obscure origin. Thus we find a small group with the typical ending in ड़, as आड़ो "opposite," ओड़ो "near," ओड़िड़ो diminutive of the preceding. Peculiar to S. is also वेझो "near," with its diminutive वेझिड़ो. सूधो "accompanied by," O. सुधा, is by Trumpp referred to Skr. सार्द्धं "with," and सञो "near," to संनिधि, probably correctly. See the remarks on the postposition से in Vol. II. p. 274, and on the Nepali ablative in सित, Vol. II. p. 235. From adverbs with the affixes आहों and आरो are formed certain adjectives which may, in their turn, be again used adverbially as well as adjectively, that is, they may either stand alone uninflected, or may agree with a substantive in gender and number. Thus—

ओरे "on this side."	ओराहों "somewhat on this side."
अगे "in front,"	अगाहों "somewhat in front."
पोइते "behind,"	पोइताहों "somewhat behind."
मथे "upon,"	मथाहों "somewhat higher up."
मंझे "in,"	मंझाहों / मंझारो } "somewhat inside."

This last word recalls the old poetic Hindi मझार used in Chand (see Vol. II. p. 293). They may also take the feminine ending आहीं, as अगाहीं, मथाहीं.[1]

Simple ablatives or locatives of nouns are also used adverbially, as—

पुठां / पुठों } "from behind,"	abl. of पोइठ "the rear."
पुठिआं "from behind,"	„ पुठि "the back."

[1] Trumpp, Sindhi Grammar, p. [illegible].

मथां "from upon,"	abl. of मथो "the head."
मथे *id.*	loc. of *id.*
माये "at all,"	" मायु "place."
मूरि "completely,"	" मूरु "capital," "stock-in-trade."
मूराहिं / मूराएं } *id.*	abl. of *id.*
मंढहि "before,"	loc. of मंढहु "beginning."
मंढहां *id.*	abl. of *id.*
पारे "on the other side,"	loc. of पारु "the other side."
पारां "from the other side,"	abl. of *id.*
अंदरे "within,"	loc. of अंदरु "the inside."
अंदरां / अंदरूं } "from within,"	abl. of *id.*
विचे "in the midst,"	loc. of विचु "the midst."
हडे / हडेही } "at all,"	" हडु "the core."
हेठि "below,"	" हेठु "the bottom."
हेठां "from below,"	abl. of *id.*

Sindhi thus preserves the case-endings more strictly than the other languages. The latter mostly take the Prakrit locative, or ablative, and entirely reject the terminations.

Hindi has अनत "elsewhere," Skr. अन्यत्र, निकट "near," also नेरे (dialectically नेड़ and नेरो); परे "on the other side," भीतर "within," Skr. अभ्यन्तरे, बाहिर, बाहर "outside," Skr. बहिस्, and others.

M., like S., has मागें, but in the sense of "before," also पुढें "before," पलीकडे "beyond," वर "above," जवळ "near," which are peculiar to itself. In the other languages there is nothing deserving special mention; the subject has already been treated in Vol. II. p. 206.

Adverbs of manner.—While the adverbs of place, being also, in their nature, postpositions, and as such used to form cases, do not call for special mention, adverbs of manner are not so used, and it is to them that the term adverb, in its more special sense, correctly applies. Such words as *āge* "before," *pichhe* "behind," and the others, may, indeed, be properly regarded as adverbs when they are used alone, but when in conjunction with nouns, they become true postpositions, giving to the relations of the noun a more extended application. Adverbs of manner, on the other hand, are, for the most part, adjectives used adverbially, and this practice is common in all Aryan languages. In Sindhi, which preserves distinctions obliterated in the other languages, adjectives may, as pointed out above, be used adverbially by being undeclined, or, in their true use as adjectives, by agreeing with the subject in gender and case. Thus, to quote the instances given by Trumpp:[1]

ओचितोईं कुअ हिकिड़े उन अटे जे भरि में बुरु कियो
"By chance one mouse made a hole near that granary."

Here *achito-ī* is an adjective in the nom. sing. masc. with emphatic *ī*, and although by the accident of the construction it is in the same case as the subject *kūo* "a mouse," yet it is evidently used adverbially.

तदिहीं बहु हारे पाण घणो रोई माउ वरिचोति
"Then having shed tears much, having wept much, his mother returned."

Here *ghaṇo* is an adjective in the nom. sing. masc., and clearly does not agree with *māū* "mother," which is feminine; it must be regarded as used adverbially.

लुकूं वञनि कोसिड़ो डाहा तपनि चौड़
"The winds strike hot, the days burn fiercely."

In this sentence I do not think we should regard the adjectives as used adverbially; लुकूं "winds," is a noun in the nom. pl. fem. and कोसिड़ो "hot" agrees with it, so also चौड़

[1] Sindhi Grammar, p. 384.

"days," is nom. sing. masc. and बाढा "fierce, excessive" (Skr. वृद्ध), agrees with it; so that we might more literally translate, "the hot winds strike, the fierce days burn."

In Marathi and Gujarati also, where adjectives have the full range of three genders, they are often made to agree with the noun in constructions, where in English they would be used adverbially. When intended to be adverbially used, they stand in the nom. sing. neuter, ending in ें M. and उं G. In Bengali and Oriya, where no gender exists, it is impossible to draw the same line of distinction, and this remark applies also to that numerous class of adjectives in Hindi and Panjabi, as also in all the other languages, which are indeclinable, or which, ending in mute *a*, do not vary their terminations. Those adjectives in H. and P. which end in *á* masc. and *í* fem., when used adverbially, stand in the former gender and do not vary with the noun.

§ 83. Conjunctions.—In Hindi the common word for "and" is और, Old-H. अरु, अवर, from Skr. अपर "other." In B. and O. it loses the final consonant, B. औ, O. अउ. In B., however, एवं, pronounced *ebong*, is very common; and आर "also." P. अते, often shortened into ते, probably from Skr. अन्ते "at the end," "afterwards," as well as अर (अपर). S. अवे, अं, ई or इ, in which the fondness of S. for the *i*-sound comes out. G. uses generally तथा literally "then." It has besides व and वी for "also," which belong to the group from अपर. G. अने, shortened ने, I am disposed to connect with P. अते, and ascribe to Skr. अन्ते. In the former case the त has been lost, in the latter the न. It may, however, be allied to M. आणि, आणखी "and," from Skr. अन्य "other." In all the languages, however, the shorter conjunction व is in use, side by side with the words given above. The ordinary Skr. च has left no descendants. The Gipsies use *te* or *ta*, which agrees with P., also *u*, which is Persian و.

"Also."—H. भी. Skr. अपि हि. Pr. वि हि. The various steps from अपि downwards are all retained in S. पि, वि, बि (for विहि), and भी. The other forms पुणु, पुणि, पिणि, are from Skr. पुनर् "again," and show a gradual change from the *u* to the *i*, in accordance with S. proclivities. P. नाळे means literally "near to," locative of नाळ "near." G. पण, meaning also "but," is from पुनर्. B. uses ओ, and O. बि.

"But" is very frequently expressed even in Hindi by the Arabic words लेकिन لیکن, बल्कि بلکه, and Persian मगर مگر; and in the other languages also. Pure Sanskrit are परन्तु and किन्तु, as well as वरन (Skr. वरं). In Hindi पर (Skr. परं) is also used, and in P., which also uses अपर, and a strange form हेपर, in the initial syllable of which we may recognize an incorporation of the near demonstrative pronoun, so that it means "rather than this." P. has also मगरों, मगों, probably corruptions of مگر. Peculiar to P. and S. are the forms P. इवों, S. इवां, इवें, and emphatic इवोंहि and इवेंहि "but rather." These are ablatives from इव, and the idiom may be paralleled by our English phrase "on the other hand." S. has also पर "but," and पण, in which latter it agrees with G. It also uses मगरि, having added a final *i* to مگر. G. and M., in addition to पण, use also परंतु, O. किन्तु and पर, B. किन्तु and वरं.

"Or."—H. या, अथवा, which are Skr., with य for व. The Arabic या يا is very common, and commoner still is कि, probably shortened from Skr. किंवा. This कि is colloquially common in nearly all the languages. G. writes it कें, where *e* is short. M. lengthens the vowel and retains the nasalization कीं, also using अथवा, as does G. P. कै, अथवा, and या. S. के and कि. B. uses several variations of किंवा, as किम्बा, किवा, कि, and वा, also अथवा. O. the same.

"If."—Skr. यदि, generally pronounced and written जदि, is universal. H. shortens it into जद् and जै (= जइ, with loss of द्) and जो, by rejection of final *i*, and द goes out, its place being supplied by ज and ड; thus यद् = जद = जड = जो. Persian अगर اگر is also very common. P. जे and जेकर. This last introduces कर for करि "having done." S. जे.

"Although."—Skr. यद्यपि is used in B. O., also in H., but more common is जो भी "if even." P. has भावें, literally "one may think," or "it may seem." B. also uses यदि वा "if even." S. जोड़े, जोड़ि, sometimes with जे prefixed, जे जोड़े: this, too, is literally "if even," for जोड़े alone is used to mean "either," "even," and is apparently really the correlative तो (तथ = तहि) with a diminutive affix. It is not found in the other languages. G. जो पण "but if." In all cases there is a correlative; thus to H. जो or जो भी answers तो or तो भी "then," or "even then;" to P. भावें answers तां भी; to G. जो पण, answers तो पण, and so in all. In B. and O., as in written H., the correlative is Skr. तथापि "yet."

"Because."—H. क्योंकि literally "for why." B. and O. use Skr. कारण "cause," and जे हेतु or जे हेतुक. G. माटे, probably Skr. मात्रके, which is also sometimes used in O. in the sense of "only," "merely," "for the simple reason that." G. has also केमके "for why," and shorter कांके. S. जेका, जेकहं, where the last syllable is for कारे "for" (see Vol. II. p. 260). S. also uses a string of forms with छा "why?" as छाकाणे, छा काइ, and छो ता, छो जो. The correlatives "therefore," etc., take the त form तेका "etc."

These instances may suffice to show the general principles on which the languages proceed in forming their conjunctions. There is, as in other respects, a general similarity of process, accompanied by variations of development.

§ 84. Interjections.—The various spontaneous or involuntary sounds, some of them hardly articulate, by which sudden emotions are expressed, are scarcely susceptible of rigid scientific analysis in any language. Everywhere we find ha! ho! or ah! oh! and the like. Surprise, fear, disgust, delight, and other sentiments are often displayed by grunts, shakes, turns of the head, or movements of the hands, and among the people of India the hands play so large a part in conversation that they may almost be said to speak for themselves. It is only the Englishman who can converse with his hands in his pockets.

In Hindi the principal interjections are हे, हो, अहो, भो "Ho!" or "Oh!" हे is used to superiors, as हे धर्मावतार "O incarnation of justice!" which is the common method of addressing a Magistrate or Judge, हे प्रभु "O Lord!" हे पिता "O father!" हो, अहो, and भो, have no special tone of respect or disrespect. Sorrow is shown by आ, आह, हाह, हा हा, हाय "alas!" whence the common cry of native suitors, or persons applying to a ruler for redress, दोहाइ literally "twice alas!" One often hears *dohde khudāwand, dohde Angrez Bahādur*, which is as much as to say "grant me justice," or "listen to my complaint." Others are छि छि "fie!" चुप "hush!" आह, ओह "ah!" a cry of pain; थू थू disgust; चल तेरी, an expression with a suspicion of indelicacy about it, like too many of the native ejaculations, meaning "begone," and at times with a menacing tone "how dare you?" I suspect the word now spelt चल was originally टल from टलना "to go away," "be stopped," and तेरी the feminine genitive of तू "thou," is explained by such filthy expressions as तेरी मा "thy mother." Two men are quarrelling, and one says to the other "Āh, terī mā," "oh thy mother." The person addressed at once understands that some gross and filthy insult to his mother is intended, for indiscriminate foul abuse of each other's female relations is a favourite weapon with the natives of India. Thus the innocent word साला or शाला "brother-in-law," has become the lowest term of abuse in those languages, the obscene imagination of the people immediately grasping the idea involved in this assumption of relationship.

Panjabi has mostly the same as Hindi. A very favourite

interjection of surprise with Panjabis, though it is also used by the other languages, is बाह, and doubled बाह बाह. The simple-minded Panjabi says "wāh! wāh!" to every new thing he sees, and this favourite exclamation helps to form the once terrible war-cry of the fighting Sikhs, "*wāh wāh! fatih guru ji!*"

All the other languages have these common interjections, several of which are also Persian or Arabic more or less corrupted. Thus the Persian شاد باش *shād bāsh*, "be joyful!" is used everywhere as a term of encouragement, "well done!" and is used to stimulate workers to increased efforts, to express approbation, or to kindle flagging courage. It appears mostly without the د, as *shābāsh*, *shābāsh*, *sābās*, according to the language in which it is used.

A few special remarks are due to a very widespread word which is claimed by the Non-Aryan writers, बरे, बरे or रे. This is used to call inferiors, to rebuke impertinence, in scolding or quarrelling, and in most languages takes also a feminine form बरी, री, री. Dr. Caldwell shows[1] that this word is also in use in the Dravidian group, and is there understood to mean "O slave!" Hemachandra, however (ii, 201), knows it as used in addressing (sambhāshaṇa), and in dalliance (ratikalahe). For reproach (kshepe) he prescribes हरे. I do not dispute the Non-Aryan origin of this word, but it must have found its way into Aryan speech at a very early date, and has there, to a great extent, lost its sense of rebuke, for it is often used merely to call attention, and in friendly condescension to an inferior, and there has sprung up beside it a form बरे, used also in the same tone. The interchange of ब and र need cause no difficulty, being, especially in early writers, extremely common. There does not appear to be any Sanskrit origin for this word, and the fact that in the

[1] Dravidian Comparative Grammar, p. 440 (first edition).

Dravidian group it can be traced to a definite meaning, is one which carries great weight.

In O. and B. रे is only used in calling males; when addressing females, O. uses लो, and B. गो. Thus O. चाल लो, मा बजारकु जिबा "Come along, mother, let us go to the bazar;" B. मिनतिये बलो शुन गो जननि "The lady entreats, 'hear me, oh my mother'" (Bhârat, Vid.-S. 338). लो, लोकटी are also used in B. in contempt or reproof. Both these words seem to be fragments of लोकटी, from Skr. लोक in the sense of "person," the word लोक or लोकाई being used to indicate the women of the speaker's family, and especially his wife, whom it is not considered proper to speak of directly.

§ 85. It is necessary to revert to the subject of postpositions, although they were partially discussed in Vol. II. p. 295, because in that place they were regarded in only one of their two aspects, namely, as factors in the declensional system. Here they must be looked at as parts of speech, corresponding to prepositions in the western Aryan languages.

In Hindi, in addition to the postpositions mentioned in Vol. II., may be cited as very common the following, some of which are also used as adverbs. Thus बाहिर "without" (Skr. बहिस्) is used as a postposition with the genitive case, as घर के बाहिर "outside the house," or even without the genitive sign, as द्वार बाहिर "outside the door." So also पार "across," "on the other side of," is very commonly used with the direct form of the noun in the phrase नदी पार "across the river," "on the other side of the river." So also समेत "with," "accompanied by," as सूर सामंत समेत "accompanied by his peers and paladins," the meaning of the postposition from सम्+आ+इ requires this construction.

बीच "in," "in the middle of," सिरे "at the end of" (Skr. शिरस्), कने "near to," "at the house of" (Skr. कर्णे), संग "with," द्वारा "by means of," ठाँ "at," "at the house of"

(Skr. पार्श्वे).[1] are also colloquially common, both with and without the sign of the genitive, but more frequently with it.

Panjabi has कोळ "near," literally, "in the bosom of," कोळों "from the side of," विच् "in," which is the regular sign of the locative, पार् "on the other side," and वार पार् "on both sides" (of a river, valley, etc.), as well as the Hindi words given above.

The postpositions in Sindhi are more numerous, and are divided, more clearly than in the other languages, into two classes, those which are added direct to the oblique form of the noun, and those which are added to the genitive. Of the first class are भर् or भरि "on," "leaning on" (Skr. भर), where in H. भर् rather means "full," as कोस भर् "a full kos;" तोड़ि and तोड़िं "up to," which Trumpp regards as an emphatic locative from तोड़ु "end;" वाँ, जियाँ, जीयाँ, जिहं, "like" (Skr. यथा); ड्रां, ड्रांह, ड्रे "towards," with an ablative form ड्राहाँ "from the direction of" (perhaps from Skr. दिश्): रे, रिया, "without" (Skr. ऋते); साँ, साणु, से, सेँ "with" (Skr. सम; cf. B. सने).

S. सूधो "along with," H. सूधा and सुधा "with," O. सुधा or सबु सुधा "together with," "all taken together," from Skr. सार्धम्, according to Trumpp and others, but the O. usage seems to refer rather to Skr. शुद्ध, in the sense of संयुक्त "completed."

S. ताँईं "up to," "till" (Skr. तावत्). P. ताँईं and तीर्ह, appears occasionally to be used as a postposition, and one or two others of less importance complete the list.

[1] Platts (Grammar, p. 196), from whom I take this list, is the first writer to give the real origin and meaning of this word, which I, in common with most of my countrymen, had hitherto confounded with yahāṅ "here." There was no need for Platts to be so very dogmatic and arrogant about this and one or two similar small discoveries. He should try to bear the weight of his stupendous erudition more meekly. We may be thankful, however, to him for condescending to make a few mistakes occasionally, to bring himself down to our level. Such are the remarkable bit of philology in note 1, page 164, and his remarks on the intransitive in notes to pp. 171, 174. He who undertakes to correct others, should be quite sure he is right himself first.

Of the second class are ब्राझां, ब्राझूं, ब्राझों "without," P. बाझ, बाझों *id.* This rather means "owing to the absence of," as in the passage quoted by Trumpp, तान सूरिह आन्हा हेकल हेजल बाझों हूंय थे "Then they were considered by the hero as thorns *in the absence of* his friend." It is probably connected with Skr. √बाध् in the sense of being bound or impeded. विना "without" (Skr. विना), is also common in H. P. B. and O. In M. विना, and G. विना and वना (*vinâ, vanâ*).

S. काए and कए "for the sake of," correspond to H. P. लिये, and are used like it, either with or without the genitive particle; but in S. the meaning is the same in both cases, while in H. it differs; thus उस लिये "for that reason," but उस के लिये "for the sake of him."

While in the other languages the postpositions, when not used as case-signs, are almost invariably joined to the genitive with the masculine oblique case-sign, in Sindhi they may take the ablative or accusative. Thus अगो "in front," may take the accusative. It is probably like O. आदौ "in the first place," or with a negative आदौ न "not at all," "at no time;" thus आदौ सेठि गला नहि literally "to begin with, he did not go there," that is to say, "he never went there at all," locative of Skr. आदि "beginning."

अंदरि "within," Skr. अन्तर्, but more probably from Persian اندر. वेझो "near to," धारे "apart, without," काणे "for the sake of," contracted from कारणे; मथे "upon," loc. of मथो "head," वांगे "like to," वेझो "near to," are also used in the same way.

In Marathi, besides the postpositions which are exclusively employed in forming cases, there are some which are added direct to the oblique form of the noun, and others which require the genitive case-sign.

Of the former kind are वर "on" (Skr. उपरि), which is generally written as one word with the noun, as घरावर "on the house," उद्यावर "till to-morrow." A longer form is वरता, which is declined as an adjective, generally meaning "up." Others are बाहेर "out," आंत "in," कडे "at," करून "by means of," वांचून "without," विषयीं "about," "concerning," literally "in the matter (of)," मागें "behind," "formerly," पुढें "before," "in future," खालीं "under."

There is nothing specially worthy of note in the remaining languages which do not vary from Hindi very widely, either in the words they use, or in the manner of using them.

§ 86. The survey of the seven languages is here ended; the thinness of matter and illustration, in some respects, is due to the want of material, the difficulty of procuring books, and the absence of persons who might be consulted. Others, who enjoy greater advantages in these respects, will, in future times, supplement and supersede much that is defective and erroneous in this outline. Amru'lkais sings—

وَما المَرْءُ ما دامَتْ حُشاشَةُ نَفْسِهِ
بِمُدْرِكِ أَطْرافِ الخُطُوبِ ولا آلِ

FINIS.

INDEX.

The Roman numeral indicates the volume, and the Arabic numeral the page. Only those words are here given which form the subject of some discussion, or illustrate some rule. A hyphen before a word indicates that it is a termination.

Note.—When the anuswâra precedes a strong consonant, it is not the nasal breathing, but the nasal letter of the varga of that consonant, and is therefore the first element in a mixed nexus. It must be looked for at the end of each varga.

A

-aïŋ, ii. 107
aïŋçâ, i. 193
aŋiŋ, ii. 311
aŋvalâ, i. 254; ii. 29
aŋa, aŋeu (aŋça), ii. 174
aŋeh, aŋeûŋ (açru), i. 337; ii. 193
-aŋhi, ii. 223
aŋhri, i. 134
-ak, ii. 29, 111
aka, ii. 345
akaḍ, ii. 102
akaḍait, *ib.*
akatar, ii. 346
akaté, *ib.*
akarâ, i. 260
akavka, ii. 343
akkh, i. 309; ii. 173
akahi, *ib.*
akhi, *ib.*
agaru, agure, ii. 296
agaro, *ib.* ii. 101
agalâ, *ib.*
agâü, ii. 296
agiár, i. 260; ii. 134
agio, ii. 296
agua, i. 172
agunis, ii. 186
agûniko, ii. 115
agg, aggi, agi (agni), i. 300; ii. 52, 218
aggéil, aggáiln, ii. 297
agru, ii. 285, 296

aglá, ii. 101
ank, ii. 120
ankaḍi, ib.
ankā, iii. 68
ankúr, ii. 282
ankhaḍi, ii. 120
ankhi, ii. 172
ang, ii. 121
angana, ii. 17
angára, i. 129; ii. 269
angiyá, ii. 121
angurijaṇu, iii. 71
anguli, i. 134
angialstno, ii. 288
acharaj, i. 186, 349
acharaṭ, ib.
achhe, achchhe, achchhá, ii. 12
√achh, achchh (as), iii. 180
achhání, ii. 80
achchhario, achchhero, ii. 286
achhi, iii. 185
aju, ajj, ajja, i. 327
anjali, i. 252
anjhu, i. 357
-aṭ, ii. 67
aṭak, ii. 31, 61
aṭakná, ib.
aṭá, aṭári, ii. 120
aṭká, ii. 63
aṭkáná, ii. 31
aṭkolo, aṭkhelo, ii. 96
aṭṭh, i. 315; ii. 133
aṭṭhi (asthi), i. 317
aṭṭhárah, ii. 134
aṭharapúk, ii. 44
aṭhál, aṭháls, i. 250
aṭhávan, ii. 141
aḍaṇá, aḍaṇoṇ, ii. 20
aḍat, aḍatya, ii. 58, 88
aḍavaṇúk, ii. 44
aḍahaṇ, ii. 184
aḍiyal, ii. 96
aḍi, aḍich, ii. 144
aḍhat (aṛhat), ii. 53
aḍhall, ii. 96
aḍhái (aṛhái), ii. 144
aḍhár, ii. 184
-aṇ, ii. 166
aṇḍá, aṇḍera (aṇḍa), ii. 5
aṇḍajá, ii. 120
-at, iii. 123
atasi, i. 130, 179
-atu, ii. 63
adhasta, ii. 298
adhu, adha, ii. 12
addhá, ii. 12
-an, ii. 166
-ana, ii. 15
ani (anya), i. 341
antar, antarúṇ (antra), ii. 174
-ando, iii. 123
andhakára, andherá, i. 299
andhá, andhalá, ii. 12
andhápaṇu, ii. 73
-anh, ii. 206
annhá, ii. 12
anahorá, ii. 299
apachchhar (apsaras), i. 309
apúpa, i. 179
apná, ii. 329
ab, ii. 336
abhyantare, i. 182
abhra, ii. 21
amangala, i. 262
amaro (-re, -ri), ii. 345
amo, ii. 307
ameṇ, ii. 302, 308
amo, ib.
amb, ambá, ambu, i. 342; ii. 21
ambavaṇi, ii. 127
ambiyá, ii. 21
ambhe, i. 362

amhe, amhap, etc. (forms of 1 pers. pron. pl.), ii. 302
-amhi, ii. 223
-aya, i. 140, 204
-ar (genitive), ii. 276, 280
araṇya, i. 179
aratti, arattatao, ii. 288
araheṭ, araṭa (araghaṭṭa), i. 266
archi, i. 318
arpa, i. 341
ardhâ, ii. 12
aliam (alika), i. 149
alsi, i. 130
ava, i. 178, 204
avaka, ii. 345
avasthâna, i. 178
avalambana, i. 262
avaçyâya, i. 346
avalo, ii. 73
avig, ii. 311
avijapo, iii. 72
avga, avgutno, ii. 268
açi (açiti), ii. 137
ashṭan, i. 315; ii. 133
ashṭâdaça, ii. 134
√as, iii. 171
asâ, ii. 302
asâḍlâ, ii. 313
asi, ii. 137
asiṇ, ii. 302
aso (me), iii. 184
asmâa, ii. 17
asthi, i. 317
-ahaṇ, ii. 220
ahal, ahahi, iii. 173
-ahi, ii. 221
ahiṇ, ii. 311
ahir, i. 268
-ahuṇ, ii. 220
ahvâṇ, ii. 311

Â

â, ii. 318, 336
√â, âla, âa, iii. 45
âiṇ, ii. 306
-âiṇ, âiṇi, ii. 90, 169
-âiṇ, ii. 166
âisâ, i. 158
-âit, ii. 104
âulâ, âolâ, ii. 29
âu, ii. 302
âuiṇ, ii. 311
âuṇ, ii. 302
âpoṇ, ii. 118
âuv, i. 254; ii. 173
âuvalâ, i. 254; ii. 29
âuviro, i. 254
âusû, i. 357
âuhiṇ, ii. 336
âkh, i. 310
âkhaḍu, i. 259
âkhu, i. 310
âg, âgun, âgi, (agni), i. 300; ii. 62, 191, 207, 209, 218
âgal, âgali, ii. 101
âgâ, i. 142
âgiâ, âgyâ (âjñâ), i. 303; ii. 159, 195
âgiog, âgu, âgo, i. 296
ânk, iii. 66
ânkh, i. 309; ii. 173
âṅgaṇ, âṅgaṇu, ii. 17
âchho, i. 316, 318; iii. 185
âj, âji, i. 327
âjikâra, ii. 279
ânch, i. 318
ânju, i. 367
-âṭ, ii. 65, 67
âṭ (ashṭan), ii. 133
âṭalo, ii. 336
âṭh (ashṭan), i. 315; ii. 133

âṭhâîn, i. 253
âṭhara, ii. 134
âṭhruṇ, ii. 247
-âṭko, ii. 114
âḍâl, ii. 144
âḍat, âḍhat (âṛhat), ii. 58
âṇ, ân (√ânî) iii. 44
âṇiko, ii. 115
âṇḍâ, ii. 8
-âti, ii. 105
âtman, i. 350; ii. 76, 328
âdṛiç, i. 158
âdhâ, ii. 12
-ân, ii. 69
âno, ii. 8
ânt, ii. 110
ântnahâ, ib.
-ândo, iii. 123
ânḍhalo, ii. 12, 73
√âp, app, iii. 41
âp, âpan, âpanâ (âtman), i. 330; ii. 328
âpalâ, ii. 330
âpaṇ, ii. 330, 348
âpelo (âpiḍa), i. 156, 196
âbh, ii. 21
âm, i. 342; ii. 219
-âmani, ii. 70
âmarâ, i. 84; ii. 302
âmi, ii. 84; ii. 302
-âmi, ii. 77
âmba, âmbo, i. 342; ii. 21
âmbaṭâṅ, ii. 127
âmhâ, âmhi, ii. 302, 306
âyâ, iii. 16
-âr, -ârâ, -âru, ii. 94
-âl, -âlu, ii. 90, 94
-âlâ, iii. 142
âlaya, i. 182; ii. 10, 93, 98
âv, iii. 44
-âv, ii. 63
-âvat, ii. 69
âvatto, i. 334
-âvan, ii. 69
-âvo, ii. 336
âçi, ii. 187
âçcharya, i. 136, 344; ii. 286
âshâḍha, i. 259
âsarâ, âsiro (âçraya), i. 182, 367; ii. 10.
-âhaṭ, ii. 65
-âhi, ii. 218
-âhiṅ, âhuṅ, ii. 220
âhe (√as), iii. 172
âhed, âhar, i. 266
-âho, ii. 218
-âḷ, -âḷa, ii. 90
âḷokh, ii. 104

I

i, ih, ii. 317, 319, 329, 336
-in, -io, iii. 135
iṅg, iii. 262
ik, ikk, ii. 131
-ika, ii. 83, 84, 111, 156
ikaḍe, ii. 146
-ikâ, ii. 164
ikrâhaṭ, ii. 141
ikshu, i. 135, 218, 310
igâraha, ii. 134
igyârahvâṅ, ii. 248
ingâlo, (angâra), i. 129, 250
ingiaṇṇo (ingitajña), 302
iṇam, i. 156
iṇâṇam, ii. 335
-iṇu, ii. 114
it, itai, iii. 260
-ita, ii. 102
iti, i. 180, 196
ittho, ii. 336, 346

itthi, ïthiká (strí), i. 353
itná, ii. 336
ildhar, ii. 336
-in, -ini, ii. 163, 164
-iní, ii. 64
imi, iii. 263
imli, i. 134
-iya, ii. 84, 88, 156
iyánám, i. 186
-íru, ii. 113
-íl, ii. 94, 95
-íla, -ílá, iii. 134
ílsí, i. 130
iva, i. 180

Í

í, ii. 317, 336
-í, ii. 89
-ío, ii. 88, 89
-íṇ, ii. 233
íṇa, ii. 336; iii. 264
íkh, i. 310
-íṇ, ii. 170, 231
-íṇo, ii. 114
-ído, iii. 128
-íya, ii. 84, 85, 156
-íro, ii. 97
-íl, -ílá, -ílo, ii. 95, 97, 98
ísurá (íçvara), i. 358
-íhi, ii. 214, 215
íḍ, ii. 95

U

u, ii. 318, 336
-ua, -uá, ii. 39
uajjháuo, i. 328
-uka, ii. 35, 112
ukhaṇḍijaṇu, iii. 71
ug, ugg, ugav (√udgam), i. 294;
iii. 39
ugár (udgára), i. 179
ugál, ugálṇá, ib.
uchakká, ii. 72
uchál, uchchhál, ii. 79
uchán, ii. 90
uchchá, ii. 13
uchchhá (ikshu), i. 135, 148,
216, 310
ujáḍṇá, ujáḍú, ii. 86
unchá, ii. 13
unchás, ii. 123
unchál, ii. 79
uṭh (√utthá) i. 294; iii. 40, 43
uṭhu, ii. 67, 92
uḍ (ur, √uḍḍí), uḍir, iii. 44
uḍako, ii. 33
uḍáu, ii. 41, 43
uḍák, ib.
uḍán, ii. 81
upṭh, ii. 134
upḍá, ii. 81
utar (√uttṛí), iii. 54
utárná, utárú, ii. 86
uti, ii. 336
-uti, ii. 108
utthe, i. 314; ii. 336, 346
utthuṇ, ii. 346
utná, ii. 336
utsava, i. 317
utsuka, ib.
uda, ii. 21
udumbara, i. 133, 160
udgára, i. 139
udra, ii. 21
udvoḍhá, i. 245, 271
udhar, ii. 336
udhálú, ii. 37
un, i. 343; ii. 48
unáç, unis, ii. 134

unáņ, unháņ, ii. 318
unájá, ii. 93
unl, ii. 319
ungalī, i. 134
undir, ii. 281
unho, i. 347
upa, i. 200
upajjháyo (upâdhyâya), i. 328
upano, iii. 141
upari, ii. 298
upavishṭa, i. 179; iii. 38
uppalam, i. 234
ubálná, ubáraņu (ujjvâlana), i. 294
ubidako, ii. 38
ubhárnā (udbhâraņa), i. 294
umrāā, ii. 152
umhaļ, i. 347
urlá, ii. 344
urân, ii. 207, 219
-ul, -ûl, ii. 99, 100
ulka, i. 180
ulko, ii. 83
uvavajjhihiti (√upapad), iii. 20
us, ii. 318
usrun, i. 172
ushma, i. 172, 347
uh, uhai, ii. 318, 336
uhajo, ii. 336

Û

û, ii. 318, 339
ûņa, ii. 338
ûkh, i. 135, 218, 310
ûngh, ii. 82, 92
ûnghás, ûnghásá, ii. 82
ûnghâju, ii. 92
ûchâņi, ii. 80
ûcho, ib.
ûnchá, ii. 13, 79
ûnchâl, ii. 79
-ûņiko, ii. 115
-ûņo, ii. 114, 115
-ûņḍo, ii. 81
ût, ii. 21
-ût, ii. 108
ûd, ii. 21
ûn, i. 348; ii. 48
ûnavinçati, ii. 154
ûnh, i. 347
ûpar, ii. 298
ûrnâ, i. 342
ûs, i. 218, 310
-ûhî, ii. 216

ṚI

ṛiksha, i. 159, 218, 310; ii. 14
ṛitu, i. 159
√ṛidh, ii. 58
ṛiddha, i. 159
ṛishabha, i. 159
ṛishi, i. 160

E

-e, ii. 262
e, ii. 317, 336
eáraha, i. 260, 243; ii. 134
-eņ, ii. 262, 271
eka, ek, eku, ekk, i. 141, 166; ii. 130, 245
eka- (in comp.), i. 253, 259, 268; ii. 134, 141
ekottara, ii. 142
ekhana, ii. 336
ekhâno, ib.
egyo (âgo), i. 142; ii. 296

eṭalo, ii. 336
eṭhā, ib.
eḍ, eḍi, i. 134
eḍo, eḍo, ii. 336
-eṇ, ii. 169
eta, ii. 336
etiro, eto, ib.
-eto, ii. 108
ethākām, ii. 220
en, enan, enanta, ii. 336
-er, ii. 276, 279
eraṇḍa, i. 180
-erā, -eru, ii. 98
-erā, ii. 199
-el, -elā, -elu, ii. 95, 97, 98
-elo, iii. 134
evaḍo, ii. 336
eva, ova, ib.
es, -esun, ii. 219
eh, ehā, ehāṇ, ii. 317
-ehi, -ehiṇ, ii. 219
ehvāṇ, ii. 336

AI

ai, i. 185
aiṅgl, ii. 137
aiḍeṇ, ii. 336
aiḍā, ii. 336
-ait, ii. 69
-aitā, ib.
-aito, ii. 103
-ail, ii. 96, 167
aisā, ii. 336

O

o, ii. 318, 336
-oṇ (ord.), ii. 143
-oṇ (pl.), ii. 218, 248
-oṇ (loc.), ii. 236, 346
oka, ii. 345
-oko, ii. 112
okovka, ii. 345
okhāne, ii. 336
ogaṇla, ii. 134
ogāl, i. 298
ojhā, i. 328
oṇjal, i. 252
oṭh, oṇṭh (oshṭha), ii. 7
oṭhāru, ii. 92
oṭhl, ii. 87
oḍe, oḍo, ii. 336
opav, opāv, opā (√svanam), iii. 57
oṇḍā, ii. 81
otiro, ii. 336
-otl, ii. 106
odava, ii. 345
ovoka, ib.
os, i. 356
oshṭha, i. 317; ii. 7
ohi, ii. 204

AU

-aut, ii. 69, 106
-autā, auti, ib.
-aun, -aunā, ii. 69
aur, ii. 341; iii. 270
aushadha, i. 138, 252
aushṭpika, ii. 87

K

ka, ii. 344
-ka, ii. 26
kaṇvel, i. 255; ii. 23
kaṇh, ii. 258
kaṇhaiyā, kaṇho, i. 163

kaṇhiṇ, kaṇṇi, ii. 323, 326
kakaḍī, i. 130, 188, 318; ii. 35
kakaḍo, i. 316
kakkho, ii. 7
kakshu, ii. 7, 87, 257
kakhana, ii. 338
kaṅkan, i. 190, 296
kaṅkar, i. 130; ii. 95
kaṅkarilá, ii. 95
kaṅgaṇ, i. 296
kachak, ii. 31, 88
kachaṇag, ii. 68
kachát, ii. 68, 89
kachiandh, ii. 126
kachim, i. 278
kachchh, ii. 7
kachchhapa, i. 153, 278
kachhkú, ii. 328
kaññá, i. 341
kanjho, i. 356
kaṭ, káṭ (√kṛit), i. 333; ii. 13; iii. 59
kaṭ, i. 145
kaṭáit, ii. 105
kaṭán, ib.
kaṭáha, i. 199
kaṭhaṇ (kaṭhiṇa), i. 145, 155; ii. 13, 62
kaṭhanáç, ii. 82
kaḍ, ii. 98
kaḍak, kaṛká, ii. 31, 38, 43
kaḍakaḍ, ii. 104
kaḍakká, kaṛkhait, ii. 105
kaḍáhi, i. 199
kaḍhiṇ, ii. 338
kaḍil, ii. 98
kaḍh, kaḍḍh (√kṛish), i. 353; iii. 57
kaṇ, ii. 324
kaṇik, ii. 231
kaṇiç, ib.
kaṇṭaka, i. 297; ii. 29, 93
kaṇṭhálá, ii. 69
kaṇṭhi, i. 270
kaṇḍá, kaṇḍiálá, i. 207; ii. 29, 93
kaṇṇo, i. 343; ii. 7
kata, ii. 336
katarna, i. 334
katl, i. 334
kath, i. 367; iii. 87
kad, ii. 338
kadala, ii. 343
kadali, i. 142
kaniá (kanyá), i. 341
kanu, i. 343; ii. 7
kanhaiyo, kangan, i. 190
kankála, kangál, i. 198
kandhi, i. 270
kandhá, i. 297; ii. 9, 100
kann, i. 343; ii. 7
kannh, i. 300
kanhaṇg, ii. 60
kanhavájú, ib.
kapaḍá (kapṛá), i. 199, 316
kapaḍiándh, ii. 126
kaparla, i. 158, 209
kapáṭa, i. 200
kapás, kapáh, etc., i. 259, 318
kapitthá, i. 273
kapúra, i. 318
kab, ii. 336; iii. 257
kabará, kaburá, etc., i. 130, 319
kamala, i. 255
kamáú, ii. 41
kamin, ii. 167
kamp, kámp, etc. (√kamp), i. 279; iii. 34
kambalá, kammal, etc., ii. 23
kaya, ii. 344
kar (√kṛi), i. 98, 160, 181; ii. 17, 19, 38, 162, 179, 265; iii. 11, 16, 18, 25, 41, 72, 75, 77

kar, kará (genitive), ii. 277, 279, 287
kara (hand), ii. 11
karapaneg, ii. 67
karál, i. 199
kariá, i. 267
karisudh, ii. 126
karisu, i. 150
karudhí (krodhin), ii. 167
karuh (kroçu), i. 269
karhaṭiká, i. 138; ii. 35
karjál, ii. 168
karṇa, i. 343; ii. 7
kartana, i. 333
kardama, i. 334; ii. 26
karpaṭa, i. 199, 318
karpaṭán, ii. 127
karpása, i. 259, 318
karsh (√krish), i. 322, 353; iii. 57
kal (kalyam), i. 356; iii. 264
kavaḍí, i. 300
kavala, ii. 24
kavá, ii. 344
kavi, ii. 191
kaçá, ii. 325
kaçmala, i. 346
kaçmira, i. 346
kashṭa, ii. 90, 93
kas, kasailá, ii. 96
kas (pron.), ii. 344
kasak, ii. 31
kasapeg, ii. 30
kasmin, kaseálá, ii. 98
kasd, ii. 336
kasta, kasu, i. 149
kah, kahná, etc. (√kath), i. 367; iii. 37
kahá, ii. 324
kaháṇ, i. 255; ii. 338
kahár, i. 299; ii. 127
kahíṇ, ii. 328
kahuṇ, ii. 253
kajá, i. 244; ii. 13
kalca, i. 171
ká, ii. 276
káṇh, ii. 167
káṇhán, ii. 338
káṇkáṇ, ii. 329
káku, kág, i. 198
káká, i. 210
kákh, káṅkh, ii. 7, 267
káṅkaḍa, i. 318
káṅkhe, i. 318; ii. 267, 268
káj (kácha), i. 199
káj (kárya), i. 340
kánchana, ii. 17
káṭ, káṭná (√krit), i. 333; ii. 20, 36; iii. 59
káṭú, ii. 36
káḍhná (√krish), i. 353, 354; ii. 20, 32, 41; iii. 67
káṇá, ii. 13
káṇṭá, i. 297; ii. 29
káṇṭil, ii. 98
kátar, i. 234
kádná, kádo (kardama), i. 334; ii. 26
kán, ii. 7
káná, ii. 18
kánkuḍl, i. 133
kángu, i. 198
kándh, kándhá (skandha), i. 297, 300; ii. 9
kánh (kṛishṇa), i. 163, 247
kápaḍ, i. 199, 318
kápṛ, i. 318
kápás, i. 169, 318
kábar, kabará, i. 130, 146, 319
kábalo, kámbalá, ii. 23, 89
kám (karma), i. 182, 346; ii. 41
káma (basm), ii. 196
káya, ii. 324

-kār, ii. 126
kār, ii. 279, 284
kāraṇlaṇu, i. 260
kāraj, kārju (kārya), i. 171, 249, 349
kāriso, ii. 325
kārīgar, ii. 167
kāṛo, i. 247
kārtiko, i. 354
kāruṇāpuṇa, i. 355
kāl, kālī, kālh (kalyam), i. 350
kālā, i. 244, 247; ii. 13
kālikār, ii. 279
kāvaḍā, ii. 80
kāvanjā, i. 106
kāçmīra, i. 346
kāchhuā, i. 316; ii. 7
kāsā, i. 149
kāh, ii. 324
kāhā, kāhāṇ, ii. 323, 326
kāhāḍavuṇ, i. 333
kāhāṇ, i. 355
kāhār, kāhāri, ii. 327
kāhāvaṇa, i. 355
kāṭhā, i. 244; ii. 13
ki, ii. 324
kiā, ib.
kiṇṇu, i. 257
kikaḍo, ii. 336
kikkur, ib.
kichhi, kichhu, ii. 328
kiṭṭa, i. 145
kiḍā, kiḍo, i. 199
kitakā, ii. 332, 338
kitaro, ii. 331, 338
kitek, ii. 333
kitthe, ii. 338
kitnā, ii. 331, 338
kiddhau, iii. 144
kidhar, ii. 338
kin, kinh, ii. 323, 326
kiyau, iii. 144
kiran, i. 130; ii. 17
kiles, i. 171; ii. 7
killā, i. 160
kis, ii. 326
kisān, i. 160
kise, ii. 324, 326
kisô, ii. 326
kihaṇḍī, ii. 331, 333
kihā, ib.
kihi, ii. 323
kī (gen.), ii. 276
kī (pron.), ii. 323, 324, 326
kīḍ, kīḍo, i. 199
kīrīṇa, i. 168; ii. 323
kīṇa, iii. 144
kuṇvar (kumāra), i. 255
kukkur, ii. 184, 200
kukh (kukshi), i. 218
kuchchho (kukshi), i. 310; ii. 218
kuchh, ii. 328
kunchi, kunji, i. 109; ii. 35
kunjaḍā, ii. 165
kuṭam, i. 146
kuṭāḍī, i. 278
kuṭṭinī, i. 146; ii. 170
kuṭil, ii. 96
kuṭhārā, i. 279, 278
kuḍāṇu, i. 334
kuḍī, kuḍh, i. 316
kuḍie, ii. 138
kuṇḍ, kuṇḍālā, ii. 93
kuṇḍala, ii. 24
kuṭho, iii. 338
kuḍaṇu kuḍāvuṇ (√kurd), i. 150, 334
kuddāl, i. 157
kubaḍā, i. 286
kubiro, i. 130
kubo, etc. (kubja), i. 285, 286
kumād, ii. 163

kumbi, kuṇbi, etc., ii. 67, 165, 170
kumhār, etc. (kumbhakāra), i. 144, 298, 346; ii. 126, 165
kurál, ii. 100
kula, i. 155, 244, 247
kulathā, ii. 164
kulīi, kurīi, ii. 24
kulhārī, kuhārā, etc., i. 270
koshṭha, i. 157; ii. 85, 167
kusaṇu, kuhaṇu, iii. 51
kuṣṭhi, ii. 167
kuhuḍī, ii. 167
kuḷa, i. 244
kūāṇ, i. 203
kūnjī, ii. 35
kūdnā (√kurd), i. 150, 334
kūpa, i. 160, 203
kūs, ii. 316
kṛipā, ii. 90
kṛipālā, id.
kṛishaka, i. 160
kṛishṇa, i. 168
ke, ii. 323, 326, 333
-ke (gen. aff.), ii. 260, 276, 278
keī, ii. 326
keuṇ, ii. 323, 328
keuṇaī, ii. 326
keṭalo, ii. 331, 338
keḍā, keḍo, ii. 333, 334, 336
keṭā, keṭo, ii. 333, 338
keṭiro, ii. 338
keḍe, id.
keṭe, id.
kemana, id.
komāne, ii. 328
ker, kerā, etc. (gen. aff.), ii. 251, 254
kerian, ii. 328
keru, ii. 323, 338
kelā, 142, 202; ii. 24
kevaṭ (kaivarta), i. 167
kevaḍo, ii. 334, 335
kevaḍhā, id.
kevāre, ii. 338
keviḍu, i. 202; ii. 24
kevo, ii. 331
koça, ii. 90
koçarī, i. 259; ii. 86
kosājā, ii. 90
koha, ii. 327
kohari, i. 259; ii. 86
kahavuṇ, (√kath), i. 126, 243; iii. 41
kehi, ii. 326
kehvāṇ, ii. 338
kaiek, ii. 327, 333
kaichhana, i. 85
kaisā, i. 158; ii. 325, 331
ko (objective aff.), i. 46; ii. 263
ko (pron.), ii. 322, 326, 338
koil (kokila), i. 187, 201; ii. 24
koī, ii. 326
koū, ii. 327
koṇvalā (komala), i. 197, 258
kokh, i. 157, 310
koṭ, i. 315, 316
koṭhā, koṭhī (koshṭha), i. 315
koṭhā, koṭhuṇ (adv.), ii. 338
koḍhī (kushṭhin), i. 157, 316; ii. 85, 89
koṇ, koṇī, koṇhī, ii. 326, 336
koro, ii. 277
kos, kosh, kohu (kroça), i. 259; ii. 7
kohu (prov.), ii. 33, 338
koliyo, ii. 24
koll, ii. 169
kauṇ, i. 48; ii. 258, 260
kauḍī, i. 158, 200, 333; ii. 164
kauṇ, ii. 328, 338
kauṇaī, ii. 326
kaun, ii. 322, 323

kaulá, ii. 91
kaulárú, *ib.*
kyá, ii. 324
kyúṇ, ii. 338
krí, iii. 64

KH

khauyo, iii. 138
khaggo (khaḍga), i. 285
khacharaṭ, ii. 68
khajapu, iii. 51
khajúr, i. 319
khaṭ (khaṭvá), ii. 48
khaṭá, khaṭṭá, ii. 83
khaṭápan, ii. 73
khaṭáu, ii. 62
khaṭiáudh, ii. 198
khaḍaka, ii. 31, 68, 98
khaḍag, i. 286, 299
khaḍkhaḍúṭ, ii. 68
khaḍá, iii. 60
khaḍí, ii. 35
khaṇ, ii. 7
khaṇa, ii. 98
khaṇapu, iii. 50
khaṇá, i. 299
khaṇápí, ii. 20
khaṇil, khaṇoṇg, ii. 98
khaṇḍa, i. 299
khaṇḍá (khaḍga), i. 285; ii. 104, 105
khaṇḍáṅ, *ib.*
khattri, ii. 88, 156
khan, i. 130; ii. 7
khani, khanu, i. 299
khano, i. 285
khandhá, i. 300, 306; ii. 9
khapayu, ii. 43, 63
khapapeṇ, ii. 35
khapati, ii. 53
khapáú, ii. 43
khapi, khapyá, ii. 33
khamá, i. 174, 310; ii. 159
khambh, i. 318
kharajyá, ii. 55
khalaḍá, ii. 190
khavaljyá, ii. 89
khavá (√khád), iii. 48
khavijapo, *ib.*
khashkhas, ii. 104
khá (√khád), i. 302, 304; ii. 96; iii. 40, 68
kháu, ii. 36, 87
kháṅ, ii. 166
khágyáin, *ib.*
kháyamá, i. 191
kháj, khájapeṇ, ii. 191
kháṭ (khaṭvá), i. 154; ii. 48
khánmlá, i. 285
kháḍho, iii. 140
khánorá, ii. 100
khánḍá, khánaḥ, i. 273, 306; ii. 9
khár, i. 310
khál (below), ii. 38
khál (skin), ii. 120
khávavipeṇ, iii. 77
khíṅh, iii. 64
khíchṛu, khícháv, ii. 68
khíṅj, iii. 64
khiṇa, i. 130; ii. 7
khitri, ii. 88, 156
khímá, i. 130; ii. 169
khilaumá, ii. 70
khiláṅ, ii. 41
khillá, ii. 86
khisaláhaṭ, ii. 65
khisiyáhaṭ, *ib.*
khír, i. 309
khujaláhaṭ, ii. 65
khuḍako, ii. 33

khadhâ, khudâhiâ, ii. 159
khumḍâni, khusrâni, ii. 70
khumpu, i. 822
khuhu, khûhu, i. 150, 191, 203; ii. 202
khuhumbo, i. 191
khe, ii. 253, 258
kheuh, khegeh, iii. 64
khetu, i. 310
kheḍ, khedavuṇ, etc. (kshetra), i. 310, 338; ii. 37
khet (kshetra), i. 218, 310, 338
khetri, ii. 88
khep (√kship), i. 196
khol, khoḷ, i. 239, 240, 244; ii. 96
khevnâ, i. 300
khogir, ii. 282
khoḍ, khoḍ, khol, etc.; ii. 20; iii. 62

G

gajak, ii. 32
gajapu, gajjnâ (√garj), i. 319
gaṭho, iii. 188
gaṭhilâ, ii. 95
gaṭhri, i. 120
gaḍ, gaḍbaḍ, etc., i. 336
gaḍaku, ii. 164
gaḍhaulâ, ii. 67, 68
gaḍḍh, iii. 49
gaḍha, ii. 95
gaḍhâl, ii. 69
gaḍhelâ, ii. 96
-gaṇ, ii. 200
gaṇḍâsâ, ii. 82
gaṇḍh (√granth), iii. 69
gadhâ, gadahâ, etc. (gardabha), i. 338
gaṇtâit, ii. 105
gandhaḷâ, ii. 101
gabbh, gabbhu, etc. (garbha), i. 319; ii. 7
gabbhin, gabhin, etc. (garbhiṇî), i. 183, 319
gambhir, i. 81, 150; ii. 13
garapu, i. 247
garahin, ii. 7, 11
garbhan, i. 183
garbhiṇi, i. 185
galâv, galâu, ii. 63
gavuḷno, ii. 288
gah, gahâ (√grah), iii. 42
gahak, gahako, ii. 31, 33
gaharâ, gahirâ, i. 81, 150; ii. 13
gâû, ii. 26, 27
gâṇ, gâṇv, etc. (grâma), i. 254; ii. 7, 26
gâṇvaḍuṇ, ii. 118
gâṇvi, ii. 66
gâjapeṇ, gâjnâ (√garj), i. 319
gâṇjâ, i. 297
gâṭu, i. 837
gâḍapu, gâḍavuṇ, etc., i. 336
gâḍâ, ii. 149
gâḍi, i. 336; ii. 149, 192
gâḍhâ, gâḍho, ii. 13
gâṇḍ, i. 147, 227
gât, i. 337
gâdâni, ii. 77
gâdhâ, i. 336
gân, i. 266
gânth, i. 257; iii. 59
gâbh, i. 319; ii. 7
gâbhin, i. 145, 183, 319; ii. 183
gâbhûṇ, ii. 100
gâm (grâma), ii. 7, 26
gâmaḍuṇ, ii. 119
gâvuṇ (√gai), ii. 37
gâhâ, i. 267

gijh. i. 160, 337; ii. 21
gidh, giddh, *ib.*
ginnâ, i. 180
gimh, gim, i. 347
giyârâp, i. 260
girâka, ii. 42
gîhapu, ii. 10
gîlru, i. 160
gîl, gidh, i. 160, 337; ii. 21
guâr, ii. 167
guj, gujho, i. 359
guḍko, ii. 83
guṇapaṇâ, ii. 73
guḍi, i. 240
gunia, ii. 135
gunth (√granth), iii. 59
guru, ii. 166
-gul, -guli, ii. 200
gusail, ii. 167
gusâin, ii. 168
guâlî, ii. 42
gûj, i. 359
gûth (√granth), iii. 59
geuh (√grah), iii. 42
geru, i. 146
geh, ii. 14
gehun, i. 81, 160, 267
go, i. 267; ii. 245
gochhâri, ii. 105
gojâ, ii. 245
goṭu, i. 337
goṭṭhil, ii. 218
goḍhu, ii. 110
goḍ, goḍil, ii. 98
goṇḍaa, ii. 62
goṇḍâ, ii. 82, 90, 98
got, i. 337
gom, i. 267
gorâ, i. 158
goro, ii. 247
gol, i. 240, 244, 247
golâ, ii. 148
golârâ, ii. 94
goli, ii. 203
gulo, i. 247
gosâin, i. 257; ii. 154
gosâvi, *ib.*
goh, i. 267; ii. 48
gohâl, i. 260
gohâp, i. 169, 267.
gyârap, gyâsah, ii. 184
granth, i. 186
grâsapan, i. 154
grâsti, i. 186
grhasta, *ib.*
gwâlin, ii. 168

GH

ghaṭaṇu, iii. 71
ghaṭilâ, ii. 79
ghaḍavuṇ, ii. 48
ghaḍâ, ghaḍi, i. 199; ii. 91. 92
ghaḍâu, ii. 43, 44
ghaḍiyâl, etc., ii. 91, 92, 94
ghaṇaghuro, ii. 127
ghaṇaghaṇâṭ, ii. 69
ghaṇâ, ii. 13
ghaṇorâ, ii. 96
ghaṇṭâ, ii. 98
ghamori, ii. 100
ghar (gṛiha), i. 192; ii. 14, 98, 183, 191, 200, 280
gharachâ, ii. 110
gharaṭu, ii. 64
gharolâ, ii. 95
ghasavaṭ, ii. 67
ghâ, ghâv (ghâta), i. 187, 202; ii. 100
ghâil, ghâyal, etc. ii. 100
ghât, ii. 89

ghâṇ, ghâṇolâ, ii. 98
ghânṭaḍi, ii. 119
ghâm, ii. 26, 69
ghâmelâ, ii. 99
ghâmoli, ii. 100
ghâsṇuṇ, ii. 67; iii. 88
ghisâv, ii. 63
ghiü, ghi, etc. (ghṛita), i. 160; ii. 156, 157
ghurnâ, etc. (√ghûrṇ), i. 150, 344; ii. 64
ghurnâ, etc., *ib.*
ghul, ghuḷ (√ghûrṇ), ii. 20, 41, 65; iii. 56
ghusnil, ii. 96
gho, ghos (√grah), iii. 42, 148, 220
gho, ii. 48, 151
ghoḍâ, ghoṛâ (ghoṭaka), i. 199; ii. 29, 69, 125, 169, 184, 185, 186
ghomâ, ii. 66
ghorâro, ii. 60
ghoro, ii. 30

CH

chhaiitho, i. 324
chhagar, i. 148; ii. 22
chak, etc. (chakra), ii. 23
chanchalâ, ii. 24
chaṭak, ii. 32
chaṭâl, i. 215
chaḍ, chaḍh, ii. 48, 53, 64, 65, 69
chatur, ii. 132
chand, etc. (chandra), i. 297, 337, 338; ii. 21
chandan, ii. 17
chapkan, etc. (chap), i. 218
chab, chabb (√charv), i. 352; iii. 40
chabiç, i. 263
chamak, ii. 32
chamatkâra, ii. 33
chamâr, i. 183, 346; ii. 126, 165
chamârin, i. 183; ii. 165
chamelo, ii. 97
chamkâvat, etc., ii. 66
chamṛâ, i. 346; ii. 120
chara, ii. 37
charchâit, ii. 103
charyâito, ii. 104
chal, chall, etc. (√chal), iii. 34, 78
chalâvan, ii. 70
chavaṇi, ii. 19
chahuṇpnâ, i. 276
-châ, -chi, etc., ii. 270, 289
châṇ, i. 182
châṇvelo, ii. 97
châṇgalepaṇ, ii. 73
châṭuyâ, ii. 39
châṇḍipo, ii. 114
chând, i. 297, 337; ii. 21
châṇḍalo, ii. 119
châp, châṇp, etc., i. 211, 212
châb, etc. (√charv), i. 352; ii. 68; iii. 40
châm (charman), i. 345, 346; ii. 61, 116
châmâr, i. 346
châmoṭâ, ii. 123
châr, ii. 132, 245
chârâni, ii. 90
chârog, ii. 245
châlaṇog, etc. (√chal), i. 156; ii. 51; iii. 34
châlani, châluni, i. 133
châlis, ii. 137
châs, i. 210, 215
chiṭo, i. 386
chiṭṭh (√sthâ), i. 230

chidiyá, ii. 159
chito, ii. 29
chitti, i. 310
chindh, etc., ii. 118, 122
chinh, chihan, etc. (chinha), i. 353; ii. 94
chip, chipṭá, etc., i. 212
chimkáṭu, ii. 64
chimṭá, etc., i. 212
-chiyá, ii. 289
chirṭá, ii. 149
chirṇá, ib.
chishṭh (√sthá), i. 280; iii. 34
chik, ii. 91
chid, ii. 191
chipṭ, i. 836
chitá, ii. 29
chiro, ii. 80
chuk, iii. 224
chukauti, ii. 106
chuṭilá, ii. 95
chuḍḍo, ii. 161
chuṇúk, ii. 44
chuná, etc., i. 344; ii. 9
chunávaṭ, ii. 66
chup, i. 212
churá, i. 348
chuhanu, chúná, i. 321
chúná, etc. (chúrṇa), i. 343, 344; ii. 9
chúrá, etc. (chúrṇa), ib.
chengaraṭ, ii. 68
cheḍá, chelá (cheṭa), i. 240; ii. 9, 40
chopaṭ, ii. 66, 123
-cho, ii. 140, 276, 278
chok, ii. 247
chokh, i. 134
chonch, choṇṭ, i. 134, 215, 297
chotho, i. 144, 334
chobá (√charv), i. 352; iii. 40
choraní, ii. 166
chori, i. 155, 349; ii. 76
chorávaṇ, ii. 73
chorápo, ii. 114, 115
choráguṇ, ii. 141
chau (chár), ii. 120, 140
chaugr, chaugri, etc. (chamara), i. 145, 256; ii. 22
chaukh, i. 134
chaugho, ii. 245
chauuk, ii. 31, 88, 96
chauṭ, chauṭá, ii. 82, 144
chauḍahág, i. 334
chauḍá (chauṛá), ii. 60
chauthá, i. 149
chaudaha, etc. (chaturdaça), i. 144, 334; ii. 184
chaudhari, ii. 166, 167
chaubai (chaturvedi), ii. 87
chaubis, i. 253
chaur, chauri, i. 148, 256; ii. 22
chauranjá, ii. 141
chauvi, i. 253

CHH

chha, i. 261; ii. 132, 140, 246
chhakaḍá, i. 198
chhaṭṭhá, i. 261; ii. 143
chhaḍ, iii. 52
chhattis, ii. 140
chhattri, ii. 88, 156
chhas, i. 130; ii. 7
chhap, etc., i. 210, 211, 213
chhappan, ii. 140
chhabilá, ii. 95
chhabbis, i. 253
chhamá, i. 130; ii. 159
chhay, i. 261; ii. 132, 140
chhabo, i. 261

chhá, i. 261; ii. 324
chháṇṇú, ii. 141
chhágr, chhágh (chhiyá), ii. 48
chhágharú, ii. 94
chháḍ, iii. 52
chhápá, etc., i. 211, 212, 213
chhápárú, ii. 112
chhásan, ii. 299
chháyalá, ii. 95, 97
chhár, i. 310
chháliyá, i. 261
chhávaḍá, ib.
chhávo, ib.
chhijaṇu, iii. 50, 138
chhiti, i. 196, 310
chhin, ii. 7, 288
chhínaṇu, iii. 50, 139
chhínamál, i. 218
chhinno, iii. 188
chhip, etc., ii. 211
chhipanjá, ii. 141
chhipáv, ii. 64
chhipávani, ii. 69
chhibará, i. 213
chhimá (kshamá), i. 120, 310; ii. 159
chhio, ii. 10
chhiṇṭ, i. 336
chhimá, i. 261
chhuṭ, ii. 43, 70; iii. 52
chhuṭáṇ, ii. 43
chhuṭápá, ii. 72
chhuṭo, iii. 188
chhuri, i. 218, 310; ii. 9
chhuhaṇu, etc., ii. 65; iii. 51
chhe (chhah), i. 261
chhe (√as), iii. 186
chhekáṇ, ii. 42
chhenchaḍámi, ii. 77
chhejhuá, i. 254
chhemi, ii. 66
chheliyá, i. 261
chheli, i. 142
chheloni, ii. 77
chheráṇ, i. 261
chho, ii. 151, 190
chhokaḍá, i. 215, 261; ii. 72, 120, 163
chhokaḍápaná, ii. 73
chhoṭá, ii. 72
chhoḍ, iii. 52

J

jaú, i. 81
jakhana, ii. 337
jag, jagg, etc. (yajna), i. 303; ii. 15
jagaṭu, i. 81
jagáná, iii. 78
jangal, i. 248
jangh, i. 81, 296; ii. 48
jaj, jajan, etc. (yajna), i. 303; ii. 15
jajmán, i. 197
jaṭá, i. 196
jaṭini, i. 168
jaḍáṇ, ii. 41
jaḍáni, ii. 70
jaḍḍho, ii. 161
jaḍná, ii. 41
jaḍyá, ii. 85
jatan (yatna), i. 171; ii. 16
jatrá (yátrá), ii. 159
jathaṇu, i. 146
jathá, i. 147
jad, ii. 337
janam, i. 171; ii. 60
janeü, janoï, janyo (yajnopavita), i. 303
japná, i. 196
jab, ii. 337
jamál, i. 192

jama, jambu, i. 297, 298
jara (jala), i. 247
jallâdani, ii. 167
javag (√yâ), i. 249; iii. 36, 213, 222
jashpur, i. 304
jasd, ii. 337
jahâg, ib.
jahig, ii. 321
jalânâ, etc. (√jval), i. 244
jalakaṭ, ii. 122
jaḷu, jaḷo, ii. 181, 193
jâ (√yâ), i. 249; iii. 36, 215, 222
jâgval, i. 255; ii. 193
jâṅhâ, ii. 337
jâg (yajna), i. 303; ii. 16
jâgaṇâ, etc. (√jâgri), ii. 35, 51; iii. 78
jâgarûk, ii. 44
jâgû, ii. 36
jângh, i. 296; ii. 46
jâchanûk, ii. 44
jâchû, ii. 37
jâṭo, i. 192
jâṇ, jân, etc. (√jnâ), i. 303; ii. 104; iii. 41
jânito, ii. 104
jât, ii. 52
jâtrâ, ii. 159
jâmâl, i. 192
jâmâtu, i. 159
jâmu, i. 297
jâmoṭa, ii. 122
jâru, jâl, etc. (jâla), i. 81, 247; ii. 7, 199
jâlapaṇa, ii. 72
jâluyâ, ii. 40
jâsti, ii. 54
jâhâ, jâhâg, ii. 321
jiaṇu, i. 242
jiâmpu, ib.
jikado, ii. 337
jijmân, i. 107
jiṭhut, ii. 106
jiḍahig, ii. 337
jitakâ, ib.
jiti, ib.
jitthe, ib.
jithâ, ib.
jithe, ib.
jidhar, ib.
jindu, ii. 117
jindaḍo, ib.
jin, jinâg, ii. 321
jibâ (√yâ), i. 249; iii. 36, 213, 222
jilânâ, i. 241
jio, ii. 321
jih, ib.
jihâ, ii. 337
jihi, ii. 321
jî (jîva), i. 252; ii. 156
jîû, ib.
jinâ, i. 241
jiban, ii. 17
jibh (jihvâ), i. 155, 185, 359; ii. 48, 191, 207, 209, 217
juâṇig, i. 192
jugala, ii. 24
juguchhâ, i. 196
jugût, i. 172, 173; ii. 232
jujh, etc. (√yudh), i. 264, 326
juṭ (√yuj), iii. 54
junâ, juneraṇ, ii. 99
jurimâna, ii. 176
juvalâ, juḷâ, etc. (yugala), ii. 24
jûth, i. 267
jûh, ib.
je, ii. 321, 337
joṅg, ib.
jokhâne, ii. 337
jeṭalo, ib.

joṭhá, ii. 337
joṭhákra, ib.
joṭhant, ii. 106
juḍá, juḍo, ii. 337
jotiro, joto, ib.
jothen, jobe, ib.
jom, jomana, ib.
jovaḍo, jovaḍhá, ib.
jovo, jovhág, ib.
joher, i. 189
joiad, ii. 337
jo (pron.), ii. 321, 337
-jo (gen. aff.), ii. 276, 289
joṅto, ii. 103
jogitá, ii. 79
joṭo, jot, etc. (yoktram), i. 249
joḍ (√yuj), iii. 54
jot, joti (jyoti), i. 197
jodhápan, i. 263
joru, ii. 207
johi, ii. 322
jau, ii. 185
jaun, ii. 321
jválg, i. 192

JH

jhagrálu, ii. 60, 94
jhaṅgali, i. 192
jhaṅgā, ib.
jhaṭak, ii. 32
jhaṭapa, ii. 52
jhaṭel, ii. 99
jhaḍák, ii. 43
jhaṇḍá, i. 139
jhañjhanáhaṭ, ii. 65
jhapak, ii. 32
jhapás, ii. 59
jhamak, ii. 32
jhambel, ii. 97
jhari, i. 272
jharokhá, i. 177
jhalak, ii. 32
jhaṭavaná, ii. 127
jhánkná, i. 176
jháṭ, ii. 52
jháḍná, i. 177; ii. 86
jháḍavo, ii. 121
jháḍú, ii. 86
jháṅṭná, i. 177
jhámá, i. 272
jhámp, i. 177, 276; ii. 91
jhámpál, ii. 91
jhálar, i. 382
jhálurá, ii. 40
jhis, jhil, etc., i. 192
jhijhak, ii. 32
jhiḍak, ib.
jhilgá, i. 332
jhilmil, ib.
jhukáraṭ, ii. 66
jhuñjhuṇiāhaṭ, ib.
jhuṭṭho, ii. 161
jhuḍálo, ii. 93
jhuḍḍo, ii. 161
jhulko, ii. 33
jhúl, jholá, etc. ii. 158, 332
jhomp, i. 139
jhok, ii. 33
jhop, jhomp, etc. ii. 91, 120

Ṭ

ṭakáū, ii. 43
ṭako, ii. 247
ṭaṭak, ii. 32
ṭaṭṭi, i. 287
ṭaṭho, i. 337
ṭaṇ, ṭan, etc., i. 227
ṭapak, ii. 32

ṭap, ṭappé, etc., i. 214
ṭapak, i. 214; ii. 32
ṭamak, ii. 32
ṭalnâ, ṭalaṇeṇ, etc. (√ṭal), i. 244; iii. 59
ṭasak, ii. 32
ṭahak, ii. 32, 33
ṭahaṇu, i. 337
ṭahnî, i. 226
ṭâkaṇuṇ, i. 224; iii. 224
ṭâṭ, i. 215
ṭâṇ, ṭânnâ, etc., i. 227
ṭâṇḍâ, i. 251
ṭâp, etc., i. 214
ṭâmo, i. 342; ii. 21
ṭâhâṭ, i. 251
ṭio, i. 150
ṭikaḍî, ṭikalî, etc. (tilaka), i. 197, 226; ii. 120
ṭikâṭ, ii. 104
ṭikâû, ii. 41
ṭip, etc., i. 214, 215
ṭilavâ, i. 314
ṭîh, i. 163, 347
ṭihâî, id.
ṭîlâ, i. 226
ṭîkâ, (tilaka), ii. 120
ṭîp, i. 214, 215
ṭîb, i. 259
ṭuṇḍ, i. 226
ṭubaṇu, i. 276; ii. 30
ṭuṭ, ṭûṭ, etc. (√truṭ), i. 330; iii. 52
ṭe, i. 337
ṭekaḍâ, ii. 120
ṭokuyâ, ii. 39
ṭekuâ, i. 142
ṭeḍâ, ṭoḍhâ, etc., i. 287, 350
ṭep, i. 215
ṭehalyâ, ii. 35
ṭokâ, i. 215, 261
ṭopnâ, i. 214, 215
ṭobo, ii. 30
ṭri, ṭru, etc. (Sindhî = Skr. tri), ii. 137, 139, 143, 246, 247.

ṬH

ṭhag, i. 314; ii. 165, 167
ṭhagun, ṭhagin, ii. 165, 167
ṭhagî, ii. 78
ṭhagnâ, i. 197, 314
ṭhaṭbol, ii. 100
ṭhaṇak, ii. 32
ṭhaṇḍâ, i. 230, 237
ṭhapâk, ii. 48
ṭhapak, ṭhapnâ, etc., i. 214; ii. 32
ṭhamak, ii. 32
ṭharaṇu, ṭhaharnâ, etc., i. 231
ṭharâv, ii. 64
ṭhâ (√sthâ), i. 230, 231; iii. 34
ṭhâk, etc. (derivs. of ṭhâ), i. 231
ṭhâkurâin, ii. 166
-ṭhâru, ii. 274, 295
-ṭhâro, ii. 296
ṭhiâ, i. 231
ṭhikânâ, id.
ṭhiṭhak, ii. 32
ṭhîpkâ, i. 214
ṭhir, i. 231
ṭhîk, id.
ṭhuṇṭho, i. 226
ṭhekîrî, ii. 87
ṭhekuyâ, ii. 39
ṭheṇṭâmi, ii. 77
ṭhep, i. 231
ṭhelnâ, i. 142
ṭhovaṇeṇ, i. 142; iii. 224
ṭhonṭh, i. 215

Ḍ

ḍaṇsnâ, i. 225
ḍakâr, i. 139, 179

ḍakait, ii. 89
ḍaknut, ii. 106
ḍank, ḍankh, etc., i. 225
ḍankílá, ii. 96
ḍangu, ii. 12
ḍangupu, i. 225
ḍachak, ii. 82
ḍaṭhapu, iii. 50
ḍaṭṭá, i. 229
ḍaṭná, *ib.*
ḍaḍhu, ii. 175
ḍadho, iii. 187
ḍanḍu, etc., i. 229, 280
ḍab, ḍabná, etc., i. 225
ḍabalo, i. 319
ḍabbú, i. 225; ii. 40
ḍamírjapu, iii. 72
ḍayá, i. 237
ḍayálu, ii. 89
ḍar, i. 226; ii. 60
ḍaráln, ii. 50
ḍal, etc., i. 228
ḍamaṛo, i. 225
ḍah, ii. 183, 247
ḍahapu, iii. 49, 137
-ḍá, -ḍí, ii. 116, 118
ḍáo, i. 310
ḍám, i. 237
ḍáṅg, etc., i. 225
ḍákuyá, ii. 39
ḍákú, ii. 86
ḍáḍh, i. 182
ḍánk, i. 226
ḍáḍh, ḍáḍhí, etc., i. 225, 237, 278; ii. 35
ḍánu, i. 237
ḍáṇṭá, etc., i. 229
ḍáṇḍ, etc., i. 229, 230; ii. 65
ḍábharo, ii. 97
ḍál, etc., i. 226
ḍálím, i. 240
ḍálná, iii. 228
ḍáhap, i. 330
ḍáháp, ii. 18
ḍáhár, i. 226
ḍáhná, i. 225; iii. 60
ḍiṅgu, i. 242; ii. 19; iii. 80, 139
ḍiṅyáṭu, ii. 109
ḍiárapu, i. 242; iii. 80
ḍio, i. 237; ii. 93
ḍigharo, ii. 117
ḍijapu, i. 242
ḍiṭho, iii. 136
ḍipu, i. 237; ii. 194
ḍinḍim, i. 228
ḍiṭi, i. 162, 315
ḍino, iii. 139
ḍibiyá, i. 226; ii. 159
ḍisapu, i. 161; iii. 136
ḍiṭh (dṛishṭi), i. 162, 237, 315
ḍukhu, i. 237
ḍudho, iii. 137
ḍubiro, i. 319
ḍubná, ii. 87
ḍubhapu, iii. 49
ḍumur, i. 133, 160
ḍulná, i. 227
ḍuhapu, iii. 49
ḍeú, ii. 12, 194
ḍekhapu, i. 242
ḍeṅkuyá, ii. 39
ḍeḍaru, i. 334; ii. 22
ḍeḍh, etc. (1½), i. 237; ii. 144
ḍepná, ii. 40
ḍeru, ii. 22
ḍed, ii. 86
ḍehu, ii. 86, 225
-ḍo, ii. 118
ḍoḍhi, i. 285; ii. 14
ḍobú, ii. 36
ḍomaḍá, i. 120
ḍol, ḍol, ḍor, etc., i. 227

ḌH

ḍhakelá, ii. 95
ḍhakká, etc., i. 227; ii. 95
ḍhabillá, ii. 95
ḍhalait, ii. 102
ḍhavál, ii. 63
ḍhál, ii. 144
ḍhálu, ii. 36
ḍhillá, etc. (çithila), i. 165, 272; ii. 24, 77, 120
ḍhomá, i. 241; ii. 69
ḍholak, ii. 121
ḍholál, ii. 62, 63

Ṇ

ṇa, ii. 128
-ṇí, -ṇí, ii. 168
ṇía, i. 300; ii. 52
ṇlattai, i. 164; iii. 60
ṇíchhum, i. 327

T

taéṇ, ii. 311
takhmaa, ii. 337
taṭṭuṇ, ii. 192
taḍák, ii. 32
taḍabaḍáhaṭ, ii. 65
taṇ, ii. 131
-taṇo, ii. 287, 288
tata, ii. 337
tato, iii. 138
tathákár, ii. 280
tatháy, i. 314
tad, ii. 337
-taná, ii. 289
tantu, tand, etc., ii. 174
tap, iii. 58
tapak, i. 214
tapáil, ii. 44
tam, tame, etc., ii. 309, 311
tar (√tṛí), iii. 54
tala, tale, etc., i. 184; ii. 296
talão, i. 240
talaiyá, ii. 121
tav (√tap), iii. 59
tasá, tasen, ii. 337
tahán, ib.
tahviṇ, ii. 309, 311
táiṇ, ii. 311
táú, i. 198, 200
táṅgú, ii. 139
táṅhág, ii. 337
táḍ, i. 240
táḍaṇá, i. 229, 334
táṇ, tán, etc. (tána), i. 227, 229; ii. 7
tánt, ii. 174
támbá, etc. (támra), i. 342; ii. 21
támbolt, etc., ii. 66
tár (√tṛí), iii. 54
tárú, ii. 88
tárúṇ, i. 247; ii. 193, 200
táro, ii. 312
táv (√tap), i. 198, 200; iii. 59
táhá, ii. 315, 319
táḷ, i. 240
ti-, tir-, etc. (triṇi in comp.), ii. 139, 140, 141
tiág (tyágn), i. 324
tikaḍe, ii. 337
tigho, ii. 245
tiṇ, tinká, etc., i. 160
titi, titthe, tidhar, ii. 337
titaká, titná, ib.
timro, ii. 345
tiṇmuliyá, i. 129
tiriyá, etc. (strí), i. 171, 314
tirkhá, i. 163, 347, 348

tirpat (tṛipta), i. 166
tilajā, ii. 129
tis, ii. 315
tih, ib.
tihedo, ii. 337
tihā (pron.), ib.
tīkhā (tṛishṇa), i. 163, 347
tiga, ii. 337
tīkhā, i. 300
tījo (tṛitīya), i. 150; ii. 142
tin, i. 337; ii. 131, 245
tinuŋ, ib.
tiyā, timi, etc. (strī), i. 171, 314
tīs, i. 155; ii. 137, 140
tīel, i. 179
tisrā, ii. 143
tu, tö, etc. (tvam), ii. 309, 310, 312
tuṭṇeṇa, etc. (√trut), i. 227, 237, 336; iii. 56
tuṭho, iii. 139
tud, etc. (√tud), i. 226
tuṇḍ, i. 227; ii. 90
tum, tumhe, etc., ii. 309, 312, 345
turant (tvaritam), i. 324
turi, tūri, etc., i. 249
tul (√tul), i. 351; iii. 60
tus, iii. 139
tusā, tuhā, etc., ii. 309
-te, ii. 295, 315
te-, tein, etc. (tripi in comp.), i. 253; ii. 139, 140
tetalo, ii. 337
teḍā, teḍe, etc., ib.
teḍhā, i. 237, 330
tetiro, ii. 337
tentuli, i. 146, 240
tebe, ii. 337
temman, ib.
terah, etc. (trayodaça), i. 136, 243; ii. 134, 135, 312
tel, i. 151; ii. 7
teli, ii. 85
tevaḍā, ii. 337
tevāro, tevo, tevhāŋ, ib.
tesi, i. 179
to, ii. 302, 310, 318, 337
-to, iii. 194
toŋ, ii. 299
toḍ (√trut), iii. 52
toṇḍ, toṇḍāl, etc., i. 227; ii. 94, 95
topaā, i. 214
tomā, etc., ii. 309, 311, 312
tol, taul, etc. (√tul), iii. 60
tyauŋ, ii. 337

TH

thaksijā, ii. 97
thaknā, i. 230
thaṭā, i. 237
thaṇa, than, etc. (stana), i. 313; ii 175
thanḍā, i. 237
thamb, etc. (√stambh), i. 313; iii. 60
tharolo, ii. 97
tharuŋ (√sthā), i. 230, 248; iii. 35
thā (√sthā), i. 230; iii. 206
thāḍhā, iii. 35
thāpā, etc., i. 230
thāmb, etc. (√stambh), i. 313; iii. 60
thāro, ii. 312, 314
thāli, i. 244
thi, thiaŋu, etc. (√sthā), i. 230; iii. 36, 211
-thi, ii. 273, 274
thoŋ, i. 226

thorwi, ii. 73
thorero, ii. 117

D

daga, ii. 12
dakhin, i. 310 ; ii. 13
dachhin, ib.
daṭṭâ, etc., i. 229
daḍ, etc., ib.
daṇḍ, etc., ib., ii. 65
dahnâ, etc., i. 224
dayâlu, ii. 59
dariâil, i. 152
darç, daro (√dṛiç), i. 162 ; iii. 16
dal, i. 225, 226
das, ii. 153
dahinâ, i. 225 ; ii. 13
dahi, i. 267 ; ii. 153
dâ, ii. 276, 291 ; iii. 42
dâghl, ii. 65
dâkh, i. 182, 310 ; ii. 48
dâṭ, etc., i. 229
dâḍh, i. 225
dâḍhî, i. 225, 237 ; ii. 35, 92
dâḍhiâlû, ii. 92
dâṇḍî, i. 229 ; ii. 55
dâd, ii. 175
dâdur, i. 334
dânâ, ii. 152
dânt, ii. 85
dâbnâ, etc., i. 224
dâm, dâv, etc., ii. 61
dâmâd, i. 199, 210
dâl, i. 226
dâs, ii. 14, 195, 214
dâh (√dah), i. 225
dâhâḍo, ii. 118, 189
dâḷ, i. 226
dikhânâ, dikhlânâ, i. 162, 241
diṭṭhi (dṛishṭi), i. 162, 315
din, ii. 8
dinnan, diyan, iii. 144
diyâ, i. 203 ; ii. 9
dirtjapo, iii. 72
dilânâ, iii. 80
divaḍḍhe, i. 236
divâ, i. 203
diç, dis (√dṛiç), i. 161
dîâ, ii. 9
dîṭh (dṛishṭi), i. 162, 237, 315
dîvo, ii. 9
duî, ii. 181
duti, ii. 248
dudhâlû, etc., ii. 91, 94, 97, 98
dapura, i. 156
dubla, i. 161, 319
duritno, ii. 268
dulhin, etc., i. 271
dusallû, ii. 101
dusori, ii. 129
dushṭumi, ii. 77
dûâ, dûjâ, i. 150 ; ii. 143
dûḍhâg, i. 257 ; ii. 26
dûdh, i. 236 ; ii. 14, 91, 94
dûnâ, i. 158, 201
dûb, i. 182 ; ii. 48
dûbo, ii. 87
dûsrâ, ii. 142, 247
dṛiḍhatâ, ii. 79
de (√dâ), i. 169 ; ii. 33 ; iii. 43, 140, 218
de (deva), i. 253
deû, i. 253
deûḷ, deval, etc. (devâlaya), i. 149 ; ii. 10, 232
dekh, i. 161 ; iii. 45
deḍh, i. 237
deyar, i. 253 ; ii. 29
dev, ii. 188, 189, 208, 210, 225, 263, 272

des (deça), ii. 8, 224, 225
dest, ii. 86
doh, ii. 173, 176
do, i. 324; ii. 129, 131, 245
doghe, ii. 245
dojiyâ, ii. 129
don, i. 324; ii. 131, 245
dunog, ii. 245
dopaṭṭâ, ii. 129
dobhâshiyâ, ib.
dor, ii. 149
dol (√dul), i. 227
doladâ, ii. 129
drum, i. 26

DH

dhak, dhakk, etc., i. 130, 227
dhakoiâ, ii. 35, 95, 161
dhajâ, ii. 9
dhaḍak, ii. 82, 83
dhaḍavâi, ii. 168
dhaṇâru, ii. 92
dhaṇlâṇl, ii. 169
dhatûrâ, ii. 22
dhani, ii. 88
dhani, ii. 34, 88
dhamakâ, i. 268
dharam, i. 171; ii. 26
dhavala, i. 268
dhavâḍavag, iii. 81
dhâṇḍalyâ, ii. 167
dhâi, ii. 174
dhân, etc. (dhânya), i. 341; ii. 78
dhâmpnâ, i. 276
dhâv, etc., ii. 51; iii 81
dhiko, i. 130, 227
dhî, etc. (duhitâ), i. 192, 210; ii. 103, 207
dhiru, ii. 164
dhuapu, i. 242
dhuâriṇl, ii. 20
dhutalâ, iii. 143
dhuttâ (dhûrta), i. 334
dhulâl, ii. 62
dhulânâ, i. 241
dhulvaḍâ, etc. (dhûl), i. 162
dhûâṅ, etc. (dhûma), i. 257; ii. 26
dhûp, i. 152
dhûpal, ii. 127
dhoṇḍâ, ii. 90, 149
dhoṇḍâl, ii. 90
dhoti, etc. (dhautra) i. 171, 338
dhonâ, i. 241; ii. 62
dhobin, etc., i. 183; ii. 167
dhobî, etc., i. 183; ii. 164, 165, 167, 169
dholâl, ii. 62
dholânâ, i. 241
dhobâ, ii. 167
dhaṅun, i. 268; ii. 62
dhamakaml, i. 268
dhaulâ, ib.
dhyân, i. 227

N

-na, ii. 334
naǵvag (√nam), iii. 19, 20, 57
nakharelo, ii. 161
nangâ (nagna), i. 191, 300
nachhattar, i. 171
naṭâ, ii. 184
nadînave, ii. 140
naṇdhapâl, i. 330; ii. 72
natait, ii. 103
nadî, ii. 190, 226
nadhânave, ii. 140
nam, iii. 19, 20, 57

nar, ii. 226
narulu, i. 201
navasri, ii. 156
navâd, ii. 140
navve, navad, etc., ii. 137, 141
nashṭâmi, ii. 77
nahâṇ (snâna), i. 347
nahiyar, i. 167
nâl, nâû, ii. 58
nâknâ, ii. 40
nâch (√nṛit), i. 327; iii. 86
nâjo, ii. 161
nât (hattâ), 246
nâti, nâtû, etc. (naptṛi), ii. 58, 155, 193
nâm, nâmv, etc. (nâman), i. 254, 266; ii. 60, 182
nâraugi, i. 180
nâriyal, etc. (nârikela), i. 201
nâri, ii. 165, 199
nâlâ, ii. 9
nâv (√nam), iii. 57
nâhaṇṇṇ, i. 347
-ni, ii. 334
niüṇ (nemi), i. 256
nikaṭ, i. 185
nikal, nikâl, etc. (√nishkṛish), i. 354; iii. 66
nikas, nikâs, etc., ib.
nigas, etc., i. 152
nind, i. 182, 337; ii. 46
nindârto, ii. 103
nidrâlu, ii. 69
ninânave, ii. 140
nimdâs, ii. 83
nipaṭâru, ii. 94
nibaḍ, nibaṛ (nivṛit), iii. 60
nimna, i. 340
nirmalâi, ii. 79
nivâ (√nam), iii. 57
niçâla, ii. 89
nihachhai, etc. (niçchaye), i. 140, 307; ii. 297
nihuḍ (√nam), iii. 57
√nî, iii. 44
-nig, ii. 262, 271
nicha, nicho, i. 184; ii. 297
nîj (nidrâ), i. 182, 337; ii. 46
nîṭ, i. 152
nînd (nidrâ), i. 182, 337; ii. 46, 82
-nuṇ, ii. 253, 261
nuṇi (√nam), iii. 57
nupûr, i. 168, 175
nûṇ, i. 144, 246
-ne, ii. 262
-neṇ, ii. 253
neü, nev, etc. (nemi), i. 191, 260
neugṭâ, i. 248, 301
neṇa, etc. (nayana), i. 140; ii. 17
nemâlto, ii. 103
noval, neul, etc. (nakula), i. 139, 187, 201
nevaṇ (navati), ii. 137, 141
nohemi, i. 189
-no, ii. 276, 287
noḍi, ii. 226
nora, noliyâ (nakula), i. 187, 201
nyâv, etc. (nyâya), i. 241
nhâ (√snâ), i. 148, 347; iii. 68

P

-pe, ii. 71
pak (√pach), iii. 58, 78
pakkâ, etc. (pakva), i. 153, 324; ii. 25
pakh, i. 310
pakhi, ii. 154
pagaḍi, i. 154

pach, iii. 12, 38
pachâṇṇû, ii. 141
pachâvan, ib.
pachhâs, ii. 137, 140
pachhis, etc., i. 253
pachhpan, ii. 141
pachhhattâv, i. 218
pachhhim, i. 307
pachhe, ii. 297
panchânna, ii. 141
panchhi, ii. 154
panj, ii. 132, 140, 246
panjâha, ii. 137, 141
paṭakâ, etc., i. 133
paṭâkâ, ii. 43
paṭvâri, ii. 154
paṭṭâ, etc., i. 224, 336
paḍ (√paṭ), i. 224; ii. 64; iii. 86, 226
paḍâv (paḍâo), ii. 64, 66
paḍi (prati), i. 321
paḍisâ, ii. 199
paḍosi (parosi), i. 321; ii. 153
paḍchhâyâ, i. 321
paḍh, paṛh (√paṭh), i. 270; ii. 37; iii. 40
paḍhama, i. 132
-paṇu, -paṇo, ii. 71, 75
paṇkappaḍâ, etc., i. 152
paṇḍitâṇi, ii. 166
paṇḍita, ii. 72, 166
paṇṇarah, ii. 134
pati, ii 134, 190
patâ, ii. 29
patthar, i. 148, 153, 218, 320; ii. 97
patthaḥarallâ, ii. 97
-pan, ii. 71, 75, 172
pan- (panchan in comp.), ii. 126
pandarah, pandhrâṇ, etc., ii. 134
pandhado, ii. 117
pannâs, ii. 137
par, pari, ii. 298, 344
parakh, etc. (parikshâ), i. 145, 182
parakkhaṇâ, ii. 187
paraṇ, paraṇâhu, etc. (√pari-ṇi), iii. 44
parab (parvvan), i. 131, 171, 322, 352; ii. 60
paralâ, ii. 344
paraloku, ii. 127
paras, i. 356
parasnâ (√spṛiçh), i. 171, 356
parosi, ii. 154
pargaṇâ, i. 320
parchhâiṇ, i. 321
parjant, i. 156
paṛti, ii. 164
paṛtu, ib.
paṛnâlâ, i. 320
parbatiyâ, ii. 86
parbhu, i. 322
parvaṇ, iii. 266
palang, i. 199, 249; ii. 119
palangaḍi, ii. 119
palâu, ii. 349
paçu, i. 133, 260; ii. 166
pasihâ (√praviç), i. 316
pastâvaṇeṇ, i. 218
pastis, ii. 140
paharû, ii. 36, 38
paharyo, i. 267; ii. 142
pahirâ, i. 131
pahirâvâ, etc., i. 177; ii. 69, 70
pahilâ, i. 131, 136, 267; ii. 142
pahuṇ, ii. 259
pahûnahnâ, etc., i. 276, 343; iii. 66
-pâ, ii. 71, 75
pâ, pâv, pâm, etc. (√prâp), i. 202; iii. 18, 41
√pâ, iii. 44, 228

pât, i. 262
pâu, ii. 144
pâṇ, i. 256
pâûṇ, ii. 144
pâe, *cf.*
pâûs, pâvus (prâvṛiṣh), i. 165
pâgv, i. 255, 256
pâkaḍ, i. 133
pâkhl, ii. 154
pâgalâmi, ii. 77
pachlw, ii. 297
pâṅch, ii. 152
pâṅchvâṅ, ii. 248
pâṭ, i. 273
pâṭala, ii. 110
pâṭaviṇoṇ, etc., i. 330
pâṭâ, i. 159
pâṭh, i. 162, 315
pâḍâ, i. 224
pâḍahâ, ii. 36
pâḍo, ii. 150
pâḍhnâ, ii. 37
pâḍhl, ii. 85
pâṇ, pân (parṇa), i. 343; ii. 14
pâṇ (âtman), i. 330; ii. 328
pâṇl, pânl, i. 149, 152; ii. 125, 156
pâpl, ii. 86, 166
pâra, i. 266
pâracho, ii. 110
pârkhaṇeṇ, i. 145
pâlaṇu, i. 247
pâlâu, i. 349
pâs, etc. (pârçva), i. 153, 355; ii. 25, 299
pâhâḍ, i. 164, 260
pâhuṇ, ii. 258
pâhunâ, i. 343
pâhoṇ, ii. 299
pi, (api), i. 175
pi (√pâ), i. 240, 241, 242; iii. 44
piu (pitâ), i. 165, 187, 202; ii. 58, 187, 194
pik, pikâ (√pach), i. 129; ii. 25; iii. 88
pichhalâ, ii. 101
pichha, ii. 297
piñaṇu, ii. 60
piñjarâ, i. 130
piṭ, i. 162; iii. 63
piṭṭh, etc. (priṣhṭha), i. 162, 165, 315
pitiyâ, ii. 90
pinilhibâ, i. 177
pînaw, ii. 345
pippala, ii. 24
piyâsâ, ii. 24
piyâsâ, i. 137, 203; ii. 81, 82
pirihl, i. 145
pirbhu (parvan), i. 131, 322, 352; ii. 60
pilsaj, i. 276
pilânâ, i. 240; iii. 80
pisâi, ii. 63
pistallo, ii. 140
pih (√praviç), i. 316; iii. 38, 139
pilaṇeṇ, i. 240
pî (priya), ii. 156
pî (√pâ), i. 240; iii. 44
pîchho, ii. 297
pîṭ, i. 162; iii. 63
pîṭh, etc. (priṣhṭha), i. 162, 315
pîṭho, iii. 139
pîḍ, ii. 48, 50
pîḍaṇu, etc. (√pîḍ), i. 240; ii. 50
pîḍhâ, i. 270
pîṭho, iii. 141
pîpala, ii. 24
pîlâ, i. 248
pîlbâ, i. 323
pîh, pîs (√piṣh), i. 259; iii. 139
pua, i. 337

puñ, ii. 297
putru, i. 108
putrein, ib.
puṭh, puṭhi (pṛishṭha), i. 316
puḍhâit, ii. 104
-puṇ, -puṇâ, ii. 71, 75
put, i. 337
putali, etc., i. 133
puturâ, i. 172, 168
purash, ii. 199
purushâtan, ii. 76
pusspeṇ, i. 218; iii. 40
puhap, puhup (pushpa), i. 191, 307, 331
puhukar, i. 307
pûchh, etc. (prachh), i. 218; iii. 40
pûjâri, ii. 58
pûnaû, ii. 174
pûrâ, i. 343, 344
pûrbe, ii. 29
pûrjeṇu, iii. 71
pekkh, i. 152
petâñ, petâ, ii. 42, 112
peṭhu, i. 316; iii. 130, 144
peḍ, i. 135
peuth, i. 139
peuû, ii. 30
peun, ii. 61
pelaṇâ, etc., i. 240; ii. 36
pelu, ii. 340
peç (praviç), i. 316; iii. 38
peharavuṇ, i. 177
pohela, i. 138, 167; ii. 142, 344
pai, ii. 298
paiṅgaṭh, i. 168
paiṭh (√praviç), i. 316; iii. 38
paiṇḍhâ, i. 168
paintâlis, i. 168, 215, 292
paintis, ib.
pairâk, ii. 43
-po, ii. 71
poû, ii. 297
pokhar, i. 133, 306
poṇâ, ii. 144
potâ, i. 188; ii. 343, 344
pothi, i. 313; ii. 29, 202
ponar, ii. 164
poh, i. 269
poke, i. 133, 260
paunu, ii. 144

PH

phakaṇu, i. 276
phaṭ, etc. (√sphaṭ), i. 308; iii. 53
phaḍ, etc. (id.), ib.
phaṇâ, ii. 9
phansa, i. 192
phandrûl, ii. 100
phus, etc. (√spṛish), i. 307, 356
phumkaṇi, ii. 77
phânsi, etc., i. 355; ii. 8
phâuk, ii. 191
phâṭ (√sphaṭ), i. 308; iii. 53
phâṭak, i. 308; ii. 31
phâḍ, etc., i. 308; iii. 53
phândnâ, i. 307
phâl, phâr, i. 247; ii. 8
phâhl, i. 356; ii. 8
phiṭ, (√sphaṭ), i. 308; iii. 53
phuṭ (√sphuṭ), i. 308; iii. 53
phup (pushpa), i. 307, 331
phûl, i. 151, 152
phuṅknâ, i. 276
pher, iii. 56
phoḍ, i. 307; iii. 54
phoḍâ, i. 307; ii. 29, 30
phoḍû, ii. 38

B

bak, i. 252
bakarâ, etc., i. 131, 144, 319; ii. 22, 150, 162

bagajá, i. 252
baghitalá, iii. 143
bachá, bachhá, etc., i. 155, 317; ii. 9, 121, 151
bachhàná, etc., i. 178, 211
baj, báj (√vad), i. 328; iii. 66
bajhaṇu, i. 328; iii. 48, 137
bajho, iii. 137
baṭe, i. 164, 216
baṭná, etc., i. 164; ii. 62
baṭhán, i. 178
baḍ (vaṭa), i. 199; ii. 6
baḍá (vṛiddha), i. 168; ii. 72, 79
baḍhal, i. 334; ii. 155, 165
baḍhápaṇu, ii. 72
baḍhia, ii. 165
baṇiáṇ, ii. 167
baṇiáṇp, ii. 168
bat- (vártá in comp.), i. 151
battí, i. 154, 334
battís, i. 331; ii. 138, 142
badho, iii. 137
banáná, iii. 78
bandhaṇu, etc., i. 300; iii. 48
banná, iii. 78
bapauti, ii. 107
bar, ii. 12
baras, barsá, etc. (varsha), i. 178, 355; ii. 9, 14
bareṭhan, ii. 165
baruchu, ii. 168
barkhá, etc. (varsha), i. 261, 355; ii. 9
barrbhání, ii. 103
barj, i. 362
barhyu, i. 355
balad, ii. 199
balá, ii. 206
bali, i. 182
bavanjá, i. 331
bahattar, i. 288, 331
bahangí, i. 131
bahin, i. 136, 155, 183, 202, 206; ii. 170
bahirá, i. 188, 257; ii. 13
bahu, bahú, etc. (vadhú), i. 183; ii. 56, 184, 216, 225
bá- (dvi in comp.), i. 253, 288, 331; ii. 138
báa (váyu), i. 147; ii. 54
báürá, báülá, etc. (vátula), ii. 100
báṇa, etc., ii. 6, 121, 164
báṇauli, ii. 121
bágh, i. 182; ii. 54, 172
bág, i. 163, 323; ii. 69
bágun, i. 196
bágh, i. 330, 351; ii. 21, 165, 169
báchhurí, i. 186
báchhná, i. 351
bájh, i. 359
báṅjhá, i. 327
báḍho, ii. 155
bát, i. 164, 182; ii. 49
báti, i. 182; ii. 49
bádul, i. 145
bándhná, i. 300
báp, ii. 191, 215
bápú, i. 191, 207, 331
bábá, ii. 182, 192, 204
báyako, ii. 161, 192
báyáṇ, ii. 26
báraṇu, i. 324
bárah, etc. (dvádaça), i. 243, 331; ii. 184, 186, 246
bálak, ii. 199, 201
bálantapaṇ, ii. 75
bálapan, i. 330; ii. 72
báli, bálú (váluká), i. 147; ii. 89
bálná, i. 324
báhoṭi, ii. 122
bi- (dvi in comp.), i. 331
bio, ii. 145

bikat, i. 182
bikâv, ii. 64
bikû, ii. 10, 157
bikh, i. 261; ii. 8, 174
bigad, etc. (√vighaṭ), i. 273; ii. 86, 70; iii. 61
bichhâná, ii. 70
bichhná, etc. (√ṛiçchikâ), ii. 146, 807
bijlî (vidyut), i. 146, 181, 182, 827
biṭapaṇ, ii. 74
bitná, i. 351
bindî, i. 147; ii. 54, 174
bindhâj, ii. 94
birânavṇ, i. 331; ii. 139
birâni, ib.
birt, i. 166
bilâito, ii. 104
bis, ii. 174
bih, i. 242
bihan, i. 202
bihân, ii. 16
bihî (√bhî), iii. 68
bilra, ii. 6
bîj (vîja), i. 331; ii. 143
bîs (vimçati), i. 165; ii. 137, 140
bîsrâṇ, ii. 248
bujh (√budh), i. 273, 328; ii. 66, 107; iii. 48, 137
bujhail, ii. 96
bujhanti, ii. 66, 107
bud, bûḍ, etc., i. 132, 276; iii. 69
buḍḍhâ, etc. (vṛiddha), i. 163; ii. 159
buḍhâpaṇ, i. 380; ii. 72, 73
bund, bûnd (vindu), i. 135; ii. 54, 174
bundhaṇu, iii. 48, 137
bulânâ, i. 211; iii. 78
be, i. 331
beâlis, i. 331; ii. 139
beünâ, i. 148
beng, i. 361
bech, iii. 64
beṭâ, ii. 136, 204, 228
beṭî, ii. 207
beṭnâ, ii. 41
bejûk, ii. 44
beḍhâ, i. 273, 316
bepârî, i. 361
ber, i. 142; ii. 22
bel, i. 157
belnâ, ii. 17
behan, i. 138, 202
beherâ, i. 138; ii. 13
baiguṇ, i. 167
baiṭh (√upaviç), i. 179, 241, 242, 316; ii. 31; iii. 88
bokar, i. 319; ii. 22
bonâ, i. 156, 200
bol (√brû), iii. 57
byauṭnâ, i. 144
byorâ, i. 143

BH

bhaṃv (√bhram), iii. 34
bhaṃvara (bhramara), i. 320; ii. 22
bhaṃvaî, ii. 65
bhage, iii. 137
bhagat, i. 287
bhang (√bhañj), iii. 39
bhajaṇu, ii. 38; iii. 50, 137
bhañjaṇu, ib.
bhañj, iii. 39
bhaṭaku, ii. 37
bhaṭuaḍî, ii. 117
bhaṭṭî, i. 134

bhaḍuá, ii. 80
bhattjá, i. 161, 165
bhanvál, ii. 156
bhabát, i. 145
bham (√bhram), iii. 34
bhay, ii. 10, 222
bhayau, iii. 195
bhar, ii. 19, 20, 38, 51, 70, 108, 109
bharam (√bhram), iii. 34
bharyatu, ii. 109
bhalá, ii. 73, 79
bhavan, ii. 66
bháiṭyo, i. 161, 165
bháito, ii. 103
bhái, bháü, etc. (bhrátri), i. 202, 320; ii. 58, 103, 164, 193, 194
bháij, i. 165
bhákhá, i. 261
bhág, bháng (√bhanj), iii. 39
bháṅ (bhágya), ii. 78
bhájavaṭ, ii. 67
bháju, ii. 38
bháñu, ib.
bháḍ, bháḍá, i. 199; ii. 29, 30
bháṇḍá, i. 199
bháṇḍámi, ii. 77
bháṇḍo, ii. 29
bháṇḍpaṇá, ii. 73
bhát, i. 286
bháph, i. 191, 331
bhár, ii. 40, 199
bháruá, ii. 40
bhálá, ii. 9
bhálú, ii. 89
bháv, ii. 14
bhávi, ii. 170
bhávin, ii. 170, 231
bháshá, i. 261
bhikári, i. 152
bhig, bhij, etc., i. 176; iii. 81
bhiḍ, iii. 63
bhinal, ii. 155
√bhí, iii. 9
bhikh (bhikshá), i. 152
bhítar, i. 176, 194
bhukhaḍo, ii. 119
bhugu, iii. 137
bhunjaṇu, iii. 50
bhuñaṇu, ib.
bhupikáṭu, ii. 54
bhulaṇu, ii. 62
√bhú, iii. 63, 194
bhú, bhúán, etc. (bhúmi), i. 267; ii. 62, 89, 194
bhúl, bhúlná, ii. 81
bhejná, i. 223; iii. 66
bheḍ, iii. 63
bheḍá, i. 316
bheḍayá, ii. 39
bheṇu, i. 187, 202; ii. 194
bheṇṭ, iii. 63
bhaiṇa, i. 192
bhaiṇ, i. 187
bholiḍo, ii. 117
bhaun (√bhram), iii. 34
bhaun, bhaunh (bhrú), ii. 66
bhaunr (bhramara), i. 220; ii. 23
bhaunl, i. 203

M

ma, ii. 302
makhi, i. 218, 310; ii. 34
mag, ii. 8
maghar, i. 323, 354
maṅaṇu, i. 319; ii. 19
machháv, ii. 64
machhuá, ii. 39, 40
maj (pron.), ii. 302

majjh, majhi, etc., (madhya), i. 327; ii. 306
majhár, ii. 293
majholá, i. 327; ii. 100
manjan, etc., i. 149, 319
manjháro, ii. 100
maṭṭi, i. 162, 333; ii. 35
maṭh, i. 270
maṇḍal, ii. 24
mat, ii. 52
matho, i. 313; ii. 29, 195, 213
madhu, ii. 191, 295
manaüll, ii. 107
mandir, ii. 22
mandhiṇḍo, ii. 117
mamatálü, ii. 91
mar (√mṛi), iii. 55
maroṭho, ii. 169
markaṇu, ii. 51
malná (çmaçána), i. 348
maslr, i. 188
mahangá, etc. (mahárgha), i. 149 273
mahátam, ii. 77
mahádevaḍo, ii. 119
mahimá, ii. 152
mahuá, ii. 40
mahüá, i. 150
mahobá, i. 317
majaṇeṇ, i. 243
má, -mál, máû, etc. (mátá), i. 165, 202; ii. 49, 58, 187, 191, 202
-má, ii. 244
-máṇ, ii. 292
máṇhi, ii. 294
máṇhaiṇ, *ib.*
mákhi, i. 310; ii. 34
mágeṇ, ii. 110
mágitalá, iii. 143
mágehá, ii. 110
mág, máng, etc. (√mṛig), i. 319; iii. 40
máchhi, i. 218; ii. 34
máchhuá, ii. 39
máj (mṛij), i. 319; iii. 9
májh, i. 327; ii. 312
mánjh, ii. 293
mánjhail, ii. 97
máṭi, ii. 35
máṭhá, i. 267
máṇhipo, ii. 72
mát, ii. 48, 217, 218
máthá, i. 313; ii. 29
-mán (plur.), ii. 199, 280, 316
mápná, i. 206
mámu, ii. 39
márná, i. 161; ii. 36, 50; iii. 55
máro, ii. 306, 312
málá, ii. 48, 216
máli, ii. 154, 165, 198, 195
máçi, i. 218, 310; ii. 34
másük, ii. 282
máso (matsya), i. 218
-mi, ii. 334
michhá, i. 327
miṭ, miṭh, etc., 162; iii. 63
miṭṭi, i. 162, 333; ii. 35
miṭhás, ii. 82
miḍyol, ii. 340
miuro, ii. 345
mirüg, ii. 72, 226
misar (miçra), i. 367
mi, ii. 302, 306
migh, i. 266
mlchh, i. 327
mu, mui, ii. 302, 304
muá (mṛita), i. 165; iii. 144
mugh, i. 266
mukhiri, i. 322
mukhi, ii. 88, 89
mugulání, ii. 166

mugdar, etc. (mudgara), i. 286
mujh, ii. 302, 304, 306
muṭhi, i. 315
muṇḍá, ii. 157
muṇḍásá, ii. 83
muṇḍó, ii. 86
mutás, ii. 82
murelá, ii. 121
musaṇa, iii. 51
múṇ, ii. 302, 304
múgará, i. 286
múchh, i. 135
múṭh, i. 191, 315
múḍh, i. 286; ii. 72
mút, i. 152, 338
múrkh, ii. 72
múrchh, i. 172
múl, i. 351
músal, i. 155
músá, ii. 9
meṇ, ii. 298
meghi, ii. 92
merjaṇeg, i. 139
merá, ii. 312, 313, 314
meleṇ, i. 165
mo, ii. 302, 318
mokh, i. 307
moti, i. 297; ii. 84, 167, 208
modi, ii. 184
mor, i. 144
mohoḍag, ii. 118, 189
mhaṇaṇeg, i. 192
mhatalá, iii. 151
mhátárá, ii. 73
mháro, ii. 312, 314
mhaiga, i. 192

Y

-yal, ii. 100
yah, ii. 317, 336
√yá, iii. 36, 213
-yá, ii. 83, 88
yárahag, i. 260; ii. 249
yáhi, ii. 319
yih, ii. 336
yúṇ, ib.
yo, ii. 317, 319
yeṇeg, ii. 249
-yo, ii. 88
yog, i. 249

R

raú, ii. 194
rakat, i. 171
rakh, etc. (√raksh), iii. 41
raṭ, etc., i. 228
raḍ, etc., ib.
raṇḍ, i. 299; ii. 48
raṇḍápo, ii. 72, 73
ratan, i. 171
ratu, i. 287
ran, i. 179, 341
rana, i. 299; ii. 48, 72
rasá, ii. 148
√rah, i. 131, 188; ii. 36, 42; iii. 40
rahag, i. 179, 266
rás, i. 202
ráut, i. 202; ii. 127
rául, i. 202
rákh (raksha), ii. 48, 110
rájá, i. 202; ii. 60, 152, 184, 190
ráḍ, i. 228
ráḍh, ráḍhi, i. 228; ii. 86
ráṇḍ, i. 299; ii. 48, 72
ráṇḍápá, ii. 72
rát, i. 337; ii. 52, 112, 203, 209, 288
rátá, i. 287

rán, i. 179, 341
ráni, i. 303
rávat, i. 202
rás, i. 348
ráh, iii. 40
richh, i. 310; ii. 14
ríṇu, i. 179, 341
richh, i. 216, 310; ii. 14
ris, ib.
-ru, ii. 273
ruaṇu, i. 202
rukhi, ii. 341
√ruch, iii. 19, 23
ruḍhi, ii. 229
√rul, iii. 16, 24
√rulh, iii. 20
runo, iii. 138
rulánâ, i. 241
rudyo, ii. 17
rúḍh, i. 316
-re, ii. 292
rekh, regh, etc. (rakhá), i. 272; ii. 48
roṭ, i. 266
roṭá, i. 170
roṇḍi, i. 180
rot, roṭi, ii. 92, 94, 101
roṭál, roṭilá, ib.
roṭuá, ii. 40
roh (√ruh), i. 138; ii. 48, 49; iii. 40
-ro, ii. 217, 281, 284
roáṇ (rumán), i. 257
rolá, ii. 82
rogi, ii. 86
roná, i. 202, 341; ii. 32

L.

lakhavaṇ, i. 266
lakhoṭi, ii. 123
√lag, i. 300; ii. 260; iii. 34, 216
laguti, ii. 53
lagin, i. 172
lagun, ii. 261
lajálú, ii. 92
lajilá, ii. 97
laṭakná, i. 228; ii. 32
laṭh, i. 250, 315
laḍká, i. 228; ii. 72, 201
laḍḍu, i. 228
laḍhaṇoṇ, i. 228; ii. 44
lad, ii. 20; iii. 61
laḍhu, i. 268; iii. 137
lanu, ii. 299
labhaṇu, iii. 49, 137
lahaṇu, i. 268; iii. 49, 137
lahar, i. 131, 138
-lá, ii. 253, 260
-lál, ib.
lákh, i. 152
lág (√lag), i. 300; ii. 51, 52; iii. 84
lágiṇ, ii. 260
láj, ii. 49, 92
láṭhi, i. 241, 250, 315
láḍ, ii. 100, 101
láḍi, ii. 85
lát, i. 248; ii. 49
látho, i. 269
lálá, ii. 159
láhaṇu, i. 269
likhṇá, i. 268
liṭ, liḍ, iii. 64
lito, iii. 138
√lip, iii. 59, 158
liḍho, iii. 141
lílá, i. 228
luchhá, ii. 72, 77
luhaṇḍá, ii. 125
luhá, ii. 15
lúká, i. 178, 180

lâj, i. 248
lûṇ, i. 144, 248
lûmaṇu, iii. 61
lûlaṇu, ib.
lo (√lubh), i. 246, 268; iii. 49, 219
-lo, ii. 281, 287
lok, ii. 8, 28, 200
long, i. 143, 191
loṇ, loṇá, i. 143, 144; ii. 33, 111, 156
lohá, ii. 15, 30
lohî, ii. 92
lohu, ii. 15
lau, ii. 261
laung, i. 143
launḍ, i. 238

V

For words not found under V, *look under* B.

vakhaṛ, i. 252
vagaḍṇá, i. 273
vangal, i. 252
vaṭi, i. 334; ii. 72
vaṭo, i. 164
vaṭho, iii. 188
vaḍhaṛ, i. 334
vaṇati, ii. 53
vathu, ii. 202
var, ii. 298
variboko, ii. 112
varia, i. 178
varu, i. 182
varttaṇuk, ii. 44
varhyu, ii. 14
√vas, i. 252; iii. 188
vasati, ii. 53
vasamli, ii. 54
vastu, ii. 190
vah, ii. 118, 334
vaháṇ, ii. 330
vahitru, ii. 45
vahû, i. 183, 267; ii. 65, 161, 190
vâî, ii. 64
vâû, i. 147; ii. 54, 158, 194
-vâṇ, ii. 244, 247
vâgh, ii. 170
vâghû, ii. 195
vâchhâjû, ii. 92
vâchchhâ, i. 168
vâjaṭu, ii. 48
vânah, iii. 66
vâṇjh, i. 327
vâpaṇu, i. 164
vâparû, ii. 192, 217
vâḍhu, i. 334; ii. 90, 202
vâṇiko, ii. 111
vât, i. 334; ii. 99
vâtûl, ii. 99
vâdula, i. 146
vâpâriko, ii. 111
vâph, i. 307
vâyaḍl, ii. 119
vârî, i. 147
vâryâsâ, ii. 114
vâserâ, ii. 99
vâkîpo, i. 330; ii. 72
vikiṇ (√vikrî), iii. 64
√vighuṭ, iii. 61
-vich, ii. 292
vichu, vinchû, i. 146, 307; ii. 193, 203
vijû, ii. 117, 194
vijuli, i. 327
viñâiṇu, ii. 42; iii. 71
viṭṭhal, i. 347
viḍahaṇu, ii. 38
virali, i. 166
virchhaṇu, i. 361; ii. 42
vih, i. 242; iii. 189

vihu, ii. 8, 174
vigu, ii. 194
vih, i. 259; ii. 137, 140
vuṭho, iii. 126
vuh, ii. 336
ve, ii. 318, 319
vaktire, ii. 81
vaṭha, i. 179; iii. 189
varu, ii. 112
vorudy, i. 143

Ç

√çak, iii. 16, 36
çatâria, i. 289
√çal, iii. 57
çambhar, i. 297; ii. 107
çabdapaṇṇ, ii. 73
çâgyçi, ii. 140
çâṇpav, ii. 140
çâç, i. 358
çâl, ii. 50
çiḍi, i. 273
çil, ii. 182
-çig, ii. 271
çina, i. 334
√çikh, iii. 68
√çir, ib.
çuṇ, ena (√çru), i. 357; iii. 15, 16, 24, 28, 41
√çushk, iii. 20
çot (kalantra), i. 216, 310; ii. 35
ço, ii. 324
çorbâ, i. 199

SH

shâṇḍh, i. 315
shola, i. 248; ii. 134

S

sak, etc (√çak), iii. 36, 224
sagar, i. 195, 207
sagâ, i. 358
sagauti, ii. 108
saghaṇu, ii. 31; iii. 38
sange, i. 184; ii. 274
sach (satya), i. 227; ii. 109
sajyâ, i. 186; ii. 40
sajhâne, ii. 102
saṭṭh, i. 316; ii. 137, 246
saḍ, iii. 57
saḍanṭh, i. 289, 293
saṇḍhâ, i. 356
sat-, satt-, etc. (saptan in comp.), i. 253, 288, 289, 290, 293; ii. 133, 134, 137, 141
sanu, ii. 275
sanh, i. 299
sapu, i. 310
sapoḍâ, i. 149
sapotâ, ii. 121
sab, sabh, etc. (sarva), i. 251, 352; ii. 25, 200, 258, 340, 341
samajhnâ, i. 211, 327; ii. 37, 107
samarun, i. 347
samundar, ii. 21
samo, i. 140
samûlha, ii. 200
sambalâ, iii. 68
sar, sâr (√sṛi), iii. 55
sarasuti, i. 354
sarâknâ, i. 171, 266, 358
savâ, i. 100; ii. 144
sasa, i. 353; ii. 194
sasur, i. 358; ii. 22
sahaṇu, ii. 38
sahapoṇ, i. 155
sâlu, i. 257; ii. 134
sâg, ii. 106

sâñjh, i. 278, 328; ii. 60
sâṭh, i. 315; ii. 137
sâḍhâ, i. 356
sâḍhe, i. 278; ii. 144
sât (saptan), i. 183; ii. 236, 268
sâmp, i. 319; ii. 121
sâmhne, ii. 298
sasurâ, i. 358; ii. 193, 216
sâsû, i. 358; ii. 192, 210
sikluṇu, i. 242; iii. 90
singh, i. 160, 262; ii. 14
sir, ii. 60
-siṇ, ii 272
sia, i. 354, 350
sukkhâ, etc., i. 307; ii. 12; iii. 80
suṇaṇu, etc. (√çru), i. 366; iii. 60, 136
sunto, ii. 219, 235, 310
sûar, i. 206
sûî, i. 187, 191, 202
sûjhâ, i. 338
-se, ii. 274
se, ii. 318, 334
sekhâne, ii. 337
seṭhâ, ib.
sendh, i. 184, 299
so, ii. 314, 322, 337
so (√svap), i. 199; iii. 36
soṇâ (suvarṇa), i. 241, 243, 353; ii. 15, 80
sonâr, i. 201; ii. 126
solah, i. 243; ii. 134
√sthambh, iii. 60
√sthâ, iii. 34, 206
√sphuṭ, etc., iii. 53, 57

H

hagnâ, ii. 83
hachâ, ii. 169, 203
hato, iii. 177
hattar, i. 291, 295
hum, etc., ii. 302, 307, 309, 312
halaṇu, ii. 19, 53
hâ, ii. 317, 288
hâḍ, i. 317
hâṇḍâ, i. 268; ii. 148
hâth, i. 268, 313; ii. 91, 109
hâthî, i. 268, 313; ii. 133, 164
hânî, ii. 52
hiyâ, i. 202; ii. 117
hundî, i 268
hunto, ii. 219, 234
heṭh, ii. 298
ho, huâ, etc., (√bhû), i. 268; ii. 236, 318; iii. 33, 197
hai (√as), iii. 173
haun, etc., ib.
hvai, hvaihai, etc., ib.

FINIS.

LINGUISTIC PUBLICATIONS

OF

TRÜBNER & CO.,

57 AND 59, LUDGATE HILL, LONDON, E.C.

Adi Granth (The); or, The Holy Scriptures of the Sikhs, translated from the original Gurmukhî, with Introductory Essays, by Dr. Ernest Trumpp, Professor Regius of Oriental Languages at the University of Munich, etc. Roy. 8vo. cloth, pp. 866. £2 12s. 6d.

Ahlwardt.—The Divans of the Six Ancient Arabic Poets, Ennâbiga, 'Antara, Tarafa, Zuhair, 'Algama, and Imruolqais; chiefly according to the MSS. of Paris, Gotha, and Leyden, and the collection of their Fragments: with a complete list of the various readings of the Text. Edited by W. Ahlwardt, 8vo. pp. xxx. 340, sewed. 1870. 12s.

Aitareya Brahmanam of the Rig Veda. 2 vols. See under Haug.

Alabaster.—The Wheel of the Law: Buddhism illustrated from Siamese Sources by the Modern Buddhist, a Life of Buddha, and an account of H.M. Consulate-General in Siam, M.R.A.S. Demy 8vo. pp. lviii. and 324. 1871. 14s.

Alif Lailat wa Lailat.—The Arabian Nights. 4 vols. 4to. pp. 495, 493, 442, 434. Cairo, A.H. 1279 (1862). £3 3s.

This celebrated Edition of the Arabian Nights is now, for the first time, offered at a price which makes it accessible to Scholars of limited means.

Amberley.—An Analysis of Religious Belief. By Viscount Amberley. 2 vols. 8vo. cl., pp. xvi. 496 and 512. 1876. 30s.

American Oriental Society, Transactions of. Subscription, £1 5s. per volume.

Andrews.—A Dictionary of the Hawaiian Language, to which is appended an English-Hawaiian Vocabulary, and a Chronological Table of Remarkable Events. By Lorrin Andrews. 8vo. pp. 560, cloth. £1 11s. 6d.

Anthropological Institute of Great Britain and Ireland (The Journal of the). Published Quarterly.

Vol. I., No. 1. January-July, 1871. 8vo. pp. 120–clix, sewed. Illustrated with 11 full page Plates, and numerous Woodcuts, and accompanied by several folding plates of Tables, etc. 7s.

Vol. I., No. 2. October, 1871. 8vo. pp. 121-264, sewed. 4s.

Vol. I., No. 3. January, 1872. 8vo. pp. 265–427, sewed. 16 full-page Plates. 4s.

Vol. II., No. 1. April, 1872. 8vo. pp. 136, sewed. Eight two-page plates and two four-page plates. 4s.

Vol. II., No. 2. July and Oct., 1872. 8vo. pp. 137-312. 9 plates and a map. 6s.

Vol. II., No. 3. January, 1873. 8vo. pp. 143. With 4 plates. 4s.

Vol. III., No. 1. April, 1873. 8vo. pp. 136. With 8 plates and two maps. 4s.

Vol. III., No. 2. July and October, 1873. 8vo. pp. 168, sewed. With 9 plates. 4s.

Vol. III., No. 3. January, 1874. 8vo. pp. 238, sewed. With 6 plates, etc. 6s.

Vol. IV., No. 1. April and July, 1874. 8vo. pp. 308, sewed. With 22 plates. 8s.

Vol. IV., No. 2. April, 1875. 8vo. pp. 200, sewed. With 11 plates. 6s.

Vol. V., No. 1. July, 1875. 8vo. pp. 120, sewed. With 3 plates. 4s.

Vol. V., No. 2. October, 1875. 8vo. pp. 132, sewed. With 8 plates. 4s.

Vol. V., No. 3. January, 1876. 8vo. pp. 156, sewed. With 8 plates. 5s.

Vol. V., No. 4. April, 1876. 8vo. pp. 128, sewed. With 2 plates. 5s.

Anthropological Institute—*continued.*

Vol. VI., No. 1. July, 1876. 8vo. pp. 100, sewed. With 8 plates. 5s.
Vol. VI., No. 2. October, 1876. 8vo. pp. 98, sewed. With 4 plates and a map. 5s.
Vol. VI., No. 3. January, 1877. 8vo. pp. 146, sewed. With 11 plates. 5s.
Vol. VI., No. 4. May, 1877. 8vo. pp. iv. and 184, sewed. With 7 plates. 5s.
Vol. VII., No. 1. August, 1877. 8vo. pp. 116, sewed. With three plates. 5s.
Vol. VII., No. 2. November, 1877. 8vo. pp. 84, sewed. With one plate. 5s.
Vol. VII., No. 3. February, 1878. 8vo. pp. 193, sewed. With three plates. 5s.
Vol. VII., No. 4. May, 1878. 8vo. pp. iv. and 136, sewed. With nine plates. 5s.
Vol. VIII., No. 1. August, 1878. 8vo. pp. 103, sewed. With one plate. 5s.
Vol. VIII., No. 2. November, 1878. 8vo. pp. 126, sewed. With three plates. 5s.

Apastambíya Dharma Sutram.—Aphorisms of the Sacred Laws of the Hindus, by Apastamba. Edited, with a Translation and Notes, by G. Bühler. By order of the Government of Bombay. 2 parts. 8vo. cloth, 1868-71. £1 4s. 6d.

Arabic and Persian Books (A Catalogue of). Printed in the East. Constantly for sale by Trübner and Co., 57 and 59, Ludgate Hill, London. 16mo. pp. 46, sewed. 1s.

Archæological Survey of India.—See under Burgess and Cunningham.

Arden.—A Progressive Grammar of the Telugu Language, with Copious Examples and Exercises. In Three Parts. Part I. Introduction.—On the Alphabet and Orthography.—Outline Grammar, and Model Sentences. Part II. A Complete Grammar of the Colloquial Dialect. Part III. On the Grammatical Dialect used in Books. By A. H. Arden, M.A., Missionary of the C. M. S. Masulipatam. 8vo. sewed, pp. xiv. and 380. 14s.

Arnold.—The Iliad and Odyssey of India. By Edwin Arnold, M.A., C.S.I., F.R.G.S., etc. Fcap. 8vo. sd., pp. 24. 1s.

Arnold.—The Indian Song of Songs. From the Sanskrit of the Gita Govinda of Jayadeva. By Edwin Arnold, M.A., C.S.I., F.R.G.S. (of University College, Oxford), formerly Principal of Poona College, and Fellow of the University of Bombay. Cr. 8vo. cl., pp. xvi. and 144. 1875. 5s.

Arnold.—A Simple Transliteral Grammar of the Turkish Language. Compiled from various sources. With Dialogues and Vocabulary. By Edwin Arnold, M.A., C.S.I., F.R.G.S. Post 8vo. cloth, pp. 80. 2s. 6d.

Asher.—On the Study of Modern Languages in General, and of the English Language in particular. An Essay. By David Asher, Ph.D. 12mo. pp. viii. and 80, cloth. 2s.

Asiatic Society.—Journal of the Royal Asiatic Society of Great Britain and Ireland, from the Commencement to 1863. First Series, complete in 20 Vols. 8vo., with many Plates. Price £10; or, in Single Numbers, as follows:—Nos. 1 to 14, 6s. each; No. 15, 2 Parts, 4s. each; No. 16, 2 Parts, 4s. each; No. 17, 2 Parts, 4s. each; No. 18, 6s. These 18 Numbers form Vols. I. to IX.—Vol. X., Part 1, op.; Part 2, 5s.; Part 3, 5s.—Vol. XI., Part 1, 6s.; Part 2 not published.—Vol. XII., 2 Parts, 6s. each.—Vol. XIII., 2 Parts, 6s. each.—Vol. XIV., Part 1, 5s.; Part 2 not published.—Vol. XV., Part 1, 6s.; Part 2, with 3 Maps, £2 2s.—Vol. XVI., 2 Parts, 6s. each.—Vol. XVII., 2 Parts, 6s. each.—Vol. XVIII., 2 Parts, 6s. each.—Vol. XIX., Parts 1 to 4, 16s.—Vol. XX., Parts 1 and 2, 4s. each. Part 3, 7s. 6d.

Asiatic Society.—Journal of the Royal Asiatic Society of Great Britain and Ireland. *New Series.* Vol. I. In Two Parts. pp. iv. and 490, sewed. 1864-5. 16s.

Contents.—I. Vajra-chhedikâ, the "Kin Kong King," or Diamond Sûtra. Translated from the Chinese by the Rev. S. Beal, Chaplain, R.N.—II. The Pâramitâ-hridaya Sûtra, or, in Chinese, "Mo-ho-pô-ye-po-lo-mih-to-sin-king," i.e. "The Great Pâramitâ Heart Sûtra." Translated from the Chinese by the Rev. S. Beal, Chaplain, R.N.—III. On the Preservation of National Literature in the East. By Colonel F. J. Goldsmid.—IV. On the Agricultural, Commercial, Financial, and Military Statistics of Ceylon. By E. R. Power, Esq.—V. Contributions to a Knowledge of the Vedic Theogony and Mythology. By J. Muir, D.C.L., LL.D.—VI. A Tabular List of Original Works and Translations, published by the late Dutch Government of Ceylon at their Printing Press at Colombo. Compiled by Mr. Mat. P. J. Ondaatje, of Colombo.—VII. Assyrian and Hebrew Chronology compared, with a view of showing the extent to which the Hebrew Chronology of Ussher must be modified, in conformity with the Assyrian Canon. By J. W. Bosanquet, Esq.—VIII. On the existing Dictionaries of the Malay Language. By Dr. H. N. van der Tuuk.—IX. Bilingual Readings: Cuneiform and Phoenician. Notes on some Tablets in the British Museum, containing Bilingual Legends (Assyrian and Phoenician). By Major-General Sir H. Rawlinson, K.C.B., Director R.A.S.—X. Translations of Three Copper-plate Inscriptions of the Fourth Century A.D., and Notices of the Chálukya and Gurjjara Dynasties. By Professor J. Dowson, Staff College, Sandhurst.—XI. Yama and the Doctrine of a Future Life, according to the Rig-Yajur-, and Atharva-Vedas. By J. Muir, Esq., D.C.L., LL.D.—XII. On the Jyotisha Observation of the Place of the Colures, and the Date derivable from it. By William D. Whitney, Esq., Professor of Sanskrit in Yale College, New Haven, U.S.—Note on the preceding Article. By Sir Edward Colebrooke, Bart., M.P., President R.A.S.—XIII. Progress of the Vedic Religion towards Abstract Conceptions of the Deity. By J. Muir, Esq., D.C.L., LL.D.—XIV. Brief Notes on the Age and Authenticity of the Work of Aryabhata, Varahamihira, Brahmagupta, Bhattotpala, and Bhaskaracharya. By Dr. Bhau Daji, Honorary Member R.A.S.—XV. Outlines of a Grammar of the Malagasy Language. By H. N. Van der Tuuk.—XVI. On the Identity of Xandrames and Krananda. By Edward Thomas, Esq.

Vol. II. In Two Parts. pp. 522, sewed. 1866-7. 16s.

CONTENTS.—I. Contributions to a Knowledge of Vedic Theogony and Mythology. No. 2. By J. Muir, Esq.—II. Miscellaneous Hymns from the Rig- and Atharva-Vedas. By J. Muir, Esq.—III. Five hundred questions on the Social Condition of the Natives of Bengal. By the Rev. J. Long.—IV. Short account of the Malay Manuscripts belonging to the Royal Asiatic Society. By Dr. H. N. van der Tuuk.—V. Translation of the Amitabha Sutra from the Chinese. By the Rev. S. Beal, Chaplain Royal Navy.—VI. The initial coinage of Bengal. By Edward Thomas, Esq.—VII. Specimens of an Assyrian Dictionary. By Edwin Norris, Esq.—VIII. On the Relations of the Priests to the other classes of Indian Society in the Vedic age. By J. Muir, Esq.—IX. On the Interpretation of the Veda. By the same.—X. An attempt to Translate from the Chinese a work known as the Confessional Services of the great compassionate Kwan Yin, possessing 1000 hands and 1000 eyes. By the Rev. S. Beal, Chaplain Royal Navy.—XI. The Hymns of the Gaupâyanas and the Legend of King Asamâti. By Professor Max Müller, M.A., Honorary Member Royal Asiatic Society.—XII. Specimen Chapters of an Assyrian Grammar. By the Rev. E. Hincks, D.D., Honorary Member Royal Asiatic Society.

Vol. III. In Two Parts. pp. 516, sewed. With Photograph. 1868. 22s.

CONTENTS.—I. Contributions towards a Glossary of the Assyrian Language. By H. F. Talbot.—II. Remarks on the Indo-Chinese Alphabets. By Dr. A. Bastian.—III. The poetry of Mohamed Rabadan, Arragonese. By the Hon. H. E. J. Stanley.—IV. Catalogue of the Oriental Manuscripts in the Library of King's College, Cambridge. By Edward Henry Palmer, B.A., Scholar of St. John's College, Cambridge; Member of the Royal Asiatic Society; Membre de la Société Asiatique de Paris.—V. Description of the Amravati Tope in Guntur. By J. Fergusson, Esq., F.R.S.—VI. Remarks on Prof. Brockhaus' edition of the Kathâsarit-sâgara, Lambaka IX. XVIII. By Dr. H. Kern, Professor of Sanskrit in the University of Leyden.—VII. The source of Colebrooke's Essay "On the Duties of a Faithful Hindu Widow." By Fitzedward Hall, Esq., M.A., D.C.L. Oxon. Supplement: Further detail of proof that Colebrooke's Essay, "On the Duties of a Faithful Hindu Widow," was not indebted to the Vivâdabhangârnava. By Fitzedward Hall, Esq.—VIII. The Sixth Hymn of the First Book of the Rig Veda. By Professor Max Müller, M.A., Hon. M.R.A.S.—IX. Sassanian Inscriptions. By E. Thomas, Esq.—X. Account of an Embassy from Morocco to Spain in 1690 and 1691. By the Hon. H. E. J. Stanley.—XI. The Poetry of Mohamed Rabadan, of Arragon. By the Hon. H. E. J. Stanley.—XII. Materials for the History of India for the Six Hundred Years of Mohammadan rule, previous to the Foundation of the British Indian Empire. By Major W. Nassau Lees, LL.D., Ph.D.—XIII. A Few Words concerning the Hill people inhabiting the Forests of the Cochin State. By Captain G. E. Fryer, Madras Staff Corps, M.R.A.S.—XIV. Notes on the Bhojpurí Dialect of Hindí, spoken in Western Behar. By John Beames, Esq., B.C.S., Magistrate of Chumparun.

Vol. IV. In Two Parts. pp. 521, sewed. 1869-70. 16s.

CONTENTS.—I. Contribution towards a Glossary of the Assyrian Language. By H. F. Talbot. Part II.—II. On Indian Chronology. By J. Fergusson, Esq., F.R.S.—III. The Poetry of Mohamed Rabadan of Arragon. By the Hon. H. E. J. Stanley.—IV. On the Magar Language of Nepal. By John Beames, Esq., B.C.S.—V. Contributions to the Knowledge of Parsee Literature. By Edward Sachau, Ph.D.—VI. Illustrations of the Lamaist System in Tibet, drawn from Chinese Sources. By Wm. Frederick Mayers, Esq., of H.B.M. Consular Service, China.—VII. Khuddaka Pátha, a Páli Text, with a Translation and Notes. By R. C. Childers, late of the Ceylon Civil Service.—VIII. An Endeavour to elucidate Rashiduddin's Geographical Notices of India. By Col. H. Yule, C.B.—IX. Sassanian Inscriptions explained by the Pahlavi of the Pársís. By E. W. West, Esq.—X. Some Account of the Senbyú Pagoda at Mengún, near the Burmese Capital, in a Memorandum by Capt. E. H. Sladen, Political Agent at Mandalé; with Remarks on the Subject by Col. Henry Yule, C.B.—XI. The Brhat-Sanhitá; or, Complete System of Natural Astrology of Varáha-Mihira. Translated from Sanskrit into English by Dr. H. Kern.—XII. The Mohammadan Law of Evidence, and its influence on the Administration of

Justice in India. By N. B. E. Baillie, Esq.—XIII. The Mohammedan Law of Evidence in connection with the Administration of Justice to Foreigners. By N. B. E. Baillie, Esq.—XIV. A Translation of a Bactrian Pali Inscription. By Prof. J. Dowson.—XV. Indo-Parthian Coins. By E. Thomas, Esq.

Vol. V. In Two Parts. pp. 463, sewed. With 10 full-page and folding Plates. 1871-2. 16s. 6d.

Contents.—I. Two Jâtakas. The original Pâli Text, with an English Translation. By V. Fausböll.—II. On an Ancient Buddhist Inscription at Keu-yung kwan, in North China. By A. Wylie.—III. The Brhat Sanhitâ; or, Complete System of Natural Astrology of Varâha-Mihira. Translated from Sanskrit into English by Dr. H. Kern.—IV. The Pongol Festival in Southern India. By Charles E. Gover.—V. The Poetry of Mohamed Rabadan, of Arragon. By the Right Hon. Lord Stanley of Alderley.—VI. Essay on the Creed and Customs of the Jangams. By Charles P. Brown.—VII. On Malabar, Coromandel, Quilon, etc. By C. P. Brown.—VIII. On the Treatment of the Nexus in the Neo-Aryan Languages of India. By John Beames, B.C.S.—IX. Some Remarks on the Great Tope at Sânchi. By the Rev. S. Beal.—X. Ancient Inscriptions from Mathura. Translated by Professor J. Dowson.—Note to the Mathura Inscriptions. By Major-General A. Cunningham.—XI. Specimen of a Translation of the Adi Granth. By Dr. Ernest Trumpp.—XII. Notes on Dhammapada, with special Reference to the Question of Nirvâna. By R. C. Childers, late of the Ceylon Civil Service.—XIII. The Brhat-Sanhitâ; or, Complete System of Natural Astrology of Varâha-mihira. Translated from Sanskrit into English by Dr. H. Kern.—XIV. On the Origin of the Buddhist Arthakathâs. By the Mudliar L. Comrilla Vijasinha, Government Interpreter to the Ratnapura Court, Ceylon. With an Introduction by R. C. Childers, late of the Ceylon Civil Service.—XV. The Poetry of Mohamed Rabadan, of Arragon. By the Right Hon. Lord Stanley of Alderley.—XVI. Proverbia Communia Syriaca. By Captain R. F. Burton.—XVII. Notes on an Ancient Indian Vase, with an Account of the Engraving thereupon. By Charles Horne, M.R.A.S., late of the Bengal Civil Service.—XVIII. The Bhar Tribe. By the Rev. M. A. Sherring, LL.D., Benares. Communicated by C. Horne, M.R.A.S., late B.C.S.—XIX. Of Jihâd in Mohammedan Law, and its application to British India. By N. B. E. Baillie.—XX. Comments on Recent Pehlvi Decipherments. With an Incidental Sketch of the Derivation of Aryan Alphabets. And Contributions to the Early History and Geography of Tabaristân. Illustrated by Coins. By Edward Thomas, F.R.S.

Vol. VI., Part I., pp. 212, sewed, with two plates and a map. 1872. 8s.

Contents.—The Ishmaelites, and the Arabic Tribes who Conquered their Country. By A. Sprenger.—A Brief Account of Four Arabic Works on the History and Geography of Arabia. By Captain S. B. Miles.—On the Methods of Disposing of the Dead at Llassa, Thibet, etc. By Charles Horne, late B.C.S. The Brhat-Sanhitâ; or, Complete System of Natural Astrology of Varâha-mihira, Translated from Sanskrit into English by Dr. H. Kern.—Notes on Hwen Thsang's Account of the Principalities of Tokhâristân, in which some Previous Geographical Identifications are Reconsidered. By Colonel Yule, C.B.—The Campaign of Ælius Gallus in Arabia. By A. Sprenger.—An Account of Jerusalem, Translated for the late Sir H. M. Elliot from the Persian Text of Nâsir ibn Khusrû's Safarnâmah by the late Major A. R. Fuller.—The Poetry of Mohamed Rabadan, of Arragon. By the Right Hon. Lord Stanley of Alderley.

Vol. VI., Part II., pp. 213 to 400 and lxxxiv., sewed. Illustrated with a Map, Plates, and Woodcuts. 1873. 8s.

Contents.—On Hiouen-Thsang's Journey from Patna to Ballabhi. By James Fergusson, D.C.L., F.R.S.—Northern Buddhism. [Note from Colonel H. Yule, addressed to the Secretary.]—Hwen Thsang's Account of the Principalities of Tokhâristân, etc. By Colonel H. Yule, C.B.—The Brhat-Sanhitâ; or, Complete System of Natural Astrology of Varâha-mihira. Translated from Sanskrit into English by Dr. H. Kern.—The Initial Coinage of Bengal, under the Early Muhammadan Conquerors. Part II. Embracing the preliminary period between A.H. 614-634 (A.D. 1217-1236-7). By Edward Thomas, F.R.S.—The Legend of Dîpañkara Buddha. Translated from the Chinese (and intended to illustrate Plates xxix. and L., 'Tree and Serpent Worship'). By S. Beal.—Note on Art. IX., ante pp. 213-274 on Hiouen-Thsang's Journey from Patna to Ballabhi. By James Fergusson, D.C.L., F.R.S.—Contributions towards a Glossary of the Assyrian Language. By H. F. Talbot.

Vol. VII., Part I., pp. 170 and 24, sewed. With a plate. 1874. 8s.

Contents.—The Upasampadâ-Kammavâcâ, being the Buddhist Manual of the Form and Manner of Ordering of Priests and Deacons. The Pâli Text, with a Translation and Notes. By J. F. Dickson, B.A., sometime Student of Christ Church, Oxford, now of the Ceylon Civil Service.—Notes on the Megalithic Monuments of the Coimbatore District, Madras. By M. J. Walhouse, late Madras C.S.—Notes on the Sinhalese Language. No. 1. On the Formation of the Plural of Neuter Nouns. By R. C. Childers, late of the Ceylon Civil Service.—The Pali Text of the Mahâparinibbâna Sutta and Commentary, with a Translation. By R. C. Childers, late of the Ceylon Civil Service.—The Brhat-Sanhitâ; or, Complete System of Natural Astrology of Varâha-mihira. Translated from Sanskrit into English by Dr. H. Kern.—Note on the Valley of Choombi. By Dr. A. Campbell, late Superintendent of Darjeeling.—The Name of the Twelfth Imâm on the Coinage of Egypt. By H. Sauvaire and Stanley Lane Poole.—Three Inscriptions of Parâkrama Bâhu the Great from Pulastipura, Ceylon (date circa 1180 A.D.). By T. W. Rhys Davids.—Of the Kharâj or Muhammadan Land Tax; its Application to British India, and Effect on the Tenure of Land. By N. B. E. Baillie.—Appendix: A Specimen of a Syriac Version of the Kalilah wa-Dimnah, with an English Translation. By W. Wright.

Vol. VII., Part II., pp. 191 to 394, sewed. With seven plates and a map. 1875. 8s.

Contents.—Sigiri, the Lion Rock, near Pulastipura, Ceylon; and the Thirty-ninth Chapter of the Mahávamsa. By T. W. Rhys Davids.—The Northern Frontagers of China. Part I. The Origines of the Mongols. By H. H. Howorth.—Inedited Arabic Coins. By Stanley Lane Poole.—Notice on the Dinars of the Abbasside Dynasty. By Edward Thomas Rogers.—The Northern Frontagers of China. Part II. The Origines of the Manchus. By H. H. Howorth.—Notes on the Old Mongolian Capital of Shangtu. By S. W. Bushell, B.Sc., M.D.—Oriental Proverbs in their Relations to Folklore, History, Sociology; with Suggestions for their Collection, Interpretation, Publication. By the Rev. J. Long.—Two Old Simhalese Inscriptions. The Sahasa Malla Inscription, date 1200 A.D., and the Ruwanwæli Dagaba Inscription, date 1191 A.D. Text, Translation, and Notes. By T. W. Rhys Davids.—Notes on a Bactrian Pali Inscription and the Samvat Era. By Prof. J. Dowson.—Note on a Jade Drinking Vessel of the Emperor Jahângîr. By Edward Thomas, F.R.S.

Vol. VIII., Part I., pp. 156, sewed, with three plates and a plan. 1876. 8s.

Contents.—Catalogue of Buddhist Sanskrit Manuscripts in the Possession of the Royal Asiatic Society (Hodgson Collection). By Professors E. B. Cowell and J. Eggeling.—On the Ruins of Sigiri in Ceylon. By T. H. Blakesley, Esq., Public Works Department, Ceylon.—The Pâtimokkha, being the Buddhist Office of the Confession of Priests. The Pali Text, with a Translation, and Notes. By J. F. Dickson, M.A., sometime Student of Christ Church, Oxford, now of the Ceylon Civil Service.—Notes on the Sinhalese Language. No. 2. Proofs of the Sanskritic Origin of Sinhalese. By R. C. Childers, late of the Ceylon Civil Service.

Vol. VIII., Part II., pp. 157-308, sewed. 1876. 8s.

Contents.—An Account of the Island of Bali. By R. Friederich.—The Pali Text of the Mahâparinibbâna Sutta and Commentary, with a Translation. By R. C. Childers, late of the Ceylon Civil Service.—The Northern Frontagers of China. Part III. The Kara Khitai. By H. H. Howorth.—Inedited Arabic Coins. II. By Stanley Lane Poole.—On the Form of Government under the Native Sovereigns of Ceylon. By A. de Silva Ekanâyaka, Mudaliyar of the Department of Public Instruction, Ceylon.

Vol. IX., Part I., pp. 156, sewed, with a plate. 1877. 8s.

Contents.—Bactrian Coins and Indian Dates. By E. Thomas, F.R.S.—The Tenses of the Assyrian Verb. By the Rev. A. H. Sayce, M.A.—An Account of the Island of Bali. By R. Friederich (continued from Vol. VIII. n.s. p. 218).—On Ruins in Makran. By Major Mockler.—Inedited Arabic Coins. III. By Stanley Lane Poole.—Further Note on a Bactrian Pali Inscription and the Samvat Era. By Prof. J. Dowson.—Notes on Persian Beluchistan. From the Persian of Mirza Mehdy Khan. By A. H. Schindler.

Vol. IX., Part II., pp. 292, sewed, with three plates. 1877. 10s. 6d.

Contents.—The Early Faith of Asoka. By E. Thomas, F.R.S.—The Northern Frontagers of China. Part II. The Manchus (Supplementary Notice). By H. H. Howorth.—The Northern Frontagers of China. Part IV. The Kin or Golden Tatars. By H. H. Howorth.—On a Treatise on Weights and Measures by Eliya, Archbishop of Nisibin. By M. H. Sauvaire.—On Imperial and other Titles. By Sir T. E. Colebrooke, Bart., M.P.—Affinities of the Dialects of the Chepang and Kusundah Tribes of Nipál with those of the Hill Tribes of Arracan. By Captain C. J. F. Forbes, F.R.G.S., M.A.S. Bengal, etc.—Notes on Some Antiquities found in a Mound near Damghan. By A. H. Schindler.

Vol. X., Part I., pp. 156, sewed, with two plates and a map. 1878. 8s.

Contents.—On the Non-Aryan Languages of India. By E. L. Brandreth, Esq.—A Dialogue on the Vedantic Conception of Brahma. By Pramadá Dása Mittra, late Officiating Professor of Anglo-Sanskrit, Government College, Benares.—An Account of the Island of Bali. By R. Friederich (continued from Vol. IX. N.S. p. 120).—Unpublished Glass Weights and Measures. By Edward Thomas Rogers.—China via Tibet. By S. C. Boulger.—Notes and Recollections on Tea Cultivation in Kumaon and Garhwál. By J. H. Batten, F.R.G.S., Bengal Civil Service Retired, formerly Commissioner of Kumaon.

Vol. X., Part II., pp. 146, sewed. 1878. 6s.

Contents.—Note on Pliny's Geography of the East Coast of Arabia. By Major-General S. B. Miles, Bombay Staff Corps.—The Maldive Islands; with a Vocabulary taken from François Pyrard de Laval, 1602—1607. By A. Gray, late of the Ceylon Civil Service.—On Tibeto-Burman Languages. By Captain C. J. F. S. Forbes, of the Burmese Civil Service Commission.—Burmese Transliteration. By H. L. St. Barbe, Esq., Resident at Mandalay.—On the Connexion of the Mons of Pegu with the Koles of Central India. By Captain C. J. F. S. Forbes, of the Burmese Civil Commission.—Studies on the Comparative Grammar of the Semitic Languages, with special Reference to Assyrian. By Paul Haupt. The Oldest Semitic Verb-Form.—Arab Metrology. II. El Djabarty. By M. H. Sauvaire.—The Migrations and Early History of the White Huns; principally from Chinese Sources. By Thomas W. Kingsmill.

Vol. X., Part III., pp. 204, sewed. 1878. 8s.

Contents.—On the Hill Canton of Sálár,—the most Easterly Settlement of the Turk Race. By Robert B. Shaw.—Geological Notes on the River Indus. By Griffin W. Vyse, B.A., M.R.A.S., etc., Executive Engineer P.W.D. Panjab.—Educational Literature for Japanese Women. By Basil Hall Chamberlain, Esq., M.R.A.S.—On the Natural Phenomenon Known in the East by the Names Sub-hi-Kāzib, etc., etc. By J. W. Redhouse, M.R.A.S., Hon. Memb. R.S.L.—On a Chinese Version of the Sānkhya Kārikā, etc., found among the Buddhist Books comprising the Tripitaka and two other works. By the Rev. Samuel Beal, M.A.—The Rock-cut Phrygian Inscriptions at Doganlu. By Edward Thomas, F.R.S.—Index.

Vol. XI., Part I., pp. 128, sewed. 5s.

Contents.—On the Position of Women in the East in the Olden Time. By Edward Thomas, F.R.S.—Notice of the Scholars who have Contributed to the Extension of our Knowledge of the Languages of British India during the last Thirty Years. By Robert N. Cust, Hon. Librarian R.A.S.—Ancient Arabic Poetry: its Genuineness and Authenticity. By Sir William Muir, K.C.S.I., LL.D.—Note on Manrique's Mission and the Catholics in the time of Shah Jahān. By H. G. Keene, Esq.—On Sandhi in Pali. By the late R. C. Childers.—On Arabic Amulets and Mottoes. By E. T. Rogers, M.R.A.S.

Asiatic Society.—Transactions of the Royal Asiatic Society of Great Britain and Ireland. Complete in 3 vols. 4to., 80 Plates of Facsimiles, etc., cloth. London, 1827 to 1835. Published at £9 5s.; reduced to £5 5s.

The above contains contributions by Professor Wilson, G. C. Haughton, Davis, Morrison, Colebrooke, Humboldt, Dorn, Grotefend, and other eminent Oriental scholars.

Asiatic Society of Bengal.—Journal of the Asiatic Society of Bengal. Edited by the Honorary Secretaries. 8vo. 8 numbers per annum, 4s. each number.

Asiatic Society of Bengal.—Proceedings of the Asiatic Society of Bengal. Published Monthly. 1s. each number.

Asiatic Society.—The Journal of the Bombay Branch of the Royal Asiatic Society. Edited by the Secretary. Nos. 1 to 35. 7s. 6d. to 10s. 6d. each number.

Asiatic Society.—Journal of the Ceylon Branch of the Royal Asiatic Society. 8vo. Published irregularly. 7s. 6d. each part.

Asiatic Society of Japan.—Transactions of the Asiatic Society of Japan. Vol. I. From 30th October, 1872, to 9th October, 1873. 8vo, pp. 110, with plates. 1874. Vol. II. From 22nd October, 1873, to 15th July, 1874. 8vo. pp. 249. 1874. Vol. III. Part I. From 16th July, 1874, to December, 1874. 1875. Vol. III. Part II. From 13th January, 1875, to 30th June, 1875. Vol. IV. From 20th October, 1875, to 12th July, 1876. Each Part 7s. 6d.

Asiatic Society.—Journal of the North China Branch of the Royal Asiatic Society. New Series. Parts 1 to 11.

Aston.—A Grammar of the Japanese Written Language. By W. G. Aston, M.A., Assistant Japanese Secretary, H.B.M.'s Legation, Yedo, Japan. Second edition, Enlarged and Improved. Royal 8vo. pp. 306. 28s.

Aston.—A Short Grammar of the Japanese Spoken Language. By W. G. Aston, M.A., H. B. M.'s Legation, Yedo, Japan. Third edition. 12mo. cloth, pp. 96. 12s.

Athar-al-Adhar.—Traces of Centuries; or, Geographical and Historical Arabic Dictionary, by Selim Khuri and Selim Sh-hadeh. Geographical Parts I. to IV., Historical Parts I. and II. 4to. pp. 788 and 384. Price 7s. 6d. each part. [*In course of publication.*

Atharva Veda Prātiçākhya.—See under Whitney.

Auctores Sanscriti. Edited for the Sanskrit Text Society, under the supervision of Theodor Goldstücker. Vol. I., containing the Jaiminiya-Nyāya-Mālā-Vistara. Parts I. to VII., pp. 582, large 4to. sewed. 10s. each part. Complete in one vol., cloth, £3 13s. 6d. Vol. II. The Institutes of Gautama. Edited with an Index of Words, by A. F. Stenzler, Ph.D., Professor of Oriental Languages in the University of Breslau. 8vo. cloth, pp. iv. 78. 4s. 6d. Vol. III. Vaitāna Sūtra. The Ritual of the Atharva Veda. Edited with Critical Notes and Indices, by Dr. Richard Garbe. 8vo. sewed, pp. 119. 5s.

Axon.—The Literature of the Lancashire Dialect. A Bibliographical Essay. By William E. A. Axon, F.R.S.L. Fcap. 8vo. sewed. 1870. 1s.

Baba.—An Elementary Grammar of the Japanese Language, with Easy Progressive Exercises. By Tatui Baba. Crown 8vo. cloth, pp. xii. and 92. 5s.

Bachmaier.—Pasigraphical Dictionary and Grammar. By Anton Bachmaier, President of the Central Pasigraphical Society at Munich. 18mo. cloth, pp. viii.; 26; 160. 1870. 3s.

Bachmaier.—Pasigraphisches Wörterbuch zum Gebrauche für die deutsche Sprache. Verfasst von Anton Bachmaier, Vorsitzendem des Central-Vereins für Pasigraphie in München. 18mo. cloth, pp. viii.; 32; 128; 120. 1870. 2s. 6d.

Bachmaier.—Dictionnaire Pasigraphique, précédé de la Grammaire. Redigé par Antoine Bachmaier, Président de la Société Centrale de Pasigraphie à Munich. 18mo. cloth, pp. vi. 26; 168; 150. 1870. 2s. 6d.

Baldwin.—A Manual of the Foochow Dialect. By Rev. C. C. Baldwin, of the American Board Mission. 8vo. pp. viii.-256. 18s.

Balfour.—Waifs and Strays from the Far East; being a Series of Disconnected Essays on Matters relating to China. By Frederic Henry Balfour. 1 vol. demy 8vo. cloth, pp. 224. 10s. 6d.

Ballad Society (The).—Subscription—Small paper, one guinea, and large paper, three guineas, per annum. List of publications on application.

Ballantyne.—A Grammar of the Mahratta Language. For the use of the East India College at Haileybury. By James R. Ballantyne, of the Scottish Naval and Military Academy. 4to. cloth, pp. 56. 5s.

Ballantyne.—Elements of Hindí and Braj Bhákhá Grammar. By the late James R. Ballantyne, LL.D. Second edition, revised and corrected. Crown 8vo., pp. 44, cloth. 5s.

Ballantyne.—First Lessons in Sanskrit Grammar; together with an Introduction to the Hitopadésa. Second edition. Second Impression. By James R. Ballantyne, LL.D., Librarian of the India Office. 8vo. pp. viii. and 110, cloth. 1873. 3s. 6d.

Ballantyne.—Hindustani Selections in the Naskhi and Devanagari Character. With a Vocabulary of the Words. Prepared for the use of the Scottish Naval and Military Academy, by James R. Ballantyne. Royal 8vo. cloth, pp. 74. 3s. 6d.

Ballantyne.—Principles of Persian Caligraphy, illustrated by Lithographic Plates of the TA"LIK characters, the one usually employed in writing the Persian and the Hindustani. Second edition. Prepared for the use of the Scottish Naval and Military Academy, by James R. Ballantyne. 4to. cloth, pp. 14, 6 plates. 2s. 6d.

Banerjea.—The Arian Witness, or the Testimony of Arian Scriptures in corroboration of Biblical History and the Rudiments of Christian Doctrine. Including Dissertations on the Original Home and Early Adventures of Indo-Arians. By the Rev. K. M. Banerjea. 8vo. sewed, pp. xviii. and 236. 8s. 6d.

Bate.—A Dictionary of the Hindee Language. Compiled by J. D. Bate. 8vo. cloth, pp. 806. £2 12s. 6d.

Beal.—Travels of Fah Hian and Sung-Yun, Buddhist Pilgrims from China to India (400 A.D. and 518 A.D.) Translated from the Chinese, by S. Beal (B.A. Trinity College, Cambridge), a Chaplain in Her Majesty's Fleet, a Member of the Royal Asiatic Society, and Author of a Translation of the Pratimôksha and the Amithâba Sûtra from the Chinese. Crown 8vo. pp. lxxiii. and 210, cloth, ornamental, with a coloured map. 10s. 6d.

Beal.—A CATENA OF BUDDHIST SCRIPTURES FROM THE CHINESE. By S. BEAL, B.A., Trinity College, Cambridge; a Chaplain in Her Majesty's Fleet, etc. 8vo. cloth, pp. xiv. and 436. 1871. 15s.

Beal.—THE ROMANTIC LEGEND OF SÂKHYA BUDDHA. From the Chinese-Sanscrit by the Rev. SAMUEL BEAL, Author of "Buddhist Pilgrims," etc. Crown 8vo. cloth, pp. 400. 1875. 12s.

Beal.—THE BUDDHIST TRIPITAKA, as it is known in China and Japan. A Catalogue and Compendious Report. By SAMUEL BEAL, B.A. Folio, sewed, pp. 117. 7s. 6d.

Beal.—TEXTS FROM THE BUDDHIST CANON, commonly known as DHAMMAPADA. Translated from the Chinese by S. BEAL, B.A., Professor of Chinese, University of London. With accompanying Narrative. Post 8vo. pp. viii. and 176, cloth. 7s. 6d.

Beames.—OUTLINES OF INDIAN PHILOLOGY. With a Map, showing the Distribution of the Indian Languages. By JOHN BEAMES. Second enlarged and revised edition. Crown 8vo. cloth, pp. viii. and 96. 5s.

Beames.—NOTES ON THE BHOJPURI DIALECT OF HINDI, spoken in Western Behar. By JOHN BEAMES, Esq., B.C.S., Magistrate of Chumparun. 8vo. pp. 26, sewed. 1868. 1s. 6d.

Beames.—A COMPARATIVE GRAMMAR OF THE MODERN ARYAN LANGUAGES OF INDIA (to wit), Hindi, Panjabi, Sindhi, Gujarati, Marathi, Uriya, and Bengali. By JOHN BEAMES, Bengal C.S., M.R.A.S., &c.

Vol. I. On Sounds. 8vo. cloth, pp. xvi and 360. 16s.
Vol. II. The Noun and the Pronoun. 8vo. cloth, pp. xii. and 348. 16s.
Vol. III. The Verb. 8vo. cloth, pp. xii. and 316. [*Just ready.*

Bede.—VENERABILIS BEDAE HISTORIA ECCLESIASTICA GENTIS ANGLORUM. Ad Fidem Codd. MSS. recensuit JOSEPHUS STEVENSON. With plan of the English Historical Society, by the late John Miller. 8vo. pp. xxxv., xxi. and 424, and 2 facsimiles. 7s. 6d.

The same, in royal 8vo., uniform with the publications of the Master of the Rolls. 10s. 6d.

Bellairs.—A GRAMMAR OF THE MARATHI LANGUAGE. By H. S. K. BELLAIRS, M.A., and LAXMAN Y. ASHKEDKAR, B.A. 12mo. cloth, pp. 90. 5s.

Bellew.—A DICTIONARY OF THE PUKKHTO, OR PUKSHTO LANGUAGE, on a New and Improved System. With a reversed Part, or English and Pukkhto. By H. W. BELLEW, Assistant Surgeon, Bengal Army. Super Royal 8vo. pp. xii. and 356, cloth. 42s.

Bellew.—A GRAMMAR OF THE PUKKHTO OR PUKSHTO LANGUAGE, on a New and Improved System. Combining Brevity with Utility, and Illustrated by Exercises and Dialogues. By H. W. BELLEW, Assistant Surgeon, Bengal Army. Super-royal 8vo., pp. xii. and 156, cloth. 21s.

Bellew.—FROM THE INDUS TO THE TIGRIS: a Narrative of a Journey through the Countries of Balochistan, Afghanistan, Khorassan, and Iran, in 1872; together with a Synoptical Grammar and Vocabulary of the Brahoe Language, and a Record of the Meteorological Observations and Altitudes on the March from the Indus to the Tigris. By H. W. BELLEW, C.S.I., Surgeon Bengal Staff Corps, Author of "A Journal of a Mission to Afghanistan in 1857-58," and "A Grammar and Dictionary of the Pukkhto Language." Demy 8vo. cloth. 14s.

Bellew.—KASHMIR AND KASHGHAR. A Narrative of the Journey of the Embassy to Kashghar in 1873-74. By H. W. BELLEW, C.S.I. Demy 8vo. cl. pp. xxxii. and 420. 16s.

Bellows.—ENGLISH OUTLINE VOCABULARY, for the use of Students of the Chinese, Japanese, and other Languages. Arranged by JOHN BELLOWS. With Notes on the writing of Chinese with Roman Letters. By Professor SUMMERS, King's College, London. Crown 8vo., pp. 6 and 368, cloth. 6s.

Bellows.—OUTLINE DICTIONARY, FOR THE USE OF MISSIONARIES, EXPLORERS, and Students of Language. By MAX MÜLLER, M.A., Taylorian Professor in the University of Oxford. With an Introduction on the proper use of the ordinary English Alphabet in transcribing Foreign Languages. The Vocabulary compiled by JOHN BELLOWS. Crown 8vo. Limp morocco, pp. xxxi. and 368. 7s. 6d.

Bellows.—DICTIONARY FOR THE POCKET, French and English, English and French. Both Divisions on same page. By JOHN BELLOWS. Masculine and Feminine Words shown by Distinguishing Types. Conjugations of all the Verbs; Liaison marked in French Part, and Hints to aid Pronunciation. Together with Tables and Maps. Revised by ALEXANDRE BELJAME, M.A., and Fellow of the University, Paris. Second Edition. 32mo. roan, with tuck, gilt edges. 10s. 6d. Persian, 10s. 6d. Morocco, 12s. 6d.

Benfey.—A GRAMMAR OF THE LANGUAGE OF THE VEDAS. By Dr. THEODOR BENFEY. In 1 vol. 8vo., of about 650 pages. [*In preparation.*

Benfey.—A PRACTICAL GRAMMAR OF THE SANSKRIT LANGUAGE, for the use of Early Students. By THEODOR BENFEY, Professor of Sanskrit in the University of Göttingen. Second, revised and enlarged, edition. Royal 8vo. pp. viii. and 296, cloth. 10s. 6d.

Benfey.—VEDICA UND VERWANDTES. Von THEODOR BENFEY. Cr. 8vo. 7s. 6d.

Beschi.—CLAVIS HUMANIORUM LITTERARUM SUBLIMIORIS TAMULICI IDIOMATIS. Auctore R. P. CONSTANTIO JOSEPHO BESCHIO, Soc. Jesu, in Madurensi Regno Missionario. Edited by the Rev. K. IHLEFELD, and printed for A. Burnell, Esq., Tranquebar. 8vo. sewed, pp. 171. 10s. 6d.

Beveridge.—THE DISTRICT OF BAKARGANJ; its History and Statistics. By H. BEVERIDGE, B.C.S. 8vo. cloth, pp. xx. and 460. 21s.

Bhagavat-Geeta.—See under WILKINS.

Bibliotheca Indica. A Collection of Oriental Works published by the Asiatic Society of Bengal. Old Series. Fasc. 1 to 235. New Series. Fasc. 1 to 408. (Special List of Contents to be had on application.) Each Fasc. in 8vo., 2s.; in 4to., 4s.

Bibliotheca Orientalis: or, a Complete List of Books, Pamphlets, Essays, and Journals, published in France, Germany, England, and the Colonies, on the History and the Geography, the Religions, the Antiquities, Literature, and Languages of the East. Edited by CHARLES FRIEDERICI. Part I., 1876, sewed, pp. 86, 2s. 6d. Part II., 1877, sewed, pp. 100, 2s. 6d.

Bibliotheca Sanskrita.—See TRÜBNER.

Bickell.—OUTLINES OF HEBREW GRAMMAR. By GUSTAVUS BICKELL, D.D. Revised by the Author; Annotated by the Translator, SAMUEL IVES CURTISS, junior, Ph.D. With a Lithographic Table of Semitic Characters by Dr. J. EUTING. Cr. 8vo. sd., pp. xiv. and 140. 1877. 3s. 6d.

Bigandet.—THE LIFE OR LEGEND OF GAUDAMA, the Buddha of the Burmese, with Annotations. The ways to Neibban, and Notice on the Phongyies, or Burmese Monks. By the Right Reverend P. BIGANDET, Bishop of Ramatha, Vicar Apostolic of Ava and Pegu. 8vo. pp. xi., 538, and v. £1 11s. 6d.

Bleek.—A COMPARATIVE GRAMMAR OF SOUTH AFRICAN LANGUAGES. By W. H. I. BLEEK, Ph.D. Volume I. I. Phonology. II. The Concord. Section I. The Noun. 8vo. pp. xxxvi. and 322, cloth. £1 16s.

Bleek.—A BRIEF ACCOUNT OF BUSHMAN FOLK LORE AND OTHER TEXTS. By W. H. I. BLEEK, Ph.D., etc., etc. Folio sd., pp. 21. 1875. 2s. 6d.

Bleek.—REYNARD IN SOUTH AFRICA; or, Hottentot Fables. Translated from the Original Manuscript in Sir George Grey's Library. By Dr. W. H. I. BLEEK, Librarian to the Grey Library, Cape Town, Cape of Good Hope. In one volume, small 8vo., pp. xxxi. and 94, cloth. 3s. 6d.

Blochmann.—The Prosody of the Persians, according to Saifi, Jami, and other Writers. By H. Blochmann, M.A. Assistant Professor, Calcutta Madrasah. 8vo. sewed, pp. 166. 10s. 6d.

Blochmann.—School Geography of India and British Burmah. By H. Blochmann, M.A. 12mo. pp. vi. and 100. 2s. 6d.

Blochmann.—A Treatise on the Ruba'i entitled Risalah i Taranah. By Agha Ahmad 'Ali. With an Introduction and Explanatory Notes, by H. Blochmann, M.A. 8vo. sewed, pp. 11 and 17. 2s. 6d.

Blochmann.—The Persian Metres by Saifi, and a Treatise on Persian Rhyme by Jami. Edited in Persian, by H. Blochmann, M.A. 8vo. sewed, pp. 62. 3s. 6d.

Bombay Sanskrit Series. Edited under the superintendence of G. Bühler, Ph. D., Professor of Oriental Languages, Elphinstone College, and F. Kielhorn, Ph. D., Superintendent of Sanskrit Studies, Deccan College. 1868-70.

1. Panchatantra iv. and v. Edited, with Notes, by G. Bühler, Ph. D. Pp. 84, 16. 6s.
2. Nâgojîbhaṭṭa's Paribhâshendusekhara. Edited and explained by F. Kielhorn, Ph. D. Part I., the Sanskrit Text and Various Readings. pp. 116. 10s. 6d.
3. Panchatantra ii. and iii. Edited, with Notes, by G. Bühler, Ph. D. Pp. 86, 14, 2. 7s. 6d.
4. Panchatantra i. Edited, with Notes, by F. Kielhorn, Ph.D. Pp. 114, 53. 7s. 6d.
5. Kâlidâsa's Raghuvaṃśa. With the Commentary of Mallinâtha. Edited, with Notes, by Shankar P. Pandit, M.A. Part I. Cantos I.-VI. 10s. 6d.
6. Kâlidâsa's Mâlavikâgnimitra. Edited, with Notes, by Shankar P. Pandit, M.A. 10s. 6d.
7. Nâgojîbhaṭṭa's Paribhâshendusekhara. Edited and explained by F. Kielhorn, Ph. D. Part II. Translation and Notes (Paribhâshâs, i.-xxxvii.) pp. 184. 10s. 6d.
8. Kâlidâsa's Raghuvaṃśa. With the Commentary of Mallinâtha. Edited, with Notes, by Shankar P. Pandit, M.A. Part II. Cantos VII.-XIII. 10s. 6d.
9. Nâgojîbhaṭṭa's Paribhâshendusekhara. Edited and explained by F. Kielhorn. Part II. Translation and Notes. (Paribhâshâs xxxviii.-lxix.) 7s. 6d.
10. Dandin's Daśakumâracharita. Edited with critical and explanatory Notes by G. Bühler. Part I. 7s. 6d.
11. Bhartrihari's Nîtiśataka and Vairâgyaśataka, with Extracts from Two Sanskrit Commentaries. Edited, with Notes, by Kâśinâth T. Telang. 9s.
12. Nâgojîbhaṭṭa's Paribhâshendusekhara. Edited and explained by F. Kielhorn. Part II. Translation and Notes. (Paribhâshâs lxx.-cxxii.) 7s. 6d.
13. Kâlidâsa's Raghuvaṃśa, with the Commentary of Mallinâtha. Edited, with Notes, by Shankar P. Pandit. Part III. Cantos XIV.-XIX. 10s. 6d.
14. Vikramânkadevacharita. Edited, with an Introduction, by G. Bühler. 7s. 6d.
15. Bhavabhûti's Mâlatî-Mâdhava. With the Commentary of Jagaddhara, edited by Ramkrishna Gopal Bhandarkar. 14s.

Borooah.—A Practical English-Sanskrit Dictionary. By Anundoram Borooah, B.A., B.C.S., of the Middle Temple, Barrister-at-Law. Vol. I. A to Falconry. pp. xx.–580–10. £1 11s. 6d.

Borooah.—A Companion to the Sanskrit-Reading Undergraduates of the Calcutta University, being a few notes on the Sanskrit Texts selected for examination, and their Commentaries. By Anundoram Borooah. 8vo. pp. 64. 2s. 6d.

Borooah.—Bhavabhuti and his Place in Sanskrit Literature. By Anundoram Borooah. 8vo. sewed, pp. 70. 5s.

Bottrell.—Traditions and Hearthside Stories of West Cornwall. By W. Bottrell (an old Celt). Demy 12mo. pp. vi. 292, cloth. 1870. Scarce.

Bottrell.—Traditions and Hearthside Stories of West Cornwall. By William Bottrell. With Illustrations by Mr. Joseph Blight. Second Series. Crown 8vo. cloth, pp. iv. and 300. 6s.

Bowditch.—Suffolk Surnames. By N. I. Bowditch. Third Edition, 8vo. pp. xxvi. and 758, cloth. 7s. 6d.

Bretschneider.—On the Knowledge Possessed by the Ancient Chinese of the Arabs and Arabian Colonies, and other Western Countries mentioned in Chinese Books. By E. Bretschneider, M.D., Physician of the Russian Legation at Peking. 8vo. pp. 28, sewed. 1871. 1s.

Bretschneider.—Notes on Chinese Mediæval Travellers to the West. By E. Bretschneider, M.D. Demy 8vo. sd., pp. 130. 5s.

Bretschneider.—Archæological and Historical Researches on Peking and its Environs. By E. Bretschneider, M.D., Physician to the Russian Legation at Peking. Imp. 8vo. sewed, pp. 64, with 4 Maps. 5s.

Bretschneider.—Notices of the Mediæval Geography and History of Central and Western Asia. Drawn from Chinese and Mongol Writings, and Compared with the Observations of Western Authors in the Middle Ages. By E. Bretschneider, M.D. 8vo. sewed, pp. 233, with two Maps. 12s. 6d.

Brhat-Sanhita (The).—See under Kern.

Brinton.—The Myths of the New World. A Treatise on the Symbolism and Mythology of the Red Race of America. By Daniel G. Brinton, A.M., M.D. Second Edition, revised. Cr. 8vo. cloth, pp. viii. and 331. 12s. 6d.

British Museum.—Catalogue of Sanskrit and Pali Books in the British Museum. By Dr. Ernst Haas. Printed by permission of the Trustees of the British Museum. 4to. pp. viii. and 188, boards. £1 1s.

British Museum Publications (List of) on Sale by Trübner & Co. [*On application.*

British Archæological Association (Journal of The). Volumes 1 to 31, 1845 to 1876, £1 11s. 6d. each. General Index to vols. 1 to 30. 8vo. cloth. 15s. Parts Quarterly, 8s. each.

Brockie.—Indian Philosophy. Introductory Paper. By William Brockie, Author of "A Day in the Land of Scott," etc., etc. 8vo. pp. 26, sewed. 1872. 6d.

Bronson.—A Dictionary in Assamese and English. Compiled by M. Bronson, American Baptist Missionary. 8vo. calf, pp. viii. and 609. £2 2s.

Brown.—The Dervishes; or, Oriental Spiritualism. By John P. Brown, Secretary and Dragoman of the Legation of the United States of America at Constantinople. With twenty-four Illustrations. 8vo. cloth, pp. viii. and 415. 14s.

Brown.—Sanskrit Prosody and Numerical Symbols Explained. By Charles Philip Brown, Author of the Telugu Dictionary, Grammar, etc., Professor of Telugu in the University of London. Demy 8vo. pp. 64, cloth. 3s. 6d.

Bühler.—Eleven Land-Grants of the Chaulukyas of Aṇhilvâḍ. A Contribution to the History of Gujarât. By G. Bühler. 16mo. sewed, pp. 126, with Facsimile. 3s. 6d.

Bühler.—Three New Edicts of Aśoka. By G. Bühler. 16mo. sewed, with Two Facsimiles. 2s. 6d.

Burgess.—Archæological Survey of Western India. Vol. I. Report of the First Season's Operations in the Belgâm and Kaladgi Districts. Jan. to May, 1874. By James Burgess. With 56 photographs and lith. plates. Royal 4to. pp. viii. and 45. £2 2s.

Vol. 2. Report of the Second Season's Operations. Report on the Antiquities of Kâṭhiâwâḍ and Kachh. 1874-5. By James Burgess, F.R.G.S., M.R.A.S., etc. With Map, Inscriptions, Photographs, etc. Roy. 4to. half bound, pp. x. and 242. £3 3s.

Vol. 3. Report of the Third Season's Operations. 1875-76. Report on the Antiquities in the Bidar and Aurangabad Districts. Royal 4to. half bound pp. viii. and 138, with 66 photographic and lithographic plates. £2 2s.

Burnell.—Catalogue of a Collection of Sanskrit Manuscripts. By A. C. Burnell, M.R.A.S., Madras Civil Service. Part I. *Vedic Manuscripts.* Fcap. 8vo. pp. 64, sewed. 1870. 2s.

Burnell.—Dayadaçaçloki. Ten Slokas in Sanskrit, with English Translation. By A. C. Burnell. 8vo. pp. 11. 2s.

Burnell.—Elements of South Indian Palæography. From the Fourth to the Seventeenth Century A.D. By A. C. Burnell. Second Corrected and Enlarged Edition, 35 Plates and Map, in One Vol. 4to. pp. xiv.-148. £2 12s. 6d.

Burnell.—On the Aindra School of Sanskrit Grammarians. Their Place in the Sanskrit and Subordinate Literatures. By A. C. Burnell. 8vo. pp. 120. 10s. 6d.

Burnell.—The Sâmavidhânabrâhmaṇa (being the Third Brâhmaṇa) of the Sâma Veda. Edited, together with the Commentary of Sâyaṇa, an English Translation, Introduction, and Index of Words, by A. C. Burnell. Volume I.—Text and Commentary, with Introduction. 8vo. pp. xxxviii. and 104. 12s. 6d.

Burnell.—The Ârsheyabrâhmaṇa (being the fourth Brâhmaṇa) of the Sâma Veda. The Sanskrit Text. Edited, together with Extracts from the Commentary of Sâyaṇa, etc. An Introduction and Index of Words. By A. C. Burnell, Ph.D. 8vo. pp. 51 and 109. 10s. 6d.

Burnell.—The Devatâdhyâyabrâhmaṇa (being the Fifth Brâhmaṇa) of the Sama Veda. The Sanskrit Text edited, with the Commentary of Sâyaṇa, an Index of Words, etc., by A. C. Burnell, M.R.A.S. 8vo. and Trans., pp. 34. 5s.

Burnell.—The Jaiminîya Text of the Ârsheyabrâhmaṇa of the Sâma Veda. Edited in Sanskrit by A. C. Burnell, Ph. D. 8vo. sewed, pp. 56. 7s. 6d.

Burnell. — The Saṃhitopanishadbrâhmaṇa (Being the Seventh Brâhmaṇa) of the Sâma Veda. The Sanskrit Text. With a Commentary, an Index of Words, etc. Edited by A. C. Burnell, Ph.D. 8vo. stiff boards, pp. 86. 7s. 6d.

Burnell.—The Vaṃçabrâhmaṇa (being the Eighth Brâhmaṇa) of the Sâma Veda. Edited, together with the Commentary of Sâyaṇa, a Preface and Index of Words, by A. C. Burnell, M.R.A.S., etc. 8vo. sewed, pp. xliii., 12, and xii., with 2 coloured plates. 10s. 6d.

Butler.—Hungarian Poems and Fables for English Readers. Selected and translated by E. D. Butler, of the British Museum. With Illustrations by A. G. Butler. Fcap. limp cloth, pp. vi.–88. 1877. 2s.

Buttmann.—A Grammar of the New Testament Greek. By A. Buttmann. Authorised translation by Prof. J. H. Thayer, with numerous additions and corrections by the author. Demy 8vo. cloth, pp. xx. and 474. 1873. 14s.

Butrus-al-Bustany.—كتاب دائرة المعارف An Arabic Encyclopædia of Universal Knowledge, by Butrus-al-Bustany, the celebrated compiler of Mohit al Mohit (محيط المحيط), and Katr el Mohit (قطر المحيط).

This work will be completed in from 12 to 15 Vols., of which Vols. I. to III. are ready, Vol. I. contains letter ا to ابب; Vol. II. ابه to ار; Vol. III. ار to اغ. Small folio, cloth, pp. 800 each. £1 11s. 6d. per Vol.

Byington.—Grammar of the Choctaw Language. By the Rev. Cyrus Byington. Edited from the Original MSS. in Library of the American Philosophical Society, by D. G. Brinton, M.D. Cr. 8vo. sewed, pp. 56. 7s. 6d.

Calcutta Review (The).—Published Quarterly. Price 8s. 6d. per number.

Caldwell.—A Comparative Grammar of the Dravidian, or South-Indian Family of Languages. By the Rev. R. Caldwell, LL.D. A Second, corrected, and enlarged Edition. Demy 8vo. pp. 805. 1875. 28s.

Callaway.—Izinganekwane, Nensumansumane, Nezindaba, Zabantu (Nursery Tales, Traditions, and Histories of the Zulus). In their own words, with a Translation into English, and Notes. By the Rev. Henry Callaway, M.D. Volume I., 8vo. pp. xiv. and 378, cloth. Natal, 1866 and 1867. 16s.

Callaway.—The Religious System of the Amazulu.

Part I.—Unkulunkulu; or, the Tradition of Creation as existing among the Amazulu and other Tribes of South Africa, in their own words, with a translation into English, and Notes. By the Rev. Canon Callaway, M.D. 8vo. pp. 128, sewed. 1868. 4s.

Part II.—Amatongo; or, Ancestor Worship, as existing among the Amazulu, in their own words, with a translation into English, and Notes. By the Rev. Canon Callaway, M.D. 1869. 8vo. pp. 127, sewed. 1869. 4s.

Part III.—Izinyanga Zokubula; or, Divination, as existing among the Amazulu, in their own words. With a Translation into English, and Notes. By the Rev. Canon Callaway, M.D. 8vo. pp. 150, sewed. 1870. 4s.

Part IV.—Abatakati, or Medical Magic and Witchcraft. 8vo. pp. 40, sewed. 1s. 6d.

Calligaris.—Le Compagnon de Tous, ou Dictionnaire Polyglotte. Par le Colonel Louis Calligaris, Grand Officier, etc. (French—Latin—Italian—Spanish—Portuguese—German—English—Modern Greek—Arabic—Turkish.) 2 vols. 4to., pp. 1157 and 746. Turin. £4 4s.

Campbell.—Specimens of the Languages of India, including Tribes of Bengal, the Central Provinces, and the Eastern Frontier. By Sir G. Campbell, M.P. Folio, paper, pp. 308. 1874. £1 11s. 6d.

Carletti.—Idh-har-ul-haqq, ou Manifestation de la Vérité de El-hage Rahmat-ullah Effendi de Dehli (un des Descendants du Calife Osman-ben-'Affan). Traduit de l'Arabe, par un éminent, quoique très-jeune, Orientaliste de Tunis. Revu sur le texte, retouché en plusieurs endroits et augmenté d'une préface et d'un appendice. Par P. V. Carletti. In Two Vols. 8vo. [*In the press.*

Carpenter.—The Last Days in England of the Rajah Rammohun Roy. By Mary Carpenter, of Bristol. With Five Illustrations. 8vo. pp. 272, cloth. 7s. 6d.

Carr.—[illegible]. A COLLECTION OF TELUGU PROVERBS, Translated, Illustrated, and Explained; together with some Sanscrit Proverbs printed in the Devanâgarî and Telugu Characters. By Captain M. W. CARR, Madras Staff Corps. One Vol. and Supplement, royal 8vo. pp. 488 and 148. 31s. 6d.

Catlin.—O-KEE-PA. A Religious Ceremony of the Mandans. By GEORGE CATLIN. With 13 Coloured Illustrations. 4to. pp. 60, bound in cloth, gilt edges. 14s.

Chalmers.—A CONCISE KHANG-HSI CHINESE DICTIONARY. By the Rev. J. CHALMERS, LL.D., Canton. Three Vols. Royal 8vo. bound in Chinese style, pp. 1800. 21s.

Chalmers.—THE ORIGIN OF THE CHINESE; an Attempt to Trace the connection of the Chinese with Western Nations in their Religion, Superstitions, Arts, Language, and Traditions. By JOHN CHALMERS, A.M. Foolscap 8vo. cloth, pp. 78. 5s.

Chalmers.—THE SPECULATIONS ON METAPHYSICS, POLITY, AND MORALITY OF "THE OLD PHILOSOPHER" LAU TSZE. Translated from the Chinese, with an Introduction by John Chalmers, M.A. Fcap. 8vo. cloth, xx. and 62. 4s. 6d.

Charnock.—LUDUS PATRONYMICUS; or, the Etymology of Curious Surnames. By RICHARD STEPHEN CHARNOCK, Ph.D., F.S.A., F.R.G.S. Crown 8vo., pp. 182, cloth. 7s. 6d.

Charnock.—VERBA NOMINALIA; or Words derived from Proper Names. By RICHARD STEPHEN CHARNOCK, Ph. Dr. F.S.A., etc. 8vo. pp. 326, cloth. 14s.

Charnock.—THE PEOPLES OF TRANSYLVANIA. Founded on a Paper read before THE ANTHROPOLOGICAL SOCIETY OF LONDON, on the 4th of May, 1869. By RICHARD STEPHEN CHARNOCK, Ph.D., F.S.A., F.R.G.S. Demy 8vo. pp. 36, sewed. 1870. 2s. 6d.

Chaucer Society's (The).—Subscription, two guineas per annum. List of Publications on application.

Childers.—A PALI-ENGLISH DICTIONARY, with Sanskrit Equivalents, and with numerous Quotations, Extracts, and References. Compiled by the late Prof. R. C. CHILDERS, late of the Ceylon Civil Service. Imperial 8vo. Double Columns. Complete in 1 Vol., pp. xxii. and 622, cloth. 1875. £3 3s.

The first Pali Dictionary ever published.

Childers.—NOTES ON THE SINHALESE LANGUAGE. No. 1. On the Formation of the Plural of Neuter Nouns. By the late Prof. R. C. CHILDERS. Demy 8vo. sd., pp. 16. 1873. 1s.

Childers.—ON SANDHI IN PALI. By the late Prof. R. C. CHILDERS. 8vo. sewed, pp. 22. 1s.

Childers.—THE MAHÂPARINIBBÂNASUTTA OF THE SUTTA-PITAKA. The Pali Text. Edited by the late Professor R. C. CHILDERS. 8vo. cloth, pp. 72. 5s.

China Review; OR, NOTES AND QUERIES ON THE FAR EAST. Published bi-monthly. Edited by E. J. EITEL. 4to. Subscription, £1 10s. per volume.

Chintamon.—A COMMENTARY ON THE TEXT OF THE BHAGAVAD-GÍTÁ; or, the Discourse between Krishna and Arjuna of Divine Matters. A Sanscrit Philosophical Poem. With a few Introductory Papers. By HURRYCHUND CHINTAMON, Political Agent to H. H. the Guicowar Mulhar Rao Maharajah of Baroda. Post 8vo. cloth, pp. 118. 6s.

Christaller.—A DICTIONARY, ENGLISH, TSHI, (ASANTE), AKRA; Tshi (Chwee), comprising as dialects Akan (Asanté, Akem, Akuapem, etc.) and Fanté; Akra (Accra), connected with Adangme; Gold Coast, West Africa.

Enyiresi, Twi ne Nkran	Enlisi, Otšui ke Gã
nsem - asekyere - nhõma.	wiemoi - ahiläilo - wolo.

By the Rev. J. G. Christaller, Rev. C. W. Locher, Rev. J. Zimmermann. 16mo. 7s. 6d.

Christaller.—A Grammar of the Asante and Fante Language, called Tshi (Chwee, Twi): based on the Akuapem Dialect, with reference to the other (Akan and Fante) Dialects. By Rev. J. G. Christaller. 8vo. pp. xxiv. and 203. 1875. 10s. 6d.

Clarke.—Ten Great Religions: an Essay in Comparative Theology. By James Freeman Clarke. 8vo. cloth, pp. x. and 528. 1871. 15s.

Clarke.—Memoir on the Comparative Grammar of Egyptian, Coptic, and Ude. By Hyde Clarke, Cor. Member American Oriental Society; Mem. German Oriental Society, etc., etc. Demy 8vo. sd., pp. 32. 2s.

Clarke.—Researches in Pre-historic and Proto-historic Comparative Philology, Mythology, and Archæology, in connection with the Origin of Culture in America and the Accad or Sumerian Families. By Hyde Clarke. Demy 8vo. sewed, pp. xi. and 74. 1875. 2s. 6d.

Clarke.—Serpent and Siva Worship, and Mythology in Central America, Africa and Asia. By Hyde Clarke, Esq. 8vo. sewed. 1s.

Cleasby.—An Icelandic-English Dictionary. Based on the MS. Collections of the late Richard Cleasby. Enlarged and completed by G. Vigfússon. With an Introduction, and Life of Richard Cleasby, by G. Webbe Dasent, D.C.L. 4to. £3 7s.

Cleasby.—Appendix to an Icelandic-English Dictionary. See Skeat.

Colebrooke.—The Life and Miscellaneous Essays of Henry Thomas Colebrooke. The Biography by his Son, Sir T. E. Colebrooke, Bart., M.P., The Essays edited by Professor Cowell. In 3 vols.

Vol. I. The Life. With Portrait and Map. Demy 8vo. cloth, pp. xii. and 492. 14s.

Vols. II. and III. The Essays. A New Edition, with Notes by E. B. Cowell, Professor of Sanskrit in the University of Cambridge. Demy 8vo. cloth, pp. xvi.-544, and x.-520. 1873. 28s.

Collecçao de Vocabulos e Frases usados na Provincia de S. Pedro, do Rio Grande do Sul, no Brasil. 12mo. pp. 32, sewed. 1s.

Contopoulos.—A Lexicon of Modern Greek-English and English Modern Greek. By N. Contopoulos. In 2 vols. 8vo. cloth. Part I. Modern Greek-English, pp. 460. Part II. English-Modern Greek, pp. 582. £1 7s.

Conway.—The Sacred Anthology. A Book of Ethnical Scriptures. Collected and edited by M. D. Conway. 4th edition. Demy 8vo. cloth, pp. xvi. and 480. 12s.

Coomára Swamy.—The Dathávansa; or, the History of the Tooth-Relic of Gotama Buddha. The Pali Text and its Translation into English, with Notes. By Sir M. Coomára Swámy, Mudeliár. Demy 8vo. cloth, pp. 174. 1874. 10s. 6d.

Coomára Swamy.—The Dathávansa; or, the History of the Tooth-Relic of Gotama Buddha. English Translation only. With Notes. Demy 8vo. cloth, pp. 100. 1874. 6s.

Coomára Swamy.—Sutta Nípáta; or, the Dialogues and Discourses of Gotama Buddha. Translated from the Pali, with Introduction and Notes. By Sir M. Coomára Swamy. Cr. 8vo. cloth, pp. xxxvi. and 160. 1874. 6s.

Cotton.—Arabic Primer. Consisting of 180 Short Sentences containing 30 Primary Words prepared according to the Vocal System of Studying Language. By General Sir Arthur Cotton, K.C.S.I. Cr. 8vo. cloth, pp. 38. 2s.

Cowell and Eggeling.—Catalogue of Buddhist Sanskrit Manuscripts in the Possession of the Royal Asiatic Society (Hodgson Collection). By Professors E. B. Cowell and J. Eggeling. 8vo. sd., pp. 56. 2s. 6d.

Cowell.—A Short Introduction to the Ordinary Prakrit of the Sanskrit Dramas. With a List of Common Irregular Prakrit Words. By Prof. E. B. Cowell. Cr. 8vo. limp cloth, pp. 40. 1875. 3s. 6d.

Cunningham.—The Ancient Geography of India. I. The Buddhist Period, including the Campaigns of Alexander, and the Travels of Hwen-Thsang. By Alexander Cunningham, Major-General, Royal Engineers (Bengal Retired). With thirteen Maps. 8vo. pp. xx. 590, cloth. 1870. 28s.

Cunningham.—The Bhilsa Topes; or, Buddhist Monuments of Central India: comprising a brief Historical Sketch of the Rise, Progress, and Decline of Buddhism; with an Account of the Opening and Examination of the various Groups of Topes around Bhilsa. By Brev.-Major Alexander Cunningham, Bengal Engineers. Illustrated with thirty-three Plates. 8vo. pp. xxxvi. 370, cloth. 1854. £2 2s.

Cunningham.—Archæological Survey of India. Four Reports, made during the years 1862-63-64-65. By Alexander Cunningham, C.S.I., Major-General, etc. With Maps and Plates. Vols. 1 to 5. 8vo. cloth. £5.

Cust.—A Sketch of the Modern Languages of the East Indies. Accompanied by Two Language Maps. By R. Cust. Post 8vo. pp. xii. and 198, cloth. 12s.

Da Cunha.—Memoir on the History of the Tooth-Relic of Ceylon; with an Essay on the Life and System of Gautama Buddha. By J. Gerson da Cunha. 8vo. cloth, pp. xiv. and 70. With 4 photographs and cuts. 7s. 6d.

Da Cunha.—The Sahyâdri Khanda of the Skanda Purana; a Mythological, Historical and Geographical Account of Western India. First edition of the Sanskrit Text, with various readings. By J. Gerson da Cunha, M.R.C.S. and L.M. Eng., L.R.C.P. Edinb., etc. 8vo. bds. pp. 580. £1 1s.

Da Cunha.—Notes on the History and Antiquities of Chaul and Bassein. By J. Gerson da Cunha, M.R.C.S. and L.M. Eng., etc. 8vo. cloth, pp. xvi. and 262. With 17 photographs, 9 plates and a map. £1 5s.

Dalton.—Descriptive Ethnology of Bengal. By Edward Tuite Dalton, C.S.I., Colonel, Bengal Staff Corps, etc. Illustrated by Lithograph Portraits copied from Photographs. 39 Lithograph Plates. 4to. half-calf, pp. 340. £6 6s.

D'Alwis.—A Descriptive Catalogue of Sanskrit, Pali, and Sinhalese Literary Works of Ceylon. By James D'Alwis, M.R.A.S., Advocate of the Supreme Court, &c., &c. In Three Volumes. Vol. I., pp. xxxii. and 244, sewed. 1870. 8s. 6d.

Davids.—Three Inscriptions of Parâkrama Bâhu the Great, from Pulastipura, Ceylon. By T. W. Rhys Davids. 8vo. pp. 20. 1s. 6d.

Davids.—Sigiri, the Lion Rock, near Pulastipura, and the 39th Chapter of the Mahâvamsa. By T. W. Rhys Davids. 8vo. pp. 30. 1s. 6d.

Delepierre.—Supercheries Littéraires, Pastiches Suppositions d'Auteur, dans les Lettres et dans les Arts. Par Octave Delepierre. Fcap. 4to. paper cover, pp. 328. 14s.

Delepierre.—Tableau de la Littérature du Centon, chez les Anciens et chez les Modernes. Par Octave Delepierre. 2 vols. small 4to. paper cover, pp. 324 and 318. 21s.

Delepierre.—Essai Historique et Bibliographique sur les Rébus. Par Octave Delepierre. 8vo. pp. 24, sewed. With 15 pages of Woodcuts. 1870. 3s. 6d.

Dennys.—China and Japan. A complete Guide to the Open Ports of those countries, together with Pekin, Yeddo, Hong Kong, and Macao; forming a Guide Book and Vade Mecum for Travellers, Merchants, and Residents in general; with 56 Maps and Plans. By Wm. Frederick Mayers, F.R.G.S. H.M.'s Consular Service; N. B. Dennys, late H.M.'s Consular Service; and Charles King, Lieut. Royal Marine Artillery. Edited by N. B. Dennys. In one volume. 8vo. pp. 600, cloth. £2 2s.

Dennys.—A Handbook of the Canton Vernacular of the Chinese Language. Being a Series of Introductory Lessons, for Domestic and Business Purposes. By N. B. Dennys, M.R.A.S., Ph.D. 8vo. cloth, pp. 4, 195, and 31. £1 10s.

Dennys.—A Handbook of Malay Colloquial, as spoken in Singapore, Being a Series of Introductory Lessons for Domestic and Business Purposes. By N. B. Dennys, Ph.D., F.R.G.S., M.R.A.S., etc., Author of "The Folklore of China," "Handbook of Cantonese," etc., etc. 8vo. cloth, pp. 204. £1 1s.

Dennys.—The Folk-Lore of China, and its Affinities with that of the Aryan and Semitic Races. By N. B. Dennys, Ph.D., F.R.G.S., M.R.A.S., author of "A Handbook of the Canton Vernacular," etc. 8vo. cloth, pp. 168. 10s. 6d.

De Vere.—Studies in English; or, Glimpses of the Inner Life of our Language. By M. Schele de Vere, LL.D., Professor of Modern Languages in the University of Virginia. 8vo. cloth, pp. vi. and 365. 12s. 6d.

De Vere.—Americanisms: the English of the New World. By M. Schele De Vere, LL.D., Professor of Modern Languages in the University of Virginia. 8vo. pp. 685, cloth. 12s.

Dickson.—The Pâtimokkha, being the Buddhist Office of the Confession of Priests. The Pali Text, with a Translation, and Notes, by J. F. Dickson, M.A. 8vo. sd., pp. 69. 2s.

Dinkard (The).—The Original Pehlwi Text, the same transliterated in Zend Characters. Translations of the Text in the Gujrati and English Languages; a Commentary and Glossary of Select Terms. By Peshotun Dustoor Behramjee Sunjana. Vols. I. and II. 8vo. cloth. £2 2s.

Döhne.—A Zulu-Kafir Dictionary, etymologically explained, with copious illustrations and examples, preceded by an introduction on the Zulu-Kafir Language. By the Rev. J. L. Döhne. Royal 8vo. pp. xlii. and 418, sewed. Cape Town, 1857. 21s.

Döhne.—The Four Gospels in Zulu. By the Rev. J. L. Döhne, Missionary to the American Board, C.F.M. 8vo. pp. 208, cloth. Pietermaritzburg, 1866. 5s.

Doolittle.—A Vocabulary and Handbook of the Chinese Language. Romanized in the Mandarin Dialect. In Two Volumes comprised in Three Parts. By Rev. Justus Doolittle, Author of "Social Life of the Chinese." Vol. I. 4to. pp. viii. and 548. Vol. II. Parts II. and III., pp. vii. and 695. £1 11s. 6d. each vol.

Douglas.—Chinese-English Dictionary of the Vernacular or Spoken Language of Amoy, with the principal variations of the Chang-Chew and Chin-Chew Dialects. By the Rev. Carstairs Douglas, M.A., LL.D., Glasg., Missionary of the Presbyterian Church in England. 1 vol. High quarto, cloth, double columns, pp. 632. 1873. £3 3s.

Douglas.—Chinese Language and Literature. Two Lectures delivered at the Royal Institution, by R. K. Douglas, of the British Museum, and Professor of Chinese at King's College. Cr. 8vo. cl., pp. 118. 1875. 5s.

Douglas.—The Life of Jenghiz Khan. Translated from the Chinese, with an Introduction, by Robert Kennaway Douglas, of the British Museum, and Professor of Chinese, King's College, London. Cr. 8vo. cloth, pp. xxxvi.-106. 1877. 5s.

Douse.—Grimm's Law; A Study: or, Hints towards an Explanation of the so-called "Lautverschiebung." To which are added some Remarks on the Primitive Indo-European K, and several Appendices. By T. Le Marchant Douse. 8vo. cloth, pp. xvi. and 230. 10s. 6d.

Dowson.—A Grammar of the Urdu or Hindustani Language. By John Dowson, M.R.A.S. 12mo. cloth, pp. xvi. and 264. 10s. 6d.

Dowson.—A Hindustani Exercise Book. Containing a Series of Passages and Extracts adapted for Translation into Hindustani. By John Dowson, M.R.A.S., Professor of Hindustani, Staff College. Crown 8vo. pp. 100. Limp cloth, 2s. 6d.

Dwight.—Modern Philology: Its Discovery, History, and Influence. New edition, with Maps, Tabular Views, and an Index. By Benjamin W. Dwight. In two vols. cr. 8vo. cloth. First series, pp. 360; second series, pp. xi. and 554. £1.

Early English Text Society's Publications. Subscription, one guinea per annum.

1. Early English Alliterative Poems. In the West-Midland Dialect of the Fourteenth Century. Edited by R. Morris, Esq., from an unique Cottonian MS. 16s.
2. Arthur (about 1440 A.D.). Edited by F. J. Furnivall, Esq., from the Marquis of Bath's unique MS. 4s.
3. Ane Compendious and Breue Tractate concernyng ye Office and Dewtie of Kyngis, etc. By William Lauder. (1556 A.D.) Edited by F. Hall, Esq., D.C.L. 4s.
4. Sir Gawayne and the Green Knight (about 1320-30 A.D.). Edited by R. Morris, Esq., from an unique Cottonian MS. 10s.
5. Of the Orthographie and Congruitie of the Britan Tongue; a treates, noe shorter than necessarie, for the Schooles, be Alexander Hume. Edited for the first time from the unique MS. in the British Museum (about 1617 A.D.), by Henry B. Wheatley, Esq. 4s.
6. Lancelot of the Laik. Edited from the unique MS. in the Cambridge University Library (ab. 1500), by the Rev. Walter W. Skeat, M.A. 8s.
7. The Story of Genesis and Exodus, an Early English Song, of about 1250 A.D. Edited for the first time from the unique MS. in the Library of Corpus Christi College, Cambridge, by R. Morris, Esq. 8s.
8. Morte Arthure; the Alliterative Version. Edited from Robert Thornton's unique MS. (about 1440 A.D.) at Lincoln, by the Rev. George Perry, M.A., Prebendary of Lincoln. 7s.
9. Animadversions uppon the Annotacions and Corrections of some Imperfections of Impressiones of Chaucer's Workes, reprinted in 1598; by Francis Thynne. Edited from the unique MS. in the Bridgewater Library. By G. H. Kingsley, Esq., M.D., and F. J. Furnivall, Esq., M.A. 10s.
10. Merlin, or the Early History of King Arthur. Edited for the first time from the unique MS. in the Cambridge University Library (about 1450 A.D.), by Henry B. Wheatley, Esq. Part I. 2s. 6d.
11. The Monarche, and other Poems of Sir David Lyndesay. Edited from the first edition by Johne Skott, in 1552, by Fitzedward Hall, Esq., D.C.L. Part I. 3s.
12. The Wright's Chaste Wife, a Merry Tale, by Adam of Cobsam (about 1462 A.D.), from the unique Lambeth MS. 306. Edited for the first time by F. J. Furnivall, Esq., M.A. 1s.

Early English Text Society's Publications—*continued.*

13. Seinte Marherete, þe Meiden ant Martyr. Three Texts of ab. 1200, 1310, 1330 A.D. First edited in 1862, by the Rev. Oswald Cockayne, M.A., and now re-issued. 2s.

14. Kyng Horn, with fragments of Floriz and Blauncheflur, and the Assumption of the Blessed Virgin. Edited from the MSS. in the Library of the University of Cambridge and the British Museum, by the Rev. J. Rawson Lumby. 3s. 6d.

15. Political, Religious, and Love Poems, from the Lambeth MS. No. 306, and other sources. Edited by F. J. Furnivall, Esq., M.A. 7s. 6d.

16. A Tretice in English breuely drawe out of þ book of Quintis essencijs in Latyn, þ Hermys þ prophete and king of Egipt after þ flood of Noe, fader of Philosophris, hadde by reuelacioun of an aungil of God to him sente. Edited from the Sloane MS. 73, by F. J. Furnivall, Esq., M.A. 1s.

17. Parallel Extracts from 29 Manuscripts of Piers Plowman, with Comments, and a Proposal for the Society's Three-text edition of this Poem. By the Rev. W. Skeat, M.A. 1s.

18. Hali Meidenhead, about 1200 A.D. Edited for the first time from the MS. (with a translation) by the Rev. Oswald Cockayne, M.A. 1s.

19. The Monarche, and other Poems of Sir David Lyndesay. Part II., the Complaynt of the King's Papingo, and other minor Poems. Edited from the First Edition by F. Hall, Esq., D.C.L. 3s. 6d.

20. Some Treatises by Richard Rolle de Hampole. Edited from Robert of Thornton's MS. (ab. 1440 A.D.), by Rev. George G. Perry, M.A. 1s.

21. Merlin, or the Early History of King Arthur. Part II. Edited by Henry B. Wheatley, Esq. 4s.

22. The Romans of Partenay, or Lusignen. Edited for the first time from the unique MS. in the Library of Trinity College, Cambridge, by the Rev. W. W. Skeat, M.A. 6s.

23. Dan Michel's Ayenbite of Inwyt, or Remorse of Conscience, in the Kentish dialect, 1340 A.D. Edited from the unique MS. in the British Museum, by Richard Morris, Esq. 10s. 6d.

24. Hymns to the Virgin and Christ; The Parliament of Devils, and Other Religious Poems. Edited from the Lambeth MS. 853, by F. J. Furnivall, M.A. 3s.

25. The Stacions of Rome, and the Pilgrim's Sea-Voyage and Sea-Sickness, with Clene Maydenhod. Edited from the Vernon and Porkington MSS., etc., by F. J. Furnivall, Esq., M.A. 1s.

26. Religious Pieces in Prose and Verse. Containing Dan Jon Gaytrigg's Sermon; The Abbaye of S. Spirit; Sayne Jon, and other pieces in the Northern Dialect. Edited from Robert of Thorntone's MS. (ab. 1440 A.D.), by the Rev. G. Perry, M.A. 2s.

27. Manipulus Vocabulorum: a Rhyming Dictionary of the English Language, by Peter Levins (1570). Edited, with an Alphabetical Index, by Henry B. Wheatley. 12s.

28. The Vision of William concerning Piers Plowman, together with Vita de Dowel, Dobet et Dobest. 1362 A.D., by William Langland. The earliest or Vernon Text; Text A. Edited from the Vernon MS., with full Collations, by Rev. W. W. Skeat, M.A. 7s.

Early English English Text Society's Publications—*continued.*

29. Old English Homilies and Homiletic Treatises. (Sawles Warde and the Wohunge of Ure Lauerd: Ureisuns of Ure Louerd and of Ure Lefdi, etc.) of the Twelfth and Thirteenth Centuries. Edited from MSS. in the British Museum, Lambeth, and Bodleian Libraries; with Introduction, Translation, and Notes. By Richard Morris. *First Series.* Part I. 7s.

30. Piers, the Ploughman's Crede (about 1394). Edited from the MSS. by the Rev. W. W. Skeat, M.A. 2s.

31. Instructions for Parish Priests. By John Myrc. Edited from Cotton MS. Claudius A. II., by Edward Peacock, Esq., F.S.A., etc., etc. 4s.

32. The Babees Book, Aristotle's A B C, Urbanitatis, Stans Puer ad Mensam, The Lytylle Childrenes Lytil Boke. The Bokes of Nurture of Hugh Rhodes and John Russell, Wynkyn de Worde's Boke of Keruynge, The Booke of Demeanor, The Boke of Curtasye, Seager's Schoole of Vertue, etc., etc. With some French and Latin Poems on like subjects, and some Forewords on Education in Early England. Edited by F. J. Furnivall, M.A., Trin. Hall, Cambridge. 15s.

33. The Book of the Knight de la Tour Landry, 1372. A Father's Book for his Daughters. Edited from the Harleian MS. 1764, by Thomas Wright, Esq., M.A., and Mr. William Rossiter. 8s.

34. Old English Homilies and Homiletic Treatises. (Sawles Warde, and the Wohunge of Ure Lauerd: Ureisuns of Ure Louerd and of Ure Lefdi, etc.) of the Twelfth and Thirteenth Centuries. Edited from MSS. in the British Museum, Lambeth, and Bodleian Libraries; with Introduction, Translation, and Notes, by Richard Morris. *First Series.* Part 2. 8s.

35. Sir David Lyndesay's Works. Part 3. The Historie of ane Nobil and Wailzeand Squyer, William Meldrum, umqwhyle Laird of Cleische and Bynnis, compylit be Sir David Lyndesay of the Mont *alias* Lyoun King of Armes. With the Testament of the said Williame Meldrum, Squyer, compylit alswa be Sir Dauid Lyndesay, etc. Edited by F. Hall, D.C.L. 2s.

36. Merlin, or the Early History of King Arthur. A Prose Romance (about 1450-1460 A.D.), edited from the unique MS. in the University Library, Cambridge, by Henry B. Wheatley. With an *Essay on Arthurian Localities*, by J. S. Stuart Glennie, Esq. Part III. 1869. 12s.

37. Sir David Lyndesay's Works. Part IV. Ane Satyre of the thrie estaits, in commendatioun of vertew and vituperatioun of vyce. Maid be Sir David Lindesay, of the Mont, *alias* Lyon King of Armes. At Edinbvrgh. Printed be Robert Charteris, 1602. Cvm privilegio regis. Edited by F. Hall, Esq., D.C.L. 4s.

38. The Vision of William concerning Piers the Plowman, together with Vita de Dowel, Dobet, et Dobest, Secundum Wit et Resoun, by William Langland (1377 A.D.). The "Crowley" Text; or Text B. Edited from MS. Laud Misc. 581, collated with MS. Rawl. Poet. 38, MS. B. 15. 17. in the Library of Trinity College, Cambridge, MS. Dd. 1. 17. in the Cambridge University Library, the MS. in Oriel College, Oxford, MS. Bodley 814, etc. By the Rev. Walter W. Skeat, M.A., late Fellow of Christ's College, Cambridge. 10s. 6d.

39. The "Gest Hystoriale" of the Destruction of Troy. An Alliterative Romance, translated from Guido De Colonna's "Hystoria Troiana." Now first edited from the unique MS. in the Hunterian Museum, University of Glasgow, by the Rev. Geo. A. Panton and David Donaldson. Part I. 10s. 6d.

Early English Text Society's Publications—*continued.*

40. English Gilds. The Original Ordinances of more than One Hundred Early English Gilds: Together with the olde usages of the cite of Wynchestre; The Ordinances of Worcester; The Office of the Mayor of Bristol; and the Costomary of the Manor of Tettenhall-Regis. From Original MSS. of the Fourteenth and Fifteenth Centuries. Edited with Notes by the late Toulmin Smith, Esq., F.R.S. of Northern Antiquaries (Copenhagen). With an Introduction and Glossary, etc., by his daughter, Lucy Toulmin Smith. And a Preliminary Essay, in Five Parts, On the History and Development of Gilds, by Lujo Brentano, Doctor Juris Utriusque et Philosophiæ. 21s.

41. The Minor Poems of William Lauder, Playwright, Poet, and Minister of the Word of God (mainly on the State of Scotland in and about 1568 A.D., that year of Famine and Plague). Edited from the Unique Originals belonging to S. Christie-Miller, Esq., of Britwell, by F. J. Furnivall, M.A., Trin. Hall, Camb. 3s.

42. Bernardus de Cura rei Famuliaris, with some Early Scotch Prophecies, etc. From a MS., KK 1. 5, in the Cambridge University Library. Edited by J. Rawson Lumby, M.A., late Fellow of Magdalen College, Cambridge. 2s.

43. Ratis Raving, and other Moral and Religious Pieces, in Prose and Verse. Edited from the Cambridge University Library MS. KK 1. 5, by J. Rawson Lumby, M.A., late Fellow of Magdalen College, Cambridge. 3s.

44. Joseph of Arimathie: otherwise called the Romance of the Seint Graal, or Holy Grail: an alliterative poem, written about A.D. 1350, and now first printed from the unique copy in the Vernon MS. at Oxford. With an appendix, containing "The Lyfe of Joseph of Armathy," reprinted from the black-letter copy of Wynkyn de Worde; "De sancto Joseph ab Arimathia," first printed by Pynson, A.D. 1516; and "The Lyfe of Joseph of Arimathia," first printed by Pynson, A.D. 1520. Edited, with Notes and Glossarial Indices, by the Rev. Walter W. Skeat, M.A. 5s.

45. King Alfred's West-Saxon Version of Gregory's Pastoral Care. With an English translation, the Latin Text, Notes, and an Introduction. Edited by Henry Sweet, Esq., of Balliol College, Oxford. Part I. 10s.

46. Legends of the Holy Rood; Symbols of the Passion and Cross-Poems. In Old English of the Eleventh, Fourteenth, and Fifteenth Centuries. Edited from MSS. in the British Museum and Bodleian Libraries; with Introduction, Translations, and Glossarial Index. By Richard Morris, LL.D. 10s.

47. Sir David Lyndesay's Works. Part V. The Minor Poems of Lyndesay. Edited by J. A. H. Murray, Esq. 3s.

48. The Times' Whistle: or, A Newe Daunce of Seven Satires, and other Poems: Compiled by R. C., Gent. Now first Edited from MS. Y. 8. 3. in the Library of Canterbury Cathedral; with Introduction, Notes, and Glossary, by J. M. Cowper. 6s.

49. An Old English Miscellany, containing a Bestiary, Kentish Sermons, Proverbs of Alfred, Religious Poems of the 13th century. Edited from the MSS. by the Rev. R. Morris, LL.D. 10s.

50. King Alfred's West-Saxon Version of Gregory's Pastoral Care. Edited from 2 MSS., with an English translation. By Henry Sweet, Esq., Balliol College, Oxford. Part II. 10s.

51. Þe Liflade of St. Juliana, from two old English Manuscripts of 1230 A.D. With renderings into Modern English, by the Rev. O. Cockayne and Edmund Brock. Edited by the Rev. O. Cockayne, M.A. Price 2s.

Early English Text Society's Publications—*continued.*

52. Palladius on Husbondrie, from the unique MS., ab. 1420 A.D., ed. Rev. B. Lodge. Part I. 10s.

53. Old English Homilies, Series II., from the unique 13th-century MS. in Trinity Coll. Cambridge, with a photolithograph; three Hymns to the Virgin and God, from a unique 13th-century MS. at Oxford, a photolithograph of the music to two of them, and transcriptions of it in modern notation by Dr. Rimbault, and A. J. Ellis, Esq., F.R.S.; the whole edited by the Rev. Richard Morris, LL.D. 8s.

54. The Vision of Piers Plowman, Text C (completing the three versions of this great poem), with an Autotype; and two unique alliterative Poems: Richard the Redeles (by William, the author of the *Vision*); and The Crowned King; edited by the Rev. W. W. Skeat, M.A. 18s.

55. Generydes, a Romance, edited from the unique MS., ab. 1440 A.D., in Trin. Coll. Cambridge, by W. Aldis Wright, Esq., M.A., Trin. Coll. Cambr. Part I. 3s.

56. The Gest Hystoriale of the Destruction of Troy, translated from Guido de Colonna, in alliterative verse; edited from the unique MS. in the Hunterian Museum, Glasgow, by D. Donaldson, Esq., and the late Rev. G. A. Panton. Part II. 10s. 6d.

57. The Early English Version of the "Cursor Mundi," in four Texts, from MS. Cotton, Vesp. A. iii. in the British Museum; Fairfax MS. 14. in the Bodleian; the Göttingen MS. Theol. 107; MS. R. 3, 8, in Trinity College, Cambridge. Edited by the Rev. R. Morris, LL.D. Part I. with two photo-lithographic facsimiles by Cooke and Fotheringham. 10s. 6d.

58. The Blickling Homilies, edited from the Marquis of Lothian's Anglo-Saxon MS. of 971 A.D., by the Rev. R. Morris, LL.D. (With a Photolithograph). Part I. 8s.

59. The Early English Version of the "Cursor Mundi;" in four Texts, from MS. Cotton Vesp. A. iii. in the British Museum; Fairfax MS. 14. in the Bodleian; the Göttingen MS. Theol. 107; MS. R. 3. 8. in Trinity College, Cambridge. Edited by the Rev. R. Morris, LL.D. Part II. 15s.

60. Meditacyuns on the Soper of our Lorde (perhaps by Robert of Brunne). Edited from the MSS. by J. M. Cowper, Esq. 2s. 6d.

61. The Romance and Prophecies of Thomas of Erceldoune, printed from Five MSS. Edited by Dr. James A. H. Murray. 10s. 6d.

62. The Early English Version of the "Cursor Mundi," in Four Texts. Edited by the Rev. R. Morris, M.A., LL.D. Part III. 15s.

63. The Blickling Homilies. Edited from the Marquis of Lothian's Anglo-Saxon MS. of 971 A.D., by the Rev. R. Morris, LL.D. Part II. 4s.

64. Francis Thynne's Emblemes and Epigrams, A.D. 1600, from the Earl of Ellesmere's unique MS. Edited by F. J. Furnivall, M.A. 4s.

65. Be Domes Dæge (Bede's De Die Judicii) and other short Anglo-Saxon Pieces. Edited from the unique MS. by the Rev. J. Rawson Lumby, B.D. 2s.

66. The Early English Version of the "Cursor Mundi," in Four Texts. Edited by Rev. R. Morris, M.A., LL.D. Part IV. 10s.

67. Notes on Piers Plowman. By the Rev. W. W. Skeat, M.A. Part I. 21s.

68. The Early English Version of the "Cursor Mundi," in Four Texts. Edited by Rev. R. Morris, M.A., LL.D. Part V. 25s.

Early English Text Society's Publications—*continued.*

69. ADAM DAVY'S FIVE DREAMS ABOUT EDWARD II. THE LIFE OF SAINT ALEXIUS. Solomon's Book of Wisdom. St. Jerome's 15 Tokens before Doomsday. The Lamentation of Souls. Edited from the Laud MS. 622, in the Bodleian Library, by F. J. FURNIVALL, M.A. 5s.

Extra Series. Subscriptions—Small paper, one guinea; large paper two guineas, per annum.

1. THE ROMANCE OF WILLIAM OF PALERNE (otherwise known as the Romance of William and the Werwolf). Translated from the French at the command of Sir Humphrey de Bohun, about A.D. 1350, to which is added a fragment of the Alliterative Romance of Alisaunder, translated from the Latin by the same author, about A.D. 1340; the former re-edited from the unique MS. in the Library of King's College, Cambridge, the latter now first edited from the unique MS. in the Bodleian Library, Oxford. By the Rev. WALTER W. SKEAT, M.A. 8vo, sewed, pp. xliv. and 328. £1 6s.

2. ON EARLY ENGLISH PRONUNCIATION, with especial reference to Shakspere and Chaucer; containing an investigation of the Correspondence of Writing with Speech in England, from the Anglo-Saxon period to the present day, preceded by a systematic Notation of all Spoken Sounds by means of the ordinary Printing Types; including a re-arrangement of Prof. F. J. Child's Memoirs on the Language of Chaucer and Gower, and reprints of the rare Tracts by Salesbury on English, 1547, and Welsh, 1567, and by Barcley on French, 1521. By ALEXANDER J. ELLIS, F.R.S. Part I. On the Pronunciation of the xivth, xvth, xvith, and xviith centuries. 8vo, sewed, pp. viii. and 416. 10s.

3. CAXTON'S BOOK OF CURTESYE, printed at Westminster about 1477–8, A.D., and now reprinted, with two MS. copies of the same treatise, from the Oriel MS. 79, and the Balliol MS. 354. Edited by FREDERICK J. FURNIVALL, M.A. 8vo, sewed, pp. xii. and 58. 5s.

4. THE LAY OF HAVELOK THE DANE; composed in the reign of Edward I., about A.D. 1280. Formerly edited by Sir F. MADDEN for the Roxburghe Club, and now re-edited from the unique MS. Laud Misc. 108, in the Bodleian Library, Oxford, by the Rev. WALTER W. SKEAT, M.A. 8vo, sewed, pp. lv. and 160. 10s.

5. CHAUCER'S TRANSLATION OF BOETHIUS'S "DE CONSOLATIONE PHILOSOPHIÆ." Edited from the Additional MS. 10,340 in the British Museum. Collated with the Cambridge Univ. Libr. MS. Ii. 3. 21. By RICHARD MORRIS. 8vo. 12s.

6. THE ROMANCE OF THE CHEVELERE ASSIGNE. Re-edited from the unique manuscript in the British Museum, with a Preface, Notes, and Glossarial Index, by HENRY H. GIBBS, Esq., M.A. 8vo, sewed, pp. xviii. and 38. 3s.

7. ON EARLY ENGLISH PRONUNCIATION, with especial reference to Shakspere and Chaucer. By ALEXANDER J. ELLIS, F.R.S., etc., etc. Part II. On the Pronunciation of the xiiith and previous centuries, of Anglo-Saxon, Icelandic, Old Norse and Gothic, with Chronological Tables of the Value of Letters and Expression of Sounds in English Writing. 10s.

8. QUEENE ELIZABETHES ACHADEMY, by Sir HUMPHREY GILBERT. A Booke of Precedence, The Ordering of a Funerall, etc. Varying Versions of the Good Wife, The Wise Man, etc., Maxims, Lydgate's Order of Fools, A Poem on Heraldry, Occleve on Lords' Men, etc., Edited by F. J. FURNIVALL, M.A., Trin. Hall, Camb. With Essays on Early Italian and German Books of Courtesy, by W. M. ROSSETTI, Esq., and E. OSWALD, Esq. 8vo. 13s.

Early English Text Society's Publications—*continued.*

9. The Fraternitye of Vacabondes, by John Awdeley (licensed in 1560-1, imprinted then, and in 1565), from the edition of 1575 in the Bodleian Library. A Caueat or Warening for Commen Cursetors vulgarely called Vagabones, by Thomas Harman, Esquiere. From the 3rd edition of 1567, belonging to Henry Huth, Esq., collated with the 2nd edition of 1567, in the Bodleian Library, Oxford, and with the reprint of the 4th edition of 1573. A Sermon in Praise of Thieves and Thievery, by Parson Haben or Hyberdyne, from the Lansdowne MS. 98, and Cotton Vesp. A. 25. Those parts of the Groundworke of Conny-catching (ed. 1592), that differ from *Harman's Caueat.* Edited by Edward Viles & F. J. Furnivall. 8vo. 7s. 6d.

10. The Fyrst Boke of the Introduction of Knowledge, made by Andrew Borde, of Physycke Doctor. A Compendyous Regyment or a Dyetary of Helth made in Mountpyllier, compiled by Andrewe Boorde, of Physycke Doctor. Barnes in the Defence of the Berde: a treatyse made, answerynge the treatyse of Doctor Borde upon Berdes. Edited, with a life of Andrew Boorde, and large extracts from his Breuyary, by F. J. Furnivall, M.A., Trinity Hall, Camb. 8vo. 18s.

11. The Bruce; or, the Book of the most excellent and noble Prince, Robert de Broyss, King of Scots: compiled by Master John Barbour, Archdeacon of Aberdeen. A.D. 1375. Edited from MS. G 23 in the Library of St. John's College, Cambridge, written A.D. 1487; collated with the MS. in the Advocates' Library at Edinburgh, written A.D. 1489, and with Hart's Edition, printed A.D. 1616; with a Preface, Notes, and Glossarial Index, by the Rev. Walter W. Skeat, M.A. Part I. 8vo. 12s.

12. England in the Reign of King Henry the Eighth. A Dialogue between Cardinal Pole and Thomas Lupset, Lecturer in Rhetoric at Oxford. By Thomas Starkey, Chaplain to the King. Edited, with Preface, Notes, and Glossary, by J. M. Cowper. And with an Introduction, containing the Life and Letters of Thomas Starkey, by the Rev. J. S. Brewer, M.A. Part II. 12s. (*Part I., Starkey's Life and Letters, is in preparation.*

13. A Supplicacyon for the Beggars. Written about the year 1529, by Simon Fish. Now re-edited by Frederick J. Furnivall. With a Supplycacion to our moste Soueraigne Lorde Kynge Henry the Eyght (1544 A.D.), A Supplication of the Poore Commons (1546 A.D.), The Decaye of England by the great multitude of Shepe (1550-3 A.D.). Edited by J. Meadows Cowper. 6s.

14. On Early English Pronunciation, with especial reference to Shakspere and Chaucer. By A. J. Ellis, F.R.S., F.S.A. Part III. Illustrations of the Pronunciation of the xivth and xvith Centuries. Chaucer, Gower, Wycliffe, Spenser, Shakspere, Salesbury, Barcley, Hart, Bullokar, Gill. Pronouncing Vocabulary. 10s.

15. Robert Crowley's Thirty-one Epigrams, Voyce of the Last Trumpet, Way to Wealth, etc., 1550-1 A.D. Edited by J. M. Cowper, Esq. 12s.

16. A Treatise on the Astrolabe; addressed to his son Lowys, by Geoffrey Chaucer, A.D. 1391. Edited from the earliest MSS. by the Rev. Walter W. Skeat, M.A., late Fellow of Christ's College, Cambridge. 10s.

17. The Complaynt of Scotlande, 1549, A.D., with an Appendix of four Contemporary English Tracts. Edited by J. A. H. Murray, Esq. Part I. 10s.

18. The Complaynt of Scotlande, etc. Part II. 8s.

19. Oure Ladyes Myroure, A.D. 1530, edited by the Rev. J. H. Blunt, M.A., with four full-page photolithographic facsimiles by Cooke and Fotheringham. 24s.

Early English Text Society's Publications—*continued.*

20. LONELICH'S HISTORY OF THE HOLY GRAIL (ab. 1450 A.D.), translated from the French Prose of SIRES ROBIERS DE BORRON. Re-edited from the Unique MS. in Corpus Christi College, Cambridge, by F. J. Furnivall, Esq. M.A. Part I. 8s.

21. BARBOUR'S BRUCE. Edited from the MSS. and the earliest printed edition by the Rev. W. W. SKEAT, M.A. Part II. 4s.

22. HENRY BRINKELOW'S COMPLAYNT OF RODERYCK MORS, somtyme a gray Fryre, unto the Parliament Howse of Ingland his naturall Country, for the Redresse of certen wicked Lawes, euel Customs, and cruel Decreys (ab. 1542); and THE LAMENTACION OF A CHRISTIAN AGAINST THE CITIE OF LONDON, made by Roderigo Mors, A.D. 1545. Edited by J. M. COWPER, Esq. 9s.

23. ON EARLY ENGLISH PRONUNCIATION, with especial reference to Shakspere and Chaucer. By A. J. ELLIS, Esq., F.R.S. Part IV. 10s.

24. LONELICH'S HISTORY OF THE HOLY GRAIL (ab. 1450 A.D.), translated from the French Prose of SIRES ROBIERS DE BORRON. Re-edited from the Unique MS. in Corpus Christi College, Cambridge, by F. J. FURNIVALL, Esq., M.A. Part II. 10s.

25. THE ROMANCE OF GUY OF WARWICK. Edited from the Cambridge University MS. by Prof. J. ZUPITZA, Ph.D. Part I. 20s.

26. THE ROMANCE OF GUY OF WARWICK. Edited from the Cambridge University MS. by Prof. J. ZUPITZA, Ph.D. (The 2nd or 15th century version.) Part II. 14s.

27. THE ENGLISH WORKS OF JOHN FISHER, Bishop of Rochester (died 1535). Edited by Professor J. E. B. MAYOR, M.A. Part I., the Text. 16s.

28. LONELICH'S HISTORY OF THE HOLY GRAIL. Edited by F. J. FURNIVALL, M.A. Part III. 10s.

29. BARBOUR'S BRUCE. Edited from the MSS. and the earliest Printed Edition, by the Rev. W. W. SKEAT, M.A. Part III. 21s.

30. LONELICH'S HISTORY OF THE HOLY GRAIL. Edited by F. J. FURNIVALL, Esq., M.A. Part. IV. 15s.

31. ALEXANDER AND DINDIMUS. Translated from the Latin about A.D. 1340-50. Re-edited by the Rev. W. W. SKEAT, M.A. 6s.

Edda Saemundar Hinns Froda—The Edda of Saemund the Learned. From the Old Norse or Icelandic. By BENJAMIN THORPE. Part I. with a Mythological Index. 12mo. pp. 152, cloth, 3s. 6d. Part II. with Index of Persons and Places. 12mo. pp. viii. and 172, cloth. 1866. 4s.; or in 1 Vol. complete, 7s. 6d.

Edkins.—INTRODUCTION TO THE STUDY OF THE CHINESE CHARACTERS. By J. EDKINS, D.D., Peking, China. Roy. 8vo. pp. 340, paper boards. 18s.

Edkins.—CHINA'S PLACE IN PHILOLOGY. An attempt to show that the Languages of Europe and Asia have a common origin. By the Rev. JOSEPH EDKINS. Crown 8vo., pp. xxiii.—403, cloth. 10s. 6d.

Edkins.—A VOCABULARY OF THE SHANGHAI DIALECT. By J. EDKINS. 8vo. half-calf, pp. vi. and 151. Shanghai, 1869. 21s.

Edkins.—A GRAMMAR OF COLLOQUIAL CHINESE, as exhibited in the Shanghai Dialect. By J. EDKINS, B.A. Second edition, corrected. 8vo. half-calf, pp. viii. and 225. Shanghai, 1868. 21s.

Edkins.—A GRAMMAR OF THE CHINESE COLLOQUIAL LANGUAGE, commonly called the Mandarin Dialect. By JOSEPH EDKINS. Second edition. 8vo. half-calf, pp. viii. and 279. Shanghai, 1864. £1 10s.

Edkins.—Progressive Lessons in the Chinese Spoken Language. With Lists of Common Words and Phrases. By J. Edkins, B.A. Third edition, 8vo. pp. 120. 1869. 14s.

Edkins.—Religion in China. A Brief Account of the Three Religions of the Chinese. By Joseph Edkins, D.D. Post 8vo. cloth. 7s. 6d.

Eger and Grime; an Early English Romance. Edited from Bishop Percy's Folio Manuscript, about 1650 A.D. By John W. Hales, M.A., Fellow and late Assistant Tutor of Christ's College, Cambridge, and Frederick J. Furnivall, M.A., of Trinity Hall, Cambridge. 1 vol. 4to., pp. 64, (only 100 copies printed), bound in the Roxburghe style. 10s. 6d.

Egyptian Calendar for the Year 1296 A.H. (1878 A.D.), corresponding with the years 1594, 1595, of the Koptic Era. Demy 8vo. sewed, pp. 98. 5s.

Eitel.—A Chinese Dictionary in the Cantonese Dialect. By Ernest John Eitel, Ph.D. Tubing. Will be completed in four parts. Part I. (A—K). 8vo. sewed, pp. 202. 12s. 6d. Part II. (K—M). pp. 202. 12s. 6d.

Eitel.—Handbook for the Student of Chinese Buddhism. By the Rev. E. J. Eitel, of the London Missionary Society. Crown 8vo. pp. viii., 224, cl., 18s.

Eitel.—Feng-Shui; or, The Rudiments of Natural Science in China. By Rev. E. J. Eitel, M.A., Ph.D. Demy 8vo. sewed, pp. vi. and 84. 6s.

Eitel.—Buddhism: its Historical, Theoretical, and Popular Aspects. In Three Lectures. By Rev. E. J. Eitel, M.A. Ph.D. Second Edition. Demy 8vo. sewed, pp. 130. 5s.

Elliot.—The History of India, as told by its own Historians. The Muhammadan Period. Complete in Eight Vols. Edited from the Posthumous Papers of the late Sir H. M. Elliot, K.C.B., East India Company's Bengal Civil Service, by Prof. John Dowson, M.R.A.S., Staff College, Sandhurst.

Vols. I. and II. With a Portrait of Sir H. M. Elliot. 8vo. pp. xxxii. and 542, x. and 580, cloth. 18s. each.
Vol. III. 8vo. pp. xii. and 627, cloth. 24s.
Vol. IV. 8vo. pp. x. and 563, cloth. 21s.
Vol. V. 8vo. pp. xii. and 576, cloth. 21s.
Vol. VI. 8vo. pp. viii. and 574, cloth. 21s.
Vol. VII. 8vo. pp. viii. and 574, cloth. 21s.
Vol. VIII. 8vo. pp. xxxii., 444, and lxviii. cloth. 24s.

Elliot.—Memoirs on the History, Folklore, and Distribution of the Races of the North Western Provinces of India; being an amplified Edition of the original Supplementary Glossary of Indian Terms. By the late Sir Henry M. Elliot, K.C.B., of the Hon. East India Company's Bengal Civil Service. Edited, revised, and re-arranged, by John Beames, M.R.A.S., Bengal Civil Service; Member of the German Oriental Society, of the Asiatic Societies of Paris and Bengal, and of the Philological Society of London. In 2 vols. demy 8vo., pp. xx., 370, and 396, cloth. With two Lithographic Plates, one full-page coloured Map, and three large coloured folding Maps. 36s.

Ellis.—On Numerals, as Signs of Primeval Unity among Mankind. By Robert Ellis, B.D., Late Fellow of St. John's College, Cambridge. Demy 8vo. cloth, pp. viii. and 94. 3s. 6d.

Ellis.—The Asiatic Affinities of the Old Italians. By Robert Ellis, B.D., Fellow of St. John's College, Cambridge, and author of "Ancient Routes between Italy and Gaul." Crown 8vo. pp. iv. 156, cloth. 1870. 5s.

Ellis.—Peruvia Scythica. The Quichua Language of Peru: its derivation from Central Asia with the American languages in general, and with the Turanian and Iberian languages of the Old World, including the Basque, the Lycian, and the Pre-Aryan language of Etruria. By Robert Ellis, B.D. 8vo. cloth, pp. xii. and 219. 1875. 6s.

Ellis.—Etruscan Numerals. By Robert Ellis, B.D. 8vo. sewed, pp. 52. 2s. 6d.

English and Welsh Languages.—The Influence of the English and Welsh Languages upon each other, exhibited in the Vocabularies of the two Tongues. Intended to suggest the importance to Philologers, Antiquaries, Ethnographers, and others, of giving due attention to the Celtic Branch of the Indo-Germanic Family of Languages. Square, pp. 30, sewed. 1869. 1s.

English Dialect Society's Publications. Subscription, 1873 to 1876, 10s. 6d. per annum; 1877 and following years, 20s. per annum.

1873.

1. Series B. Part 1. Reprinted Glossaries. Containing a Glossary of North of England Words, by J. H.; five Glossaries, by Mr. Marshall; and a West-Riding Glossary, by Dr. Willan. 7s. 6d.

2. Series A. Bibliographical. A List of Books illustrating English Dialects. Part I. Containing a General List of Dictionaries, etc.; and a List of Books relating to some of the Counties of England. 4s.

3. Series C. Original Glossaries. Part I. Containing a Glossary of Swaledale Words. By Captain Harland. 4s.

1874.

4. Series D. The History of English Sounds. By H. Sweet, Esq. 4s. 6d.

5. Series B. Part II. Reprinted Glossaries. Containing seven Provincial English Glossaries, from various sources. 7s.

6. Series B. Part III. Ray's Collection of English Words not generally used, from the edition of 1691; together with Thoresby's Letter to Ray, 1703. Re-arranged and newly edited by Rev. Walter W. Skeat. 8s.

6*. Subscribers to the English Dialect Society for 1874 also receive a copy of 'A Dictionary of the Sussex Dialect.' By the Rev. W. D. Parish.

1875.

7. Series D. Part II. The Dialect of West Somerset. By F. T. Elworthy, Esq. 3s. 6d.

8. Series A. Part II. Containing a List of Books Relating to some of the Counties of England. 6s.

9. Series C. A Glossary of Words used in the Neighbourhood of Whitby. By F. K. Robinson. Part I. 7s. 6d.

10. Series C. A Glossary of the Dialect of Lancashire. By J. H. Nodal and G. Milner. Part I. 3s. 6d.

1876.

11. On the Survival of Early English Words in our Present Dialects. By Dr. R. Morris. 6d.

12. Series C. Original Glossaries. Part III. Containing Five Original Provincial English Glossaries. 7s.

13. Series C. A Glossary of Words used in the Neighbourhood of Whitby. By F. K. Robinson. Part II. 6s 6d.

14. A Glossary of Mid-Yorkshire Words, with a Grammar. By C. Clough Robinson. 9s.

1877.

15. A Glossary of Words used in the Wapentakes of Manley and Corringham, Lincolnshire. By Edward Peacock, F.S.A. 9s. 6d.

16. A Glossary of Holderness Words. By F. Ross, R. Stead, and T. Holderness. With a Map of the District. 4s.

17. On the Dialects of Eleven Southern and South-Western Counties, with a new Classification of the English Dialects. By Prince Louis Lucien Bonaparte. With Two Maps. 1s.

18. Bibliographical List. Part III. completing the Work, and containing a List of Books on Scottish Dialects, Anglo-Irish Dialect, Cant and Slang, and Americanisms, with additions to the English List and Index. Edited by J. H. Nodal. 4s. 6d.

19. An Outline of the Grammar of West Somerset. By F. T. Elworthy, Esq. 5s.

1878.

20. A Glossary of Cumberland Words and Phrases. By William Dickinson, F.L.S. 6s.

21. Tusser's Five Hundred Pointes of Good Husbandrie. Edited with Introduction, Notes and Glossary, by W. Payne and Sidney J. Herrtage, B.A. 12s. 6d.

22. A Dictionary of English Plant Names. By James Britten, F.L.S., and Robert Holland. Part I. (A to F). 8s. 6d.

1879.

23. Five Reprinted Glossaries, including Wiltshire, East Anglian, Suffolk, and East-Yorkshire Words, and Words from Bishop Kennett's *Parochial Antiquities*. Edited by the Rev. Professor Skeat, M.A. 7s.

24. Supplement to the Cumberland Glossary (No. 20). By W. Dickinson, F.L.S. 1s.

Etherington.—The Student's Grammar of the Hindí Language. By the Rev. W. Etherington, Missionary, Benares. Second edition. Crown 8vo. pp. xiv., 250, and xiii., cloth. 1873. 12s.

Faber.—A Systematical Digest of the Doctrines of Confucius, according to the Analects, Great Learning, and Doctrine of the Mean, with an Introduction on the Authorities upon Confucius and Confucianism. By Ernst Faber, Rhenish Missionary. Translated from the German by P. G. von Möllendorff. 8vo. sewed, pp. viii. and 131. 1875. 12s. 6d.

Facsimiles of Two Papyri found in a Tomb at Thebes. With a Translation by Samuel Birch, LL.D., F.S.A., Corresponding Member of the Institute of France, Academies of Berlin, Herculaneum, etc., and an Account of their Discovery. By A. Henry Rhind, Esq., F.S.A., etc. In large folio, pp. 30 of text, and 16 plates coloured, bound in cloth. 21s.

Fallon.—A New Hindustani-English Dictionary. With Illustrations from Hindustani Literature and Folk-lore. By S. W. Fallon, Ph.D. Halle. Parts I. to XIX. Roy. 8vo. Price 4s. 6d. each Part.

To be completed in about 25 Parts of 48 pages each Part, forming together One Volume.

Farley.—Egypt, Cyprus, and Asiatic Turkey. By J. Lewis Farley, Author of "The Resources of Turkey," etc. Demy 8vo. cl., pp. xvi.–270. 10s. 6d.

Fausböll.—The Dasaratha-Jātaka, being the Buddhist Story of King Rāma. The original Pāli Text, with a Translation and Notes by V. Fausböll. 8vo. sewed, pp. iv. and 48. 2s. 6d.

Fausböll.—Five Jātakas, containing a Fairy Tale, a Comical Story, and Three Fables. In the original Pāli Text, accompanied with a Translation and Notes. By V. Fausböll. 8vo. sewed, pp. viii. and 72. 6s.

Fausböll.—The Jātaka. The Original Pāli Text, with a Translation and Notes. By V. Fausböll. 8vo. sewed, pp. xiii. and 128. 7s. 6d.

Fausböll.—Jātaka. See under Jātaka.

Fiske.—Myths and Myth-Makers: Old Tales and Superstitions interpreted by Comparative Mythology. By John Fiske, M.A., Assistant Librarian, and late Lecturer on Philosophy at Harvard University. Crown 8vo. cloth, pp. viii. and 252. 10s. 6d.

Fornander.—An Account of the Polynesian Race: Its Origin and Migrations. By A. Fornander. Vol. I. Post 8vo., cloth. 7s. 6d.

Forsyth.—Report of a Mission to Yarkund in 1873, under Command of Sir T. D. Forsyth, K.C.S.I., C.B., Bengal Civil Service, with Historical and Geographical Information regarding the Possessions of the Ameer of Yarkund. With 45 Photographs, 4 Lithographic Plates, and a large Folding Map of Eastern Turkestan. 4to. cloth, pp. iv. and 573. £5 5s.

Foss.—Norwegian Grammar, with Exercises in the Norwegian and and English Languages, and a List of Irregular Verbs. By Frithjof Foss, Graduate of the University of Norway. Crown 8vo., pp. 40, cloth limp. 2s.

Foster.—Pre-Historic Races of the United States of America. By J. W. Foster, LL.D., Author of the "Physical Geography of the Mississippi Valley," etc. With 72 Illustrations. 8vo. cloth, pp. xvi. and 416. 14s.

Fryer.—Vuttodaya. (Exposition of Metre.) By Sangharakkhita Thera. A Pali Text, Edited, with Translation and Notes, by Major G. E. Fryer. 8vo. pp. 44. 2s. 6d.

Furnivall.—Education in Early England. Some Notes used as Forewords to a Collection of Treatises on "Manners and Meals in the Olden Time," for the Early English Text Society. By Frederick J. Furnivall, M.A., Trinity Hall, Cambridge, Member of Council of the Philological and Early English Text Societies. 8vo. sewed, pp. 74. 1s.

Garrett.—A Classical Dictionary of India, Illustrative of the Mythology, Philosophy, Literature, Antiquities, Arts, Manners, Customs, etc., of the Hindus. By John Garrett. 8vo. pp. x. and 793. cloth. 28s.

Garrett.—Supplement to the above Classical Dictionary of India. By John Garrett, Director of Public Instruction at Mysore. 8vo. cloth, pp. 160. 7s. 6d.

Gautama.—The Institutes of Gautama. *See Auctores Sanscriti.*

Gesenius.—Hebrew and English Lexicon of the Old Testament, including the Biblical Chaldee, from the Latin. By Edward Robinson. Fifth Edition. 8vo. cloth, pp. xii. and 1160. £1 16s.

Gesenius.—Hebrew Grammar. Translated from the Seventeenth Edition. By Dr. T. J. Conant. With Grammatical Exercises, and a Chrestomathy by the Translator. 8vo. cloth, pp. xvi.–364. £1.

Giles.—Chinese Sketches. By Herbert A. Giles, of H.B.M.'s China Consular Service. 8vo. cl., pp. 204. 10s. 6d.

Giles.—A Dictionary of Colloquial Idioms in the Mandarin Dialect. By Herbert A. Giles. 4to. pp. 65. £1 8s.

Giles.—Synoptical Studies in Chinese Character. By Herbert A. Giles. 8vo. pp. 118. 15s.

Giles.—Chinese without a Teacher. Being a Collection of Easy and Useful Sentences in the Mandarin Dialect. With a Vocabulary. By Herbert A. Giles. 12mo. pp. 60. 5s.

Giles.—Record of the Buddhistic Kingdoms. Translated from the Chinese by H. A. Giles, of H.M. Consular Service. 8vo. sewed, pp. x.–129. 5s.

Giles.—The San Tzu Ching; or, Three Character Classic; and the Ch'Jen Tsu Wen; or, Thousand Character Essay. Metrically Translated by Herbert A. Giles. 12mo. pp. 28. 2s. 6d.

Giles.—A Glossary of Reference on Subjects connected with the Far East. By H. A. Giles, of H.M. China Consular Service. 8vo. sewed, pp. v.–183. 7s. 6d.

Giles.—Hebrew and Christian Records. An Historical Enquiry concerning the Age and Authorship of the Old and New Testaments. By the Rev. Dr. Giles, Rector of Sutton, Surrey, and formerly Fellow of Corpus Christi College, Oxford. Now first published complete, 2 Vols. Vol. I., Hebrew Records; Vol. II., Christian Records. 8vo. cloth, pp. 442 and 440. 1877. 24s.

Gliddon.—Ancient Egypt, Her Monuments, Hieroglyphics, History, Archæology, and other subjects connected with Hieroglyphical Literature. By George R. Gliddon, late United States Consul, at Cairo. 10th Edition. Revised and Corrected, with an Appendix. 4to. sewed, pp. 68. 2s. 6d.

God.—Book of God. By ☉. 8vo. cloth. Vol. I.: The Apocalypse. pp. 647. 12s. 6d.—Vol. II. An Introduction to the Apocalypse, pp. 752. 14s.—Vol. III. A Commentary on the Apocalypse, pp. 854. 16s.

Goldstücker.—A Dictionary, Sanskrit and English, extended and improved from the Second Edition of the Dictionary of Professor H. H. Wilson, with his sanction and concurrence. Together with a Supplement, Grammatical Appendices, and an Index, serving as a Sanskrit-English Vocabulary. By Theodor Goldstücker. Parts I. to VI. 4to. pp. 400. 1856-1863. 6s. each.

Goldstücker.—Panini: His Place in Sanskrit Literature. An Investigation of some Literary and Chronological Questions which may be settled by a study of his Work. A separate impression of the Preface to the Facsimile of MS. No. 17 in the Library of Her Majesty's Home Government for India, which contains a portion of the Mânava-Kalpa-Sûtra, with the Commentary of Kumârila-Swâmin. By Theodor Goldstücker. Imperial 8vo. pp. 268, cloth. £2 2s.

Goldstücker.—On the Deficiencies in the Present Administration of Hindu Law; being a paper read at the Meeting of the East India Association on the 8th June, 1870. By Theodor Goldstücker, Professor of Sanskrit in University College, London, &c. Demy 8vo. pp. 56, sewed. 1s. 6d.

Gover.—The Folk-Songs of Southern India. By Charles E. Gover. 8vo. pp. xxiii. and 299, cloth. 10s. 6d.

Grammatography.—A Manual of Reference to the Alphabets of Ancient and Modern Languages. Based on the German Compilation of F. Ballhorn. Royal 8vo. pp. 80, cloth. 7s. 6d.

The "Grammatography" is offered to the public as a compendious introduction to the reading of the most important ancient and modern languages. Simple in its design, it will be consulted with advantage by the philological student, the amateur linguist, the bookseller, the corrector of the press, and the diligent compositor.

ALPHABETICAL INDEX.

Afghan (or Pushto).	Czechian (or Bohemian).	Hebrew (current hand).	Polish.
Amharic.	Danish.	Hebrew (Judæo-Ger-	Pushto (or Afghan).
Anglo-Saxon.	Demotic.	Hungarian. [man).	Romaic (Modern Greek
Arabic.	Estrangelo.	Illyrian.	Russian.
Arabic Ligatures.	Ethiopic.	Irish.	Runes.
Aramaic.	Etruscan.	Italian (Old).	Samaritan.
Archaic Characters.	Georgian.	Japanese.	Sanscrit.
Armenian.	German.	Javanese.	Servian.
Assyrian Cuneiform.	Glagolitic.	Lettish.	Slavonic (Old).
Bengali.	Gothic.	Mantshu.	Sorbian (or Wendish).
Bohemian (Czechian).	Greek.	Median Cuneiform.	Swedish.
Búgis.	Greek Ligatures.	Modern Greek (Romaic)	Syriac.
Burmese.	Greek (Archaic).	Mongolian.	Tamil.
Canarese (or Carnâtaca).	Gujerati (or Guzzeratte).	Numidian.	Telugu.
Chinese.	Hieratic.	Old Slavonic (or Cyrillic).	Tibetan.
Coptic.	Hieroglyphics.	Palmyrenian.	Turkish.
Croato-Glagolitic.	Hebrew	Persian.	Wallachian.
Cufic.	Hebrew (Archaic).	Persian Cuneiform.	Wendish (or Sorbian).
Cyrillic (or Old Slavonic).	Hebrew (Rabbinical).	Phœnician.	Zend.

Grassmann.—Wörterbuch zum Rig-Veda. Von Hermann Grassmann, Professor am Marienstifts-Gymnasium zu Stettin. 8vo. pp. 1775. £1 10s.

Green.—Shakespeare and the Emblem-Writers: an Exposition of their Similarities of Thought and Expression. Preceded by a View of the Emblem-Book Literature down to A.D. 1616. By Henry Green, M.A. In one volume, pp. xvi. 572, profusely illustrated with Woodcuts and Photolith. Plates, elegantly bound in cloth gilt, large medium 8vo. £1 11s. 6d.; large imperial 8vo. 1870. £2 12s. 6d.

Grey.—Handbook of African, Australian, and Polynesian Philology, as represented in the Library of His Excellency Sir George Grey, K.C.B., Her Majesty's High Commissioner of the Cape Colony. Classed, Annotated, and Edited by Sir George Grey and Dr. H. I. Bleek.

Vol. I. Part 1.—South Africa. 8vo. pp. 186. 20s.
Vol. I. Part 2.—Africa (North of the Tropic of Capricorn). 8vo. pp. 70. 4s.
Vol. I. Part 3.—Madagascar. 8vo. pp. 24. 2s.
Vol. II. Part 1.—Australia. 8vo. pp. iv. and 44. 3s.
Vol. II. Part 2.—Papuan Languages of the Loyalty Islands and New Hebrides, comprising those of the Islands of Nengone, Lifu, Aneitum, Tana, and others. 8vo. p. 12. 1s.
Vol. II. Part 3.—Fiji Islands and Rotuma (with Supplement to Part II., Papuan Languages, and Part I., Australia). 8vo. pp. 34. 2s.
Vol. II. Part 4.—New Zealand, the Chatham Islands, and Auckland Islands. 8vo. pp. 76. 7s.
Vol. II. Part 4 (continuation).—Polynesia and Borneo. 8vo. pp. 77-154. 7s.
Vol. III. Part 1.—Manuscripts and Incunables. 8vo. pp. viii. and 24. 2s.
Vol. IV. Part 1.—Early Printed Books. England. 8vo. pp. vi. and 266. 12s.

Grey.—Maori Mementos: being a Series of Addresses presented by the Native People to His Excellency Sir George Grey, K.C.B., F.R.S. With Introductory Remarks and Explanatory Notes; to which is added a small Collection of Laments, etc. By Ch. Oliver B. Davis. 8vo. pp. iv. and 228, cloth. 12s.

Griffin.—The Rajas of the Punjab. Being the History of the Principal States in the Punjab, and their Political Relations with the British Government. By Lepel H. Griffin, Bengal Civil Service, Under Secretary to the Government of the Punjab, Author of "The Punjab Chiefs," etc. Second edition. Royal 8vo., pp. xiv. and 630. 21s.

Griffis.—The Mikado's Empire. Book I. History of Japan from 660 B.C. to 1872 A.D. Book II. Personal Experiences, Observations, and Studies in Japan, 1870-74. By W. E. Griffis. Illustrated. 8vo. cl., pp. 626. £1.

Griffith.—Scenes from the Ramayana, Meghaduta, etc. Translated by Ralph T. H. Griffith, M.A., Principal of the Benares College. Second Edition. Crown 8vo. pp. xviii., 244, cloth. 6s.

Contents.—Preface—Ayodhya—Ravan Doomed—The Birth of Rama—The Heir apparent—Manthara's Guile—Dasaratha's Oath—The Step-mother—Mother and Son—The Triumph of Love—Farewell!—The Hermit's Son—The Trial of Truth—The Forest—The Rape of Sita—Rama's Despair—The Messenger Cloud—Khumbakarna—The Suppliant Dove—True Glory—Feed the Poor—The Wise Scholar.

Griffith.—The Rámáyan of Válmíki. Translated into English verse. By Ralph T. H. Griffith, M.A., Principal of the Benares College. 5 vols.

Vol. I., containing Books I. and II. Demy 8vo. pp. xxxii. 440, cloth. 1870. 18s.
Vol. II., containing Book II., with additional Notes and Index of Names. Demy 8vo. pp. 504, cloth. 18s.
Vol. III. Demy 8vo. pp. v. and 371, cloth. 1872. 15s.
Vol. IV. Demy 8vo. pp. viii. and 432. 1873. 18s.
Vol. V. Demy 8vo. pp. 368, cloth. 1875. 15s.

Griffith.—The Birth of the War God. A Poem by Kalidasa. Translated from the Sanskrit into English Verse. By Ralph T. H. Griffith, M.A., Principal of Benares College. Second edition, post 8vo. cloth, pp. xii. and 116. 5s.

Grout.—The Isizulu: a Grammar of the Zulu Language; accompanied with an Historical Introduction, also with an Appendix. By Rev. Lewis Grout. 8vo. pp. lii. and 432, cloth. 21s.

Gubernatis.—Zoological Mythology; or, the Legends of Animals. By Angelo de Gubernatis, Professor of Sanskrit and Comparative Literature in the Istituto di Studii Superiori e di Perfezionamento at Florence, etc. In 2 vols. 8vo. pp. xxvi. and 432, vii. and 442. 28s.

Gundert.—A Malayalam and English Dictionary. By Rev. H. Gundert, D. Ph. Royal 8vo. pp. viii. and 1116. £2 10s.

Haas.—Catalogue of Sanskrit and Pali Books in the Library of the British Museum. By Dr. Ernst Haas. Printed by Permission of the Trustees of the British Museum. 4to. cloth, pp. 200. £1 1s.

Háfiz of Shíráz.—Selections from his Poems. Translated from the Persian by Herman Bicknell. With Preface by A. S. Bicknell. Demy 4to., pp. xx. and 384, printed on fine stout plate-paper, with appropriate Oriental Bordering in gold and colour, and Illustrations by J. R. Herbert, R.A. £2 2s.

Haldeman.—Pennsylvania Dutch: a Dialect of South Germany with an Infusion of English. By S. S. Haldeman, A.M., Professor of Comparative Philology in the University of Pennsylvania, Philadelphia. 8vo. pp. viii. and 70, cloth. 1872. 3s. 6d.

Hall.—Modern English. By Fitzedward Hall, M.A., Hon. D.C.L., Oxon. Cr. 8vo. cloth, pp. xvi. and 394. 10s. 6d.

Hall.—On English Adjectives in -Able, with Special Reference to Reliable. By Fitzedward Hall, C.E., M.A., Hon. D.C.L. Oxon.; formerly Professor of Sanskrit Language and Literature, and of Indian Jurisprudence, in King's College, London. Crown 8vo. cloth, pp. viii. and 238. 7s. 6d.

Hans Breitmann.—See under Leland.

Hardy.—Christianity and Buddhism Compared. By the late Rev. R. Spence Hardy, Hon. Member Royal Asiatic Society. 8vo. sd. pp. 138. 6s.

Hassoun.—The Diwan of Hatim Tai. An Old Arabic Poet of the Sixth Century of the Christian Era. Edited by R. Hassoun. With Illustrations. 4to. pp. 43. 3s. 6d.

Haswell.—Grammatical Notes and Vocabulary of the Peguan Language. To which are added a few pages of Phrases, etc. By Rev. J. M. Haswell. 8vo. pp. xvi. and 160. 15s.

Haug.—The Book of Arda Viraf. The Pahlavi text prepared by Destur Hoshangji Jamaspji Asa. Revised and collated with further MSS., with an English translation and Introduction, and an Appendix containing the Texts and Translations of the Gosht-i Fryano and Hadokht Nask. By Martin Haug, Ph.D., Professor of Sanskrit and Comparative Philology at the University of Munich. Assisted by E. W. West, Ph.D. Published by order of the Bombay Government. 8vo. sewed, pp. lxxx., v., and 316. £1 5s.

Haug.—A Lecture on an Original Speech of Zoroaster (Yasna 45), with remarks on his age. By Martin Haug, Ph.D. 8vo. pp. 28, sewed. Bombay, 1865. 2s.

Haug.—The Aitareya Brahmanam of the Rig Veda: containing the Earliest Speculations of the Brahmans on the meaning of the Sacrificial Prayers, and on the Origin, Performance, and Sense of the Rites of the Vedic Religion. Edited, Translated, and Explained by Martin Haug, Ph.D., Superintendent of Sanskrit Studies in the Poona College, etc., etc. In 2 Vols. Crown 8vo. Vol. I. Contents, Sanskrit Text, with Preface, Introductory Essay, and a Map of the Sacrificial Compound at the Soma Sacrifice, pp. 312. Vol. II. Translation with Notes, pp. 544. £2 2s.

Haug.—AN OLD ZAND-PAHLAVI GLOSSARY. Edited in the Original Characters, with a Transliteration in Roman Letters, an English Translation, and an Alphabetical Index. By DESTUR HOSHENGJI JAMASPJI, High-priest of the Parsis in Malwa, India. Rev. with Notes and Intro. by MARTIN HAUG, Ph.D. Publ. by order of Gov. of Bombay. 8vo. sewed, pp. lvi. and 132. 15s.

Haug.—AN OLD PAHLAVI-PAZAND GLOSSARY. Ed., with Alphabetical Index, by DESTUR HOSHANGJI JAMASPJI ASA, High Priest of the Parsis in Malwa. Rev. and Enl., with Intro. Essay on the Pahlavi Language, by M. HAUG, Ph.D. Pub. by order of Gov. of Bombay. 8vo. pp. xvi. 152, 268, sd. 1870. 28s.

Haug.—ESSAYS ON THE SACRED LANGUAGE, WRITINGS, AND RELIGION OF THE PARSIS. By MARTIN HAUG, Ph.D., late Professor of Sanskrit and Comparative Philology at the University of Munich. Second Edition. Edited by E. W. WEST, Ph.D. Post 8vo. pp. xvi. and 428, cloth. 16s.

Hawken.—UPA-SASTRA: Comments, Linguistic and Doctrinal, on Sacred and Mythic Literature. By J. D. HAWKEN. 8vo. cloth, pp. viii.–288. 7s. 6d.

Heaviside.—AMERICAN ANTIQUITIES; or, the New World the Old, and the Old World the New. By JOHN T. C. HEAVISIDE. 8vo. pp. 46, sewed. 1s. 6d.

Hebrew Literature Society (Publications of). Subscription £1 1s. per Series. 1872-3. *First Series.*

Vol. I. Miscellany of Hebrew Literature. Demy 8vo. cloth, pp. viii. and 228. 10s.

Vol. II. The Commentary of Ibn Ezra on Isaiah. Edited from MSS., and Translated with Notes, Introductions, and Indexes, by M. FRIEDLÄNDER, Ph.D. Vol. I. Translation of the Commentary. Demy 8vo. cloth, pp. xxviii. and 332. 10s. 6d.

Vol. III. The Commentary of Ibn Ezra. Vol. II. The Anglican Version of the Book of the Prophet Isaiah amended according to the Commentary of Ibn Ezra. Demy 8vo. cloth, pp. 112. 4s. 6d.

1877. *Second Series.*

Vol. I. Miscellany of Hebrew Literature. Vol. II. Edited by the Rev. A. LÖWY. Demy 8vo. cloth, pp. vi. and 276. 10s. 6d.

Vol. II. The Commentary of Ibn Ezra. Vol. III. Demy 8vo. cloth, pp. 172. 7s.

Vol. III. Ibn Ezra Literature. Vol. IV. Essays on the Writings of Abraham Ibn Ezra. By M. FRIEDLÄNDER, Ph.D. Demy 8vo. cloth, pp. x.–252 and 78. 12s. 6d.

Hepburn.—A JAPANESE AND ENGLISH DICTIONARY. With an English and Japanese Index. By J. C. HEPBURN, M.D., LL.D. Second edition. Imperial 8vo. cloth, pp. xxxii., 632 and 201. £8 8s.

Hepburn.—JAPANESE-ENGLISH AND ENGLISH-JAPANESE DICTIONARY. By J. C. HEPBURN, M.D., LL.D. Abridged by the Author from his larger work. Small 4to. cloth, pp. vi. and 206. 1873. 18s.

Hernisz.—A GUIDE TO CONVERSATION IN THE ENGLISH AND CHINESE LANGUAGES, for the use of Americans and Chinese in California and elsewhere. By STANISLAS HERNISZ. Square 8vo. pp. 274, sewed. 10s. 6d.

The Chinese characters contained in this work are from the collections of Chinese groups, engraved on steel, and cast into moveable types, by Mr. Marcellin Legrand, engraver of the Imperial Printing Office at Paris. They are used by most of the missions to China.

Hincks.—SPECIMEN CHAPTERS OF AN ASSYRIAN GRAMMAR. By the late Rev. E. HINCKS, D.D., Hon. M.R.A.S. 8vo., pp. 44, sewed. 1s.

Hodgson.—ESSAYS ON THE LANGUAGES, LITERATURE, AND RELIGION OF NEPAL AND TIBET; together with further Papers on the Geography, Ethnology, and Commerce of those Countries. By B. H. HODGSON, late British Minister at Nepal. Royal 8vo. cloth, pp. 288. 14s.

Hoffmann.—Shopping Dialogues, in Japanese, Dutch, and English. By Professor J. Hoffmann. Oblong 8vo. pp. xiii. and 44, sewed. 3s.

Hoffmann, J. J.—A Japanese Grammar. Second Edition. Large 8vo. cloth, pp. viii. and 352, with two plates. £1 1s.

Holbein Society.—Subscription £1 1s. per annum. A List of Publications to be had on application.

Hopkins.—Elementary Grammar of the Turkish Language. With a few Easy Exercises. By F. L. Hopkins, M.A., Fellow and Tutor of Trinity Hall, Cambridge. Cr. 8vo. cloth, pp. 48. 3s. 6d.

Howse.—A Grammar of the Cree Language. With which is combined an analysis of the Chippeway Dialect. By Joseph Howse, Esq., F.R.G.S. 8vo. pp. xx. and 324, cloth. 7s. 6d.

Hunter.—A Statistical Account of Bengal. By W. W. Hunter, B.A., LL.D. Director-General of Statistics to the Government of India; one of the Council of the Royal Asiatic Society; M.R.G.S.; and Honorary Member of various Learned Societies.

VOL.
I. 24 Parganas and Sundarbans.
II. Nadiya and Jessor.
III. Midnapur, Hugli and Howrah.
IV. Bardwan, Birbhum and Bankura.
V. Dacca, Bakarganj, Faridpur and Maimansinh.
VI. Chittagong Hill Tracts, Chittagong, Noakhali, Tipperah, and Hill Tipperah State.
VII. Maldah, Rangpur and Dinajpur.
VIII. Rajshahi and Bogra.
IX. Murshidabad and Pabna.
X. Darjiling, Jalpaiguri and Kuch Behar State.
XI. Patna and Saran.
XII. Gaya and Shahabad.
XIII. Tirhut and Champaran.
XIV. Bhagalpur and Santal Parganas.
XV. Monghyr and Purniah.
XVI. Hazaribagh and Lohardaga.
XVII. Singbhum, Chutia, Nagpur Tributary States and Manbhum.
XVIII. Cuttack and Balasore.
XIX. Puri and Orissa Tributary States.
XX. Fisheries, Botany, and General Index.

Published by command of the Government of India. In 20 Vols. 8vo. half-morocco. £5.

Hunter (F. M.)—An Account of the British Settlement of Aden in Arabia. Compiled by Captain F. M. Hunter, F.R.G.S., F.R.A.S., Assistant Political Resident, Aden. Demy 8vo. half-morocco, pp. xii. 232. 7s. 6d.

Ikhwánu-s Safá; or, Brothers of Purity. Describing the Contention between Men and Beasts as to the Superiority of the Human Race. Translated from the Hindustani by Professor J. Dowson, Staff College, Sandhurst. Crown 8vo. pp. viii. and 156, cloth. 7s.

Indian Antiquary (The).—A Journal of Oriental Research in Archæology, History, Literature, Languages, Philosophy, Religion, Folklore, etc. Edited by James Burgess, M.R.A.S., F.R.G.S. 4to. Published 12 numbers per annum. Subscription £2.

Ingleby.—Shakespeare: the Man and the Book. By C. M. Ingleby, M.A., LL.D. 8vo. boards, pp. 172. 6s.

Inman.—Ancient Pagan and Modern Christian Symbolism Exposed and Explained. By Thomas Inman, M.D. Second Edition. With Illustrations. Demy 8vo. cloth, pp. xl. and 148. 1874. 7s. 6d.

Jaiminiya-Nyáya-Málá-Vistara.—See under Auctores Sanscriti.

Jami, Mulla.—Salámán U Absál. An Allegorical Romance; being one of the Seven Poems entitled the Haft Aurang of Mulla Jami, now first edited from the Collation of Eight Manuscripts in the Library of the India House, and in private collections, with various readings, by Forbes Falconer, M.A., M.R.A.S. 4to. cloth, pp. 92. 1850. 7s. 6d.

Jataka (The); together with its Commentary. Being Tales of the Anterior Birth of Gotama Buddha. For the first time Edited in the original Pali by V. Fausboll, and Translated by T. W. Rhys Davids. Vol. I. Text. Demy 8vo. cloth, pp. 512. 28s.

The "Jataka" is a collection of legends in Pali, relating the history of Buddha's transmigrations before he was born as Gotama. The great antiquity of this work is authenticated by its forming part of the sacred canon of the Southern Buddhists, which was finally settled at the last Council in 246 B.C. The collection has long been known as a storehouse of ancient fables, and as the most original attainable source to which almost the whole of this kind of literature, from the Panchatantra and Pilpay's fables down to the nursery stories of the present day, is traceable; and it has been considered desirable, in the interest of Buddhistic studies as well as for more general literary purposes, that an edition and translation of the complete work should be prepared. The present publication is intended to supply this want.—*Athenæum.*

Jenkins's Vest-Pocket Lexicon.—An English Dictionary of all except Familiar Words; including the principal Scientific and Technical Terms, and Foreign Moneys, Weights and Measures. By James Jenkins. 64mo., pp. 564, cloth. 1s. 6d.

Johnson.—Oriental Religions. *See* Trübner's Oriental Series.

Kalid-i-Afghani.—Translation of the Kalid-i-Afghani, the Text-book for the Pakkhto Examination, with Notes, Historical, Geographical, Grammatical, and Explanatory. By Trevor Chichele Plowden. Imp. 8vo. pp. xx. and 406, with a Map. *Lahore*, 1875. £2 2s.

Kâśikâ.—A Commentary on Pâṇini's Grammatical Aphorisms. By Pandit Jayâditya. Edited by Pandit Bâla Śâstrî, Prof. Sansk. Coll., Benares. First part. 8vo. pp. 490. 16s.

Kellogg.—A Grammar of the Hindi Language, in which are treated the Standard Hindî, Braj, and the Eastern Hindî of the Ramayan of Tulsi Das; also the Colloquial Dialects of Marwar, Kumaon, Avadh, Baghelkhand, Bhojpur, etc., with Copious Philological Notes. By the Rev. S. H. Kellogg, M.A. Royal 8vo. cloth, pp. 400. 21s.

Kern.—The Âryabhaṭîya, with the Commentary Bhaṭadîpikâ of Paramâdiçvara, edited by Dr. H. Kern. 4to. pp. xii. and 107. 9s.

Kern.—The Bṛhat-Sanhitâ; or, Complete System of Natural Astrology of Varâha-Mihira. Translated from Sanskrit into English by Dr. H. Kern, Professor of Sanskrit at the University of Leyden. Part I. 8vo. pp. 50, stitched. Parts 2 and 3 pp. 51–154. Part 4 pp. 155–210. Part 5 pp. 211–266. Part 6 pp. 267–330. Price 2s. each part. [*Will be completed in Nine Parts.*

Khirad-Afroz (The Illuminator of the Understanding). By Maulavî Hafîzu'd-dîn. A new edition of the Hindûstânî Text, carefully revised, with Notes, Critical and Explanatory. By Edward B. Eastwick, M.P., F.R.S., F.S.A., M.R.A.S., Professor of Hindûstânî at the late East India Company's College at Haileybury. 8vo. cloth, pp. xiv. and 321. 18s.

Kidd.—Catalogue of the Chinese Library of the Royal Asiatic Society. By the Rev. S. Kidd. 8vo. pp. 58, sewed. 1s.

Kielhorn.—A Grammar of the Sanskrit Language. By F. Kielhorn, Ph.D., Superintendent of Sanskrit Studies in Deccan College. Registered under Act xxv of 1867. Demy 8vo. pp. xvi. 260. cloth. 1870. 10s. 6d.

Kielhorn.—Kâtyâyana and Patanjali. Their Relation to each other and to Panini. By F. Kielhorn, Ph. D., Prof. of Orient. Lang. Poona. 8vo. pp. 64. 1876. 2s. 6d.

Kilgour.—The Hebrew or Iberian Race, including the Pelasgians, the Phenicians, the Jews, the British, and others. By Henry Kilgour. 8vo. sewed, pp. 76. 1872. 2s. 6d.

Kistner.—Buddha and his Doctrines. A Bibliographical Essay. By Otto Kistner. Imperial 8vo., pp. iv. and 32, sewed. 2s. 6d.

Koch.—A Historical Grammar of the English Language. By C. F. Koch. Translated into English. Edited, Enlarged, and Annotated by the Rev. R. Morris, LL.D., M.A. [*Nearly ready.*

Koran (The). Arabic text, lithographed in Oudh, A.H. 1284 (1867). 16mo. pp. 942. 7s. 6d.

Koran (The).—*See* Sale, and Trubner's Oriental Series.

Kramers' New Pocket Dictionary of the English and Dutch Languages. Royal 32mo. cloth, pp. xvi. and 714. 4s.

Kroeger.—The Minnesinger of Germany. By A. E. Kroeger. 12mo. cloth, pp. vi and 284. 7s.

Contents.—Chapter I. The Minnesinger and the Minnesong.—II. The Minnelay.—III. The Divine Minnesong.—IV. Walther von der Vogelweide.—V. Ulrich von Lichtenstein.—VI. The Metrical Romances of the Minnesinger and Gottfried von Strassburg's "Tristan and Isolde."

Lacombe.—Dictionnaire et Grammaire de la Langue des Cris, *par le* Rev. Père Alb. Lacombe. 8vo. paper, pp. xx. and 713, iv. and 190. 21s.

Laghu Kaumudí. A Sanskrit Grammar. By Varadarája. With an English Version, Commentary, and References. By James R. Ballantyne, LL.D., Principal of the Sanskrit College, Benares. 8vo. pp. xxxvi. and 424, cloth. £1 11s. 6d.

Land.—The Principles of Hebrew Grammar. By J. P. N. Land, Professor of Logic and Metaphysics in the University of Leyden. Translated from the Dutch by Reginald Lane Poole, Balliol College, Oxford. Part I. Sounds. Part II. Words. Crown 8vo. pp. xx. and 220, cloth. 7s. 6d.

Legge.—Confucianism in Relation to Christianity. A Paper Read before the Missionary Conference in Shanghai, on May 11, 1877. By Rev. James Legge, D.D., LL.D. 8vo. sewed, pp. 12. 1877. 1s. 6d.

Legge.—The Chinese Classics. With a Translation, Critical and Exegetical Notes, Prolegomena, and Copious Indexes. By James Legge, D.D., of the London Missionary Society. In seven vols.

Vol. I. containing Confucian Analects, the Great Learning, and the Doctrine of the Mean. 8vo. pp. 526, cloth. £2 2s.

Vol. II., containing the Works of Mencius. 8vo. pp. 634, cloth. £2 2s.

Vol. III. Part I. containing the First Part of the Shoo-King, or the Books of Tang, the Books of Yu, the Books of Hea, the Books of Shang, and the Prolegomena. Royal 8vo. pp. viii. and 280, cloth. £2 2s.

Vol. III. Part II. containing the Fifth Part of the Shoo-King, or the Books of Chow, and the Indexes. Royal 8vo. pp. 281—736, cloth. £2 2s.

Vol. IV. Part I. containing the First Part of the She-King, or the Lessons from the States; and the Prolegomena. Royal 8vo. cloth, pp. 182-244. £2 2s.

Vol. IV. Part II. containing the 2nd, 3rd and 4th Parts of the She-King, or the Minor Odes of the Kingdom, the Greater Odes of the Kingdom, the Sacrificial Odes and Praise-Songs, and the Indexes. Royal 8vo. cloth, pp. 540. £2 2s.

Vol. V. Part I. containing Dukes Yin, Hwan, Chwang, Min, He, Wan, Seuen, and Ch'ing; and the Prolegomena. Royal 8vo. cloth, pp. xii., 148 and 410. £2 2s.

Vol. V. Part II. Contents:—Dukes Seang, Ch'aou, Ting, and Gai, with Tso's Appendix, and the Indexes. Royal 8vo. cloth, pp. 526. £2 2s.

Legge.—The Chinese Classics. Translated into English. With Preliminary Essays and Explanatory Notes. By James Legge, D.D., LL.D.

Vol. I. The Life and Teachings of Confucius. Crown 8vo. cloth, pp. vi. and 338. 10s. 6d.

Vol. II. The Life and Works of Mencius. Crown 8vo. cloth, pp. 412. 12s.

Vol. III. The She King, or The Book of Poetry. Crown 8vo., cloth, pp. viii. and 432. 12s.

Legge.—Inaugural Lecture on the Constituting of a Chinese Chair in the University of Oxford. Delivered in the Sheldonian Theatre, Oct. 27th, 1876, by Rev. James Legge, M.A., LL.D., Professor of the Chinese Language and Literature at Oxford. 8vo. pp. 28, sewed. 6d.

Leigh.—The Religion of the World. By H. Stone Leigh. 12mo. pp. xii. 66, cloth. 1869. 2s. 6d.

Leitner.—Introduction to a Philosophical Grammar of Arabic. Being an Attempt to Discover a Few Simple Principles in Arabic Grammar. By G. W. Leitner. 8vo. sewed, pp. 52. *Lahore.* 4s.

Leitner.—Sinin-I-Islam. Being a Sketch of the History and Literature of Muhammadanism and their place in Universal History. *For the use of Maulvis.* By G. W. Leitner. Part I. The *Early History of Arabia to the fall of the Abbassides.* 8vo. sewed. *Lahore.* 6s.

Leland.—The English Gipsies and their Language. By Charles G. Leland. Second Edition. Crown 8vo. cloth, pp. 276. 7s. 6d.

Leland.—The Breitmann Ballads. The only Authorized Edition. Complete in 1 vol., including Nineteen Ballads illustrating his Travels in Europe (never before printed), with Comments by *Fritz Schwackenhammer.* By Charles G. Leland. Crown 8vo. handsomely bound in cloth, pp. xxviii. and 292. 6s.

Hans Breitmann's Party. With other Ballads. By Charles G. Leland. Tenth Edition. Square, pp. xvi. and 74, cloth. 2s. 6d.

Hans Breitmann's Christmas. With other Ballads. By Charles G. Leland. Second edition. Square, pp. 80, sewed. 1s.

Hans Breitmann as a Politician. By Charles G. Leland. Second edition. Square, pp. 72, sewed. 1s.

Hans Breitmann in Church. With other Ballads. By Charles G. Leland. With an Introduction and Glossary. Second edition. Square, pp. 80, sewed. 1s.

Hans Breitmann as an Uhlan. Six New Ballads, with a Glossary. Square, pp. 72, sewed. 1s.

Leland.—Fusang; or, the Discovery of America by Chinese Buddhist Priests in the Fifth Century. By Charles G. Leland. Cr. 8vo. cloth, pp. xix. and 212. 7s. 6d.

Leland.—English Gipsy Songs. In Rommany, with Metrical English Translations. By Charles G. Leland, Author of "The English Gipsies," etc.; Prof. E. H. Palmer; and Janet Tuckey. Crown 8vo. cloth, pp. xii. and 276. 7s. 6d.

Leland.—Pidgin-English Sing-Song; or Songs and Stories in the China-English Dialect. With a Vocabulary. By Charles G. Leland. Fcap. 8vo. cl., pp. viii. and 140. 1876. 5s.

Leo.—Four Chapters of North's Plutarch. Containing the Lives of Caius Marcius Coriolanus, Julius Cæsar, Marcus Antonius, and Marcus Brutus, as Sources to Shakespeare's Tragedies, Coriolanus, Julius Cæsar, and Antony and Cleopatra; and partly to Hamlet and Timon of Athens. Photolithographed in the size of the Edition of 1595. With Preface, Notes comparing the Text of the Editions of 1579, 1595, 1603, and 1612; and Reference Notes to the Text of the Tragedies of Shakespeare. Edited by Prof. F. A. Leo, Ph.D. In one volume, folio, elegantly bound, pp. 22 of letterpress and 130 pp. of facsimiles. £1 11s. 6d.

The Library Edition is limited to 250 copies, at the price £1 11s. 6d.

Of the Amateur Edition 50 copies have been struck off on a superior large hand-made paper, price £3 3s. per copy.

Leonowens.—The English Governess at the Siamese Court: being Recollections of six years in the Royal Palace at Bangkok. By Anna Harriette Leonowens. With Illustrations from Photographs presented to the Author by the King of Siam. 8vo. cloth, pp. x. and 332. 1870. 12s.

Leonowens.—The Romance of Siamese Harem Life. By Mrs. Anna H. Leonowens, Author of "The English Governess at the Siamese Court." With 17 Illustrations, principally from Photographs, by the permission of J. Thomson, Esq. Crown 8vo. cloth, pp. viii. and 278. 14s.

Literature.—Transactions of the Royal Society of Literature of the United Kingdom. First Series, 6 parts in 3 vols. 4to. plates; 1827-39. Second Series, 10 vols. or 30 parts, and vol. xi. parts 1 and 2, 8vo. plates, 1843-76. A complete set, as far as published, £10 10s. A list of the contents of the volumes and parts on application.

Lobscheid.—English and Chinese Dictionary, with the Punti and Mandarin Pronunciation. By the Rev. W. Lobscheid, Knight of Francis Joseph, C.M.I.R.G.S.A., N.Z.B.S.V., etc. Folio, pp. viii. and 2016. In Four Parts. £8 8s.

Lobscheid.—Chinese and English Dictionary, Arranged according to the Radicals. By the Rev. W. Lobscheid, Knight of Francis Joseph, C.M.I.R.G.S.A., N.Z.B.S.V., &c. 1 vol. imp. 8vo. double columns, pp. 600, bound. £2 8s.

Ludewig.—The Literature of American Aboriginal Languages. By Hermann E. Ludewig. With Additions and Corrections by Professor Wm. W. Turner. Edited by Nicolas Trübner. 8vo. fly and general Title, 2 leaves; Dr. Ludewig's Preface, pp. v.—viii.; Editor's Preface, pp. iv.—xii.; Biographical Memoir of Dr. Ludewig, pp. xiii.—xiv.; and Introductory Biographical Notices, pp. xiv.—xxiv., followed by List of Contents. Then follow Dr. Ludewig's Bibliotheca Glottica, alphabetically arranged, with Additions by the Editor, pp. 1—209; Professor Turner's Additions, with those of the Editor to the same, also alphabetically arranged, pp. 210—246; Index, pp. 247—256; and List of Errata, pp. 257, 258. Handsomely bound in cloth. 10s. 6d.

Luzzatto.—Grammar of the Biblical Chaldaic Language and the Talmud Babylonical Idioms. By S. D. Luzzatto. Translated from the Italian by J. S. Goldammer. Cr. 8vo. cl., pp. 122. 7s. 6d.

Macgowan.—A Manual of the Amoy Colloquial. By Rev. J. Macgowan, of the London Missionary Society. 8vo. sewed, pp. xvii. and 200. Amoy, 1871. £1 1s.

Mackay.—The Gaelic Etymology of the Languages of Western Europe, and more especially of the English and Lowland Scotch, and of their Slang, Cant, and Colloquial Dialects. By Charles Mackay, LL.D. Royal 8vo. cloth, pp. xxxii. and 604. 42s.

McClatchie. — A Translation of Section Forty-nine of the "Complete Works" of the Philosopher Choo-Foo-Tze, with Explanatory Notes. By the Rev. Thomas McClatchie, M.A. Small 4to. pp. xviii. and 162. 18s. 6d.

Maclay and Baldwin.—An Alphabetic Dictionary of the Chinese Language of the Foochow Dialect. By Rev. R. S. Maclay, D.D., of the Methodist Episcopal Mission, and Rev. C. C. Baldwin, A.M., of the American Board of Mission. 8vo. half-bound, pp. 1132. Foochow, 1871. £4 4s.

Mahabharata. Translated into Hindi for Madan Mohun Bhatt, by Krishnachandradharmadhikarin of Benares. (Containing all but the Harivansa.) 3 vols. 8vo. cloth, pp. 574, 810, and 1106. £3 3s.

Maha-Vira-Charita; or, the Adventures of the Great Hero Rama. An Indian Drama in Seven Acts. Translated into English Prose from the Sanskrit of Bhavabhûti. By John Pickford, M.A. Crown 8vo. cloth. 5s.

Mainyo-i-Khard (The Book of the).—The Pazand and Sanskrit Texts (in Roman characters) as arranged by Neriosengh Dhaval, in the fifteenth century. With an English translation, a Glossary of the Pazand texts, containing the Sanskrit, Persian, and Pahlavi equivalents, a sketch of Pazand Grammar, and an Introduction. By E. W. West. 8vo. sewed, pp. 484. 1871. 16s.

Maltby.—A Practical Handbook of the Uriya or Odiya Language. By Thomas J. Maltby, Esq., Madras C.S. 8vo. pp. xiii. and 201. 1874. 10s. 6d.

Manava-Kalpa-Sutra; being a portion of this ancient Work on Vaidik Rites, together with the Commentary of Kumarila-Swamin. A Facsimile of the MS. No. 17, in the Library of Her Majesty's Home Government for India. With a Preface by Theodor Goldstücker. Oblong folio, pp. 268 of letterpress and 121 leaves of facsimiles. Cloth. £4 4s.

Manipulus Vocabulorum; A Rhyming Dictionary of the English Language. By Peter Levins (1570). Edited, with an Alphabetical Index, by Henry B. Wheatley. 8vo. pp. xvi. and 370, cloth. 14s.

Manning.—An Inquiry into the Character and Origin of the Possessive Augment in English and in Cognate Dialects. By the late James Manning, Q.A.S., Recorder of Oxford. 8vo. pp. iv. and 90. 2s.

March.—A Comparative Grammar of the Anglo-Saxon Language; in which its forms are illustrated by those of the Sanskrit, Greek, Latin, Gothic, Old Saxon, Old Friesic, Old Norse, and Old High-German. By Francis A. March, LL.D. Demy 8vo. cloth. pp. xi. and 253. 1877. 10s.

Mariette.—The Monuments of Upper Egypt. A Translation of the Itinéraire de la Haute Egypte, of Auguste Mariette Bey. By Alphonse Mariette. Fcap. 8vo. cloth, pp. viii.–261. 7s. 6d.

Markham.—Quichua Grammar and Dictionary. Contributions towards a Grammar and Dictionary of Quichua, the Language of the Yncas of Peru; collected by Clements R. Markham, F.S.A., Corr. Mem. of the University of Chile, Author of "Cuzco and Lima," and "Travels in Peru and India." In one vol. crown 8vo., pp. 223, cloth. £1. 11s. 6d.

Markham.—Ollanta: A Drama in the Quichua Language. Text, Translation, and Introduction. By Clements R. Markham, F.R.G.S. Crown 8vo., pp. 128, cloth. 7s. 6d.

Markham.—A Memoir of the Lady Ana de Osorio, Countess of Chinchon, and Vice-Queen of Peru, A.D. 1629–39. With a Plea for the Correct Spelling of the Chinchona Genus. By Clements R. Markham, C.B., F.R.S., Commendador da Real Ordem de Christo, Socius Academiæ Cæsareæ Naturæ Curiosorum Cognomen Chinchon. Small 4to, pp. 112. With a Map, 2 Plates, and numerous Illustrations. Roxburghe binding. 28s.

Markham.—The Narratives of the Mission of George Bogle, B.C.S., to the Teshu Lama, and of the Journey of Thomas Manning to Lhasa. Edited, with Notes and Introduction, and lives of Mr. Bogle and Mr. Manning, by Clements R. Markham, C.B., F.R.S. Demy 8vo., with Maps and Illustrations, pp. clxi. 314, cl. 21s.

Marsden's Numismata Orientalia. New International Edition. See under Numismata Orientalia.

Mason.—THE PALI TEXT OF KACHCHAYANO'S GRAMMAR, WITH ENGLISH ANNOTATIONS. By FRANCIS MASON, D.D. I. The Text Aphorisms, 1 to 673. II. The English Annotations, including the various Readings of six independent Burmese Manuscripts, the Singalese Text on Verbs, and the Cambodian Text on Syntax. To which is added a Concordance of the Aphorisms. In Two Parts. 8vo. sewed, pp. 208, 75, and 28. Toungoo, 1871. £1 11s. 6d.

Mathews.—ABRAHAM BEN EZRA'S UNEDITED COMMENTARY ON THE CANTICLES, the Hebrew Text after two MS., with English Translation by H. J. MATHEWS, B.A., Exeter College, Oxford. 8vo. cl. limp, pp. x., 34, 24. 2s. 6d.

Mathuráprasáda Misra.—A TRILINGUAL DICTIONARY, being a comprehensive Lexicon in English, Urdú, and Hindí, exhibiting the Syllabication, Pronunciation, and Etymology of English Words, with their Explanation in English, and in Urdú and Hindí in the Roman Character. By MATHURÁPRASÁDA MISRA, Second Master, Queen's College, Benares. 8vo. pp. xv. and 1330, cloth. Benares, 1865. £2 2s.

Matthews.—ETHNOLOGY AND PHILOLOGY OF THE HIDATSA INDIANS. By WASHINGTON MATTHEWS, Assistant Surgeon, U.S. Army. *Contents*:—Ethnography, Philology, Grammar, Dictionary, and English-Hidatsa Vocabulary. 8vo cloth. £1 11s. 6d.

Mayers.—ILLUSTRATIONS OF THE LAMAIST SYSTEM IN TIBET, drawn from Chinese Sources. By WILLIAM FREDERICK MAYERS, Esq., of Her Britannic Majesty's Consular Service, China. 8vo. pp. 24, sewed. 1869. 1s. 6d.

Mayers.—THE CHINESE READER'S MANUAL. A Handbook of Biographical, Historical, Mythological, and General Literary Reference. By W. F. MAYERS, Chinese Secretary to H. B. M.'s Legation at Peking, F.R.G.S., etc., etc. Demy 8vo. pp. xxiv. and 440. £1 5s.

Mayers.—TREATIES BETWEEN THE EMPIRE OF CHINA AND FOREIGN POWERS, together with Regulations for the Conduct of Foreign Trade, etc. Edited by W. F. MAYERS, Chinese Secretary to H.B.M.'s Legation at Peking. 8vo. cloth, pp. 246. 1877. 25s.

Mayers.—THE CHINESE GOVERNMENT. A Manual of Chinese Titles, Categorically arranged, and Explained with an Appendix. By W. F. MAYERS, Chinese Secretary to H.B.M.'s Legation at Peking. Royal 8vo. cloth, pp. viii.-160. 1878. £1 4s.

Mayers.—THE ANGLO-CHINESE CALENDAR MANUAL. A Handbook of Reference for the Determination of Chinese Dates during the period from 1860 to 1879. With Comparative Tables of Annual and Mensual Designations, etc. Compiled by W. F. MAYERS, Chinese Secretary, H.B.M.'s Legation, Peking. 2nd Edition. Sewed, pp. 28. 7s. 6d.

Medhurst.—CHINESE DIALOGUES, QUESTIONS, and FAMILIAR SENTENCES, literally translated into English, with a view to promote commercial intercourse and assist beginners in the Language. By the late W. H. MEDHURST, D.D. A new and enlarged Edition. 8vo. pp. 226. 18s.

Megasthenês.—ANCIENT INDIA AS DESCRIBED BY MEGASTHENÊS AND ARRIAN. Being a Translation of the Fragments of the Indika of Megasthenês collected by Dr. SCHWANBECK, and of the First Part of the Indika of Arrian. By J. W. MCCRINDLE, M.A., Principal of the Government College, Patna, etc. With Introduction, Notes, and Map of Ancient India. Post 8vo. cloth, pp. xii.-224. 1877. 7s. 6d.

Megha-Duta (The). (Cloud-Messenger.) By Kâlidâsa. Translated from the Sanskrit into English verse, with Notes and Illustrations. By the late H. H. WILSON, M.A., F.R.S., Boden Professor of Sanskrit in the University of Oxford, etc., etc. The Vocabulary by FRANCIS JOHNSON, sometime Professor of Oriental Languages at the College of the Honourable the East India Company, Haileybury. New Edition. 4to. cloth, pp. xi. and 180. 10s. 6d.

Memoirs read before the Anthropological Society of London, 1863-1864. 8vo., pp. 542, cloth. 21s.

Memoirs read before the Anthropological Society of London, 1865-6. Vol II. 8vo., pp. x. 464, cloth. 21s.

Mills.—The Indian Saint; or, Buddha and Buddhism.—A Sketch Historical and Critical. By C. D. B. Mills. 8vo. cl., pp. 192. 7s. 6d.

Minocheherji.—Pahlavi, Gujarati, and English Dictionary. By Jamaspji Dastur Minocheherji Jamasp Asana, Fellow of the University of Bombay, and Member of the Bombay Branch of the Royal Asiatic Society. Vol. I. (To be completed in three volumes.) Demy 8vo. pp. clxxiv and 168, with Photographic Portrait of the Author. 14s.

Mirkhond.—The History of the Atábeks of Syria and Persia. By Muhammed Ben Kháwendshah Ben Mahmud, commonly called Mirkhond. Now first Edited from the Collation of Sixteen MSS., by W. H. Morley, Barrister-at-law, M.R.A.S. To which is added a Series of Facsimiles of the Coins struck by the Atábeks, arranged and described by W. S. W. Vaux, M.A., M.R.A.S. Roy. 8vo. cloth, 7 plates, pp. 118. 1848. 7s. 6d.

Mitra.—The Antiquities of Orissa. By Rajendralala Mitra. Vol. I. Published under Orders of the Government of India. Folio, cloth, pp. 160. With a Map and 36 Plates. £4 4s.

Molesworth.—A Dictionary, Marathi and English. Compiled by J. T. Molesworth assisted by George and Thomas Candy. Second Edition, revised and enlarged. By J. T. Molesworth. Royal 4to. pp. xxx and 922, boards. Bombay, 1857. £3 3s.

Molesworth.—A Compendium of Molesworth's Marathi and English Dictionary. By Baba Padmanji. Second Edition. Revised and Enlarged. Demy 8vo. cloth, pp. xx. and 624. 21s.

Möllendorff.—Manual of Chinese Bibliography, being a List of Works and Essays relating to China. By P. G. and O. F. von Möllendorff, Interpreters to H.I.G.M.'s Consulates at Shanghai and Tientsin. 8vo. pp. viii. and 378. £1 10s.

Morley.—A Descriptive Catalogue of the Historical Manuscripts in the Arabic and Persian Languages preserved in the Library of the Royal Asiatic Society of Great Britain and Ireland. By William H. Morley, M.R.A.S. 8vo. pp. viii. and 160, sewed. London, 1854. 2s. 6d.

Morris.—A Descriptive and Historical Account of the Godavery District in the Presidency of Madras. By Henry Morris, formerly of the Madras Civil Service. Author of a "History of India for Use in Schools" and other works. 8vo. cloth (with a map), pp. xii. and 390. 1878. 12s.

Morrison.—A Dictionary of the Chinese Language. By the Rev. R. Morrison, D.D. Two vols. Vol. I. pp. x. and 762; Vol. II. pp. 828, cloth. Shanghae, 1865. £6 6s.

Muhammed.—The Life of Muhammed. Based on Muhammed Ibn Ishak. By Abd El Malik Ibn Hisham. Edited by Dr. Ferdinand Wüstenfeld. The Arabic Text. 8vo. pp. 1026, sewed. Price 21s. Introduction, Notes, and Index in German. 8vo. pp. lxxii. and 266, sewed. 7s. 6d. Each part sold separately.

The text based on the Manuscripts of the Berlin, Leipsic, Gotha and Leyden Libraries, has been carefully revised by the learned editor, and printed with the utmost exactness.

Muir.—Original Sanskrit Texts, on the Origin and History of the People of India, their Religion and Institutions. Collected, Translated, and Illustrated by John Muir, Esq., D.C.L., LL.D., Ph.D.

Vol. I. Mythical and Legendary Accounts of the Origin of Caste, with an Inquiry into its existence in the Vedic Age. Second Edition, re-written and greatly enlarged. 8vo. pp. xx. 532, cloth. 1868. 21s.

Vol. II. The Trans-Himalayan Origin of the Hindus, and their Affinity with the Western Branches of the Aryan Race. Second Edition, revised, with Additions. 8vo. pp. xxxii. and 512, cloth. 1871. 21s.

Vol. III. The Vedas: Opinions of their Authors, and of later Indian Writers, on their Origin, Inspiration, and Authority. Second Edition, revised and enlarged. 8vo. pp. xxxii. 312, cloth. 1868. 16s.

Vol. IV. Comparison of the Vedic with the later representations of the principal Indian Deities. Second Edition Revised. 8vo. pp. xvi. and 524, cloth. 1873. 21s.

Vol. V. Contributions to a Knowledge of the Cosmogony, Mythology, Religious Ideas, Life and Manners of the Indians in the Vedic Age. 8vo. pp. xvi. 492, cloth, 1870. 21s.

Müller.—The Sacred Hymns of the Brahmins, as preserved to us in the oldest collection of religious poetry, the Rig-Veda-Sanhita, translated and explained. By F. Max Müller, M.A., Fellow of All Souls' College; Professor of Comparative Philology at Oxford; Foreign Member of the Institute of France, etc., etc. Volume I. Hymns to the Maruts or the Storm Gods. 8vo. pp. clii. and 264. 12s. 6d.

Müller.—The Hymns of the Rig-Veda in the Samhita and Pada Texts. Reprinted from the Editio Princeps. By F. Max Müller, M.A., etc. Second edition. With the Two Texts on Parallel Pages. In 2 vols. 8vo., pp. 1700, sewed. 32s.

Müller.—Lecture on Buddhist Nihilism. By F. Max Müller, M.A., Professor of Comparative Philology in the University of Oxford; Member of the French Institute, etc. Delivered before the General Meeting of the Association of German Philologists, at Kiel, 28th September, 1869. (Translated from the German.) Sewed. 1869. 1s.

Nagananda; or the Joy of the Snake-World. A Buddhist Drama in Five Acts. Translated into English Prose, with Explanatory Notes, from the Sanskrit of Sri-Harsha-Deva. By Palmer Boyd, B.A., Sanskrit Scholar of Trinity College, Cambridge. With an Introduction by Professor Cowell. Crown 8vo., pp. xvi. and 100, cloth. 4s. 6d.

Nalopákhyánam.—Story of Nala; an Episode of the Mahá-Bhárata. The Sanskrit Text, with Vocabulary, Analysis, and Introduction. By Monier Williams, M.A. The Metrical Translation by the Very Rev. H. H. Milman, D.D. 8vo. cl. 15s.

Naradiya Dharma Sastram; or, the Institutes of Narada. Translated for the First Time from the unpublished Sanskrit original. By Dr. Julius Jolly, University, Wurzburg. With a Preface, Notes chiefly critical, an Index of Quotations from Narada in the principal Indian Digests, and a general Index. Crown 8vo., pp. xxxv. 144, cloth. 10s. 6d.

Newman.—A Dictionary of Modern Arabic.—1. Anglo-Arabic Dictionary. 2. Anglo-Arabic Vocabulary. 3. Arabo-English Dictionary. By F. W. Newman, Emeritus Professor of University College, London. In 2 vols. crown 8vo., pp. xvi. and 376—464, cloth. £1 1s.

Newman.—A Handbook of Modern Arabic, consisting of a Practical Grammar, with numerous Examples, Dialogues, and Newspaper Extracts, in a European Type. By F. W. Newman, Emeritus Professor of University College, London; formerly Fellow of Balliol College, Oxford. Post 8vo. pp. xx. and 192, cloth. London, 1866. 6s.

Newman.—The Text of the Iguvine Inscriptions, with interlinear Latin Translation and Notes. By Francis W. Newman, late Professor of Latin at University College, London. 8vo. pp. xvi. and 54, sewed. 2s.

Newman.—Orthoëpy: or, a simple mode of Accenting English, for the advantage of Foreigners and of all Learners. By Francis W. Newman, Emeritus Professor of University College, London. 8vo. pp. 28, sewed. 1869. 1s.

Nodal.—Elementos de Gramática Quichua ó Idioma de los Yncas. Bajo los Auspicios de la Redentora, Sociedad de Filántropos para mejorar la suerte de los Aborijenes Peruanos. Por el Dr. José Fernandez Nodal, Abogado de los Tribunales de Justicia de la República del Perú. Royal 8vo. cloth, pp. xvi. and 441. Appendix, pp. 9. £1 1s.

Nodal.—Los Vinculos de Ollanta y Cusi-Kcuyllor. Drama en Quichua. Obra Compilada y Espurgada con la Version Castellana al Frente de su Texto por el Dr. José Fernandez Nodal, Abogado de los Tribunales de Justicia de la República del Perú. Bajo los Auspicios de la Redentora Sociedad de Filántropos para Mejorar la Suerte de los Aborijenes Peruanos. Roy. 8vo. bds. pp. 70. 1874. 7s. 6d.

Notley.—A Comparative Grammar of the French, Italian, Spanish, and Portuguese Languages. By Edwin A. Notley. Crown oblong 8vo. cloth, pp. xv. and 396. 7s. 6d.

Numismata Orientalia.—The International Numismata Orientalia. Edited by Edward Thomas, F.R.S., etc. Vol. I. Illustrated with 20 Plates and a Map. Royal 4to. cloth. £3 13s. 6d.

Also in 6 Parts sold separately, viz.—

Part I.—Ancient Indian Weights. By E. Thomas, F.R.S., etc. Royal 4to. sewed, pp. 84, with a Plate and a Map of the India of Manu. 9s. 6d.

Part II.—Coins of the Urtuki Turkumans. By Stanley Lane Poole, Corpus Christi College, Oxford. Royal 4to. sewed, pp. 44, with 6 Plates. 9s.

Part III. The Coinage of Lydia and Persia, from the Earliest Times to the Fall of the Dynasty of the Achæmenidæ. By Barclay V. Head, Assistant-Keeper of Coins, British Museum. Royal 4to. sewed, pp. viii. and 56, with three Autotype Plates. 10s. 6d.

Part IV. The Coins of the Tuluni Dynasty. By Edward Thomas Rogers. Royal 4to. sewed, pp. iv. and 22, and 1 Plate. 5s.

Part V. The Parthian Coinage. By Percy Gardner, M.A. Royal 4to. sewed, pp. iv. and 65, with 8 Autotype Plates. 18s.

Part VI. On the Ancient Coins and Measures of Ceylon. With a Discussion of the Ceylon Date of the Buddha's Death. By T. W. Rhys Davids, Barrister-at-Law, late of the Ceylon Civil Service. Royal 4to. sewed, pp. 60, with Plate. 10s.

Nutt.—Fragments of a Samaritan Targum. Edited from a Bodleian MS. With an Introduction, containing a Sketch of Samaritan History, Dogma, and Literature. By J. W. Nutt, M.A. Demy 8vo. cloth, pp. viii., 172, and 84. With Plate. 1874. 15s.

Nutt.—A Sketch of Samaritan History, Dogma, and Literature. Published as an Introduction to "Fragments of a Samaritan Targum." By J. W. Nutt, M.A. Demy 8vo. cloth, pp. viii. and 172. 1874. 5s.

Nutt.—Two Treatises on Verbs containing Feeble and Double Letters by R. Jehuda Hayug of Fez, translated into Hebrew from the original Arabic by R. Moses Gikatilia, of Cordova; with the Treatise on Punctuation by the same Author, translated by Aben Ezra. Edited from Bodleian MSS. with an English Translation by J. W. Nutt, M.A. Demy 8vo. sewed, pp. 312. 1870. 7s. 6d.

Oera Linda Book, from a Manuscript of the Thirteenth Century, with the permission of the Proprietor, C. Over de Linden, of the Helder. The Original Frisian Text, as verified by Dr. J. O. Ottema; accompanied by an English Version of Dr. Ottema's Dutch Translation, by William R. Sandbach. 8vo. cl. pp. xxvii. and 223. 5s.

Ollanta: A Drama in the Quichua Language. See under Markham and under Nodal.

Oriental Congress.—Report of the Proceedings of the Second International Congress of Orientalists held in London, 1874. Roy. 8vo. paper, pp. 76. 5s.

Oriental Congress.—Transactions of the Second Session of the International Congress of Orientalists, held in London in September, 1874. Edited by Robert K. Douglas, Honorary Secretary. Demy 8vo. cloth, pp. viii. and 456. 21s.

Osburn.—The Monumental History of Egypt, as recorded on the Ruins of her Temples, Palaces, and Tombs. By William Osburn. Illustrated with Maps, Plates, etc. 2 vols. 8vo. pp. xii. and 461; vii. and 643, cloth. £2 2s.

Vol. I.—From the Colonisation of the Valley to the Visit of the Patriarch Abram.
Vol. II.—From the Visit of Abram to the Exodus.

Otté.—How to Learn Danish (Dano-Norwegian). A Manual for Students of Danish (Dano-Norwegian). Based on the Ollendorffian System of Teaching Languages, and adapted for Self-Instruction. By E. C. Otté. Crown 8vo. cloth, pp. xix.–338. 7s. 6d.

Key to the Exercises. Cloth, pp. 84. 3s.

Palmer.—Egyptian Chronicles, with a harmony of Sacred and Egyptian Chronology, and an Appendix on Babylonian and Assyrian Antiquities. By William Palmer, M.A., and late Fellow of Magdalen College, Oxford. 2 vols., 8vo. cloth, pp. lxxiv. and 428, and viii. and 636. 1861. 12s.

Palmer.—A Concise Dictionary of the Persian Language. By E. H. Palmer, M.A., Professor of Arabic in the University of Cambridge. Square 16mo. pp. viii. and 364, cloth. 10s. 6d.

Palmer.—Leaves from a Word Hunter's Note Book. Being some Contributions to English Etymology. By the Rev. A. Smythe Palmer, B.A., sometime Scholar in the University of Dublin. Cr. 8vo. cl. pp. xii.–316. 7s. 6d.

Palmer.—The Song of the Reed; and other Pieces. By E. H. Palmer, M.A., Cambridge. Crown 8vo. pp. 208, handsomely bound in cloth. 5s.

Among the Contents will be found translations from Hafiz, from Omer el Kheiyâm, and from other Persian as well as Arabic poets.

Pand-Nâmah.—The Pand-Nâmah; or, Books of Counsels. By Âdarbâd Mârâsfand. Translated from Pehlevi into Gujerathi, by Harbad Sheriarjee Dadabhoy. And from Gujerathi into English by the Rev. Shapurji Edalji. Fcap. 8vo. sewed. 1870. 6d.

Pandit's (A) Remarks on Professor Max Müller's Translation of the "Rig-Veda." Sanskrit and English. Fcap. 8vo. sewed. 1870. 6d.

Paspati.—Études sur les Tchinghianés (Gypsies) ou Bohémiens de l'Empire Ottoman. Par Alexandre G. Paspati, M.D. Large 8vo. sewed, pp. xii. and 652. Constantinople, 1871. 28s.

Patanjali.—The Vyâkarana-Mahâbhâshya of Patanjali. Edited by F. Kielhorn, Ph.D., Professor of Oriental Languages, Deccan College. Vol. I., Part I. pp. 200. 8s. 6d.

Patell.—Cowasjee Patell's Chronology, containing corresponding Dates of the different Eras used by Christians, Jews, Greeks, Hindûs, Mohamedans, Parsees, Chinese, Japanese, etc. By Cowasjee Sorabjee Patell. 4to. pp. viii. and 184, cloth. 50s.

Peking Gazette.—Translation of the Peking Gazette for 1872, 1873, 1874, 1875, 1876, and 1877. 8vo. cloth. 10s. 6d. each.

Percy.—Bishop Percy's Folio Manuscripts—Ballads and Romances. Edited by John W. Hales, M.A., Fellow and late Assistant Tutor of Christ's College, Cambridge; and Frederick J. Furnivall, M.A., of Trinity Hall, Cambridge; assisted by Professor Child, of Harvard University, Cambridge, U.S.A., W. Chappell, Esq., etc. In 3 volumes. Vol. I., pp. 610; Vol. 2, pp. 681.; Vol. 3, pp. 640. Demy 8vo. half-bound, £4 4s. Extra demy 8vo. half-bound, on Whatman's ribbed paper, £6 6s. Extra royal 8vo., paper covers, on Whatman's best ribbed paper, £10 10s. Large 4to., paper covers, on Whatman's best ribbed paper, £12.

Pfoundes.—Fu So Mimi Bukuro.—A Budget of Japanese Notes. By Capt. Pfoundes, of Yokohama. 8vo. sewed, pp. 184. 7s. 6d.

Philological Society (Transactions of The). A Complete Set, including the Proceedings of the Philological Society for the years 1842-1853. 6 vols. The Philological Society's Transactions, 1854 to 1876. 15 vols. The Philological Society's Extra Volumes. 9 vols. In all 30 vols. 8vo. £19 13s. 6d.

Proceedings (The) of the Philological Society 1842-1853. 6 vols. 8vo. £3.

Transactions of the Philological Society, 1854-1876. 15 vols. 8vo. £10 16s.

*** The Volumes for 1867, 1868-9, 1870-2, and 1873-4, are only to be had in complete sets, as above.

Separate Volumes.

For 1854: containing papers by Rev. J. W. Blakesley, Rev. T. O. Cockayne, Rev. J. Davies, Dr. J. W. Donaldson, Dr. Theod. Goldstücker, Prof. T. Hewitt Key, J. M. Kemble, Dr. R. G. Latham, J. M. Ludlow, Hensleigh Wedgwood, etc. 8vo. cl. £1 1s.

For 1855: with papers by Dr. Carl Abel, Dr. W. Bleek, Rev. Jno. Davies, Miss A. Gurney, Jas. Kennedy, Prof. T. H. Key, Dr. R. G. Latham, Henry Malden, W. Ridley, Thos. Watts, Hensleigh Wedgwood, etc. In 4 parts. 8vo. £1 1s.

*** Kamilaroi Language of Australia, by W. Ridley; and False Etymologies, by H. Wedgwood, separately. 5s.

For 1856-7: with papers by Prof. Aufrecht, Herbert Coleridge, Lewis Kr. Daa, M. de Haan, W. C. Jourdain, James Kennedy, Prof. Key, Dr. G. Latham, J. M. Ludlow, Rev. J. J. S. Perowne, Hensleigh Wedgwood, R. F. Weymouth, Jas. Yates, etc. 7 parts. 8vo. (The Papers relating to the Society's Dictionary are omitted.) £1 1s. each volume.

For 1858: including the volume of Early English Poems, Lives of the Saints, edited from MSS. by F. J. Furnivall; and papers by Ern. Adams, Prof. Aufrecht, Herbert Coleridge, Rev. Francis Crawford, M. de Haan Hettema, Dr. R. G. Latham, Dr. Lottner, etc. 8vo. cl. 12s.

For 1859: with papers by Dr. E. Adams, Prof. Aufrecht, Herb. Coleridge, F. J. Furnivall, Prof. T. H. Key, Dr. C. Lottner, Prof. De Morgan, F. Pulszky, Hensleigh Wedgwood, etc. 8vo. cl. 12s.

For 1860-1: including The Play of the Sacrament; and Pascon agan Arluth, the Passion of our Lord, in Cornish and English, both from MSS., edited by Dr. Whitley Stokes; and papers by Dr. E. Adams, T. F. Barham, Rev. Derwent Coleridge, Herbert Coleridge, Sir John F. Davis, Danby P. Fry, Prof. T. H. Key, Dr. C. Lottner, Bishop Thirlwall, Hensleigh Wedgwood, R. F. Weymouth, etc. 8vo. cl. 12s.

For 1862-3: with papers by C. B. Cayley, D. P. Fry, Prof. Key, H. Malden, Rich. Morris, F. W. Newman, Robert Peacock, Hensleigh Wedgwood, R. F. Weymouth, etc. 8vo. cl. 12s.

For 1864: containing 1. Manning's (Jas.) Inquiry into the Character and Origin of the Possessive Augment in English, etc.; 2. Newman's (Francis W.) Text of the Iguvine Inscriptions, with Interlinear Latin Translation; 3. Barnes's (Dr.

Philological Society (Transactions of The)—*continued.*

W.) Grammar and Glossary of the Dorset Dialect; 4. Gwreans An Bys—The Creation: a Cornish Mystery, Cornish and English, with Notes by Whitley Stokes, etc. 8vo. cl. 12s.

*** Separately: Manning's Inquiry, 3s.—Newman's Iguvine Inscription, 3s.—Stokes's Gwreans An Bys, 8s.

For 1865: including Wheatley's (H. B.) Dictionary of Reduplicated Words in the English Language; and papers by Prof. Aufrecht, Ed. Brock, C. B. Cayley, Rev. A. J. Church, Prof. T. H. Key, Rev. R. H. Kennedy, Prof. H. Malden, Hon. G. P. Marsh, John Rhys, Guthbrand Vigfusson, Hensleigh Wedgwood, H. B. Wheatley, etc. 8vo. cl. 12s.

For 1866: including 1. Gregor's (Rev. Walter) Banffshire Dialect, with Glossary of Words omitted by Jamieson; 2. Edmondston's (T.) Glossary of the Shetland Dialect; and papers by Prof. Cassal, C. B. Cayley, Danby P. Fry, Prof. T. H. Key, Guthbrand Vigfusson, Hensleigh Wedgwood, etc. 8vo. cl. 12s.

*** The Volumes for 1867, 1868-9, 1870-2, and 1873-4, are out of print. Besides contributions in the shape of valuable and interesting papers, the volume for 1867 also includes: 1. Peacock's (Rob. B.) Glossary of the Hundred of Lonsdale; and 2. Ellis (A. J.) On Palaeotype representing Spoken Sounds; and on the Diphthong "Oy." The volume for 1868-9—1. Ellis's (A. J.) Only English Proclamation of Henry III. in Oct. 1258; to which are added "The Cuckoo's Song and "The Prisoner's Prayer," Lyrics of the XIII. Century, with Glossary; and 2. Stokes's (Whitley) Cornish Glossary. That for 1870-2—1. Murray's (Jas. A. H.) Dialect of the Southern Counties of Scotland, with a linguistical map. That for 1873-4—Sweet's (H.) History of English Sounds.

For 1875-6: containing the Rev. Richard Morris (President), Fourth and Fifth Annual Addresses. 1. Some Sources of Aryan Mythology by E. L. Brandreth; 2. C. B. Cayley on Certain Italian Diminutives; 3. Changes made by four young Children in Pronouncing English Words, by Jas. M. Menzies; 4. The Manx Language, by H. Jenner; 5. The Dialect of West Somerset, by F. T. Elworthy; 6. English Metre, by Prof. J. B. Mayor; 7. Words, Logic, and Grammar, by H. Sweet; 8. The Russian Language and its Dialects, by W. R. Morfill; 9. Relics of the Cornish Language in Mount's Bay, by H. Jenner; 10. Dialects and Prehistoric Forms of Old English. By Henry Sweet, Esq.; 11. On the Dialects of Monmouthshire, Herefordshire, Worcestershire, Gloucestershire, Berkshire, Oxfordshire, South Warwickshire, South Northamptonshire, Buckinghamshire, Hertfordshire, Middlesex, and Surrey, with a New Classification of the English Dialects. By Prince Louis Lucien Bonaparte (with Two Maps), Index, etc. Part I., 6s.; Part II., 6s.; Part III., 2s.

For 1877-8-9: containing the President's (Henry Sweet, Esq.) Sixth and Seventh Annual Addresses. 1. Accadian Phonology, by Professor A. H. Sayce; 2. On *Here* and *There* in Chaucer, by Dr. R. Weymouth; 3. The Grammar of the Dialect of West Somerset, by F. T. Elworthy, Esq.; 4. English Metre, by Professor J. B. Mayor; 5. The Malagasy Language, by the Rev. W. E. Cousins; 6. The Anglo-Cymric Score, by A. J. Ellis, Esq., F.R.S. 8vo. Part I., 3s.; Part II., 7s.

The Society's Extra Volumes.

Early English Volume, 1862-64, containing: 1. Liber Cure Cocorum, A.D. c. 1440.—2. Hampole's (Richard Rolle) Pricke of Conscience, A.D. c. 1340.—3. The Castell off Love, A.D. c. 1320. 8vo. cloth. 1865. £1.

Or separately: Liber Cure Cocorum, Edited by Rich. Morris, 3s.; Hampole's (Rolle) Pricke of Conscience, edited by Rich. Morris, 12s.; and The Castell off Love, edited by Dr. R. F. Weymouth, 6s.

Philological Society (Transactions of the)—*continued.*

Dan Michel's Ayenbite of Inwyt, or Remorse of Conscience, in the Kentish Dialect, A.D. 1340. From the Autograph MS. in Brit. Mus. Edited with Introduction, Marginal Interpretations, and Glossarial Index, by Richard Morris. 8vo. cloth. 1866. 12s.

Levins's (Peter, A.D. 1570) Manipulus Vocabulorum: a Rhyming Dictionary of the English Language. With an Alphabetical Index by H. B. Wheatley. 8vo. cloth. 1867. 16s.

Skeat's (Rev. W. W.) Mœso-Gothic Glossary, with an Introduction, an Outline of Mœso-Gothic Grammar, and a List of Anglo-Saxon and old and modern English Words etymologically connected with Mœso-Gothic. 1868. 8vo. cl. 9s.

Ellis (A. J.) on Early English Pronunciation, with especial Reference to Shakspere and Chaucer: containing an Investigation of the Correspondence of Writing with Speech in England from the Anglo-Saxon Period to the Present Day, etc. 4 parts. 8vo. 1869–75. £2.

Mediæval Greek Texts: A Collection of the Earliest Compositions in Vulgar Greek, prior to A.D. 1500. With Prolegomena and Critical Notes by W. Wagner. Part I. Seven Poems, three of which appear for the first time. 1870. 8vo. 10s. 6d.

Phillips.—The Doctrine of Addai the Apostle. Now first Edited in a Complete Form in the Original Syriac, with an English Translation and Notes. By George Phillips, D.D., President of Queen's College, Cambridge. 8vo. pp. 122, cloth. 7s. 6d.

Picard.—A New Pocket Dictionary of the English and Dutch Languages. By H. Picard. Revised and augmented by A. R. Maatjes and H. J. Vos. *Fifth edition.* Small 4to. cloth, pp. xvi. and 1186. 1877. 10s.

Pimentel.—Cuadro descriptivo y comparativo de las Lenguas Indígenas de México, o Tratado de Filología Mexicana. Par Francisco Pimentel. 2 Edicion unica completa. 3 Volume 8vo. *México*, 1875. £2 2s.

Pischel.—Hemacandra's Grammatik der Prâkritsprachen (Siddhahemacandram Adhyâya VIII.) mit Kritischen und Erläuternden Anmerkungen. Herausgegeben von Richard Pischel. Part I. Text und Wortverzeichniss. 8vo. pp. xiv. and 236. 8s.

Pope.—A Tamil Handbook; or, Full Introduction to the Common Dialect of that Language, on the plan of Ollendorff and Arnold. With copious Vocabularies, Appendices, containing Reading Lessons, Analyses of Letters, Deeds, Complaints, Official Documents, and a Key to the Exercises. By Rev. G. U. Pope. Third edition, 8vo. cloth, pp. iv. and 388. 21s.

Prakrita-Prakasa; or, The Prakrit Grammar of Vararuchi, with the Commentary (Manorama) of Bhamaha. The first complete edition of the Original Text with Various Readings from a Collation of Six Manuscripts in the Bodleian Library at Oxford, and the Libraries of the Royal Asiatic Society and the East India House; with copious Notes, an English Translation, and Index of Prakrit words, to which is prefixed an easy Introduction to Prakrit Grammar. By E. B. Cowell. Second issue, with new Preface, and corrections. 8vo. pp. xxxii. and 204. 14s.

Priaulx.—Quæstiones Mosaicæ; or, the first part of the Book of Genesis compared with the remains of ancient religions. By Osmond de Beauvoir Priaulx. 8vo. pp. viii. and 548, cloth. 12s.

Rámáyan of Válmíki.—5 vols. See under Griffith.

Ram Jasan.—A Sanskrit and English Dictionary. Being an Abridgment of Professor Wilson's Dictionary. With an Appendix explaining the use of Affixes in Sanskrit. By Pandit Ram Jasan, Queen's College, Benares. Published under the Patronage of the Government, N.W.P. Royal 8vo. cloth, pp. ii. and 707. 28*s*.

Ram Raz.—Essay on the Architecture of the Hindus. By Ram Raz, Native Judge and Magistrate of Bangalore. With 48 plates. 4to. pp. xiv. and 64, sewed. London, 1834. £2 2*s*.

Rask.—A Grammar of the Anglo-Saxon Tongue. From the Danish of Erasmus Rask, Professor of Literary History in, and Librarian to, the University of Copenhagen, etc. By Benjamin Thorpe. Second edition, corrected and improved. 18mo. pp. 200, cloth. 5*s*. 6*d*.

Rawlinson.—A Commentary on the Cuneiform Inscriptions of Babylonia and Assyria, including Readings of the Inscription on the Nimrud Obelisk, and Brief Notice of the Ancient Kings of Nineveh and Babylon, by Major H. C. Rawlinson. 8vo. pp. 84, sewed. London, 1850. 2*s*. 6*d*.

Rawlinson.—Outlines of Assyrian History, from the Inscriptions of Nineveh. By Lieut. Col. Rawlinson, C.B., followed by some Remarks by A. H. Layard, Esq., D.C.L. 8vo., pp. xliv., sewed. London, 1852. 1*s*.

Rawlinson.—Inscription of Tiglath Pileser I., King of Assyria, B.C. 1150, as translated by Sir H. Rawlinson, Fox Talbot, Esq., Dr. Hincks, and Dr. Oppert. Published by the Royal Asiatic Society. 8vo. sd., pp. 74. 2*s*.

Rawlinson.—Notes on the Early History of Babylonia. By Colonel Rawlinson, C.B. 8vo. sd., pp. 48. 1*s*.

Redhouse.—The Turkish Campaigner's Vade-Mecum of Ottoman Colloquial Language; containing a concise Ottoman Grammar; a carefully selected Vocabulary, alphabetically arranged, in two parts, English and Turkish, and Turkish and English; also a few Familiar Dialogues; the whole in English characters. By J. W. Redhouse, F.R.A.S. Oblong 32mo. limp cloth, pp. iv. and 332. 6*s*.

Redhouse.—كتاب لهجة المعاني لجيمس ردحاوس الانكليزي. A Lexicon English and Turkish, shewing in Turkish the Literal, Incidental, Figurative, Colloquial, and Technical Significations of the English Terms, indicating their pronunciation in a new and systematic manner, and preceded by a Sketch of English Etymology to facilitate to Turkish Students the acquisition of the English Language. By J. W. Redhouse, M.R.A.S. Second edition, pp. xvii. and 827. 15*s*.

Redhouse.—A Vindication of the Ottoman Sultan's Title to "Caliph," shewing its Antiquity, Validity, and Universal Acceptance. By J. W. Redhouse. 8vo. paper, pp. 20. 2*s*.

Renan.—An Essay on the Age and Antiquity of the Book of Nabathæan Agriculture. To which is added an Inaugural Lecture on the Position of the Shemitic Nations in the History of Civilization. By M. Ernest Renan, Membre de l'Institut. Crown 8vo., pp. xvi. and 148, cloth. 3*s*. 6*d*.

Revue Celtique (The).—A Quarterly Magazine for Celtic Philology, Literature, and History. Edited with the assistance of the Chief Celtic Scholars of the British Islands and of the Continent, and Conducted by H. Gaidoz. 8vo. Subscription, £1 per Volume.

Rhys.—Lectures on Welsh Philology. By John Rhys, M.A., Professor of Celtic at Oxford. Second edition, revised and enlarged. Crown 8vo. cloth, pp. viii. and 466. 15*s*.

Rig-Veda.—*See* Muller.

Rig-Veda-Sanhita: THE SACRED HYMNS OF THE BRAHMANS. Translated and explained by F. MAX MÜLLER, M.A., LL.D., Fellow of All Souls' College, Professor of Comparative Philology at Oxford, Foreign Member of the Institute of France, etc., etc. Vol. I. HYMNS TO THE MARUTS, OR THE STORM-GODS. 8vo. pp. clii and 264. cloth. 1869. 12s. 6d.

Rig-Veda Sanhita.—A COLLECTION OF ANCIENT HINDU HYMNS. Constituting the First Ashtaka, or Book of the Rig-veda; the oldest authority for the religious and social institutions of the Hindus. Translated from the Original Sanskrit by the late H. H. WILSON, M.A. 2nd Ed., with a Postscript by Dr. FITZEDWARD HALL. Vol. I. 8vo. cloth, pp. lii. and 348, price 21s.

Rig-Veda Sanhita.—A Collection of Ancient Hindu Hymns, constituting the Fifth to Eighth Ashtakas, or books of the Rig-Veda, the oldest Authority for the Religious and Social Institutions of the Hindus. Translated from the Original Sanskrit by the late HORACE HAYMAN WILSON, M.A., F.R.S., etc. Edited by E. B. COWELL, M.A., Principal of the Calcutta Sanskrit College. Vol. IV., 8vo., pp. 214, cloth. 14s.

A few copies of Vols. II. and III. still left. [*Vols. V. and VI. in the Press.*

Riola.—HOW TO LEARN RUSSIAN. A Manual for Students of Russian, based upon the Ollendorffian system of teaching languages, and adapted for self instruction. By HENRY RIOLA, Teacher of the Russian Language. With a Preface by W. R. S. RALSTON, M.A. Crown 8vo. cloth, pp. 576. 1878. 12s.

Key to the above. Crown 8vo. cloth, pp. 126. 1878. 5s.

Roberts.—ARYAN PHILOLOGY, according to the most recent Researches (Glottologia Aria Recentissima), Remarks Historical and Critical. By DOMENICO PEZZI, Membro della Facolta de Filosofia e lettere della R. Universit. di Torino. Translated by E. S. ROBERTS, M.A., Fellow and Tutor of Gonville and Caius College. Crown 8vo. cloth, pp. xvi. and 199. 6s.

Roe and Fryer.—TRAVELS IN INDIA IN THE SEVENTEENTH CENTURY. By Sir THOMAS ROE and Dr. JOHN FRYER. Reprinted from the "Calcutta Weekly Englishman." 8vo. cloth, pp. 474. 7s. 6d.

Rohrig.—THE SHORTEST ROAD TO GERMAN. Designed for the use of both Teachers and Students. By F. L. O. ROEHRIG. Cr. 8vo. cloth, pp. vii. and 225. 1874. 7s. 6d.

Rogers.—NOTICE ON THE DINARS OF THE ABBASSIDE DYNASTY. By EDWARD THOMAS ROGERS, late H.M. Consul, Cairo. 8vo. pp. 44, with a Map and four Autotype Plates. 5s.

Rosny.—A GRAMMAR OF THE CHINESE LANGUAGE. By Professor LEON DE ROSNY. 8vo. pp. 48. 1874. 3s.

Ross.—A MANDARIN PRIMER. Being Easy Lessons for Beginners, Transliterated according to the European mode of using Roman Letters. By Rev. JOHN ROSS, Newchang. 8vo. wrapper, pp. 122. 6s.

Ross—A COREAN PRIMER. Being Lessons in Corean on all Ordinary Subjects. Transliterated on the principles of the Mandarin Primer by the same author. By the Rev. JOHN ROSS, Newchang. Demy 8vo. stitched, pp. 90. 10s.

Routledge.—ENGLISH RULE AND NATIVE OPINION IN INDIA. From Notes taken in the years 1870-74. By JAMES ROUTLEDGE. Post 8vo. cloth, pp. 344. 10s. 6d.

Royal Society of Literature of the United Kingdom (Transactions of The). First Series, 6 Parts in 3 Vols., 4to., Plates; 1827-39. Second Series, 10 Vols. or 30 Parts, and Vol. XI. Parts 1 and 2, 8vo., Plates; 1843-76.

A complete set, so far as published, £10 10s. Very scarce. The first series of this important series of contributions of many of the most eminent men of the day has long been out of print and is very scarce. Of the Second Series, Vol. I.–IV., each containing three parts, are quite out of print, and can only be had in the complete series, noticed above. Three Numbers, price 4s. 6d. each, form a volume. The price of the volume complete, bound in cloth, is 13s. 6d.

Separate Publications.

I. Fasti Monastici Aevi Saxonici: or an Alphabetical List of the Heads of Religious Houses in England previous to the Norman Conquest, to which is prefixed a Chronological Catalogue of Contemporary Foundations. By Walter de Gray Birch. Royal 8vo. cloth. 1872. 7s. 6d.

II. Li Chantari di Lancelotto; a Troubadour's Poem of the XIV. Cent. Edited from a MS. in the possession of the Royal Society of Literature, by Walter de Gray Birch. Royal 8vo. cloth. 1874. 7s.

III. Inquisitio Comitatus Cantabrigiensis, nunc primum, è Manuscripto unico in Bibliothecâ Cottonianâ asservato, typis mandata: subjicitur Inquisitio Eliensis: curâ N. E. S. A. Hamilton. Royal 4to. With map and 3 facsimiles. 1876. £2 2s.

IV. A Commonplace-Book of John Milton. Reproduced by the autotype process from the original MS. in the possession of Sir Fred. U. Graham, Bart., of Netherby Hall. With an Introduction by A. J. Horwood. Sq. folio. Only one hundred copies printed. 1876. £2 2s.

V. Chronicon Adae de Usk, A.D. 1377–1404. Edited, with a Translation and Notes, by Ed. Maunde Thompson. Royal 8vo. 1876. 10s. 6d.

Rudy.—The Chinese Mandarin Language, after Ollendorff's New Method of Learning Languages. By Charles Rudy. In 3 Volumes. Vol. I. Grammar. 8vo. pp. 248. £1 1s.

Sabdakalpadruma, the well-known Sanskrit Dictionary of Rajah Radhakanta Deva. In Bengali characters. 4to. Parts 1 to 40. (In course of publication.) 3s. 6d. each part.

Sakuntala.—Kâlidâsa's Çakuntalâ. The Bengali Recension. With Critical Notes. Edited by Richard Pischel. 8vo. cloth, pp. xi. and 210. 14s.

Sakuntala.—A Sanskrit Drama in Seven Acts. Edited by Monier Williams, M.A. Second Edition. 8vo. cl. £1 1s.

Sale.—The Koran; commonly called The Alcoran of Mohammed. Translated into English immediately from the original Arabic. By George Sale, Gent. To which is prefixed the Life of Mohammed. Crown 8vo. cloth, pp. 472. 7s.

Sâma-Vidhâna-Brâhmana. With the Commentary of Sâyana. Edited, with Notes, Translation, and Index, by A. C. Burnell, M.R.A.S. Vol. I. Text and Commentary. With Introduction. 8vo. cloth, pp. xxxviii. and 104. 12s. 6d.

Sanskrit Works.—A Catalogue of Sanskrit Works Printed in India, offered for Sale at the affixed nett prices by Trübner & Co. 16mo. pp. 52. 1s.

Sarva-Sabda-Sambodhini; or, The Complete Sanskrit Dictionary. In Telugu characters. 4to. cloth, pp. 1078. £2 15s.

Satow.—An English Japanese Dictionary of the Spoken Language. By Ernest Mason Satow, Japanese Secretary to H.M. Legation at Yedo, and Ishibashi Masakata, of the Imperial Japanese Foreign Office. Imp. 32mo., pp. xx. and 366, cloth. 12s.

Sayce.—An Assyrian Grammar for Comparative Purposes. By A. H. Sayce, M.A. 12mo. cloth, pp. xvi. and 188. 7s. 6d.

Sayce.—The Principles of Comparative Philology. By A. H. Sayce, Fellow and Tutor of Queen's College, Oxford. Second Edition. Cr. 8vo. cl., pp. xxxii. and 416. 10s. 6d.

Scarborough.—A Collection of Chinese Proverbs. Translated and Arranged by William Scarborough, Wesleyan Missionary, Hankow. With an Introduction, Notes, and Copious Index. Cr. 8vo. pp. xliv. and 278. 10s. 6d.

Schleicher.—Compendium of the Comparative Grammar of the Indo-European, Sanskrit, Greek, and Latin Languages. By August Schleicher. Translated from the Third German Edition by Herbert Bendall, B.A., Chr. Coll. Camb. Part I. Grammar. 8vo. cloth, pp. 184. 7s. 6d.

Part II. Morphology. 8vo. cloth, pp. viii. and 104. 6s.

Schemeil.—El Mubtaker; or, First Born. (In Arabic, printed at Beyrout). Containing Five Comedies, called Comedies of Fiction, on Hopes and Judgments, in Twenty-six Poems of 1092 Verses, showing the Seven Stages of Life, from man's conception unto his death and burial. By Emin Ibrahim Schemeil. In one volume, 4to. pp. 160, sewed. 1870. 5s.

Schlagintweit.—Buddhism in Tibet. Illustrated by Literary Documents and Objects of Religious Worship. With an Account of the Buddhist Systems preceding it in India. By Emil Schlagintweit, LL.D. With a Folio Atlas of 20 Plates, and 20 Tables of Native Prints in the Text. Royal 8vo., pp. xxiv. and 404. £2 2s.

Schlagintweit.—Glossary of Geographical Terms from India and Tibet, with Native Transcription and Transliteration. By Hermann de Schlagintweit. Forming, with a "Route Book of the Western Himalaya, Tibet, and Turkistan," the Third Volume of H., A., and R. de Schlagintweit's "Results of a Scientific Mission to India and High Asia." With an Atlas in imperial folio, of Maps, Panoramas, and Views. Royal 4to., pp. xxiv. and 293. £4.

Semitic (Songs of The). In English Verse. By G. E. W. Cr. 8vo. cloth, pp. 140. 5s.

Shakspere Society (The New).—Subscription £1 1s. per annum. List of publications on application.

Shápurjí Edaljí.—A Grammar of the Gujarátí Language. By Shápurjí Edaljí. Cloth, pp. 127. 10s. 6d.

Shápurjí Edaljí.—A Dictionary, Gujrati and English. By Shápurjí Edaljí. Second Edition. Crown 8vo. cloth, pp. xxiv. and 874. 21s.

Shaw.—A Sketch of the Turki Language. As Spoken in Eastern Turkistan (Kàshghar and Yarkand). By Robert Barkley Shaw, F.R.G.S., Political Agent. In Two Parts. With Lists of Names of Birds and Plants by J. Scully, Surgeon, H.M. Bengal Army. 8vo. sewed, Part I., pp. 130. 7s. 6d.

Sherring.—The Sacred City of the Hindus. An Account of Benares in Ancient and Modern Times. By the Rev. M. A. Sherring, M.A., LL.D.; and Prefaced with an Introduction by Fitzedward Hall, Esq., D.C.L. 8vo. cloth, pp. xxxvi. and 388, with numerous full-page illustrations. 21s.

Sherring.—The Hindoo Pilgrims. By the Rev. M. A. Sherring. Fcap. 8vo. cloth, pp. vi. and 125. 5s.

Singh.—Sakhee Book; or, The Description of Gooroo Gobind Singh's Religion and Doctrines, translated from Gooroo Mukhi into Hindi, and afterwards into English. By Sirdar Attar Singh, Chief of Bhadour. With the author's photograph. 8vo. pp. xviii. and 205. 15s.

Skeat.—A LIST OF ENGLISH WORDS, the Etymology of which is illustrated by Comparison with Icelandic. Prepared in the form of an Appendix to Cleasby and Vigfusson's Icelandic-English Dictionary. By the Rev. WALTER W. SKEAT, M.A., English Lecturer and late Fellow of Christ's College, Cambridge; and M.A. of Exeter College, Oxford; one of the Vice-Presidents of the Cambridge Philological Society; and Member of the Council of the Philological Society of London. 1876. Demy 4to. sewed. 2s.

Smith.—A VOCABULARY OF PROPER NAMES IN CHINESE AND ENGLISH. of Places, Persons, Tribes, and Sects, in China, Japan, Corea, Assam, Siam, Burmah, The Straits, and adjacent Countries. By F. PORTER SMITH, M.B., London, Medical Missionary in Central China. 4to. half-bound, pp. vi., 72. and x. 1870. 10s. 6d.

Smith.—CONTRIBUTIONS TOWARDS THE MATERIA MEDICA AND NATURAL HISTORY OF CHINA. For the use of Medical Missionaries and Native Medical Students. By F. PORTER SMITH, M.B. London, Medical Missionary in Central China. Imp. 4to. cloth, pp. viii. and 240. 1870. £1 1s.

Sophocles.—A GLOSSARY OF LATER AND BYZANTINE GREEK. By E. A. SOPHOCLES. 4to., pp. iv. and 624, cloth. £2 2s.

Sophocles.—ROMAIC OR MODERN GREEK GRAMMAR. By E. A. SOPHOCLES. 8vo. pp. xxviii. and 196.

Sophocles.—GREEK LEXICON OF THE ROMAN AND BYZANTINE PERIODS (from B.C. 146 to A.D. 1100). By E. A. SOPHOCLES. Imp. 8vo. pp. xvi. 1188, cloth. 1870. £2 10s.

Spurrell.—A GRAMMAR OF THE WELSH LANGUAGE. By WILLIAM SPURRELL. 3rd Edition. Fcap. cloth, pp. viii.-206. 1870. 3s.

Spurrell.—A WELSH DICTIONARY. English-Welsh and Welsh-English. With Preliminary Observations on the Elementary Sounds of the English Language, a copious Vocabulary of the Roots of English Words, a list of Scripture Proper Names and English Synonyms and Explanations. By WILLIAM SPURRELL. Third Edition. Fcap. cloth, pp. xxv. and 732. 8s. 6d.

Steele.—AN EASTERN LOVE STORY. KUSA JÁTAKAYA: a Buddhistic Legendary Poem, with other Stories. By THOMAS STEELE, Ceylon Civil Service. Crown 8vo. cloth, pp. xii. and 260. 1871. 6s.

Steere.—SHORT SPECIMENS OF THE VOCABULARIES OF THREE UNPUBLISHED African Languages (Gindo, Zaramo, and Angazidja). Collected by EDWARD STEERE, LL.D. 12mo. pp. 20. 6d.

Steere.—COLLECTIONS FOR A HANDBOOK OF THE NYAMWEZI LANGUAGE, as spoken at Unyanyembe. By EDWARD STEERE, LL.D. Fcap. cloth, pp. 100. 1s. 6d.

Stent.—THE JADE CHAPLET, in Twenty-four Beads. A Collection of Songs, Ballads, etc. (from the Chinese). By GEORGE CARTER STENT, M.N.C.B.R.A.S., Author of "Chinese and English Vocabulary," "Chinese and English Pocket Dictionary," "Chinese Lyrics," "Chinese Legends," etc. Cr. 8o. cloth, pp. 176. 5s.

Stent.—A CHINESE AND ENGLISH VOCABULARY IN THE PEKINESE DIALECT. By G. E. STENT. 8vo. pp. ix. and 677. 1871. £1 10s.

Stent.—A CHINESE AND ENGLISH POCKET DICTIONARY. By G. E. STENT. 16mo. pp. 250. 1874. 10s. 6d.

Stoddard.—GRAMMAR OF THE MODERN SYRIAC LANGUAGE, as spoken in Oroomiah, Persia, and in Koordistan. By Rev. D. T. STODDARD, Missionary of the American Board in Persia. Demy 8vo. bds., pp. 190. 10s. 6d.

Stokes.—Beunans Meriasek. The Life of Saint Meriasek, Bishop and Confessor. A Cornish Drama. Edited, with a Translation and Notes, by Whitley Stokes. Medium 8vo. cloth, pp. xvi., 280, and Facsimile. 1872. 15s.

Stokes.—Goidelica—Old and Early-Middle Irish Glosses: Prose and Verse. Edited by Whitley Stokes. Second edition. Medium 8vo. cloth, pp. 192. 18s.

Strangford.—Original Letters and Papers of the late Viscount Strangford, upon Philological and Kindred Subjects. Edited by Viscountess Strangford. Post 8vo. cloth, pp. xxii. and 284. 1878. 12s. 6d.

Stratmann.—A Dictionary of the Old English Language. Compiled from the writings of the xiiith, xivth, and xvth centuries. By Francis Henry Stratmann. Third Edition. 4to. In wrapper. £1 10s.

Stratmann.—An Old English Poem of the Owl and the Nightingale. Edited by Francis Henry Stratmann. 8vo. cloth, pp. 60. 3s.

Strong.—Selections from the Bostan of Sadi, translated into English Verse. By Dawsonne Melancthon Strong, Captain H.M. 10th Bengal Lancers. 12mo. cloth, pp. ii. and 56. 2s. 6d.

Sunjana.—A Grammar of the Pahlvi Language, with Quotations and Examples from Original Works and a Glossary of Words bearing affinity with the Semitic Languages. By Peshotun Dustoor Behramjee Sunjana, Principal of Sir Jamsetjee Jejeebhoy Zarthosti Madressa. 8vo. cl., pp. 18–457. 25s.

Surya-Siddhanta (Translation of the).—*See* Whitney.

Sweet.—A History of English Sounds, from the Earliest Period, including an Investigation of the General Laws of Sound Change, and full Word Lists. By Henry Sweet. Demy 8vo. cloth, pp. iv. and 164. 4s. 6d.

Syed Ahmad.—A Series of Essays on the Life of Mohammed, and Subjects subsidiary thereto. By Syed Ahmad Khan Bahador, C.S.I., Author of the "Mohammedan Commentary on the Holy Bible," Honorary Member of the Royal Asiatic Society, and Life Honorary Secretary to the Allygurh Scientific Society. 8vo. pp. 532, with 4 Genealogical Tables, 2 Maps, and a Coloured Plate, handsomely bound in cloth. £1 10s.

Syro-Egyptian Society.—Original Papers read before the Syro-Egyptian Society of London. Volume I. Part 1. 8vo. sewed, 2 plates and a map, pp. 144. 3s. 6d.

Including, among other papers, Remarks on the Obelisks of Ancient Egypt. By W. H. Yates, M.D.—Notes on the Hieroglyphics of Horapollo Nilous. By S. Sharpe.—Remarks on the Wedge Inscription recently discovered on the Upper Euphrates. By G. F. Grotefend, Ph.D. (With a Copy of the Original Inscription).

Taittiriya-Pratiçakhya.—See Whitney.

Tarkavachaspati.—Vachaspatya, a Comprehensive Dictionary, in Ten Parts. Compiled by Taranatha Tarkavachaspati, Professor of Grammar and Philosophy in the Government Sanskrit College of Calcutta. An Alphabetically Arranged Dictionary, with a Grammatical Introduction and Copious Citations from the Grammarians and Scholiasts, from the Vedas, etc. Parts I. to VII. 4to. paper. 1873–6. 18s. each Part.

Technologial Dictionary.—Pocket Dictionary of Technical Terms used in Arts and Sciences. English-German-French. Based on the larger Work by Karmarsch. 3 vols. imp. 16mo. cloth. 12s.

Technological Dictionary of the terms employed in the Arts and Sciences; Architecture, Civil, Military and Naval; Civil Engineering, including Bridge Building, Road and Railway Making; Mechanics, Machine and Engine Making; Shipbuilding and Navigation; Metallurgy, Mining and Smelting; Artillery; Mathematics; Physics; Chemistry; Mineralogy, etc. With a Preface by Dr. K. KARMARSCH. Second Edition. 3 vols.

Vol. I. English—German—French. 8vo. cloth, pp. 666. 12*s*.
Vol. II. German—English—French. 8vo. cloth, pp. 646. 12*s*.
Vol. III. French—German—English. 8vo. cloth, pp. 618. 12*s*.

The Boke of Nurture. By JOHN RUSSELL, about 1460–1470 Anno Domini. The Boke of Keruynge. By WYNKYN DE WORDE, Anno Domini 1513. The Boke of Nurture. By HUGH RHODES, Anno Domini 1577. Edited from the Originals in the British Museum Library, by FREDERICK J. FURNIVALL, M.A., Trinity Hall, Cambridge, Member of Council of the Philological and Early English Text Societies. 4to. half-morocco, gilt top, pp. xix. and 146, 28, xxviii. and 56. 1867. 1*l*. 11*s*. 6*d*.

Thibaut.—THE SULVASÚTRAS. English Translation, with an Introduction. By G. THIBAUT, Ph.D., Anglo-Sanskrit Professor Benares College. 8vo. cloth, pp. 47, with 4 Plates. 5*s*.

Thibaut.—CONTRIBUTIONS TO THE EXPLANATION OF JYOTISHA-VEDÂNGA. By G. THIBAUT, Ph.D. 8vo. pp. 27. 1*s*. 6*d*.

Thomas.—EARLY SASSANIAN INSCRIPTIONS, SEALS AND COINS, illustrating the Early History of the Sassanian Dynasty, containing Proclamations of Ardeshir Babek, Sapor I., and his Successors. With a Critical Examination and Explanation of the Celebrated Inscription in the Hâjîâbad Cave, demonstrating that Sapor, the Conqueror of Valerian, was a Professing Christian. By EDWARD THOMAS, F.R.S. Illustrated. 8vo. cloth, pp. 148. 7*s*. 6*d*.

Thomas.—THE CHRONICLES OF THE PATHÁN KINGS OF DEHLI. Illustrated by Coins, Inscriptions, and other Antiquarian Remains. By EDWARD THOMAS, F.R.S., late of the East India Company's Bengal Civil Service. With numerous Copperplates and Woodcuts. Demy 8vo. cloth, pp. xxiv. and 467. 1871. £1 8*s*.

Thomas.—THE REVENUE RESOURCES OF THE MUGHAL EMPIRE IN INDIA, from A.D. 1593 to A.D. 1707. A Supplement to "The Chronicles of the Pathân Kings of Delhi." By EDWARD THOMAS, F.R.S. Demy 8vo., pp. 60, cloth. 3*s*. 6*d*.

Thomas.—COMMENTS ON RECENT PEHLVI DECIPHERMENTS. With an Incidental Sketch of the Derivation of Aryan Alphabets, and contributions to the Early History and Geography of Tabaristân. Illustrated by Coins. By EDWARD THOMAS, F.R.S. 8vo. pp. 56, and 2 plates, cloth, sewed. 3*s*. 6*d*.

Thomas.—SASSANIAN COINS. Communicated to the Numismatic Society of London. By E. THOMAS, F.R.S. Two parts. With 3 Plates and a Woodcut. 12mo. sewed, pp. 43. 5*s*.

Thomas.—RECORDS OF THE GUPTA DYNASTY. Illustrated by Inscriptions, Written History, Local Tradition and Coins. To which is added a Chapter on the Arabs in Sind. By EDWARD THOMAS, F.R.S. Folio, with a Plate, handsomely bound in cloth, pp. iv. and 64. Price 14*s*.

Thomas.—JAINISM; or, The Early Faith of Asoka. With Illustrations of the Ancient Religions of the East, from the Pantheon of the Indo-Scythians. To which is added a Notice on Bactrian Coins and Indian Dates. By EDWARD THOMAS, F.R.S. 8vo. pp. viii., 24 and 82. With two Autotype Plates and Woodcuts. 7*s*. 6*d*.

Thomas.—THE THEORY AND PRACTICE OF CREOLE GRAMMAR. By J. J. THOMAS. Port of Spain (Trinidad), 1869. 1 vol. 8vo. bds. pp. viii. and 135. 12*s*.

Thorburn.—BANNÚ; or, Our Afghán Frontier. By S. S. THORBURN, I.C.S., Settlement Officer of the Bannú District. 8vo. cloth, pp. x. and 480. 18s.

Thorpe.—DIPLOMATARIUM ANGLICUM ÆVI SAXONICI. A Collection of English Charters, from the reign of King Æthelberht of Kent, A.D., DCV., to that of William the Conqueror. Containing: I. Miscellaneous Charters. II. Wills. III. Guilds. IV. Manumissions and Acquittances. With a Translation of the Anglo-Saxon. By the late BENJAMIN THORPE, Member of the Royal Academy of Sciences at Munich, and of the Society of Netherlandish Literature at Leyden. 8vo. pp. xlii. and 682, cloth. 1865. £1 1s.

Tiele.—OUTLINES OF THE HISTORY OF RELIGION to the Spread of the Universal Religions. By C. P. TIELE, Dr. Theol. Professor of the History of Religions in the University of Leiden. Translated from the Dutch by J. ESTLIN CARPENTER, M.A. Post 8vo. cloth, pp. xix. and 249. 7s. 6d.

Tindall.—A GRAMMAR AND VOCABULARY OF THE NAMAQUA-HOTTENTOT LANGUAGE. By HENRY TINDALL, Wesleyan Missionary. 8vo. pp. 124, sewed. 6s.

Trübner's Bibliotheca Sanscrita. A Catalogue of Sanskrit Literature, chiefly printed in Europe. To which is added a Catalogue of Sanskrit Works printed in India; and a Catalogue of Pali Books. Constantly for sale by Trübner & Co. Cr. 8vo. sd., pp. 84. 2s. 6d.

Trübner's Oriental Series

I. ESSAYS ON THE SACRED LANGUAGE, WRITINGS, AND RELIGION OF THE PARSIS. By MARTIN HAUG, Ph.D. late Professor of Sanskrit and Comparative Philology at the University of Munich. Edited by Dr. E. W. WEST. Second Edition. Post 8vo. cloth, pp. xvi. and 428. 1878. 16s.

II. TEXTS FROM THE BUDDHIST CANON, commonly known as Dhammapada. With accompanying Narratives. Translated from the Chinese by S. BEAL, B.A., Professor of Chinese, University College, London. Post 8vo. cloth, pp. viii. and 176. 1878. 7s. 6d.

III. THE HISTORY OF INDIAN LITERATURE. By ALBRECHT WEBER. Translated from the German by JOHN MANN, M.A., and THEODOR ZACHARIAE, Ph.D., with the sanction of the Author. Post 8vo. cloth, pp. xxiii. and 360. 1878. 18s.

IV. A SKETCH OF THE MODERN LANGUAGES OF THE EAST INDIES. By ROBERT CUST. Accompanied by Two Language Maps. Post 8vo. cloth, pp. xii. and 198. 1878. 12s.

V. THE BIRTH OF THE WAR GOD. A Poem by KALIDASA. Translated from the Sanskrit into English Verse. By RALPH T. H. GRIFFITH, M.A., Principal of Benares College. Second Edition. Post 8vo. cloth, pp. xii.-116. 1879. 5s.

The following Works are in Preparation.

A CLASSICAL DICTIONARY OF HINDU MYTHOLOGY AND HISTORY, GEOGRAPHY AND LITERATURE. By JOHN DOWSON, M.R.A.S., late Professor in the Staff College. In One Volume, post 8vo., about 400 pages, price not to exceed 21s.

SELECTIONS FROM THE KU-RAN. With a COMMENTARY. Translated by the late EDWARD WILLIAM LANE, Author of an "Arabic-English Lexicon," etc. A New Edition, Revised, with an Introduction on the History and Development of Islam, especially with reference to India. By STANLEY LANE POOLE. Post 8vo. cloth.

PASSAGES RELIGIOUS, MORAL, PRUDENTIAL, AND NARRATIVE, from the Mahabharata and other Sanskrit Works. Freely Translated or Paraphrased in English Verse. With an Appendix containing Prose Versions of the Original Texts. By JOHN MUIR, LL.D. Post 8vo. cloth.

Trübner's Oriental Series—*continued.*

ORIENTAL RELIGIONS in their Relation to Universal Religion. By SAMUEL JOHNSON. *First Section—India. Second Section—China.* In Two Volumes, post 8vo. cloth.

MISCELLANEOUS ESSAYS Relating to Indian Subjects. By B. H. HODGSON, late British Minister at Nepal. In Two Volumes, post 8vo. cloth.

THE GULISTAN; or, Rose Garden of Shekh Mushliu'd-din Sadi of Shiraz. Translated for the first time into Prose and Verse, with an Introductory Preface, and a Life of the Author, from the Atish Kadah, by EDWARD B. EASTWICK, F.R.S., M.R.A.S., etc. Second Edition, post 8vo. cloth.

THE JATAKA STORIES. With the Commentary and Collection of Buddhist Fairy Tales, Fables, and Folk Lore. Translated from the original Pali by T. W. RHYS DAVIDS. (The first part of the Commentary contains the most complete account we yet have of the Life of Buddha.) Vol. I., post 8vo. cloth.

CHINESE BUDDHISM. A Volume of Sketches, Historical and Critical. By J. EDKINS, D.D., Author of "China's Place in Philology," "Religion in China," etc., etc. Post 8vo. cloth.

BUDDHIST RECORDS OF THE WESTERN WORLD. Being the Si-yu-ki by HYEN THSANG. Translated from the original Chinese, with Introduction, Index, etc. By SAMUEL BEAL, Trinity College, Cambridge; Professor of Chinese, University College, London. In Two Vols., post 8vo. cloth.

THE POEMS OF HAFIZ OF SHIRAZ. Translated from the Persian into English Verse by E. H. PALMER, M.A., Professor of Arabic in the University of Cambridge. Post 8vo. cloth.

HISTORY OF THE PORTUGUESE IN INDIA. Based upon Documentary Evidence, now for the first time made available. By J. GERSON DA CUNHA, M.D. Post 8vo. cloth.

INDIAN TALES FROM TIBETAN SOURCES. Translated from the Tibetan into German by ANTON SCHIEFNER. Rendered into English, with Notes, by W. R. S. RALSTON. In One Volume, post 8vo.

ON THE VICISSITUDES OF ARYAN CIVILIZATION IN INDIA. One of the Florence Prize Essays. By Dr. J. GERSON DA CUNHA. In Two Volumes, post 8vo.

Trumpp.—GRAMMAR OF THE PAŠTO, or Language of the Afghans, compared with the Iranian and North-Indian Idioms. By Dr. ERNEST TRUMPP. 8vo. sewed, pp. xvi. and 412. 21s.

Trumpp.—GRAMMAR OF THE SINDHI LANGUAGE. Compared with the Sanskrit-Prakrit and the Cognate Indian Vernaculars. By Dr. ERNEST TRUMPP. Printed by order of Her Majesty's Government for India. Demy 8vo. sewed, pp. xvi. and 590. 15s.

Van der Tuuk.—OUTLINES OF A GRAMMAR OF THE MALAGASY LANGUAGE. By H. N. VAN DER TUUK. 8vo., pp. 28, sewed. 1s.

Van der Tuuk.—SHORT ACCOUNT OF THE MALAY MANUSCRIPTS BELONGING TO THE ROYAL ASIATIC SOCIETY. By H. N. VAN DER TUUK. 8vo., pp. 52. 2s. 6d.

Vedarthayatna (The); or, an Attempt to Interpret the Vedas. A Marathi and English Translation of the Rig Veda, with the Original Samhitâ and Pada Texts in Sanskrit. Parts I. to XXVIII. 8vo. pp. 1—896. Price 3s. 6d. each.

Vishnu-Purana (The); a System of Hindu Mythology and Tradition. Translated from the original Sanskrit, and Illustrated by Notes derived chiefly from other Purânas. By the late H. H. WILSON, M.A., F.R.S., Boden Professor of Sanskrit in the University of Oxford, etc., etc. Edited by FITZEDWARD

HALL. In 6 vols. 8vo. Vol. I. pp. cxl. and 200; Vol. II. pp. 348; Vol. III. pp. 348; Vol. IV. pp. 346, cloth; Vol. V. Part 1. pp. 192, cloth. 10s. 6d. each. Vol. V., Part 2, containing the Index, compiled by Fitzedward Hall. 8vo. cloth, pp. 268. 12s.

Vissering, W.—ON CHINESE CURRENCY. Coin and Paper Money. With Facsimile of a Bank Note. Royal 8vo. cloth, pp. xv. and 219. *Leiden*, 1877. 18s.

Wade.—YÜ-YEN TZŬ-ERH CHI. A progressive course designed to assist the Student of Colloquial Chinese, as spoken in the Capital and the Metropolitan Department. In eight parts, with Key, Syllabary, and Writing Exercises. By THOMAS FRANCIS WADE, C.B., Secretary to Her Britannic Majesty's Legation, Peking. 3 vols. 4to. Progressive Course, pp. xx. 296 and 16; Syllabary, pp. 126 and 36; Writing Exercises, pp. 48; Key, pp. 174 and 140, sewed. £4.

Wade.—WÊN-CHIEN TZŬ-ERH CHI. A series of papers selected as specimens of documentary Chinese, designed to assist Students of the language, as written by the officials of China. In sixteen parts, with Key. Vol. I. By THOMAS FRANCIS WADE, C.B., Secretary to Her Britannic Majesty's Legation at Peking. 4to., half-cloth, pp. xii. and 455; and iv., 72, and 52. £1 16s.

Wake.—CHAPTERS ON MAN. With the Outlines of a Science of comparative Psychology. By C. STANILAND WAKE, Fellow of the Anthropological Society of London. Crown 8vo. pp. viii. and 344, cloth. 7s. 6d.

Wake.—THE EVOLUTION OF MORALITY. Being a History of the Development of Moral Culture. By C. STANILAND WAKE, author of "Chapters on Man," etc. Two vols. 8vo. cloth, pp. xvi. and 506, xii. and 474. 21s.

Watson.—INDEX TO THE NATIVE AND SCIENTIFIC NAMES OF INDIAN AND OTHER EASTERN ECONOMIC PLANTS AND PRODUCTS, originally prepared under the authority of the Secretary of State for India in Council. By JOHN FORBES WATSON, M.A., M.D., F.L.S., F.R.A.S., etc., Reporter on the Products of India. Imperial 8vo., cloth, pp. 650. £1 11s. 6d.

Weber.—ON THE RÂMÂYANA. By DR. ALBRECHT WEBER, Berlin. Translated from the German by the Rev. D. C. Boyd, M.A. Reprinted from "The Indian Antiquary." Fcap. 8vo. sewed, pp. 130. 5s.

Weber.—THE HISTORY OF INDIAN LITERATURE. By ALBRECHT WEBER. Translated from the German by JOHN MANN, M.A., and DR. THEODOR ZACHARIAE, with the Author's sanction. Post 8vo. pp. xxiii. and 360, cloth. 1878. 18s.

Wedgwood.—A DICTIONARY OF ENGLISH ETYMOLOGY. By HENSLEIGH WEDGWOOD. Third Edition, thoroughly revised and enlarged. With an Introduction on the *Formation of Language*. Imperial 8vo., double column, pp. lxxii. and 746. 21s.

Wedgwood.—*ON THE ORIGIN OF LANGUAGE.* By HENSLEIGH WEDGWOOD, late Fellow of Christ's College, Cambridge. Fcap. 8vo. pp. 176, cloth. 3s. 6d.

West.—GLOSSARY AND INDEX OF THE PAHLAVI TEXTS OF THE BOOK OF Arda Viraf, The Tale of Gosht-I Fryano, The Hadokht Nask, and to some extracts from the Din-Kard and Nirangistan; prepared from Destur Hoshangji Asa's Glossary to the Arda Viraf Namak, and from the Original Texts, with Notes on Pahlavi Grammar. By E. W. WEST, Ph.D. Revised by MARTIN HAUG, Ph.D. Published by order of the Government of Bombay. 8vo. sewed, pp. viii. and 352. 25s.

West and Bühler.—A DIGEST OF THE HINDU LAW OF INHERITANCE and Partition, from the Replies of the Sâstris in the several Courts of the Bombay Presidency. With Introduction, Notes and Appendix. Edited by RAYMOND WEST and J. G. BÜHLER. Second Edition. Demy 8vo. sewed, pp. 674. £1 11s. 6d.

Wheeler.—THE HISTORY OF INDIA FROM THE EARLIEST AGES. By J. TALBOYS WHEELER, Assistant Secretary to the Government of India in the Foreign Department, Secretary to the Indian Record Commission, author of "The Geography of Herodotus," etc. etc. Demy 8vo. cl.

Vol. I. The Vedic Period and the Maha Bharata. pp. lxxv. and 576.

Vol. II., The Ramayana and the Brahmanic Period. pp. lxxxviii. and 680, with two Maps. 21s.

Vol. III. Hindu, Buddhist, Brahmanical Revival. pp. 484, with two maps. 18s.

Vol. IV. Part I. Mussulman Rule. pp. xxxii. and 320. 14s.

Vol. IV. Part II. In the press.

Wheeler.—EARLY RECORDS OF BRITISH INDIA. A History of the English Settlement in India, as told in the Government Records, the works of old travellers and other contemporary Documents, from the earliest period down to the rise of British Power in India. By J. TALBOYS WHEELER. Royal 8vo. cloth, pp. xxxii. and 392. 1878. 15s.

Whitmee.—A GRAMMAR AND DICTIONARY OF THE SAMOAN LANGUAGE. By Rev. GEORGE PRATT, forty years a Missionary of the London Missionary Society in Samoa. Second Edition. Edited by Rev. S. J. WHITMEE, F.R.G.S. Crown 8vo. cloth, pp. 380. 18s.

Whitney.—ORIENTAL AND LINGUISTIC STUDIES. By WILLIAM DWIGHT WHITNEY, Professor of Sanskrit and Comparative Philology in Yale College. First Series. The Veda; the Avesta; the Science of Language. Cr. 8vo. cl., pp. x. and 419. 12s.

Second Series.—The East and West—Religion and Mythology—Orthography and Phonology—Hindu Astronomy. Crown 8vo. cloth, pp. 446. 12s.

Whitney.—ATHARVA VEDA PRÁTIÇÁKHYA; or, Çáunakíyá Caturádhyá-yiká (The). Text, Translation, and Notes. By WILLIAM D. WHITNEY, Professor of Sanskrit in Yale College. 8vo. pp. 286, boards. £1 11s. 6d.

Whitney.—LANGUAGE AND THE STUDY OF LANGUAGE: Twelve Lectures on the Principles of Linguistic Science. By W. D. WHITNEY. Third Edition, augmented by an Analysis. Crown 8vo. cloth, pp. xii. and 504. 10s. 6d.

Whitney.—LANGUAGE AND ITS STUDY, with especial reference to the Indo-European Family of Languages. Seven Lectures by W. D. WHITNEY, Professor of Sanskrit, and Instructor in Modern Languages in Yale College. Edited with Introduction, Notes, Tables of Declension and Conjugation, Grimm's Law with Illustrations, and an Index, by the Rev. R. MORRIS, M.A., LL.D. Cr. 8vo. cl., pp. xxii. and 318. 5s.

Whitney.—SURYA-SIDDHANTA (Translation of the): A Text-book of Hindu Astronomy, with Notes and an Appendix, containing additional Notes and Tables, Calculations of Eclipses, a Stellar Map, and Indexes. By W. D. WHITNEY. 8vo. pp. iv. and 354, boards. £1 11s. 6d.

Whitney.—TAITTIRÍYA-PRÁTIÇÁKHYA, with its Commentary, the Tribháshyaratna: Text, Translation, and Notes. By W. D. WHITNEY, Prof. of Sanskrit in Yale College, New Haven. 8vo. pp. 469. 1871. £1 5s.

Williams.—A DICTIONARY, ENGLISH AND SANSCRIT. By MONIER WILLIAMS, M.A. Published under the Patronage of the Honourable East India Company. 4to. pp. xii. 862, cloth. 1851. £3 3s.

Williams.—A SANSKRIT-ENGLISH DICTIONARY, Etymologically and Philologically arranged, with special reference to Greek, Latin, German, Anglo-Saxon, English, and other cognate Indo-European Languages. By MONIER WILLIAMS, M.A., Boden Professor of Sanskrit. 4to. cloth, pp. xxv. and 1186. £4 14s. 6d.

Williams.—A Practical Grammar of the Sanskrit Language, arranged with reference to the Classical Languages of Europe, for the use of English Students, by Monier Williams, M.A. 1877. Fourth Edition, Revised. 8vo. cloth. 15s.

Williams.—A Syllabic Dictionary of the Chinese Language, arranged according to the Wu-Fang Yuen Yin, with the pronunciation of the Characters as heard in Peking, Canton, Amoy, and Shanghai. By S. Wells Williams. 4to. cloth, pp. lxxxiv. and 1252. 1874. £5 5s.

Williams.—First Lessons in the Maori Language. With a Short Vocabulary. By W. L. Williams, B.A. Fcap. 8vo. pp. 98, cloth. 5s.

Williams.—Modern India and the Indians. Being a Series of Impressions, Notes, and Essays. By Monier Williams, D.C.L. Second Edition. Post 8vo. cloth, pp. 344. 1878. 7s 6d.

Wilson.—Works of the late Horace Hayman Wilson, M.A., F.R.S., Member of the Royal Asiatic Societies of Calcutta and Paris, and of the Oriental Soc. of Germany, etc., and Boden Prof. of Sanskrit in the University of Oxford.

Vols. I. and II. Essays and Lectures chiefly on the Religion of the Hindus by the late H. H. Wilson, M.A., F.R.S., etc. Collected and edited by Dr. Reinhold Rost. 2 vols. cloth, pp. xiii. and 399, vi. and 416. 21s.

Vols. III, IV. and V. Essays Analytical, Critical, and Philological, on Subjects connected with Sanskrit Literature. Collected and Edited by Dr. Reinhold Rost. 3 vols. 8vo. pp. 408, 406, and 390, cloth. Price 36s.

Vols. VI., VII., VIII., IX. and X., Part I. Vishnu Purána, a System of Hindu Mythology and Tradition. Vols. I. to V. Translated from the original Sanskrit, and Illustrated by Notes derived chiefly from other Puránas. By the late H. H. Wilson. Edited by Fitzedward Hall, M.A., D.C.L., Oxon. 8vo., pp. cxl. and 200; 344; 344; 346, cloth. 2l. 12s. 6d.

Vol. X., Part 2, containing the Index to, and completing the Vishnu Purána, compiled by Fitzedward Hall. 8vo. cloth pp. 268. 12s.

Vols. XI. and XII. Select Specimens of the Theatre of the Hindus. Translated from the Original Sanskrit. By the late Horace Hayman Wilson, M.A., F.R.S. 3rd corrected Ed. 2 vols. 8vo. pp. lxi. and 384; and iv. and 418, cl. 21s.

Wilson.—Select Specimens of the Theatre of the Hindus. Translated from the Original Sanskrit. By the late Horace Hayman Wilson, M.A., F.R.S. Third corrected edition. 2 vols. 8vo., pp. lxxi. and 384; iv. and 418, cloth. 21s.

CONTENTS.

Vol. I.—Preface—Treatise on the Dramatic System of the Hindus—Dramas translated from the Original Sanskrit—The Mrichchakati, or the Toy Cart—Vikrama and Urvasi, or the Hero and the Nymph—Uttara Ráma Cheritra, or continuation of the History of Ráma.

Vol. II.—Dramas translated from the Original Sanskrit—Málati and Mádhava, or the Stolen Marriage—Mudrá Rakshasa, or the Signet of the Minister—Ratnávalí, or the Necklace—Appendix, containing short accounts of different Dramas.

Wilson.—The Present State of the Cultivation of Oriental Literature. A Lecture delivered at the Meeting of the Royal Asiatic Society. By the Director, Professor H. H. Wilson. 8vo. pp. 26, sewed. London, 1852. 6d.

Wilson.—A Dictionary in Sanskrit and English. Translated, amended, and enlarged from an original compilation prepared by learned Natives for the College of Fort William by H. H. Wilson. The Third Edition edited by Jagunmohana Tarkalankara and Khettramohana Mookerjee. Published by Gyanendrachandra Rayachoudhuri and Brothers. 4to. pp. 1008. Calcutta, 1874. £3 3s.

Wilson (H. H.).—See also Megha Duta, Rig-Veda, and Vishnu-Purána.

Wise.—COMMENTARY ON THE HINDU SYSTEM OF MEDICINE. By T. A. WISE, M.D., Bengal Medical Service. 8vo., pp. xx. and 442, cloth. 7s. 6d.

Wise.—REVIEW OF THE HISTORY OF MEDICINE. By THOMAS A. WISE, M.D. 2 vols. 8vo. cloth. Vol. I., pp. xcviii. and 397; Vol. II., pp. 574. 10s.

Withers.—THE ENGLISH LANGUAGE SPELLED AS PRONOUNCED, with enlarged Alphabet of Forty Letters. With Specimen. By GEORGE WITHERS. Royal 8vo. sewed, pp. 84. 1s.

Wordsworth.—THE CHURCH OF THIBET, and the Historical Analogies of Buddhism and Christianity. A Lecture delivered at Bombay by W. WORDSWORTH, B.A., Principal of Elphinstone College. 1877. 8vo. pp. 51. 2s. 6d.

Wright.—FEUDAL MANUALS OF ENGLISH HISTORY. A Series of Popular Sketches of our National History, compiled at different periods, from the Thirteenth Century to the Fifteenth, for the use of the Feudal Gentry and Nobility. Now first edited from the Original Manuscripts. By THOMAS WRIGHT, Esq., M.A. Small 4to. cloth, pp. xxix. and 184. 1872. 15s.

Wright.—THE HOMES OF OTHER DAYS. A History of Domestic Manners and Sentiments during the Middle Ages. By THOMAS WRIGHT, Esq., M.A., F.S.A. With Illustrations from the Illuminations in contemporary Manuscripts and other Sources, drawn and engraved by F. W. Fairholt, Esq., F.S.A. 1 Vol. medium 8vo. handsomely bound in cloth, pp. xv. and 512. 350 Woodcuts. £1 1s.

Wright.—THE CELT, THE ROMAN, AND THE SAXON; a History of the Early Inhabitants of Britain down to the Conversion of the Anglo-Saxons to Christianity. Illustrated by the Ancient Remains brought to Light by Recent Research. By THOMAS WRIGHT, Esq., M.A., F.S.A., etc., etc. Third Corrected and Enlarged Edition. Numerous Illustrations. Crown 8vo. cloth, pp. xiv. and 562. 14s.

Wright.—ANGLO-SAXON AND OLD-ENGLISH VOCABULARIES, Illustrating the Condition and Manners of our Forefathers, as well as the History of the Forms of Elementary Education, and of the Languages spoken in this Island from the Tenth Century to the Fifteenth. Edited by THOMAS WRIGHT, Esq., M.A., F.S.A., etc. Second Edition, edited, collated, and corrected by RICHARD WÜLCKER. [*In the press.*

Wylie.—NOTES ON CHINESE LITERATURE; with introductory Remarks on the Progressive Advancement of the Art; and a list of translations from the Chinese, into various European Languages. By A. WYLIE, Agent of the British and Foreign Bible Society in China. 4to. pp. 296, cloth. Price, £1 16s.

Yajurveda.—THE WHITE YAJURVEDA IN THE MADHYANDINA RECENSION. With the Commentary of Mahidhara. Complete in 36 parts. Large square 8vo. pp. 571. £4 10s.

Yates.—A BENGÁLÍ GRAMMAR. By the late Rev. W. YATES, D.D. Reprinted, with improvements, from his Introduction to the Bengálí Language. Edited by I. WENGER. Fcap. 8vo., pp. iv. and 150, bds. Calcutta, 1864. 3s. 6d.

www.ingramcontent.com/pod-product-compliance
Lightning Source LLC
Chambersburg PA
CBHW030350230426
43664CB00007BB/596

* 9 7 8 3 3 3 7 4 1 3 9 3 4 *

This is a timely, well-researched volume that advances Christian biblical scholarship and ministry at a time of global instability and unrest. Dr. Kevin Chen is sensitive to the lexical intricacies of the text, intertexts, and how the book of Daniel is coherent within the larger context of the Old and New Testaments. He writes in an elegant style that is unpretentious and easy to read. Having the best of international scholarship, this volume also demonstrates a good range of Asian scholarship. In connection to the motifs in the book of Daniel, I am impressed by how Dr. Chen brings readers through Asian names, dreams, the Great Banyan tree, lycanthropy, the Great Ming code, Chinese cosmic wars, imperial exams, the perseverance of faith in a foreign land, and more – a worthy and significant addition to the Asia Bible Commentary Series!

Peter C. W. Ho
Academic Dean and Associate Professor of Old Testament,
School of Theology, English,
Singapore Bible College

Kevin S. Chen's commentary on Daniel as a part of the Asia Bible Commentary Series is outstanding. The commentary moves through the twelve chapters based on the Hebrew/Aramaic text of Daniel, giving interesting contextual introductions, section by section explanations, and several excurses. The contextual introductions bring together parallels from Asian history and culture, and an overview of each biblical chapter. The commentary itself not only moves through the overall content of the chapter but also makes constant reference to parallels in Daniel, the rest of the Old Testament, and at times, the New Testament, and draws out important points of application. The excurses function in a similar way but bring together a larger amount of material for each key theme. Chen does all this in such a way that a broad audience is served, from an avid Bible reader to those experienced in biblical studies and biblical theology, rich in footnotes pointing to more.

Jordan M. Scheetz
Professor of Biblical Studies,
Western Seminary, Oregon, USA

In this refreshing commentary you'll realize that Daniel and his friends met with the real-world experiences of many who have been forced from their homeland. Many of our families were forced to change identity, learn a new language, eat a new diet, and abandon their cultural religion. In this work, Chen assures the reader that God has gifted believers, like Daniel, with spiritual gifts so as to be a witness despite cultural changes in our lives. Overall, any believer who uses this commentary will find modern, real world experience and application when teaching and preaching the text of Daniel.

Mario M. C. Melendez
Auguie Henry Chair of Bible,
Assistant Professor of Old Testament and Biblical Studies,
Oklahoma Baptist University, USA